W9-AMY-310

Kierkegaard's Thought

KIERKEGAARD'S THOUGHT
by Gregor Malantschuk

EDITED AND
TRANSLATED BY
HOWARD V. HONG
AND
EDNA H. HONG

PRINCETON
UNIVERSITY PRESS
1971

"The main obstacle in understanding
SK is his use of language."

B 4377
M 2613

Translation copyright © 1971
by Howard V. Hong
ALL RIGHTS RESERVED
L. C. Card: 77-155000
ISBN: 0-691-07166-7

This book has been composed in
Primer with Melior display

Original work entitled
Dialektik og Eksistens
hos Søren Kierkegaard
Published by
Hans Reitzels Forlag
Copenhagen 1968

Printed in the United States
of America by
Princeton University Press

*Dedicated to the
Memory of Charlotte Reeh
(née Voss Schrader)*

07773

ὁ μὲν γὰρ συνοπτικὸς διαλεκτικός

He who can view things in their connexion
is a dialectician.

Plato, Republic, vii, 537 c

Foreword

When this book by Gregor Malantschuk appeared in Danish, Professor N. H. Søe wrote in a review: "Kierkegaard study has been enriched by a brilliant work. It ought to be translated very soon into a world language."

After reading the book, we agreed on both points, and now we are happy to have a hand in extending the range of this superb work, the best book currently available on Kierkegaard in any language.

What makes this a good book? In his *Kierkegaards Verhältnis zu Hegel* (Stuttgart, 1969) Niels Thulstrup accounts for the merits of the book by saying that it is "one of the best substantiated and best worked out studies in the entire literature on Kierkegaard" and in pointing out that "the composition is tight, the method sure," and that "every detail, as well as the whole, is well considered."

All this is the case—and more. For one thing, although this book is the yield of a lifetime of careful, sensitive reading of Kierkegaard's works as well as the journals and papers, Gregor Malantschuk does not tell us what Kierkegaard "really means" but rather uses Kierkegaard to interpret Kierkegaard. Of course, the writer is present, but the reader, rather than being served the writer's special version of Kierkegaard, is continually presented with the rich, insightful substance of Kierkegaard's thought in all its movement and interrelations. Furthermore, he is invited to approach and to read Kierkegaard organically and collaterally, not linearly or atomistically as some hapless writers on Kierkegaard have suggested, using a single work (usually a pseudonymous work) as the basis of interpretation and critique.

Another merit is that this book centers on Kierkegaard's

thought, a rarity among the plethora of pieces committed to the genetic fallacy of psychologizing and historicizing Kierkegaard's works as autobiography, purportedly "explaining" them thereby. No thinker and writer ever tried as Kierkegaard did to leave the reader alone with the work. The dialectic of thought and existence is properly that of the reader with the work, not of the reader's curious interest in the writer. Therefore Gregor Malantschuk concentrates on the thought in its interconnectedness and wholeness and on its relation to personal, human existence. At the same time, with some deft, telling aside about Søren Kierkegaard, he makes us aware that for Kierkegaard himself the dialectic of thought was as penetrating and existential as it should be and can be for the reader who is freed, as Kierkegaard says, from gossipy interest in the writer.

In preparation of the English edition, we have been aided first of all by the author, who has clarified some knotty points, by Gail Sundem and Dorothy Bolton, who have helped at various stages of the typing and retyping, and by Carol Orr of Princeton University Press, who has seen the manuscript through the intricacies of publication. Our thanks to them all.

Howard V. Hong and Edna H. Hong

St. Olaf College
October 19, 1970

Preface

In my study of Søren Kierkegaard's writings I have been especially interested in exploring the points of departure and the basic underlying principles of his thought, since in my opinion intimate knowledge of these presuppositions can lead to a new understanding of Kierkegaard's intentions with his authorship and also make it possible to assess the value of that authorship.

My work, therefore, is first of all an attempt to penetrate the authorship on this primary basis, without at this time intermingling my own views. In that respect I more or less follow the instruction Kierkegaard himself gave for any eventual interpretation of his works when he has such an imaginary interpreter say: "No, whether the author gets angry about it or not, I will convert everything into direct communication and myself into a serviceable interpreter." Moreover, since I do not belong to "the bustlers and the hustlers in the world of the spirit," this procedure, when it involves a thinker of Kierkegaard's stature, has been the only viable one for me.

With this point of view in mind, I have concentrated on giving an account of Kierkegaard's own understanding of his authorship and have not allowed myself to take a position in any extensive way on the many contributions Kierkegaard research has yielded to the interpretation of Kierkegaard's works up to now. To do so would not only have greatly increased the length of this book, but it would also give the present account a completely different character. In many ways, however, the conclusions advanced in the book do indirectly express a position with regard to other conceptions of Søren Kierkegaard's life and works.

I am deeply grateful to the Carlsberg Fund for financial

assistance in this work and to both the Carlsberg Fund and the Rask-Ørsted Fund for aid in the publication of this book. I also express my gratitude to the University of Copenhagen for awarding me a research fellowship and giving me the possibility for additional scholarly work. May I use this opportunity to thank the Swenson-Kierke-gaard Memorial Fund of Minneapolis, Minnesota, U.S.A., whose grant at the time was a special encouragement to me in that it was the first I received for my work with Søren Kierkegaard.

A warm thank you to Professor F. J. Billeskov Jansen for the interest he has shown in my work. I thank Pastor Otto Bertelsen for scrutinizing the manuscript and Grethe Kjær for her help by typing the manuscript and reading proof.

Gregor Malantschuk

Contents

Kierkegaard's
Thought

Introduction

Exploring Søren Kierkegaard's authorship and clarifying its intentions involve great difficulties. These are due not only to the special themes which are his concern and his characteristic manner of stating the problems but also to his conscious attempt to make a penetration of his work more difficult, something he expresses in many places, both directly and indirectly. For example, Kierkegaard's principal pseudonym, Johannes Climacus, very significantly declares that he has understood it as his "task to create difficulties everywhere."[1] In referring to the structure of *Stages on Life's Way* he says, "It is thus left to the reader himself to put two and two together, if he so desires, but nothing is done to minister to a reader's indolence."[2]

The difficulties we encounter in Kierkegaard's authorship can be classified under the following points:

    1. As a result of his personal experiences and his strictly logical reasoning Kierkegaard "discovered capacities which do not exist as such for others";[3] but since he has not given a coherent account of these discoveries it is as if he has "thrown away the key" to this great "treasure," as he himself metaphorically expresses it.

    2. Kierkegaard's scrupulously sustained use of pseudo-

[1] *Concluding Unscientific Postscript*, p. 166.

[2] Ibid., pp. 264-65.

[3] *Søren Kierkegaards Papirer*, X¹ A 115 (*Søren Kierkegaard's Journals and Papers*, V); see Bibliography on the Danish and English editions of Kierkegaard's journals and papers. Hereafter the *Papirer* will be referred to by volume, category, and entry (X¹ A 115) together with the volume number of *Journals and Papers* (*J. and P.*, V) as well as the serial entry number, except for entries in Volumes IV and V, which are still in preparation.

nyms makes it difficult to find an unbroken line in the authorship.

3. This pseudonymity makes it extremely difficult to determine Kierkegaard's own position at a given point. That is to say, Kierkegaard planned his authorship in such a way that his own person must be brought into the research. Regarding this he says among other things: ". . . this is why the time will come when not only my writings but my whole life, the intriguing secret of the whole machinery, will be studied and studied."[4]

4. Furthermore, Kierkegaard gave his literary production, especially in the period up to and including *Concluding Unscientific Postscript*, "the appearance of chance and caprice"[5] in order to baffle those with no intention of penetrating deeper into his authorship. Only a searching study can lead to the discovery of "the ingenuity" of this "major work"[6] and show "what an exceedingly rigorous ordering"[7] has underlaid the development of the authorship.

5. There is a special obstacle to understanding in the intentionally difficult formulations of many of the central thoughts in Kierkegaard's works. Often these formulations are developments of the aphoristic style Kierkegaard frequently used in his journal entries in his first statement of a problem.

6. Kierkegaard made his authorship hard to get at partly for pedagogical reasons also, as the following remark testifies: "The task must be made difficult, for only the difficult inspires the noble-hearted. . . ."[8]

The obstacles referred to have made it difficult even for philosophical experts[9] to grasp the general line which runs

---

[4] VIII[1] A 424 (*J. and P.,* V).

[5] VII[1] A 104, p. 50 (*J. and P.,* V).

[6] VII[2] B 235, p. 72 (omitted from *Authority and Revelation,* p. 54).

[7] VII[1] A 104, p. 50 (*J. and P.,* V).

[8] VIII[2] B 88, pp. 184-85 (*J. and P.,* I, 656).

[9] For example, Professor H. L. Martensen, who even in 1849 in the Foreword to his *Dogmatics* characterized Kierkegaard's

through the whole authorship and renders it the precisely thought-out "dialectical structure"[10] which it is.

Kierkegaard's method of making his writings difficult succeeded so well that he eventually feared that in studying his authorship people would stop with this multiplicity of individual works without discovering that the whole should be understood within a "comprehensive plan" [*Total-Anlæg*] which puts the individual works in place in relation to each other. To prevent anyone in the future from explaining the dissimilarity of the works simply by the "poor comment that the author changed" and "to insure a comprehensive view"[11] of his work, Kierkegaard drafted in 1848 *The Point of View for My Work as an Author*. When Kierkegaard wrote this book, he was already working with the rough draft and ideas of his two last great works: *The Sickness Unto Death* and *Practice [Training] in Christianity*. It can therefore be said that the notion of a "comprehensive plan" applies in a way to the whole of Kierkegaard's authorship proper, stretching from *Either/Or* to *Two Discourses at the Communion on Fridays* (August 7, 1851). This assumption is reinforced by the fact that Kierkegaard (in the later revised and abridged edition of *Point of View for my Work as an Author*, under the title *On My Work as an Author*, which came out together with *Two Discourses at the Communion on Fridays*) seeks to encompass his authorship proper within the idea of integral unity; concerning the production all the way from *Either/Or* up to and including *Christian Discourses* he says: "This movement was completed or gone through *uno tenore*, in one breath, if I dare say so, thus the authorship, viewed *comprehensively*, is religious from first to last, something anyone who can see must see if he wants to

---

thinking as: ". . . thinking in axioms and aphorisms, by flashes and impulse. . . ." For Kierkegaard's reaction to Martensen's characterization of his thinking see especially X^6 B 137, p. 187 (*J. and P.*, V) and references.

[10] *The Point of View*, p. 103.   [11] X^1 A 116 (*J. and P.*, V).

see."[12] This unity is also underscored by Kierkegaard in his conversation with Mynster after the latter received the two books sent to him: *On My Work as an Author* and *Two Discourses at the Communion on Fridays*. Kierkegaard quotes from his conversation with Mynster: " 'Yes, there is a thread to the whole,' he said, 'but spun later, but after all, you do not say any more yourself.' I answered that the thing to notice was my having been so possessed by one thing over many years and amid so much productivity that my pen had not made one single detour."[13]

Kierkegaard's emphasis on the dialectical coherence in his whole authorship, as given in the two books mentioned and later in the posthumously published book, *The Point of View for My Work as an Author*, can, however, only brief us on the idea of the authorship. We still have the task of showing how Kierkegaard arrives at the basic assumptions and fundamental concepts for all his thought and according to what laws he utilizes these concepts in the development of his authorship. Such an investigation will first and foremost clarify Kierkegaard's dialectical method and will unravel the "criss-crossing of the strands"[14] which the great "Combinateur"[15] with his dialectical talent wove into the web of his authorship.

For the elucidation of the above-mentioned relationships and for the disclosing of the structure of the authorship in defiance of Kierkegaard's consciously incorporated difficul-

[12] *On My Work as an Author*, together with *The Point of View*, p. 147.

[13] X⁴ A 373 (*J. and P.*, V); it must be noted at the same time that in X⁴ A 380 (*J. and P.*, V) Kierkegaard is ironical about a review of the two books because the review came to the conclusion that Kierkegaard had now definitely terminated his authorship. Kierkegaard, however, regarded the publication of these two books simply as a termination of a connected period in his production without thereby feeling excluded from picking up his pen again.

[14] *On My Work as an Author*, together with *The Point of View*, p. 147 (ed. tr.)

[15] X² A 285 (*J. and P.*, V).

ties, it is expedient to use the procedure Kierkegaard himself recommends for checking an author's works, its truth and general thrust. This procedure consists of "imitating"[16] the process of thought and the dialectical movements the author has undertaken.

With this the task for this investigation is established.

This task is carried out in three stages.

1. First of all it will be shown how Kierkegaard, while studying the various themes and subjects which were of particular interest to him, showed a tendency to concentrate on the actuality of the subject, and how he thereby gradually moved away from the objective branches of knowledge toward a steadily stronger emphasis on the subjective elements which bear on man's existential development.

2. Together with this preoccupation with the subjective in human life, Kierkegaard attempted to achieve clarity on the viewpoints which should be used in clearing up all the problems related to the actuality of subjects. These efforts resulted in his shaping the foundation for his dialectical method.

The material for the first two parts of this investigation is found primarily in Kierkegaard's journal entries from 1833 to 1843. It is apparent that both Kierkegaard's transition from technical subjects to a conscious concentration on the actuality of the subject (man's inner actuality) and his development of a basis for the dialectical method took place before the year 1843.

In the first two parts direct quotations from the journals in the period prior to the actual authorship will frequently be used to illustrate concretely his work with this problem.

3. In the third part of the book Kierkegaard's authorship will be studied in the light of his dialectical method, and it will be shown here, with the help of this method, how Kierkegaard coherently sets the individual works in place in the large context, so that even the conflict between the

16 IV B 59, p. 214 (J. and P., V); Postscript, p. 14 (tr. "reproduce").

principal pseudonyms, Climacus and Anti-Climacus, serves to elucidate the principal ideas of the authorship.

Kierkegaard's first two books, *From the Papers of One Still Living* and *The Concept of Irony*, are included in the study of the works, since they can help enlighten us on the extent to which Kierkegaard, prior to beginning the actual authorship, had achieved clarity on certain fundamental features in his method. His doctoral dissertation, *The Concept of Irony* (1841), in particular can inform us more specifically of progress with respect to the dialectical method.

I   Anthropological Contemplation

Søren Kierkegaard's earliest notes give evidence that he is trying to proceed methodically and that he had set a goal for his studies and research. This goal, which he calls his "project,"[1] the Danish editors of Kierkegaard's journals and papers have described briefly as "the collection of material for *a characterization of the spirit of the Middle Ages* through a *general historical* study of the age's distinctive features in all the areas of spiritual-intellectual life, in literature, art, religion, science, and social conditions, concentrating on a *more thorough and concrete* study of the reflection of the folk genius of the Middle Ages in poetry, legends, fairy tales, and stories, *especially* on the personifications of the representative ideas rising out of the medieval folk-life's world of consciousness (see *Either/Or*, I, pp. 86-92): Don Juan, Faust, the Wandering Jew, and all this in the light of a *more abstract Hegelian-philosophic parallel interest* in a comprehensive delineation of the stages of intellectual-spiritual development, including 'world-history' as well as the single individual's 'Microcosm,' by way of defining concepts such as: the classical, the romantic ('dialectical'), the modern, comedy, tragedy, irony, humor, resignation, etc. etc."[2]

What is lacking in this compressed description is a more pronounced underscoring of the idea of unity pervading all these studies, binding together the several parts and pointing toward the recognition of man's inner actuality through introspection and all the existential possibilities it contains. Likewise missing is a special emphasis on Kierke-

---

[1] I C 83, p. 236 (*J. and P.*, V).
[2] *Papirer*, I, pp. xv-xvi.

gaard's study of works in dogmatics during this first period.[3]

Later Kierkegaard finds his own unifying expression for these efforts in referring to "the authentic anthropological contemplation,"[4] which he believed to be the most urgent task for thought in his age. When he wrote these words in July, 1840, he had himself already become clear as to how this task could be carried out.

Kierkegaard's first resolve methodically to place the most weight on self-knowledge and thereby on knowledge of subjective actuality can be dated from his Gilleleje-sojourn in the summer of 1835, when he wrote these words: "One must first learn to know himself before knowing anything else (γνωθι σεαυτον)."[5] Later in 1839 the idea of the centrality of human actuality in existence is clearly expressed: "Individuality is the true period in the development of creation. As everyone knows, a period is written when the meaning is completed, which can also be expressed (looking backwards) by saying that the meaning is there. Thus not until individuality is given is the meaning completed or is there meaning in creation, and in this way we see the possibility of reducing all philosophy to one single proposition."[6] This sentence must be understood as an underscoring of the idea that truth is to be found only in the subject, which is related to the later thesis that "subjectivity is truth."[7]

In his "project" and "anthropological contemplation," Kierkegaard concentrated on essentially the same problem

---

[3] See, for example, II C 30 (*J. and P.*, V), from the year 1838, where Kierkegaard writes that for "some years" he has been occupied with dogmatics.

[4] III A 3 (*J. and P.*, I, 37); in this entry Kierkegaard refers to an entry from 1838 (II C 55; *J. and P.*, III, 3260) in which he inquires about "the concretions" which "have real significance for the Christian consciousness."

[5] I A 75, p. 56 (*J. and P.*, V).

[6] II A 474 (*J. and P.*, II, 1981).

[7] *Postscript*, p. 182.

as Hegel in his *Phenomenology of Mind*, but in a more comprehensive and concrete way.

Before going further into Kierkegaard's interest in the above-mentioned themes, a few observations must be made to show that even before writing his journals Kierkegaard was predisposed to being led in the direction of "anthropological contemplation."

Even with a cautious estimate of Kierkegaard's or his pseudonymous authors' statements about his childhood, it must be taken for granted that his father's powerful influence was of decisive significance in developing the very aptitudes he needed as a thinker, aptitudes which he himself has emphasized as being important for him as a thinker[8]—namely, training in clear, logical explication of the content of an idea ("dialectic") and training in the creation of his own objects for cogitation ("imagination"). Kierkegaard's subsequent tremendous dialectical proficiency can be explained by the fact that he learned very early to train himself in the art "which was to be the serious business of his life."[9]

But without a doubt what especially encouraged his movement toward "anthropological contemplation" was an abundance of painful and unsolved problems, also due in part to his father's influence and upbringing. These problems and conflicts eventually called for more definite exploration and clarification. The opportunity for this presented itself after some years of study at the University. His university studies themselves were of little assistance in the problems with which he grappled, but his years as a student from 1830 to 1835 provided orientation, also in the areas to which he later gave such thorough consideration.

In the summer of 1834 Kierkegaard began in his own independent way to achieve clarification, first and fore-

[8] IV B 1, pp. 107ff. (*Johannes Climacus, or De omnibus dubitandum est*, pp. 106-108).

[9] IV B 1, p. 109 (ibid., p. 108).

most, of his personal problems. He outlined this way in his journals (at first on slips and scraps of paper, later in notebooks), which he kept under strict discipline and in which he did not fully confide. At this point the comment must be inserted that Kierkegaard's jottings of excerpts and notes from lectures he heard as a student in this first period are not to be underestimated. These entries, too, are important in understanding his working method. But to show their special significance in preparing Kierkegaard for his own independent studies is a task in itself. The present study has its point of departure in Kierkegaard's earliest recorded ideas and reflections expressing his own attitude to themes in his sphere of interest.

The great variety of entries may be best surveyed if classified according to the following basic considerations: in a broad sense the theme "anthropological contemplation" means that an attempt is made to consider man on various levels of mental-spiritual development and from various perspectives. On this basis the material in the journals and papers may be grouped under the following headings: mythology, esthetics, anthropology, philosophy, philosophy of religion, ethics, and—first and last—theology, with its subdivisions, of which dogmatics is the most important. Such concepts as irony and humor, as well as Kierkegaard's work with the "three great ideas (Don Juan, Faust, and the Wandering Jew)"[10] may also be classified under one or another of these headings. By and large it may be said that every entry can be classified under one of the headings. In this connection it is of interest to note that Kierkegaard is quickly finished with certain groups and subgroups, while other areas, such as theology and also ethics, persistently continue to be primary objects of concern, and others, again, for example, the dialectic of communication, gradually come more and more to the foreground.

Entries in the journals and papers on the above-mentioned themes of interest are intermingled, and Kierke-

[10] I A 150 (*J. and P.*, I, 795).

gaard works with these areas concurrently, conditioned, as will appear later, by methodological considerations, possibly from the very beginning.

Before we look more closely at Kierkegaard's entries within the different groupings, the following must be added: Kierkegaard considers the independent notations beginning in April, 1834 as being primarily ideas and observations, usually prompted by his reading on the various themes which were the object of his study and interest.[11] These earliest recorded notations as yet have a twofold character; they can be considered to be the results partly of influences from an external tradition and partly of Kierkegaard's independent work with specific problems. On the possibility of considerable dependence on outside influences in the writing of his first notes Kierkegaard says: "We often deceive ourselves by embracing as our own many an idea and observation which either springs forth vividly now out of a time when we read it or lies in the consciousness of the whole age—yes, even now as I write this observation—this, too, perhaps, is a fruit of the experience of the age."[12]

But from this as yet partially derivative attempt to reflect on certain problems Kierkegaard moves toward his own characteristic manner of posing the questions and solving them. Later Kierkegaard looks critically upon his first journal entries, declaring even of his "old journal for 1839" that in it not much "really felicitous or thorough"[13] is to be found. But precisely for this very reason those notes are important for this investigation, for they show us a Kierkegaard who is still uncertain about his "project."

The majority of Kierkegaard's early entries fall within the sphere of theology. These entries commence at the conclusion of Kierkegaard's substantial work with exegeti-

[11] See Niels Thulstrup's Introduction to *Philosophical Fragments*, pp. xlv-lxvii.

[12] I A 109 (*J. and P.*, V).

[13] VIII[1] A 231 (*J. and P.*, III, 2598).

cal and dogmatic questions, of which we have evidence in the journals and papers.[14] Here Kierkegaard intersperses his own observations among the excerpts, for example, those from his study of Schleiermacher's *Der christliche Glaube*.[15]

It is with the entry on predestination[16] in May, 1834, that Kierkegaard begins to present his own attitude to theological problems. The entry reads: "A strict doctrine of predestination traces the origin of evil back to God and thereby does not remain even as consistent as Manichæism, for the latter system posits two beings; the former unites these two contradictories in one being."

Kierkegaard's reflections on predestination, beginning with this memorandum, span a considerable period of time, and he records his various thoughts about it.[17] After that the reflections come to a relative termination in entries I A 295 (*J and P.*, III, 3547), and C 40 (*J. and P.*, III, 3547), and C 40 (*J. and P.*, I, 227), in which Kierkegaard believes he has found the "solution to predestination." In following Kierkegaard's line of thought in these entries, one discovers that his critical focus on the idea of absolute predestination is connected with a growing emphasis upon the significance of "human freedom." The notes on predestination are a good example of how Kierkegaard works with a par-

[14] I C 1-45 (*J. and P.*, I, 227; IV; V). With regard to these various excerpts and notes and their connection with Kierkegaard's studies at the University, see Waldemar Ammundsen, *Den unge Søren Kierkegaard* (Copenhagen, 1912), pp. 77-93.

[15] *Der christliche Glaube nach den Grundsätzen der evangelischen Kirke in Zusammenhange dargestellt*, I-II (Berlin, 2nd ed., 1830), I, pp. 3-72; see I C 20 (*J. and P.*, V) and editors' reference.

[16] I A 2 (*J. and P.*, II, 1302); the entry might conceivably be regarded as an echo of Kierkegaard's reading of *Der christliche Glaube* with Martensen as tutor. On this see p. 90 in Ammundsen's book (n. 14 above).

[17] See the following entries: I A 5 (*J. and P.*, II, 1230); A 7 (*J. and P.*, II, 1231); A 19 (*J. and P.*, III, 3543); A 20 (*J. and P.*, III, 3544); A 22 (*J. and P.*, III, 3545); A 43 (*J. and P.*, III, 3546); C 40 (*J. and P.*, I, 227).

ticular problem concurrently with others until he finds a solution, and of how working with this particular problem leads him into new trains of thought.

For example, Kierkegaard begins to jot down many different ideas touching on theological questions, and when they are not free and unattached thoughts outside the complex of deeper problems, these entries become points of departure for the study of specific theological problems.

Here we must be content to point out the most important of these theological problems, those which Kierkegaard's methodical reasoning later places into a larger context.

As early as November, 1834 Kierkegaard advances a view of Christianity which gradually develops into the nucleus of his understanding of Christianity. Kierkegaard's intention is not to concentrate on Christianity as doctrine but to take Christ's own life as the basis for a presentation of Christianity. He writes of this: "Christian dogmatics, it seems to me, must grow out of Christ's activity, and all the more so because Christ did not establish any doctrine; he acted. He *did not teach* that there was redemption for men, but he *redeemed men*. A Mohammedan dogmatics (*sit venia verbo*) would grow out of Mohammed's teaching, but a Christian dogmatics grows out of Christ's activity. Through Christ's activity (which actually was the main thing) his nature was also given; Christ's relationship to God, man, nature, and the human situation *was conditioned by his activity*. Everything else is to be regarded only as introduction."[18]

This quotation clearly indicates how Kierkegaard's primary interest focuses on Christ's activity and the conflicts this activity in the world must involve.

The deeper ground for Kierkegaard's preoccupation with this aspect of Christianity lies in his seeking to achieve clarity about the extent to which Christ's life should be a binding example for man, and, if so, how far man ought to go in his attempt at imitation.[19] That Kierkegaard would

[18] I A 27 (*J. and P.*, I, 412).
[19] A clear answer to this, resting on Kierkegaard's own exis-

transfer the thought of "Christ's activity" over to the life
of the individual Christian appears in these words: ". . . all
Christianity is a life-course."[20]

As time goes on, Kierkegaard gives much careful thought
to these questions and discovers that they belong to "the
most difficult of all" questions. He accuses "contemporary
theologians and philosophers" of overlooking this problem.
For Kierkegaard personally the problem becomes a burning
one because he is led to it by his "anthropological contemplation," which insists upon a more concrete qualification
of man's ethical and religious obligations. In the following
entry we see very clearly how Kierkegaard summarizes the
difficulties of the problem: "That the Son of God became
man is certainly the highest metaphysical and religious
paradox, but it is nevertheless not the deepest ethical paradox. Christ's appearance contains a polemic against existence. He became a human being like all others, but he
stood in a polemical relationship to the concrete-ethical
elements of actuality. He went about and taught the people.
He owned nothing; he did not even have a place to lay his
head. Truly it is uplifting to see the faith and trust in
providence which makes a man carefree as the birds of
the air and the flowers of the field, but to what extent is
this an ethical expression for a human life? Shall a man
not work in order to live; is it not superior; do I dare ignore
providing for tomorrow in this way? Here the most difficult
problems come together. Christ's life had a negative-polemical relation to the church and state. It would be the highest ethical paradox if God's son entered into the whole of
actuality, became part of it, submitted to all its triviality,
for even if I have the courage and trust and faith to die of
starvation, this is worthy of admiration, and in each generation there probably are not ten who have it, but all the

---

tential experience, is first given in entry X[1] A 134 (*J. and P.,*
IV).

[20] II A 377 (*J. and P.,* III, 3377).

same we teach and proclaim that it would be even greater to submit to the actualities of life.

"God help the poor head which entertains this kind of doubt, the unhappy man who has sufficient passion to think, the silent letter incapable of doing anything for other men except to keep still about what he suffers and possibly to smile so that no one may detect it."[21]

There is a connection between these reflections and Kierkegaard's own existential involvement in Christianity and his subsequent strong emphasis on imitation. Through his attempt to advance "Christ's activity" as the pattern for Christian life, Kierkegaard simultaneously completes the task which he regards as the culmination of Protestantism's historical development—namely, to present Christ's life as the prototype. Of this he says: "The Middle Ages culminates in Raphael, his conception of the Madonna. Protestantism will culminate in the Christ-image; but this will be the flower of the most thorough dialectical development."[22]

Another essential point of departure for Kierkegaard's work with theological questions is the relation between the human and the Christian. It is characteristic of Kierkegaard that from the beginning he advances and maintains two incompatible (so it seems) factors: (1) the justification of the human position and (2) Christianity's claim upon the whole man.

The following entry is an example of Kierkegaard's accentuation of the human side: "The trouble with philosophers in respect to Christianity is that they use continental maps when they ought to use special large-scale maps, *for every dogma is nothing but a more concrete extension* of the universally human consciousness."[23] Kierkegaard here believes that the philosophers' error consists in speaking all

[21] IV A 62 (*J. and P.*, III, 3076); see also A 47 (*J. and P.*, III, 3075) and A 103 (*J. and P.*, III, 3077).

[22] IX A 110 (*J. and P.*, I, 164).

[23] II A 440 (*J. and P.*, III, 3272). See also II A 443 (*J. and P.*, I, 446).

too abstractly about man, but the more concretely a man thinks about himself, the more he discovers the conflicts which Christianity alone resolves. In an earlier journal entry Kierkegaard warns directly against occupying oneself with "speculating about dogma" before one gets clear on the human standpoint: "If one does not maintain strictly the relation between philosophy (the purely human view of the world, the *human* standpoint) and Christianity but begins straightway, without special penetrating investigations of this relation, to speculate about dogma, one can easily achieve apparently rich and satisfying results. But things can also turn out as with marl at one time, when, without having investigated it and the soil, people used it on any sort of land—and got excellent yields for a few years but afterwards found that the soil was exhausted."[24]

But parallel with these entries Kierkegaard can give expression to the impossibility of going through "all the experiences"[25] mentioned by Paul before arriving at faith.

Kierkegaard then seeks to determine more explicitly the relation between the human position and Christianity. Entry III A 39 (*J. and P.*, I, 1100), which states that "faith is a more concrete qualification than immediacy, because from a purely human point of view the secret of all knowledge is to concentrate upon what is given in immediacy; in faith we assume something which is not given and can never be deduced from the preceding consciousness—that is, the consciousness of sin and the assurance of the forgiveness of sins," may be regarded as a direct continuation of reflections upon this relationship.

In a later entry Kierkegaard justifies a simultaneous adherence to the two standpoints when he says that "the two terms are equally necessary—namely, that Christianity is something which did not arise in any man's thought and yet since it is given to man is natural to him because here also God is creating."[26]

[24] II A 77 (*J. and P.*, III, 3253).
[25] II A 190 (*J. and P.*, II, 1097).
[26] III A 211 (*J. and P.*, II, 2277).

Thereafter it becomes important for Kierkegaard to insist on the significance of both elements and at the same time to determine with the greatest exactitude the point at which the human position reaches its culmination so that the other standpoint can get a hearing. The following entry describes the condition which is an indication that the human outlook is at its critical point: "In a spiritual sense, too, there comes a moment when we feel that we ourselves achieve nothing at all, when we go as if naked out of our self-scrutiny, as we did formerly from the womb."[27] The way which leads man to Christianity goes through "the crushing of the individual."[28] In becoming aware of this relationship Kierkegaard has taken the first step in explaining one of the most central concepts within his existential thought, namely, "the double movement of infinity."

The reflections about the relation between man and Christianity are continued, and they become essentially deepened by Kierkegaard's elucidation of the relation of absolute contrast between Socrates and Christ, man and God.

These have been only a few crucial thoughts which show up clearly in the numerous theological entries. But in going through the other groupings we will still encounter entries touching on theological problems, inasmuch as Kierkegaard, in all consistency, places these spheres in relation to theology as the central point of departure.

Mythology is the subject Kierkegaard finishes first. He devotes himself especially to this subject in the year 1836, while still working simultaneously with other topics, as was his custom. In mythology, as well as in other spheres, Kierkegaard's concern is to find an adequate definition of the concept. He attempts to set up such a comprehensive concept of mythology that he can include under it not only all the phenomena which appear in national mytho-

[27] II A 357 (*J. and P.*, IV).
[28] III A 212 (*J. and P.*, II, 2278); compare II A 758 (*J. and P.*, II, 1310).

logical figures, folk legends, and fairy stories, but also other possible manifestations of mythology in human history.

Kierkegaard certainly had some thoughts about mythology prior to 1836, but during that year he makes an effort to get a good grasp on the subject. Comments in his journal and papers specifiy the books on mythology of greatest interest to him that year.[29]

In the autumn of 1836 Kierkegaard asks the following question, which already contains certain elements of a reply: "What is involved in the concept *myth* and *mythology*—does not every age have its mythology—Novalis, etc. —how is it different from poetry (the subjective—the novel, poetic prose)—a hypothetical proposition in the indicative."[30]

Two entries, I A 269 (*J. and P.*, III, 2700) and 285 (*J. and P.*, IV), point to new aspects in the definition of the nature of mythology; these notations show that Kierkegaard ascribes a more comprehensive meaning to the concept "mythology" when he uses it as a foundation for his reflections on this topic. This allows him to embrace under mythology not only "genuine mythology,"[31] the older forms of mythology, but also man's later attempts to creat mythology.

The epitomizing definition of the concept "mythology" which he then gives in I A 300 (*J. and P.*, III, 2799) shows that his extension of the sphere of mythology comes legitimately out of his own selected premises. We quote this important note and add a few clarifying comments. "Mythology is the compacting (suppressed being) of the idea of eternity (the eternal idea) in the categories of time and space—in time, for example, Chiliasm, or the doctrine of

[29] For information on Kierkegaard's reading in mythology and fairy tales, see Carl Koch, *Søren Kierkegaard og Eventyret*, supplement to *Søren Kierkegaard og Emil Boesen* (Copenhagen, 1901), pp. 68-89, and editors' notes on this literature in the *Papirer*. See *J. and P.*, III, MYTH, MYTHOLOGY.

[30] I A 241 (*J. and P.*, III, 2798).

[31] I A 285 (*J. and P.*, IV).

a kingdom of heaven which begins in time; in space, for example, an idea construed as being a finite personality. Just as the poetic is the subjunctive but does not claim to be more (poetic actuality), mythology, on the other hand, is a hypothetical statement in the indicative (see p. 1 in this book [i.e., I A 241]) and lies in the very middle of the conflict between them, because the ideal, losing its gravity, is compacted in earthly form."[32]

In this entry we find first of all the encompassing definition of the concept "mythology": "Mythology is the compacting (suppressed being) of the idea of eternity (the eternal idea) in the categories of time and space. . . ." In mythology, then, the eternal, which is unlimited, is embraced within the categories of limitation—time and space. Therefore the eternal finds itself in mankind's mythological period in "suppressed being," since the nature of the eternal cannot be expressed in forms belonging to the world of limitations.

Secondly, this entry refers to examples of the development of mythological formations outside of the mythological eras in the strict sense. These developments will always fall under the two qualifying conditions of finitude—time and space. The development of mythological formations in relation to time expresses faith that the eternal eventually can be realized within time ("Chiliasm");[33] with respect to space it expresses faith in the possibility that an individual human being is able to accommodate the fullness of eternity and thereby act as the visible representative of the eternal.[34]

Thirdly, Kierkegaard marks the boundary between the poetic and the mythological. Mythology and poetry are

[32] With regard to "the poetic" and "the subjunctive" see also II A 161 (*J. and P.*, III, 2315).

[33] This also includes "the doctrine of the kingdom of God" here on earth, all socialist utopias which promise a perfect social order.

[34] According to Kierkegaard it could be said only of one man that he had actualized the eternal, but the eternal in this case could not be seen directly.

similar in that both are the products of creative imagination and thereby differ from what is called factual, actual. The essential difference between them is that the poet is conscious that he operates only in the sphere of possibility, while myths come to be regarded as solid actuality by those among whom they have arisen. On the basis of this distinction Kierkegaard characterizes poetic productions as "subjunctive," since they represent possibilities created by the imagination; whereas the mythological is referred to as "a hypothetical statement in the indicative," therefore something man himself creates but nevertheless conceives as factual, actual.

With entry I A 300 Kierkegaard achieves a definition of the concept mythology which seems so adequate that he makes no more changes.

After carefully defining the nature of mythology, Kierkegaard utilizes the definition along two lines, a procedure which is gradually extended to other conceptual areas.

Kierkegaard first relates mythology to man's mental-spiritual development. Mythology, which in its first manifestation corresponds to the childhood of mankind, is set in relation to every subsequent individual, and it is assumed that mythology, as a mental-spiritual phenomenon, is repeated in foreshortened perspective in the childhood of every individual.[35] Knowledge of these relationships can be of significance in the rearing of children. Most likely influenced by P. M. Møller's little essay "On Telling Fairy Stories to Children," Kierkegaard gives his own practical instructions[36] on how to influence the child in early childhood. This interest in applying a concept to practical life is an indication of Kierkegaard's efforts to give the concepts an existential direction.

Kierkegaard's second application of the concept mythology also points to his interest in linking it to existence. Kierkegaard searches for individual representatives of the different periods in mythology and finds them in Mozart's

[35] I A 319 (*J. and P.*, V).   [36] II A 12 (*J. and P.*, I, 265).

operas. He concludes that in *The Marriage of Figaro, The Magic Flute*, and *Don Juan*, Mozart in these three stages "has consummately and perfectly presented a development of love on the level of immediacy."[37]

Kierkegaard then uses the figure of the page in *The Marriage of Figaro* and of Papageno in *The Magic Flute* as individual representatives of Oriental eroticism and of Greek eroticism, respectively, in the era of mythology. Kierkegaard portrays these two types of eroticism on the basis of essential elements in Oriental and Greek mythology; therefore it is correct to say that the page and Papageno can serve as representatives of Oriental and Greek mythology.

It should be added here that as early as October 1835, while reading Schleiermacher's *Vertraute Briefe über die Lucinde*,[38] Kierkegaard became excited about Schleiermacher's method of presenting the "various points of view" through several individual characters. Mozart's operas gave Kierkegaard the possibility of applying the idea he got while reading this review of Friedrich von Schlegel's *Lucinde*—namely, that of having particular individuals represent the ideas within the first sphere of interest he had just completed. Thus as early as the beginning of 1837 Kierkegaard took his first step on the way to his subsequent very comprehensive use of pseudonyms.

It is significant that seven years later Kierkegaard was able to incorporate without alteration his interpretation of the above-mentioned operas by Mozart in his great pseudonymous work *Either/Or.*

In designating "Anthropological contemplation" as an essential task for modern thought, Kierkegaard primarily focuses attention on the significance of psychology, in the wider sense, as a prerequisite for a philosophical and theological renewal. At the time Kierkegaard wrote his observation on "anthropological contemplation" he was, to repeat, already well on the way himself to working out the desig-

[37] I C 125, p. 304 (*J. and P.*, IV).
[38] I C 69 (*J. and P.*, V).

nated task. The branch of knowledge on which Kierkegaard for personal reasons concentrated at first was psychology, and the two aspects of it which occupied him most were able to provide the first foundation for completing the task he assigned to "anthropological contemplation."

One may almost say that Kierkegaard's exploration of psychology was a necessity for him.[39] His own complex nature and his relationship to his father compelled him early to turn his attention to the hidden mechanisms of the psyche. Thus he gradually developed into an observer of his own and his father's mental states.

This connection between the exploration of his own self and of his father had its basis not only in the idea that his deepest conflicts stemmed from his father's influence upon him but also in his presentiment of certain secrets in his father's life which were the direct cause of his father's melancholy and an indirect cause of his own. Thus, apart from Kierkegaard himself, the father became the first and most important object of his observant, spying attention. Primarily out of sympathy for his father, Kierkegaard felt impelled to ferret out the reason for his father's closed-upness and melancholy. Later he was to regard the uncovering of the hidden causalities in a man's life as the most difficult but also the principal task for the psychologist. Of this he writes: "All of us have a little psychological insight, some powers of observation, but when this science or art manifests itself in its infinitude, when it abandons minor transactions on the streets and in dwellings in order to scurry after its favorite: the person shut up within himself —then men grow weary."[40]

As early as 1834 Kierkegaard may have reached the point of attempting to wrest the secret from his melancholy father, for in that year he asked himself to what extent a person, even with a good purpose, has the right to intrude into another person's private domain. This prob-

---

[39] *Stages*, p. 221; *Purity of Heart*, p. 174: ". . . he makes a virtue of necessity. . . ."

[40] V B 147 (*J. and P.*, V).

lem is treated in several journal entries of 1834 on "the idea of a master-thief."[41]

The striking thing about Kierkegaard's "master-thief" is "that he lives for an idea";[42] at the same time Kierkegaard endows him with "a touch of melancholy, a closed-up-ness within himself, a dim view of life, an inner dissatisfaction" —consequently with traits apparently borrowed from Kierkegaard himself. In my opinion Kierkegaard's speculations on "the master-thief" were motivated by a desire to find moral support for his spying observation of his father.[43] Kierkegaard justified his quest by the fact that he did it out of love for his father.

Apart from his intensified observation of his father, there were particular presentiments which especially drew Kierkegaard's attention to several hidden elements in his father's life. It is suggestive that Kierkegaard devoted some of the notations during this period to the nature of presentiment and the modes of its manifestation.[44] Presentiment became for him the reliable occasion for a sustained investigation of hidden psychic motives.

Kierkegaard's efforts to penetrate his father's secret finally led to a result. He records this in the following entry: "Then it was that the great earthquake occurred, the frightful upheaval which suddenly drove me to a new infallible principle for interpreting all the phenomena."[45] This brief statement explains two things: first, that the discovery of the secret thread was a personal catastrophe to Kierkegaard. The reason for the upheaval the entry does not tell —only the results. Next, Kierkegaard, in the expression "a new infallible law for interpreting," reveals that already

[41] See I A 11-18 (*J. and P.*, V).

[42] I A 15 (*J. and P.*, IV).

[43] Kierkegaard is in a conflict which he later calls "a teleological suspension of the ethical." That objective observation without sympathy for one's object is wrong, he declares in X¹ A 223 (*J. and P.*, IV).

[44] II A 18 (*J. and P.*, I, 91); II A 584 (*J. and P.*, IV).

[45] II A 805 (*J. and P.*, V).

for some time he had been preoccupied with this problem and thought he had found the solution. But after further investigation something occurred which suddenly made him certain of his conclusions. Note that Kierkegaard says "suddenly"; it signifies that the solution came unexpectedly and with an irresistible force of conviction.

A profound irony in Kierkegaard's great achievement in the sphere of observation is apparent, for his great triumph is overshadowed by the responsibility laid upon him by this fresh knowledge; his father's guilt obliged him to come under the common guilt, whereby he was led into the same despair under which his father suffered.

In September, 1835 Kierkegaard jots down a sentence from E.T.A. Hoffmann's story *Meister Floh*, which reproduces exactly the same situation. A person in the story gets a microscopic glass in his eye which enables him to read other people's secret thoughts and thereby to become a perfect observer. But he discovers at the same time that this "gift" of being able to unveil other people's secrets leads to despair. Kierkegaard enters the following significant words from *Meister Floh* in his journal: "How did a man who searched out the most secret thoughts of his brethren speak to himself? Does not this fatal gift bring over him that frightful condition which came over the eternal Jew, who wandered through the bright tumult of the world without joy, without hope, without pain, in apathetic indifference which is the *caput mortuum* of despair, as if through an unprofitable, comfortless waste-land?"[46]

Most likely Kierkegaard discovered his father's guilt before entering this quotation from Hoffmann. This supposition is strengthened by the fact that in the autumn of 1835 Kierkegaard began to remove himself from his father's strong influence. As yet he seemed to refuse to undertake the burdensome obligation of standing with his father in his guilt, but several years later he assumed this guilt as his own. It is unmistakable that Kierkegaard was fleeing from

[46] I C 60 (*J. and P.*, V). E.T.A. Hoffmann, *Ausgewählte Schriften*, I-X (Berlin, 1927-28), X, p. 287.

his father in the autumn of 1835; he speaks of this later as follows: ". . . for it was, after all, anxiety which brought me to go astray, and where was I to seek a safe stronghold when I knew or suspected that the only man I had admired for his strength was tottering."[47]

The autumn of 1835 thus becomes a turning point in Kierkegaard's life. Up until then he was very absorbed in "a sickly brooding" over his own "wretched history!"[48] He also discovers at this time the truth he writes in his journal a few years later: "There is nothing more dangerous for a man, nothing more paralyzing, than a certain isolating self-scrutiny, in which world-history, human life, society—in short, everything—disappears, and like the ομφαλψύχιται in an egotistical circle one constantly stares only at his own navel."[49]

After arriving at the dismal result of his analysis of the situation in his home, he seeks freedom from it by throwing himself into political life and by replacing his theological studies with a very comprehensive study of esthetics. Of this period in Kierkegaard's life it can be said that he turns away from an intense preoccupation with his own internal problems to life in the external world.

Despite his absorption in esthetic themes, however, Kierkegaard could not entirely give up working concurrently in other areas. Neither could he abandon his training in identifying himself with other people's states of mind after having learned so much about exploring man through his father's situation, which he regarded as the most difficult.

In explaining his own and his father's psychical life Kierkegaard had learned to use a particular method which later was to be useful in his psychological scrutiny of various characters drawn from the esthetic as well as the ethical spheres. One of the most important principles in this method is the identification of the observer with the object of observation. This principle, which Kierkegaard had al-

[47] IV A 107 (*J. and P.*, V).
[48] II A 172 (*J. and P.*, II, 1970).
[49] II A 187 (*J. and P.*, II, 1971).

ready used in observing his father, now becomes the basis of his whole experimental psychology. Most often, as in the case with his father, it is sympathy which moves him to identification.

Kierkegaard most likely became aware of this principle through his absorption in the art of drama, where it is of essential importance for an actor to be able to identify himself with the person he is to present if a rendering of the person's psychical life is to be achieved.

The first prompting to this identification came to Kierkegaard in the form of presentiments or intimations, the significance of which has already been mentioned. One of the pseudonymous authors, the ironist Constantin Constantius, later gives a very striking account of presentiment's part in an attempt to grasp the innermost structure of man in his relating the following about himself as an observer: "At the first shudder of presentiment my soul has in an instant followed through the whole chain of consequences, which in reality often require a long lapse of time to come to evidence. The concentration of presentiment one never forgets. So it is, I believe, an observer ought to be built, but when he is built in this fashion he will also suffer much."[50] The final observation about suffering much can be applied directly to Kierkegaard's first attempt at being an observer with respect to his father, an attempt which led him into suffering.

An indirect reference is made in the above quotation to a quality which is necessary in order that identification fostered by intimation can be accomplished fully. The observer must have a capacious receptivity for impressions. He must allow himself to be "overwhelmed" by the object of his observation. Kierkegaard, who possessed such a receptivity, speaks of it a few places in his earlier journal entries. He says, for example, that "there is a certain receptivity which is so strong that it is almost productive."[51]

[50] *Repetition*, p. 29.   [51] II A 19 (*J. and P.*, IV).

A fuller description of this receptivity would reveal that it comes very close to anxiety and that it turns particularly toward the dark side of the psychical life, but this problem will come up later.

Meanwhile the center of gravity of Kierkegaard's interest shifted to esthetics, and we will now see what happens when he finds in the world about him characters who become objects for his observation.

Kierkegaard had perceived the danger of morbidity in his pondering on his own situation, but increased identification with others also has its dangers. Full identification, which is the prerequisite for adequate empathy with the person or character being observed, can be so powerful that it can threaten the observer's psychic health. In order to identify himself with the other without losing himself, the observer must be able to endure the split which takes place by being himself and yet becoming another. Kierkegaard now uses this splitting process in observing himself and others.[52] At the time of the transition to his esthetic period he became skilled in this difficult art of balancing, but we discover that he had much difficulty initially in the redoubling of his own person required by the identification. Certain journal entries indicate that there were dangers of disruption.

Kierkegaard calls himself in his attempt at identification a "double-thinker," consequently a person who is split in two: a first original "I" and "another I" which comes out in his empathetic experiments. Every time the "other I" thinks something through, the "first I" discovers that it also bears upon itself, because the relived character situation is one of his own possibilities, which thus becomes a present possibility for him. Of this empathetic process Kierkegaard says: "The trouble is that as soon as one has

[52] Kierkegaard thereby unites the two sides of observation which Frater Taciturnus (one of the pseudonymous authors) later describes thus: to "exist in himself" and "to peer into life and into other men." *Stages*, p. 405.

thought up something, he becomes that himself. The other day I told you about an idea for a Faust, but now I feel that *it was myself* I described; I barely read or think about an illness before I have it." And further: "It is just as if I were a double-thinker and that my other *I* continually anticipates me. . . ."[53]

With these words Kierkegaard describes the process within himself which lets him identify himself with a character in order to make room again for the next identification.

The tension in Kierkegaard between wanting to maintain a thought and not letting himself be completely bound by it could take the form of evanescent thoughts. He describes this situation thus: "One thought succeeds another, just as soon as it is thought and I want to write it down, there is a new one—hold it, seize it—madness—dementia!"[54]

It is not to be wondered that Kierkegaard had some anxiety about this splitting process, something he gives expression to in the following remark: "Something very strange that has often disquieted me has been the thought that the life I lived was not my own but, without my being able to prevent it, was completely identified with another particular person, and each time I did not become aware of this until it had been partially lived through."[55]

Through this splitting process and temporary identification with various characters and possibilities, Kierkegaard prepares the types which later can be used in the authorship as representatives of different attitudes and positions in life. The simplest of these splits he uses in his first book, *From the Papers of One Still Living* (1838), when he speaks in the preface of the first and the second "I" and sensitively indicates the distance but also the solidarity between the two, expressing the latter by saying that they

[53] I A 333 (*J. and P.*, V).
[54] I A 336 (*J. and P.*, IV). See also Kierkegaard's entry on a quite similar situation of an insane person who experiences situations and characters, I C 123 (*J. and P.*, V).
[55] II A 444 (*J. and P.*, V).

"are linked together by the most profound, most holy, indissoluble bond."[56]

Kierkegaard calls this living into the many and various human possibilities experimental psychology, and by means of it the way was open for him continually to create new characters, to set them into relationship to each other or to make them the objects of his observation. This whole process was also to have great significance in the creation of the ingeniously developed system of pseudonymous authorship.[57]

It is noteworthy that Kierkegaard seeks identification particularly with characters who reveal a certain consistency in their life-attitudes, whether positive or negative according to Kierkegaard's view. Of the positive characters Socrates especially may be mentioned; of the negative, Don Juan, Faust, and Ahasuerus.

In addition to his concern with experimental psychology, Kierkegaard attempts to become clear about the origin of such psychological states as anxiety, despair, and melancholy. Once again his personal situation provided the occasion. Kierkegaard personally suffered under feelings of anxiety, as this entry among others indicates: "All existences make me anxious, from the smallest fly to the mysteries of the Incarnation; the whole thing is inexplicable to me, most of all my own self; to me all existence is infected, most of all my own self. My distress is enormous, boundless. . . ."[58]

Despair and melancholy are also apparent in the young Kierkegaard. But of principal importance is the fact, as has been indicated, that Kierkegaard experienced these mental states in intensified form through transference from his father.

Thus when Kierkegaard seeks a deeper understanding of

[56] Samlede Værker, I-XIV (Copenhagen, Gyldendal, 1901-1906), XIII, p. 45 (p. iv of Preface).

[57] On this see also Arild Christensen, "Der junge Kierkegaard," *Orbis litterarum*, XVIII, 1963, pp. 31-32.

[58] II A 420 (*J. and P.*, V).

the nature of anxiety and despair, he again works with his own difficult problems. He tries to fathom these negative conditions and find the positive counterpart to them. He finds this positive quality in the state of mind inherent in the sphere of faith.

Kierkegaard's deeply penetrating analysis of the nature of anxiety brings to light its many forms. He points out the close relationship of anxiety to presentiment, and he perceives more profoundly that the deepest ground of anxiety is in original sin. This discovery lays the foundation for explaining all the forms of anxiety from one standpoint, which he does later in *The Concept of Anxiety*. In the following entry (1842) Kierkegaard records his insight into the nature of anxiety: "The nature of original sin has often been explained, and still a primary category has been lacking—it is anxiety [*Angst*]; this is the essential determinant. Anxiety is a desire for what one fears, a sympathetic antipathy; anxiety is an alien power which grips the individual, and yet one cannot tear himself free from it and does not want to, for one fears, but what he fears he desires."[59]

Just about the same time Kierkegaard also arrives at a clear definition of the concept of despair [*Fortvivlelse*], which is an intensified form of anxiety [*Angst*].

In delving into the nature of anxiety and despair, Kierkegaard encounters the question of mood as a psychic quality. Mood, its nature together with its role in psychic life, is also subjected to a thorough investigation.

The deep psychological insight Kierkegaard gains by his experimenting and analyzing furnishes him with a mass of concrete material which he can use in his work in other areas. In this connection it should be noted that it was this very absorption with more penetrating analyses of different psychological conditions which led Kierkegaard to the viewpoint that *every dogma is nothing more than a more concrete extension* of the universally human consciousness."[60] We have a particular example of this transition from a uni-

[59] III A 233 (*J. and P.*, I, 94).
[60] II A 440 (*J. and P.*, III, 3272).

versal psychological phenomenon to dogmatics in Kierkegaard's penetration into the nature of anxiety, which ultimately leads to the dogmatic question of original sin.

Meeting Regine forced Kierkegaard to make new experimental observations. In order to help Regine through the
tragic outcome of the engagement, Kierkegaard had to become engrossed in the nature and essence of woman, and
at the same time acquaint himself with all the psychic conditions which characterize the relationship between man
and woman. Later use of these experiences in his authorship reveals the depth and comprehensiveness of the
knowledge acquired in these areas.

Mention could also be made at this time of Kierkegaard's
experience on May 19, 1838, *"an indescribable joy"* which
"inexplicably flames up" in him,[61] which gave him an insight into a new and specific mental condition which also
needed to be defined more closely in relation to the universal laws of the psychic life.

In his psychological investigations Kierkegaard profited
especially from Karl Rosenkranz's book *Psychologie oder
die Wissenschaft vom subjectiven Geist*. Here he found a
psychology which, beginning with the lower psychic states,
rises to a description of the higher forms of mental-spiritual
life. This psychology, developed according to Hegel's
scheme, appealed to Kierkegaard primarily because of its
ascending scale in the presentation of psychological
themes.

In these various ways Kierkegaard was well equipped
with psychological knowledge and experience before he
actually began his authorship; by that time he was already
practiced in making psychological experiments on the persons whom he thought qualified to enlighten him on certain aspects of mental-spiritual life or on the various existential approaches.[62] By means of ever new experiments

[61] II A 228 (*J. and P.*, V). See also G. Malantschuk, "Pælen i
Kjødet hos Søren Kierkegaard" (*Dansk teologisk Tidsskrift*, III,
1940).

[62] See V B 72:22 (*J. and P.*, V); Hans Brøchner, *Erindringer*

Kierkegaard extended his psychological knowledge, and throughout his whole life psychology remained a very important tool in his activity as an author.

Later Kierkegaard makes a distinction between general psychology and Christian psychology. General psychology has two parts: the first concerns the empirical and visible aspect of man, and the second characterizes man's condition after the eternal in man has begun to assert itself. Christian psychology, on the other hand, has to do with the psychic conditions and forms of the conscious life which have their origin in the collision between the purely human outlook and the new outlook with which Christianity confronts men.[63] Psychology is thereby arranged in the tripartite order of the stages.

It is of interest to note that Kierkegaard's concern with the sphere of psychology in his later years resembles that of his early years. Here we find, as in the beginning, a concentration on his personal experiences, which is apparent in his entitling many journal entries "About myself." This similarity appears at still another important point. Just as Kierkegaard as "the master-thief" wanted to explore certain hidden and unpleasant facts, so the later Kierkegaard as "a secret agent in the service of the highest" is interested in exploring certain (to use his expression) "criminal" situations in the religious life of Christendom. In both cases the investigation is undertaken for the sake of the good, but nonetheless it occurs by means of what Kierkegaard calls the suspension of the ethical.

Of Kierkegaard's interest in psychology as a whole, it

---

om Søren Kierkegaard, ed. Steen Johansen (Copenhagen, 1953), p. 24 et passim; H. Martensen, Af mit Levnet, I-II (Copenhagen, 1882-83), II, pp. 141-42.

[63] An example of how this collision between the human and Christianity can be expounded from a point of view hostile to Christianity is found in Nietzsche's numerous comments on *"die Psychologie des Christentums."* See, for example, *The Genealogy of Morals.*

can be said that he places man in the center as the principal object of all his observations. His "anthropological contemplation" is ultimately grounded in the realization that "Individuality is the true period [terminal point] in the development of creation. . . ."[64] It is along this road that he comes to his central concept: the single individual.

Søren Kierkegaard's discovery of the secret in his father's life and the resultant flight from his father's strict ethical and religious influence set him on two courses during the next years. In the first place, in protest against his father's upbringing, Kierkegaard was attracted to the figures which he regarded as representatives of the negative position toward Christianity—namely Faust, Don Juan, and Ahasuerus. From as early as the spring of 1835 there are signs of a special interest in the Faust figure, whose critical and inquiring spirit best corresponded to his own attitude. Kierkegaard at that time says of Faust: "World significance ought to be attributed to the idea of Faust," inasmuch as Faust represents "doubt personified."[65] Kierkegaard, who with respect to Christianity himself took the path of doubt in the autumn of 1835,[66] was tempted to set out into the external world with its pleasures and dangers under the guidance of Mephistopheles. He later describes this temptation: "Yes, therefore I believe I would surrender to Satan so that he could show me every abomination, every sin in its most dreadful form—it is this inclination, this taste for the secret of sin."[67] But with a remarkable foresight that he would not find satisfaction in this pilgrimage, Kierkegaard says, using Faust as a cover name: "Faust did not want to learn to know evil in order that he might rejoice over not being so bad (only the philistines do this); on the contrary, he wanted to feel all the sluice gates of sin open

[64] II A 474 (J. and P., II, 1981).

[65] I A 72, p. 47 (J. and P., V).

[66] See I A 94 (J. and P., III, 3245) and I A 95 (J. and P., I, 416).

[67] II A 603 (J. and P., IV).

within his own breast, the whole kingdom of incalculable possibilities. Everything, however, will not be sufficient. His expectations will be disappointed."[68] That is to say, Kierkegaard, protesting his strict upbringing and despite anticipation of a disappointing result, wanted to test thoroughly these three negative types, beginning with Faust. Since this aspect of the flight had obvious existential significance for his ethical and religious outlook, we shall discuss these three ideas in more detail under the subject of Kierkegaard's view of ethics.

But the flight from his father's influence also took a more intellectual form. Kierkegaard turned away from the study of theology and sought through independent study to fathom the various domains of scientific scholarship, beginning with the esthetic-literary.

Kierkegaard's study of literary and esthetic issues was initiated in March, 1836, with the reading of Molbech's *Forelæsninger over den nyere danske Poesi* (*Lectures on Modern Danish Poetry*, I-II; Copenhagen, 1832)[69] and thereafter with Friedrich von Diez's *Die Poesie der Troubadours* (*The Poetry of the Troubadors*; Zwickau, 1926).[70] Excerpts and comments on the text witness to the interest with which he studied these books. Other works followed.

This reading engendered a host of distinctive ideas and comments in the journals (beginning in March, 1936), attempts to clarify the central issues in esthetics. His first entry in March, 1836 indicates how exuberant and original his imagination was even when working with dry grammatical formulations: "All of human life could well be conceived as a great discourse in which different people come to represent the different parts of speech (this might also be applicable to nations in relation to each other). How many people are merely adjectives, interjections, conjunctions, adverbs; how few are nouns, action words, etc.; how many are copulas.

"People in relation to each other are like the irregular

---

[68] II A 605 (*J. and P.*, II, 1185).
[69] I C 87 (*J. and P.*, V).   [70] I C 83 (*J. and P.*, V).

verbs in various languages—almost all the verbs are irregular."[71]

In his absorbing study of literary and esthetic issues Kierkegaard concentrates mainly on the following points:

(1) He attempts to distinguish poetry from two other spheres which in his view stand on a lower plane but which nevertheless have certain points of contact with poetry—namely, mythology and music.

Mythology first and foremost expresses the primitive man's religious mentality, but if it has lost this significance, it is to be regarded only as a branch of poetry. At the same time Kierkegaard believes that if poetry is to give an ideal picture of actuality it must contain an element of mythology, inasmuch as mythology is temporal actuality seen in the light of imagination's anticipation of the eternal. Kierkegaard says of this contact between mythology and poetry: "What I call the mythological-poetic in history is the nimbus which hovers near every genuine striving in history, not an abstraction but a *transfiguration*, not the prosaic actuality, and every genuine historical trend will also give rise to such an idea-mythology."[72]

On the other hand, the lyricism of poetry places it in relation to music. It is possible to arrange a whole scale of relations between word and sound, between poetry and music. Kierkegaard's reflections on this subject give him a clear idea of when music or poetry, as the case may be, is dominant in a poetical work. Kierkegaard finds that: "Musical quality resides in the rhyme and rhythm."[73] He regards music as a medium to communicate moods and passions, and as a medium of communication it must be considered to be on a lower level than language. These reflections together with certain experiences related to man's first immediate form of existence lead Kierkegaard to his theory of music as the medium for the demonic.[74]

[71] I A 126 (*J. and P.*, I, 25).
[72] I A 264 (*J. and P.*, II, 1629).
[73] I A 261 (*J. and P.*, III, 2306).
[74] On the connecting link between the musical and the

(2) Kierkegaard seeks to place the lyrical in relation to the epic. For a brief time he was uncertain about which of the two branches of poetry comes first in mankind's spiritual development. His first thoughts on this issue appear in the following entry (which also reveals his interest in linking it together with the existential): "What a προτυπος for individual human life lies in the fact that we always see a nation's poetic development begin with the epic and only then does the lyrical follow."[75] In this journal entry Kierkegaard advances the same order of succession as Hegel—without having at this time any firsthand knowledge of Hegel. At the same time Kierkegaard is aware that Heiberg in his schematization places the lyrical first, and he asks: "To what extent, for that matter, is it right to begin with the lyrical; the history of poetry seems to indicate a beginning with the epic."[76] Nevertheless Kierkegaard quickly comes to the conclusion that the lyrical ought to be regarded as the initial stage. In *From the Papers of One Still Living*, published in 1838, this ordering is incorporated in a large context. One may now ask what brought Kierkegaard to this viewpoint. The first journal entry (I A 212 [*J. and P.*, I, 126]) concerning the ordering of the lyrical and the epic in relation to one another suggests the answer to this question. We have noted that in this entry the ordering of these two branches of poetry is supposed to be exemplary (προτυπος) for individual human life. Thus Kierkegaard promptly places the question of the ordering of the lyrical and the epic in relation to the existential development of the single individual. From here it really is not a long way to placing the lyrical first, since the lyrical stands closest to the immediate, and since the single individual begins his life in immediacy.[77]

---

demonic, see I C 125 (*J. and P.*, IV) and especially II A 180 (*J. and P.*, II, 1631) and note.

[75] I A 212 (*J. and P.*, I, 126); prototype.

[76] I A 225 (*J. and P.*, II, 1565).

[77] For Kierkegaard's placing of the lyrical in relation to the epic and of the difference between his and Hegel's view of the

(3) As far as the dramatic is concerned, there can be no doubt of its placement uppermost in the three stages of poetry. Just as the lyrical and the epic refer respectively to feeling and cognition, the conflicts and reconciliations of drama relate to the will. Kierkegaard, whose life was filled with conflicts and contradictions, must have felt especially attracted to the dramatic. We note that long before he actually became absorbed in esthetic problems Kierkegaard was absorbed in drama's primary categories: the tragic and the comic. As early as 1834, assuredly influenced by his own existential situation, Kierkegaard was reflecting on that aspect of the tragic which arises where one is misunderstood by those around him. More explicitly, Kierkegaard sees this misunderstanding grounded in the fact that the person who wills the good and himself actualizes this good releases elements which give offense and can bring the acting person into a tragic situation. Kierkegaard's first attempt to create such a tragic figure is his idea for "the master-thief," who in Kierkegaard's view "lives for an idea"[78] but uses means which are unjustifiable. In the next entry on the tragic, Kierkegaard arranges a whole scale of tragic situations which are due to misunderstanding. He begins his examples in the highest sphere, that is, with the life of Christ, saying: "Doubtless the most sublime tragedy consists in being *misunderstood*. For this reason the life of Christ is supreme tragedy, misunderstood as he was by the people, the Pharisees, the disciples, in short by everybody, and this in spite of the most exalted ideas which he wished to communicate."[79]

Thereupon Kierkegaard goes down the scale, mentioning a figure such as Job, "surrounded by misunderstanding friends, by a ridiculing wife." Next he mentions "the situation of the wife in *The Riquebourg Family*."[80] Then Clara's

---

matter, see Emanuel Hirsch, *Kierkegaard-Studien*, I-II (Gütersloh, 1933), vol. 1 pp. 13ff.

[78] I A 15 (*J. and P.*, IV). [79] I A 33 (*J. and P.*, I, 118).
[80] *The Riquebourg Family*, a drama by Scribe, translated by J. L. Heiberg (Copenhagen, 1832).

situation in Goethe's *Egmont*. Kierkegaard also mentions
Holberg's comic character "the busybody," who moans and
groans under the burden of many enterprises without being understood by others. Finally he mentions "the tragedy
in the hypochondriac's life" and the tragedy of the person
"who is seized with a longing for something higher and
who then encounters people who misunderstand him."

It could be pointed out that most of these examples have
a certain connection with Kierkegaard's own situations.
This is most apparent in the last two examples.

An example of the tragic that comes a bit later has reference to Kierkegaard himself and touches on his inability
to confide completely in anyone: "It is the tragedy of not
having anyone to whom one can make himself intelligible,
which is so beautifully expressed in Genesis, where Adam
gives all the animals names but finds *none* for himself."[81]

Kierkegaard also discovers that the tragic in a man's life
first finds its proper expression when it is regarded as something universally human. Of this he says, "Everything becomes still more tragic, if I may say so, when it is made
historical, is made into something which happens not only
to me but to the whole world, but of course only in case
one has first of all grasped his own need and then gives it
this historical background."[82]

From other entries we see how Kierkegaard continually
discovers new tragic collisions.[83]

In his work with the tragic Kierkegaard is constantly
aware of its opposite, the comic. The first journal entry
about this is joined to the first mention of the tragic and
reads: "The proximity of the tragic to the comic (an observation particularly attributable to Holberg's use of
comedy—for example, his *Jeppe paa Bjerget, Erasmus*

[81] I A 149 (*J. and P.*, I, 26).
[82] I A 208 (*J. and P.*, II, 1626).
[83] See, for example, II A 234 (*J. and P.*, I, 429); III A 199
(*J. and P.*, IV).

Montanus, den Stundesløse, etc.) seems to account also for the fact that a person *can laugh until he begins to cry*."[84]

Kierkegaard asks why the tragic isolates a person while the comic is more encompassing. He writes: "Why do we prefer to read comedy in society and tragedy in solitude?"[85] Kierkegaard discovers that the transition to the comic lies, as he says, in *"clothing the same idea in other dress."*[86] He can also become aware of a comic situation in a completely concrete event.[87] As a general view he takes note of the Aristotelian standpoint that "the category of the comic is essentially contradiction."[88]

In this way Kierkegaard encircles the domains of the tragic and the comic prior to devoting himself in 1841-42 to Hegel's esthetics, and here again he makes it abundantly clear that his special interest is *"dramatic poetry."*[89] While reading Hegel on drama, Kierkegaard pays particular attention to Hegel's delineation of the difference between classical and modern drama. Hegel shows that in Greek drama the subjective element, consequently the significance of the individual, was as yet not predominant in the same manner as in modern drama. Kierkegaard notes two passages about this from Hegel. The one is from Hegel's commentary on several statements from Aristotle's *Poetics*. "It is thus that we recognize the truth of Aristotle's dictum (*Poetics* c. 6) that tragic action possesses two sources (αἴτια δύο), opinion and character (διάνοια καὶ ἦθος), but what is most important is the end (τέλος), and individuals do not act in order to display diverse characters, but these latter are united with a common bond of imaginative conception to the former in the interest of the action."[90] The other passage is from

[84] I A 34 (*J. and P.*, IV).
[85] I A 198 (*J. and P.*, I, 125).
[86] I A 244 (*J. and P.*, V).   [87] III A 198 (*J. and P.*, V).
[88] III A 205 (*J. and P.*, II, 1737).
[89] III C 34, p. 271 (*J. and P.*, V).
[90] Ibid., p. 272; the reference is to Hegel's *Vorlesungen über die Aesthetik* (Berlin, 1838), III, pp. 506-507; G.W.F. Hegel,

Hegel's explanation that "the principal collision in Greek tragedy"[91] lies in the hero's relation to objective forces such as the family and the state, consequently not in the hero's own inner conflicts.

But quite probably Kierkegaard has fastened particularly upon Hegel's remark that in Sophocle's drama *Philoctetes*[92] —in contrast to the general trend in Greek dramas—the subjective factor is clearly predominant. Prompted perhaps by this Hegelian observation, Kierkegaard, after having read *Philoctetes*[93] himself, subsequently places even greater emphasis on this drama as an intermediate link between classical and modern drama. He says of it: "In *Philoctetes* even the situation itself is reflected." And further: "*Philoctetes* does border on being drama, as well as being interesting. Philoctetes' mounting bitterness and the progressive self-contradiction in his behavior connected with it is a profound psychological truth; but the whole thing is not classical."[94]

In addition to these comments on the differing significance of the subjective in classical and modern drama, we find reading notes of Hegel's treatment of dramatic art, especially on Hegel's interpretation of Aristotle's idea that the purpose in presenting the tragic is "to arouse fear and pity"[95] in the spectator. One gets the impression that Kierkegaard was extremely interested in this, and this interest may be explained as his seeking to clarify what meaning the presentation of the tragic can have for the individual. It may well have been this issue in particular which led him to study Aristotle's *Poetics* after reading Hegel's *Aesthetics*.

The Philosophy of Fine Art, tr. F.P.B. Osmaston (London, Bell, 1920), IV, p. 275.

[91] Ibid., pp. 317-18.

[92] On this see Hegel's *Vorlesungen über die Aesthetik*, III, pp. 552-58, especially p. 557; *The Philosophy of Fine Art*, IV, pp. 306-307.

[93] III C 38 (*J. and P.*, V).   [94] III C 39-40 (*J. and P.*, V).

[95] III C 34, p. 272 (*J. and P.*, V).

With his concentration on Aristotle's *Poetics* Kierkegaard approaches the final phase of his endeavor to define precisely the dimensions and the boundaries of the esthetic. Concurring with Aristotle's classification of "tragic actions according to their tragic value,"[96] Kierkegaard obtains a clear perspective of all kinds of tragic conflicts, and he can now compare his own attempts along this line with Aristotle's treatment of the same questions.

Kierkegaard also comes to a final appraisal of Aristotle's claims as to the meaning of the presentation of the tragic material which is supposed to produce a "purification" in the spectator because the hero's conflicts "arouse fear and pity" within him. By seeing the hero's tragic situation dramatized, the individual becomes involved with him, is torn out of his narrow outlook, and in this way is "reconciled" "with actuality."[97] Kierkegaard, however, regards the "reconciliation" won in this manner as inadequate, since it happens primarily "through the loss [of oneself] in contemplation of the esthetic itself"[98] and provides no deeper meaning for the spectators' existential situations.

Concurrently with work on these problems, Kierkegaard undertakes the demarcation of esthetics from metaphysics and ethics. This demarcation becomes important for him during his more comprehensive and methodical work of placing the various spheres of existence in relation to each other.

Thanks to his journal entries on this, we are able to describe accurately the stages along the way to this demarcation. In defining the boundaries of the esthetic Kierkegaard agrees with Hegel, who concludes his *Aesthetics* with the comic as the final stage. After naming the different kinds of poetry in rising scale, Hegel writes: "Doch auf diesem Gipfel führt die Komödie zugleich zur Auflösung der Kunst überhaupt."[99]

[96] IV C 125 (*J. and P.*, IV).   [97] IV C 113 (*J. and P.*, IV).
[98] IV C 110 (*J. and P.*, IV).
[99] Hegel, *Vorlesungen über die Aesthetik*, III, p. 580; *The Philosophy of Fine Art*, IV, p. 348: "Nevertheless we find that

If to Kierkegaard and also Hegel the esthetic culminates in the comic, the question then is what sphere comes next. Kierkegaard believes it to be the metaphysical and his basis for his argument for this stand is as follows: in comedy as well as in metaphysics there is a reconciliation of the conflicting factors, while in tragedy these factors continue to be irreconcilable. Kierkegaard can therefore regard the comic as related to the metaphysical: "The comic is really a metaphysical concept. It brings about a metaphysical reconciliation–."[100]

But seen also from another angle the comic moves in the direction of the metaphysical. "That comedy approaches the metaphysical is also seen in its having the universal as its object in a sense different than tragedy."[101] Kierkegaard tries to show that whereas historical verification is always sought for the collisions of tragedy, comedy can do without it. This reveals comedy's more abstract character compared to tragedy. Kierkegaard regards this concern for historical witness as a defect in tragedy, which becomes apparent when tragedy is considered from an ethical standpoint. That is to say, the ethical applies to everybody, but only a few can share the "extraordinary"[102] quality of the tragic characters. This reduces the value of the "reconciliation" poetry offers, and "the reconciliation" must therefore be sought on a higher plane.

Moreover, as Aristotle had already pointed out, the fact that poetry must employ such ethical distinctions as "better, worse, like us" points to a higher order of things or, to

---

in this very consummation it is Comedy which opens the way to a dissolution of all that human art implies."

[100] IV C 108 (*J. and P.*, II, 1738).

[101] IV C 120 (*J. and P.*, IV); this isolating tendency of the tragic has already been mentioned in I A 198 (*J. and P.*, I, 125); it is fully explained in Kierkegaard's published works, especially *Stages*, pp. 396-404.

[102] IV C 121, p. 418 (*J. and P.*, IV).

esthetics → ethics

say it in Kierkegaard's words: "Hereby poetry points beyond itself to *actuality* and to the metaphysical ideality."[103]

Because of these considerations Kierkegaard is obliged to rank esthetics under metaphysics, since metaphysics represents a higher and more comprehensive totality than esthetics.

Kierkegaard goes even further than "metaphysical ideality" when he places esthetics in relation to spheres lying outside the esthetic as well as the metaphysical. Thus, in the following incomplete sentences, Kierkegaard places esthetics in relation to ethics: "The relation between esthetics and ethics—the transition—*pathos-filled*, not dialectical—there a qualitatively different dialectic begins."[104]

That Kierkegaard perceives the separation of the two spheres from an existential perspective is shown in the first place by the underlining of the phrase "pathos-filled" and in the next place by his assertion that with ethics "begins a qualitatively different dialectic."

With these "sentences" Kierkegaard draws a very precise line of demarcation between esthetics and ethics which later has fundamental significance in the construction of his theory of the stages.

In many annotations to this observation about the relation between esthetics and ethics, Kierkegaard treats in greater detail the inadequacy of the esthetic when it comes to reconciling man with existence. In that connection Kierkegaard makes a note of Kant's definition of the esthetic as "disinterested satisfaction."[105] Kierkegaard may now cite this definition in support of his own already clearly expressed conception that the esthetic does not touch a man's deepest interest; this interest first makes its appearance in ethics.

That Kierkegaard believes he has arrived at a conclusive view of the esthetic with the above-mentioned treatment of

[103] IV C 109 (*J. and P.*, I, 144).
[104] IV C 105 (*J. and P.*, I, 808).
[105] IV C 114 (*J. and P.*, IV).

esthetic problems can be seen at the end of his journal entries on the esthetic, where he speaks of "the idea for my lectures" (IV C 127 [*J. and P.*, V]). The first point in these lectures is to be "concerning the concept poetry." This indicates that Kierkegaard must have thought he was perfectly clear about this concept.

The next point in these lectures, "movements through esthetics," informs us that in dealing with the esthetic questions Kierkegaard wants to delineate a progressive line which would culminate in what becomes point three, namely "the comic." Thereby—as is also explained under point three—"esthetics is abrogated," and thereafter it is possible to deal with the relation of esthetics to other spheres.

It is very interesting that at the end of his little outline for lectures on esthetics Kierkegaard adds the phrase *"Cultus des Genius."* As far as I understand it, Kierkegaard thereby wants to say that if esthetics were to become the central focus in existence, the geniuses of history would logically come to be regarded as the highest ideals, a thought similar to one found in Nietzsche.

Within this discussion of Kierkegaard's work with esthetic issues mention should be made of a concept which belongs under the heading of esthetics but points beyond it —namely, the concept of the romantic. Kierkegaard's intense preoccupation with the romantic begins, just as with the esthetic in general, after his reading of Christian Molbech's *Forelæsninger over den nyere danske Poesie* (*Lectures on Modern Danish Poetry*). Kierkegaard's very detailed quotations from Molbech's lectures pertain particularly to the romantic. He prefaces these quotations with the following comment: "The twenty-first lecture has several illuminating yet not new ideas on the concept of 'the romantic.' "[106] The excerpts that follow together with Kierkegaard's critical comments form the point of departure for Kierkegaard's more extensive work on the romantic.

[106] I C 88, p. 243 (*J. and P.*, V).

In his treatment of the romantic, Molbech leans especially on Jean Paul's *Vorschule der Aesthetik* and like him assembles various elements of the romantic without, however, being able to cite essential features as particularly characteristic. A few sentences Kierkegaard makes note of may be taken as an example: " 'Thus it is not the sentimental or the chivalrous or the marvelous element which constitutes the essential or necessary substance of the romantic—it is rather the infinitude, the freedom emancipated from physical barriers, in the working of the imagination, in intuiting the ideal, in the fullness and depth of feeling, in the idea-oriented power of reflection to which we must look for that fundamental condition for the romantic and also for a large and significant share of modern art. The romantic, declares Jean Paul, is the beautiful without boundaries or the beautiful infinite, just as there is a sublime infinite.' "[107]

Kierkegaard also takes note of Molbech's grading of the branches of art and his calling music " 'the most romantic of all the beaux arts; after that come poetry, painting, sculpture. . . .' "[108]

Kierkegaard is also aware of Molbech's comparison of the romantic with its opposites or with related concepts.

With these impulses from Molbech as his starting point, Kierkegaard proceeds to investigate romanticism further. In all probability it is during the reading of Molbech's lectures in March, 1836, that Kierkegaard characteristically jots down this sentence: "The *novel* has become reflective."[109] At this point the German romanticists and German romanticism come within Kierkegaard's scholarly horizon, and he does not let them go before he gains clarity about the concept of romanticism.

Kierkegaard's journal entries testify that none of the

[107] I C 88 (*J. and P.*, V).

[108] I C 88, p. 244 (*J. and P.*, V).

[109] I A 128 (*J. and P.*, III, 3697); with this sentence Kierkegaard no doubt expresses that it is his intention to submit the whole problem of romanticism to reflective exploration.

other concepts occupying his attention was as difficult to define and to relate to other concepts as was the concept of the romantic. Therefore the notes which discuss romanticism may serve as the best illustration of how Kierkegaard is able to experiment with a concept according to all the rules of art in order to grasp its focal point and thereby be in a position to define its relation to other concepts.

After first examining Kierkegaard's treatment of the relation between the romantic and the classical, we will consider his demarcation of the concepts related to the romantic.

Molbech discusses the contrast between the classical and the romantic, but Kierkegaard tries to illuminate the relation between the two positions with new examples which illustrate the contrasts more sharply. From the very beginning he emphasizes that this contrast places its mark on all parts of esthetics: "When I speak of the contrast between the classical and the romantic, I of course do not have in mind any particular esthetic category but rather a basic contrast which must lend different coloration to every particular segment in esthetics."[110]

The primary difference between the classical and the romantic is that the classical represents the limited and the finalized, while the romantic is characterized by its "flowing over all boundaries."[111] Thus the Greeks, as representatives of the classical, shun the infinite and the unlimited and feel at home within the calculable situation of the finite. On the other hand, Christianity, with its emphasis on a striving beyond the limited, visible world, contains a romantic element which becomes especially prevalent in the Middle Ages.

[110] I A 171 (*J. and P.*, III, 3804). Kierkegaard notes down the point that there is also a difference in the actor's appearance in the classical and in the modern world: masks *contra* mobile facial expressions; see I A 219 (*J. and P.*, III, 3811) for more about this.

[111] I A 130 (*J. and P.*, III, 3796).

In the modern period, when scientific scholarship is attempting to control all phenomena and explain them, a classical trend arises once again. According to Kierkegaard these classical propensities emerge quite clearly in Hegel's philosophy, in which the course of the whole world is viewed as "an inevitable development,"[112] which excludes the free play of possibilities. Accordingly, Hegel has "emphasized especially" the side of Christianity in which the romantic is least prominent, namely "the doctrine of the God-man."[113]

Kierkegaard tries also to include Thorvaldsen's art in the same tendency he finds in Hegel. He says of this: "Now I understand something I frequently have wondered about for a long time—namely, that Thorvaldsen has emerged in our age. He really belongs to Hegel's generation. The romantic has vanished and the present tense of necessity (the classical) has commenced (sculpture belongs to the classical), and thus we have experienced a new classical stage."[114]

The dawn of romanticism particularly in Germany was a development in contrast to the classical trend in the modern age. Kierkegaard compares this romanticism with Greek classicism, and by quoting some verse by Tieck he shows that compared to the Greek mentality the romantic mentality is restless even in its repose. "Even the most classical restlessness (for example, Laocöon, crushed by serpents) is still serene,—the most romantic serenity is restlessness—for example:

> *Waldeinsamkeit*
> *Wie liegst Du weit!*
> *O dich gereut*
> *Einst mit der Zeit.—*

[112] I A 205 (*J. and P.*, II, 1232).
[113] I A 215 (*J. and P.*, I, 421).
[114] I A 200 (*J. and P.*, III, 3805). See I A 215 (*J. and P.*, I, 421) on Hegel's tendency to subjugate the romantic in Christianity.

> *Ach einzige Freud*
> *Waldeinsamkeit.*"[115]

In his research into the relationship between classicism and romanticism Kierkegaard finds many examples of how the romantic craving and restlessness go over to their opposites when satisfied. Here is just one of the examples: "When Adam was created, Adam's idea craved its supplement in Eve (the animals came to him and he gave them names—multiplicity is here—the chorus, if I may call it that, is here—irony is here—); Eve comes, and the romantic is over, there is repose."[116] Kierkegaard often dwells on this transition from the romantic to the classical and contrariwise. Such a possible transition from a romantic period to a classical one is described in the *Papirer* I A 307 (*J. and P.*, IV).

We may now turn from Kierkegaard's treatment of the contrasts between the classical and the romantic to his attempt to draw the boundary lines between the romantic and related concepts. Mention must first be made of Kierkegaard's correction and conceptual determination of the term "romanticism" itself, in order thereby to identify the rise of genuine romanticism in his own time.

The term "romanticism" is broadened by some to comprise three cultural movements widely separated in time: Indian antiquity, the Middle Ages, and the German romantic stream.[117]

[115] I A 203 (*J. and P.*, III, 3806).

> Alone in wood so gay,
> Ah, far away!
> But thou wilt say
> Some other day,
> 'Twere best to stay
> Alone in wood so gay.

From "The Fair-haired Eckbert," tr. Thomas Carlyle, in *German Romance*, I-II (New York, Scribner's, n.d.), I, p. 281.

[116] I A 140 (*J. and P.*, III, 3801).

[117] For example, Jean Paul, *Vorschule der Aesthetik* (Vienna, 1915), I, pp. 90ff., and Chr. Molbech, *Forelæsninger over den nyere danske Poesie*, I-II (Copenhagen, 1832), II, p. 190.

Kierkegaard challenges, however, the appropriateness of characterizing India's intellectual-spiritual life as romantic. According to his conception ancient India had not differentiated between finite and infinite, which is the first condition for the rise of romanticism. That is to say, one cannot go beyond the finite before one has an idea of the infinite. Kierkegaard criticizes designating ancient India as romantic in these words: "The prolixity and diversity found in Indian poetry—which has led some to characterize it as romantic—is not romantic; it is *vegetative-prolification*; on the whole, life in the East is vegetative; indeed, their gods are borne by a calyx, grow out of flowers."[118]

Kierkegaard acknowledges that it is more justifiable to use the designation "romantic" for the Middle Ages. He also gives many examples of the manifestations of romanticism in the Middle Ages, such as in the following entry: "The romantic was also expressed in a distinctive way in the Middle Ages by all the wandering about that went on: wandering knights, traveling scholars, itinerant singers, musicians, monks, etc."[119]

Kierkegaard voices the same view in another journal entry where he also shows how in a given period a contrasting tendency can appear alongside the dominating outlook: "Corresponding phenomena: scholasticism in the Middle Ages' fantasy-period; the romantic school in our day's period of reason."[120]

Gradually Kierkegaard comes to use the term "romantic" only for the German romantic movement. Undoubtedly one of the reasons for this was the fact that the German romantic school arose against the background of the strong emphasis in J. G. Fichte's philosophy on the infinitude of the subject in contrast to finitude.[121] In addition, the romantic

[118] I A 315 (*J. and P.*, III, 3817).

[119] I A 262 (*J. and P.*, III, 3814).

[120] I A 216 (*J. and P.*, III, 3808). Regarding the age of imagination and the age of reason, see also I A 125 (*J. and P.*, II, 1669), A 139 (*J. and P.*, IV), and A 236 (*J. and P.*, I, 371).

[121] See Kierkegaard's view on this in *The Concept of Irony*,

current in Germany had its existential representatives whereby the concept romantic did not remain an abstraction but took on meaning for existence.

Kierkegaard's attempt to distinguish the romantic from related concepts first touches the relationship between the romantic and the dialectical. In Kierkegaard's opinion their resemblance consists in their containing the unfinished, the continuously sought after, as a characteristic element. Kierkegaard characterizes the "pendulum-movement" of life and of thought between two opposite positions as both romantic and dialectical. He says of it: "It is quite curious that, after being occupied so long with the concept of the romantic, I now see for the first time that the romantic becomes what Hegel calls the dialectical, the other position where

> Stoicism—fatalism
> Pelagianism—Augustinianism
> humor—irony
> etc.

are at home, positions which do not have any continuance by themselves, but life is a constant pendulum-movement between them."[122]

In a somewhat later entry, in which Kierkegaard says what he thinks about our age, he equates the two qualifications.[123] But despite their resemblance in an essential point, Kierkegaard later makes a sharp distinction between them when he realizes that they do, after all, lie on two different planes: the romantic as the expression of a philosophy of life, and the dialectical as reflection's constantly questioning search.

Kierkegaard also relates the romantic to the moral,

---

pp. 289-92, which merely echoes Hegel's statement: "But this irony issues from the Fichtian philosophy. . . ." *Lectures on the History of Philosophy*, tr. E. S. Haldane, I-III (New York, Humanities Press, 1955), II, p. 400.

[122] I A 225 (*J. and P.*, II, 1565). See also III A 92 (*J. and P.*, I, 755).

[123] I A 307 (*J. and P.*, IV).

which in his view, as already mentioned, stands on a lower level than the ethical. When the moral outlook lies within the confines of the finite and thereby resembles the classical Greek way of life, it is unlike the romantic, which bursts these boundaries. In considering the relationship between these two philosophies of life, Kierkegaard says: "Antiquity does not have an ideal to strive for; the romantic, on the other hand, does have. This is because antiquity must disapprove every endeavor which goes beyond the world of actuality, since perfection, or at least the most perfect that is possible in the world (which here are conflated, because otherwise men would have to be counseled to strive beyond the actual), is in the realm of actuality. It has no ideal, neither moral, intellectual, nor esthetic. It has no ideal—or, what amounts to the same thing—it has an ideal attainable in this world."[124]

Kierkegaard does not again juxtapose the classical (the moral) and the romantic as in the example just cited. The reason is quite clear: from the romantic current in his day he learns that there is a danger in romantic striving after it bursts its narrow middle-class bounds if one does not have in advance the ethical as a bulwark against romanticism's arbitrary use of the idea of infinity.

As already mentioned, Kierkegaard is entirely justified in indicating the romantic character of Christianity, for Christianity points out and beyond the finite and the confined. Kierkegaard advances an interesting reason for Christianity's romantic character, saying, "The fact that Christianity has not outgrown the principle of contradiction demonstrates precisely its romantic character. What is it that Goethe wanted to illuminate in his *Faust* but this very thesis?"[125] This note obviously contains an indirect polemic against Hegel's point about abolishing the principle of contradiction. Kierkegaard believes that this abro-

[124] I A 221 (*J. and P.*, I, 852).
[125] I A 324 (*J. and P.*, I, 699); for Goethe's relationship to "the classical," see I A 230 (*J. and P.*, III, 3813), also Carl Roos, *Kierkegaard og Goethe* (Copenhagen, 1955).

gation leads to the abolishing of the absolute standard, but
without this Christianity would be a relative entity.[126] Already in this entry we find expressed Kierkegaard's subsequent charge against Hegel—that his system lacks ethics.
Kierkegaard believes that Christianity and romanticism can
properly be joined, and among other things he writes this
about it: "Insofar as Christianity does not divorce itself
from romanticism, no matter how much Christian knowledge increases, it will still always remember its origin and
therefore *know* everything ἐν μυστερίῳ."[127]

But after using the term "romantic" to characterize the
German romantic movement in particular, Kierkegaard had
to give up using it for Christianity. Since Kierkegaard did
not regard this movement as being positively oriented to
Christianity, he could no longer apply the word "romantic"
to Christianity.

Of all the concepts related to the romantic, irony is the
one to which Kierkegaard links the romantic most closely.
Besides being absorbed in esthetic problems after 1836
Kierkegaard was also intensely interested in investigating
the concepts of irony and humor. Reading in Jean Paul
and later in Hegel could have prompted him to relate the
romantic to irony.

Kierkegaard's first entry concerning the relation between
irony and the romantic emphasizes, however, the contrast
between the two concepts more than the resemblance: on
the one side Kierkegaard points to how Socrates in his "ironical gratification" as "the single individual hovered above
the world," and on the other side points to "the romantic
position, where everything is struggle. . . ."[128]

The contrast is found in the relation between Socrates's

---

[126] See also II A 454 (*J. and P.*, II, 1578).

[127] II A 78 (*J. and P.*, II, 1682); in a mystery. See also Kierkegaard's answer to the question about the extent to which the
language which best reproduces inwardness and psychic currents may be called Christian or romantic in I A 250 (*J. and P.*,
III, 2304).

[128] II A 38 (*J. and P.*, II, 1680).

gratification and romanticism's restlessness; the likeness between Socrates's hovering above the world and romanticism's struggling beyond the boundaries of actuality.

But a little later, when jotting down several thoughts about irony and humor, Kierkegaard relates irony and the romantic in such a way that the concept of irony in its expanded meaning also manages to embrace the romantic. Kierkegaard refers to two forms of irony: Socratic irony, which acquires positive attributes[129] within the negativity which irony represents, and romantic irony, in which irony as a philosophy of life is used negatively, consequently egotistically, and which "runs the risk of ending with an egotistical 'Go to the devil!' "[130]

In the first case we have an irony which, by emancipating the individual from the bounds of finitude, is a step on the way to a new positivity and thereby to a new commitment; in the second case this emancipation through irony comes to be misused by the individual for his own egotistical purposes. The difference between these two forms indicates the relationship between Socratic irony and the romantic philosophy of life, which Kierkegaard now places under this expanded definition of the concept of irony.[131]

Thus Kierkegaard approaches the conclusion of his "study of irony and humor,"[132] now that the romantic can be included as a link in this study. The clarification of these relations is, in fact, the preparatory basis for Kierkegaard's exhaustive treatment of irony in his doctoral dissertation *The Concept of Irony*. Kierkegaard places romanticism between Socratic irony and humor.

Hand in hand with Kierkegaard's engagement with the esthetic problems and the romantic movement goes a study

[129] II A 103 and A 104 (*J. and P.*, II, 1691, 1692).

[130] II A 102, p. 63 (*J. and P.*, II, 1690).

[131] Compare Kierkegaard's statement in *The Concept of Irony* (p. 293): "Throughout the discussions I use the expressions: *irony* and *the ironist*, but I could as easily say: *romanticism* and *the romanticist*. Both expressions designate the same thing."

[132] II A 186 (*J. and P.*, IV).

of works by romanticists. Jean Paul must be mentioned, who in his *Vorschule der Aesthetik* treats themes from esthetics in condensed, aphoristic form.

Kierkegaard's reading includes the Schlegel brothers, Tieck, Hoffmann, and others. Reading Hegel's works while working on *The Concept of Irony* helps Kierkegaard to reach his final position in the treatment of irony and the romantic.

The special concern with the romantic and irony and humor was in the larger context of Kierkegaard's preoccupation with philosophy. At the time Kierkegaard was particularly engrossed in philosophy, Hegel's influence in Denmark was steadily increasing. Kierkegaard could not avoid taking a position on this philosophy, both in the formulation of it by Danish Hegelians and in its original form in Hegel's writings. Kierkegaard first learned about Hegel's philosophy through the Danish intermediaries;[133] his own study of Hegel's works came later.

Generally speaking Kierkegaard took a negative position toward Hegelian "speculation," but it is interesting to note that he was able to use much of what he learned from Hegel.

Kierkegaard's first comment on Hegel in his journal entries is polemical in character. In a letter (1835) to Peter Wilhelm Lund, his brother-in-law's brother, Kierkegaard writes about his plans for scholarly studies and discusses at the same time certain ways in which various types of men try to solve their life problems. Of those who turn to Hegelian philosophy he says: "The majority will live to experience what the Hegelian dialectic really means."[134] In a note to this letter, the first of Kierkegaard's objections to Hegel's philosophy stands out clearly and at the same time

[133] See Niels Thulstrup's commentary to *Concluding Unscientific Postscript*, but particularly his doctoral dissertation, *Kierkegaards Forhold til Hegel* (*Kierkegaard's Relation to Hegel*), Copenhagen, 1967.

[134] I A 72, p. 46 (*J. and P.*, V).

casts a light on the statement just quoted. Pointing to life "in all its abundance" and "differences in abilities and attitudes," he states his conviction that it does not suffice that "a cold philosophy will explain the whole thing from pre-existence and does not see it as the endless panorama of life with its varied colorfulness and its innumerable nuances."[135] This indictment of the abstract and unreal character of Hegel's philosophy subsequently becomes one of Kierkegaard's main objections to Hegelian philosophy as a whole.

The next objection to Hegel is no less significant. In his system Hegel carries out a fusion of philosophy and theology, although with the result that philosophy comes to take first place.[136] Kierkegaard understood it as his task to repudiate Hegel's infringement by pointing to the qualitative difference between the two spheres and thereby to show that in relation to philosophy Christianity lies on a completely different and higher plane than all human, philosophical speculation.

The individual steps in Kierkegaard's efforts to accomplish a clear differentiation between philosophy and Christianity can be followed in his journal entries. The first comment on this issue is in October, 1835. Kierkegaard gives his reasons for the following underlined sentence: *"Philosophy and Christianity can never be united. . . ."*[137] One of his main arguments is that "The philosopher must either accept optimism or—despair." We note that Kierkegaard here again confronts abstract philosophy with the actuality of life. He is not speaking of philosophy as such but refers to "the philosopher," who in his practical life can be led to

[135] I A 74 (*J. and P.*, I, 22). That Kierkegaard, to some extent, includes the whole idealistic orientation in this criticism is seen in II A 47 (*J. and P.*, II, 2087) and II A 198 (*J. and P.*, III, 3257).

[136] Kierkegaard's charge, "It is clear that modern philosophy makes the historical Christ a kind of *natural son*, at most an *adopted* son" (II A 765 [*J. and P.*, I, 291]), applies particularly to Hegel.

[137] I A 94 (*J. and P.*, III, 3245).

perceive the limitations of philosophy. With this observation Kierkegaard wishes to emphasize that as long as "the philosopher" can hang on to optimism as the foundation for his life he can be satisfied with philosophy, but if the optimistic view of life can no longer cope with life-situations, despair makes its appearance, which means that philosophy has gone bankrupt as a view of life that explains life.

In his efforts to show the limitations of philosophy and distinguish it from faith, Kierkegaard finds his reading of Hamann's works particularly helpful, to which entry I A 100 (*J. and P.*, II, 1539) already testifies. But the most important development is that through Hamann Kierkegaard is made aware that Christian truths, seen from a philosophical angle, have the character of the absurd.[138]

Kierkegaard records the following comment by Hamann about this: "Ist es nicht ein alter Einfall, den du oft von mir gehört: incredibile sed verum? Lügen und Romane müssen wahrscheinlich sein, Hypothesen und Fabeln; aber nicht die Wahrheiten und Grundlehren unseres Glauben."[139] Several days later Kierkegaard refers to concrete cases in which the absurd and *"self-contradicting"* in Christian truths can be pointed out. He declares: "How little the understanding [*Forstanden*] can achieve in a speculative sense is best seen in this that when it reaches the highest level it must explain the highest by using a *self-contradictory* expression. Numerous expressions in the Formula of Concord serve as examples."[140] Through the concept of the

138 See Niels Thulstrup, "Incontro di Kierkegaard e Hamann" in *Studi Kierkegaardiani* (Brescia, 1957), pp. 325-27, and "To af Forudsætningerne for Hamanns Opgør med sin Samtid," in *Dansk teologisk Tidsskrift*, XXIII, 1960.

139 I A 237 (*J. and P.*, II, 1540). From Hamann, *Schriften*, I-VIII (Berlin, 1821-43), I, p. 405. "Isn't it an old inspiration which you have often heard from me: incredible but true? Lies and stories must be probable, hypotheses and fables, but not the truth and basic doctrines of our faith."

140 I A 243 (*J. and P.*, III, 3656).

absurd Kierkegaard comes to a crucial qualification for characterizing the substance of Christianity in relation to philosophy. The following selected entries about this concept sharpen the relationship even more precisely: "But there is a view of the world according to which the paradox is higher than every system."[141] "Philosophy's idea is mediation—Christianity's, the paradox."[142]

The decisive borderline between philosophy and Christianity is reached for the first time when philosophy is confronted with the *"absolute paradox,"* which for Kierkegaard means Christ as the God-man. Kierkegaard later explains this: "Insofar as philosophy is mediation, it holds true that it is not complete before it has seen the ultimate paradox before its own eyes. This paradox is the God-man and is to be developed solely out of the idea, and yet with constant reference to Christ's appearance, in order to see whether this is sufficiently paradoxical, whether Christ's human existence [*Existents*] does not bear the mark of his not being the *individual* human being in the profoundest sense, to what extent his earthly existence does not fall within the metaphysical and the esthetic."[143]

When the relationship between philosophy and Christianity is brought out to this boundary, it is not the Christian truths which stand in opposition to philosophy but "Christ's human existence," consequently the truth as personal existence. A further sharpening of this relationship is possible by presenting a personal representative for philosophy as "the human point of view." This occurs by means of Kierkegaard's contrasting Socrates with Christ. This contrast acquires a crucial significance for Kierkegaard in the working out of his authorship.[144]

Yet another important point in Kierkegaard's polemic

[141] II A 439 (*J. and P.*, III, 3071).
[142] III A 108 (*J. and P.*, III, 3072).
[143] IV C 84 (*J. and P.*, III, 3074).
[144] This antithesis is treated thoroughly in *The Concept of Irony.*

against Hegel is his criticism of "the theory that the course of world events is an inevitable development."[145] Kierke-gaard asks how this theory works in life and answers: "Must it not paralyze all activity, inasmuch as it abolishes not only the obviously egotistical but also the natural and enthusiastic assurance, at least in the moment of battle, that what one is working for is the one right thing? Or is this philosophy practicable only for the past, so that it teaches me to solve its riddle and then lets the present life stand again as a riddle which the following generation has to solve. But of what use is that philosophy to me? And are those who like this philosophy in a position to resign and let the world go its crooked way, and what is one to think about them? Is it their fault or the system's?"

With this criticism Kierkegaard calls attention to a fundamental defect in Hegel's conception of historical actuality. From now on Kierkegaard deems it important to show why this view is untenable, and also to give his solution to the whole issue by way of a thorough analysis of the concept of freedom and of the development of history.

Kierkegaard's criticism of "an inevitable development" also touches on Hegel's concept of mediation. In this concept Hegel tries to stipulate the very plan according to which the inevitable development takes place. The "logical movement" in this plan occurs in three stages: a given position goes over to its opposite; the two opposites become harmonized (mediated), and this gives a new position, which again forms the point of departure for movements along the same pattern.

Kierkegaard does not care much for this "logical trinity," and he is sharply ironical about this so-called logical movement by means of mediation. Here are a few examples of his irony toward Hegel's logical scheme: "The Hegelian cud-chewing involves three stomachs—first, immediacy—then it is regurgitated—then down once more; perhaps a successor mastermind could continue this with four stom-

145 I A 205 (*J. and P.*, II, 1232).

achs etc., down again and then up again. I do not know whether the mastermind understands what I mean."[146]

And further: "Of course, Hegel's logical trinity can be treated the way everything can—it can be carried to the extreme by applying it to the simplest of all objects, where it no doubt is true, but unfortunately ridiculous. Thus someone might make use of it on boots and show the immediate position, then the dialectical position (that they begin to squeak), and the third position of synthesis."[147]

Hegel's claim that philosophy must begin without presuppositions, consequently with "nothing," also becomes an object of Kierkegaard's criticism. This claim is clearly rejected at an early date, although in 1838 in *From the Papers of One Still Living* he seems to pass over it leniently.[148]

The issue of the absence of presuppositions in philosophy is usually linked with Descartes's thesis: "De omnibus dubitandum est." By doubting everything, one begins with nothing and thereby begins without presuppositions. Kierkegaard, therefore, subjects Descartes's thesis to a rigorous analysis in order to show what empty talk had been attracted to this methodological postulate, but more about that later. At present just this jesting comment by Kierkegaard on the possibility of beginning philosophy with doubt: "The method of beginning with doubt in order to philosophize seems as appropriate as having a soldier slouch in order to get him to stand erect."[149]

A special kind of indictment is found in Kierkegaard's charge against Hegel that he hates that which edifies and builds up. Kierkegaard writes: "It is strange what hate, conspicuous everywhere, Hegel has for the upbuilding or the edifying, but that which builds up is not an opiate which lulls to sleep. It is the "Amen" of the finite spirit

[146] I A 229 (*J. and P.*, II, 1566).

[147] I A 317 (*J. and P.*, II, 1567); compare with I A 328, p. 140 (*J. and P.*, IV).

[148] S. V., XIII, pp. 53-56.

[149] IV A 150 (*J. and P.*, I, 775).

and is an aspect of knowledge which ought not to be ignored."[150]

What Kierkegaard says here about the edifying and up-building as representing "an aspect of knowledge which ought not to be ignored" is in harmony with his own efforts to make the upbuilding the value standard in determining truth, consequently to make it the criterion of truth. Kierkegaard believes that whereas the battle over "the criterion of truth" has usually moved along abstract lines, he himself, by making the upbuilding the standard for truth, has found a criterion of truth which could not be given "a more concrete expression."[151]

Despite these essential indictments against Hegel, there were, as mentioned, specific points where Kierkegaard could learn from him. This is why he pokes fun at those who maintained that they had gone "beyond Hegel." Of them he says: "When certain people maintain that they have gone beyond Hegel, it must be regarded at best as a bold *metaphor*, by which they are trying to express and illustrate the thoroughness with which they have studied him, to describe the terrific running start they have made to get into his thought—and with their momentum they have not been able to stop but have gone beyond him."[152]

As previously indicated, during his study of esthetics Kierkegaard was very stimulated by his reading of Hegel's *Aesthetics*. Also while writing *The Concept of Irony* he was able to profit from Hegel's description of irony in Socrates and from his discussion of Fichte as creator of the philosophical foundation for the manifestation of irony in modern times, as well as of the Schlegel brothers as the first representatives of this trend.

[150] III A 6 (*J. and P.*, II, 1588).

[151] IV A 42 (*J. and P.*, IV).

[152] II A 260 (*J. and P.*, II, 1573); see also II A 697 (*J. and P.*, II, 1572). In contrast to these entries Kierkegaard ironizes in II A 371 (*J. and P.*, II, 1576) over those who "abuse" "their master's categories." Compare also Sibbern's remarks on going beyond Hegel in *Hegels Philosophie* (Copenhagen, 1838), pp. 11ff.

Kierkegaard read Hegel's account of Socrates's irony critically, but he acknowledges later that even while working on *The Concept of Irony* he was very dependent on Hegel's views. This applies especially to Hegel's view of Socrates's relation to the state.[153]

It is noteworthy that the main plan for mapping out the material in the first part of *The Concept of Irony* is taken from Hegel. Hegel arranges his three principal ontological categories in this order: possibility, actuality, necessity, whereby necessity becomes the union of possibility and actuality. Kierkegaard uses this scheme, although in 1840 he had already drawn up another, in which actuality is the union of possibility and necessity, a plan which he retains later. In this connection it is of interest to note that in three places in the text of *The Concept of Irony* where this issue is treated, Kierkegaard works with his own plan. Thus it can be said that certain Hegelian views, which are later abandoned, do emerge in the doctoral dissertation, along with his own reflections on these problems.

Very likely Kierkegaard also learned the use of the ascending scale from Hegel. In any case it is very significant that the first time Kierkegaard mentions the name Johannes Climacus he uses it for Hegel, because Hegel, like Johannes Climacus, *"enters"* heaven "by means of his syllogisms."[154] When Kierkegaard himself later tries to describe a man's step-by-step progress toward the eternal, it is Johannes Climacus, his principal pseudonymous writer, who provides this description.

Hegel's great influence upon Kierkegaard was, however, indirect. The errors Kierkegaard discovered in Hegel's system and which had a decisive negative influence upon his understanding of central philosophical and theological themes had to be corrected, and Kierkegaard saw

[153] See Kierkegaard's comments in X³ A 477 (*J. and P.*, IV) and XI² A 108 (*J. and P.*, IV).

[154] II A 335 (*J. and P.*, 1575). See also Climacus's appreciative remarks on Hegel: VI B 54 (*J. and P.*, II, 1608) and X⁶ B 128, p. 171 (*J. and P.*, V).

this as one of his tasks. In moving now to a consideration of Kierkegaard's study of other philosophers than Hegel, it must not be forgotten that this study is also the preparation of positive correctives to the errors which Kierkegaard thought to be present in Hegel's system.

Kierkegaard's decisive work with the ideas of other philosophers comes in the years 1842-43, but this does not mean that he had not been occupied previously with the thought of these particular philosophers.

One of the first philosophers Kierkegaard mentions in his journals and papers is J. G. Fichte, passages of whose book *Die Bestimmung des Menschen* he refers to.[155] Kierkegaard points out quite early that J. G. Fichte's philosophical point of departure must be regarded as insufficient. His main charge against Fichte is that he scorns empirical actuality. This is clearly expressed in these two journal entries: "To a high degree Fichte had this spidermoistness, so that as soon as he got the slightest hold he promptly plunged down with the complete security of the form of the conclusion."[156] "The whole idealistic development in Fichte certainly did find, for example, an immortality, but without fullness, like the husband of Aurora, who was immortal, to be sure, but, lacking eternal youth, ended by becoming a grasshopper—

"In despair Fichte threw the empirical ballast overboard and foundered."[157]

Kierkegaard takes a more positive position toward I. H. Fichte. It is very interesting that in a longer entry, where Kierkegaard gives a glimpse of his philosophical and theological ideas, among these the existential development of the individual and his relation to God, he denies at the outset that he had found some of these ideas through reading I. H. Fichte's *Die Idee der Personlichkeit* in 1834.

[155] See, for example, I A 68, p. 43 (*J. and P.*, V) and I C 50 (*J. and P.*, II, 1186), and see a more detailed account of this in Hirsch, *Kierkegaard-Studien*, II, pp. 25ff.

[156] I A 231 (*J. and P.*, II, 1187).

[157] I A 302 (*J. and P.*, II, 1189).

On this same occasion Kierkegaard admits that I. H. Fichte's position is a positive advance beyond Hegel's. Of this Kierkegaard writes: "Fichte has made an advance insofar as he has gone beyond Hegel's abstraction to intuition."[158]

Kierkegaard's attitude to Kant is characterized from the start by a certain sympathetic criticism which he later finds possible to sustain. In his first entry on Kant, in connection with his claim that H. N. Clausen approaches a "Kantian standpoint" on a particular issue, Kierkegaard declares that according to this point of view it is "our reason" [Fornuft] which "tells us" that we ought "to improve ourselves," which in Kierkegaard's view has the result that "God comes to play a very subordinate role."[159]

In commenting on "the transcendence" which Kant "counsels against" Kierkegaard makes an important observation which also shows their divergent points of view. We see here that Kierkegaard not only advances the idea of the paradox as an intellectual determinant in contrast to Kant's philosophy of reason but mentions the possibility of a movement which goes beyond the universal and thereby results in the paradox in an existential sphere. The journal entry which touches on this question reads thus: "Isidorus Hisp. refers to a transcendence quite different from that which Kant counsels against—isti (namely, seculo huic renunciantes) praecepta generalia perfectius vivendo transcendunt, although Kant would probably say that it is the same except in the domain of action, and equally dangerous, since it stands in opposition to the concept of the universally valid."[160]

As far as the Greek philosophers are concerned, Kierkegaard, in his work on his doctoral dissertation had to make

[158] II A 31, p. 31 (J. and P., II, 1190).

[159] I A 30 (J. and P., II, 1305). Kierkegaard expresses the same idea but in different words in a journal entry in 1850 (X² A 396 [J. and P., I, 188]).

[160] II A 486 (J. and P., II, 2234). Those (renouncing this age) transcend general precepts by living more perfectly.

a special study of Plato. *The Concept of Irony* witnesses to the comprehensiveness and thoroughness of this study.

The other philosophers who occupied Kierkegaard in a special way and who have not as yet been mentioned will be discussed in the account of his concluding study of philosophy in 1842-43.

During these years Kierkegaard concentrates earnestly on arriving at a final understanding of philosophical issues of particular interest to him. He places his ponderings on these issues in a separate group called *"Philosophica."*[161] One special section of these entries is called *"Problemata."* In using this latter term Kierkegaard wishes to state that his preoccupation with philosophy had run up against some very special problems, the solution of which had particular significance for his further elaboration of philosophical and theological ideas. Therefore *"Problemata"* are the most central part of *"Philosophica."* The significance of this section of *"Philosophica"* is further emphasized by Kierkegaard's marking of most of these problems with the letters "a-p" "in margin with pencil."[162]

On the whole, the entries called *"Philosophica"* show how Kierkegaard selects specific philosophical authors to find answers to particular philosophical problems and how he then himself poses the very special questions to be solved, the solutions of which are already suggested by the way the questions are posed.

For general orientation on philosophical problems Kierkegaard used Tennemann's[163] history of philosophy in particular, but also Marbach's[164] and Erdmann's[165] his-

[161] IV C 2-101. (*J. and P.*, I-V; see collation of entries in each volume.)

[162] See *Papirer*, IV, under *Kilde-Angivelse, Manuscript-Beskrivelse . . . (Indication of Sources, Description of Manuscripts . . .)*, pp. 469-70.

[163] W. G. Tennemann, *Geschichte der Philosophie*, I-XI (Leipzig, 1798-1819).

[164] G. O. Marbach, *Lehrbuch der Geschichte der Philosophie*, I-II (Leipzig, 1838-41).

[165] J. E. Erdmann, *Versuch einer wissenschaftlichen Darstel-*

tories of philosophy. Many references testify at the same time to special study of the works of individual philosophers.

No attempt will be made here to give an exhaustive account of all the questions touched on in "Philosophica"; only the most essential ones will be pointed out. With a certain simplification, it can be said that in the main there are three kinds of problems which predominate in "Philosophica," namely (1) ontological problems, (2) the problem of freedom and together with it the problem of history, and (3) the question of the boundary between metaphysics and ethics.

The first journal entry in "Philosophica" concerns ontology. Kierkegaard learns from Tennemann's history of philosophy the different conceptions of "being" held by the Greeks. Little is said of modern views of ontology. This no doubt is due to Kierkegaard's being already rather well informed on this in various ways, for example, through Martensen's lectures[166] and Schelling's lectures on his view of "Seinslehre."[167]

In "Problemata" Kierkegaard formulates many questions which directly touch various aspects of ontology. He begins his more detailed reflections on this by asking: "What is a category?"[168] and whether "being" is a category—which he later denies.[169] Going on, he relates being to quantity and quality. He refers to several "notations" on being that he made while reading Spinoza.[170] He likewise records Plato's definition of being in *Parmenides*.[171]

---

lung der Geschichte der neueren Philosophie, I-II (Riga, Leipzig, 1836-42).

[166] II C 12-28. (*J. and P.*, III, V; see collation of entries in each volume.)

[167] III A 179 (*J. and P.*, V); see also A. M. Koktanek, *Schellings Seinslehre und Kierkegaard* (Munich, 1962).

[168] IV C 63 (*J. and P.*, II, 1595).

[169] IV C 66 (*J. and P.*, II, 1598).

[170] IV C 69 (*J. and P.*, IV).

[171] IV C 70 (*J. and P.*, III, 3324).

One may ask why Kierkegaard is so intensely interested in the difficult issues of ontology. He answers this himself in an extremely focal notation which declares: "Every qualification for which being is an essential qualification lies outside of immanental thought, consequently outside of logic."[172]

In writing this, Kierkegaard resolves the issue in the sphere of ontology which was most significant to him—namely, how a Christian ontology is possible. This short note points to an ontology which cannot be contained within human "immanental thought" and thereby within the confines of scientific logic, but which by means of the terminology of this logic can be described as absurd being. Kierkegaard then formulates the forms of being which metaphysics tries to describe with categorical qualifications, in contrast to the kind of being which cannot be encompassed by these qualifications. Drawing this boundary between human and Christian ontology also indicates at an essential point the difference between the spheres of knowledge and faith. The culmination in this qualifying of Christian being forms the "*absolute paradox*," which as we have seen[173] is contrasted to the being with which philosophical knowledge is concerned.

In connection with the problems of ontology Kierkegaard touches on the significance of experience for knowledge. For Kierkegaard the stuff of experience is being as "empirical mass." Kierkegaard denies that the normative can be formed out of experience or the stuff of experience alone. In the following remark he is in line with Kant: "As soon as I frame a law from experience, I insert something more into it than there is in the experience."[174] For Kierkegaard this conception becomes very significant, especially for his view of the historical sciences.

In pursuing the question of the knowledge of being which is gained through observation of empirically given

[172] IV C 88 (*J. and P.*, I, 196).
[173] See p. 61 above.
[174] IV C 75 (*J. and P.*, I, 1072).

actuality, Kierkegaard advances a contrast between positive and negative knowledge. In Kierkegaard's interpretation the given and seemingly positive knowledge of empirical actuality becomes a negative knowledge; whereas
what in the first phase is negative knowledge about the
infinite and eternal becomes positive knowledge.[175] By
means of a leap from this positive knowledge of the infinite to the realization of this knowledge in existence the
kind of being is achieved for which being is "an essential
qualification" and which can be placed in contrast to
ontology from a human point of view.

The next principal issue in "*Philosophica*" concerns
freedom and history, two concepts which Kierkegaard
often comprises under the common term "motion." Kierkegaard had to struggle for clarity on "motion," initially for
the reason (evident in many journal entries) that he
wanted to rectify Hegel's notion of "the course of world
events as an inevitable development."[176] However, it was
clear to Kierkegaard that the whole issue of motion "is
perhaps one of the most difficult problems in all philosophy."[177]

Kierkegaard claims that modern philosophy neglects
the exploration of this issue. In a journal entry in 1843 he
says: "Ancient philosophy, the most ancient in Greece,
was preeminently occupied with the question of the motion whereby the world came into existence [*blev til*], the
constitutive relationship of the elements to each other.
—The most recent philosophy is essentially occupied with
motion—that is, motion in logic. It would not be without
significance to collate the various theses from these two
spheres. The newer philosophy has never accounted for
motion. Similarly, in its otherwise profuse slates of categories there is no category which is called mediation,
which for the newest philosophy is nevertheless the most

[175] IV C 74 (*J. and P.*, II, 2282); see the supplementary notes
in IV A 56 (*J. and P.*, V).

[176] I A 205 (*J. and P.*, II, 1232).

[177] IV C 97 (*J. and P.*, V).

essential of all, in fact, the essential nerve in it, whereby it seeks to dissociate itself from every older philosophy."[178]

In naming "mediation" Kierkegaard's criticism finally gets a more concrete address. The same criticism finds expression in this comment in "*Philosophica*," which includes Plotinus: "The secret of the whole of existence Hegel explains easily enough, for he says somewhere in *Phenomenology* that something goes on behind the back of consciousness (see Introduction, p. 71n.). Plotinus manages in a similar manner in order to make one into two: Beginning as one (reason), it does not persevere as one but *without being aware* of it becomes plurality, sinking down, as it were under its own burden. (See Marbach, *Geschichte der Philosophie*, II, p. 82.)."[179]

In working out and forming his own view on "motion" Kierkegaard seeks direction in Aristotle and especially in Leibniz.

While reading Tennemann's *History of Philosophy*, Kierkegaard is attentive to his translation of the word κίνησις in Aristotle. Kierkegaard writes of this: "The transition from possibility to actuality is a change—thus Tennemann translates κίνησις; if this is correct, this sentence is of utmost importance."[180] The manner in which Kierkegaard expresses himself on this translation shows that he already is thinking about the concept of motion and that he finds Tennemann's translation of κίνησις appropriate. The definition of motion as "the transition from possibility to actuality" forms a central point of departure for his further work on the question of freedom and historical actuality.

In reading Leibniz's *Theodicy* Kierkegaard finds a penetrating and enlightening treatment of this whole question. In this work Leibniz, as he advances his own views, gives an extensive survey of all the disputes related to the prob-

---

[178] IV A 54 (*J. and P.*, III, 3294).

[179] IV C 59 (*J. and P.*, II, 1594); see also IV C 80 (*J. and P.*, I, 260) and IV C 81 (*J. and P.*, I, 1603). For information on Kierkegaard's references see editors' notes.

[180] IV C 47 (*J. and P.*, I, 258).

lem of freedom over the centuries. Kierkegaard takes note of several of the authors Leibniz mentions and turns his attention to two of them in particular: Bayle, against whom Leibniz strongly polemicizes, and Boethius.

Some of the points in this polemic noted by Kierkegaard are important for our consideration of freedom and history. He believes that Leibniz is right in opposition to Bayle when the latter wants "to make man the sole measure of all things,"[181] which is analogous to the familiar *homo mensura* thesis of Protagoras. But on the other hand, Kierkegaard points to "a weakness in all the answers" Bayle gets when Leibniz defends the view that specific concrete examples of the imperfection of this world are annulled in light of the perfection of the universe as whole. It is understandable that on the basis of his own experiences Kierkegaard must protest against Leibniz's abstract view of right and wrong in this world. Of Leibniz's defense of his views Kierkegaard says: "This is ridiculous, for if there is just one individual man who has valid reason to complain, then the universe does not help."[182] It is of interest to note that Kierkegaard seems to know how Bayle's charges should be answered. He goes on to say: "The answer is that even in sin man is greater and more fortunate than if it had not appeared, for even the split in man has more significance than immediate innocence."[183] The above is another example of how Kierkegaard comes to the reading of other authors with his own well-considered points of view.

Kierkegaard does, however, find one essential point on which Leibniz and Bayle agree, namely, the denial of *liberum arbitrium*, on which Kierkegaard also agrees. He writes of this: "A perfectly disinterested will (equilibrium) is a nothing, a chimera. Leibniz demonstrates this superbly in

[181] IV C 32 (*J. and P.*, I, 40).

[182] IV C 33 (*J. and P.*, I, 41).

[183] Ibid.; here Kierkegaard takes the same line of thought as Augustine with "*felix culpa.*" Compare this with "*beata culpa*" (*The Concept of Irony*, p. 199).

many places; Bayle also acknowledges this (in opposition to Epicurus)."[184] Kierkegaard summarizes his views on the controversy between Leibniz and Bayle thus: "The whole conflict between Leibniz and Bayle is very much to the point, and one is astonished if he compares it with controversy in our time, for we have actually gone backward, and I believe that Hegel has not really understood what it was all about."[185]

Boethius is mentioned by Leibniz in connection with speculations on the difficulty of uniting "God's foreknowledge with freedom."[186] The problem here is how one can avoid assuming the determination of future events if God knows them in advance. On this issue Boethius sets forth some very profound reflections, to which Leibniz refers. Kierkegaard's interest here is in line with that of Leibniz and Boethius, who tried to maintain God's foreknowledge together with the acknowledgement of man's freedom. This is no doubt Kierkegaard's first acquaintance with Boethius.

It is important for Kierkegaard to point out that not only the future-oriented historical process contains elements of freedom but that this also must hold for past events as well. Without the latter, repentance would be an illusion.

Kierkegaard then formulates the following question, which is the first in *"Problemata"*: "Is the past more necessary than the future?"[187] In working to clarify this problem, too, Kierkegaard receives help through Leibniz's page references to Boethius's *De consolatione philosophiae*,[188] where this specific question is treated.

Kierkegaard also takes note of Leibniz's resolution of the

[184] IV C 39 (*J. and P.*, II, 1241). In an earlier entry (III A 48; *J. and P.*, II, 1240) Kierkegaard clearly defines his understanding of *liberum arbitrium*.

[185] IV C 29 (*J. and P.*, III, 3073).

[186] IV C 40 (*J. and P.*, III, 3347).

[187] IV C 62 (*J. and P.*, II, 1245).

[188] See Boethius's *De consolatione philosophiae*, V (Agriae, 1758).

difficulties in the sphere of freedom, namely, his "theory of the infinite possible worlds."[189] It may be added here that Kierkegaard observes that Leibniz works out from the same theory his justification of the thesis that God is conscious. The fact that God must choose among "many possible worlds" presupposes "a choice, and a choice presupposes consciousness." This consciousness, moreover, embraces "God's foreknowledge of the fortuitous."[190] According to Leibniz this foreknowledge is not detrimental to the meaning of freedom in historical development. The subsequent notations prompted by Kierkegaard's reading of Leibniz's *Theodicy* permit us to see the direction Kierkegaard thinks should be taken in dealing with the question of Christianity's historical side and its paradoxical character.

Kierkegaard touches on Leibniz's definition of faith in relation to reason in another entry: "What I usually express by saying that Christianity consists in paradox, philosophy in mediation, Leibniz expresses by distinguishing between what is above reason and what is against reason. Faith is above reason."[191] In the sentences following, Kierkegaard defines more clearly his own understanding of faith, which seen from the side of thought is a paradox.

In discussing Leibniz's elucidation of the truths "which are right for all ages and for particular ages,"[192] Kierkegaard points out how important it is to get a clear idea of the relation of history to Christianity, "because it is precisely the historical which is the essential. . . ." We will look more closely at this and other significant notations on the historicity of Christianity in discussing Kierkegaard's study of religious-philosophical questions.

Kierkegaard adopts an important point of view on the concepts of motion and freedom in connection with his

[189] IV C 40 (*J. and P.*, III, 3547).
[190] IV C 31 (*J. and P.*, III, 2365).
[191] IV C 29 (*J. and P.*, III, 3073).
[192] IV C 35 (*J. and P.*, II, 1635).

rendition of several of Descartes's central ideas.[193] Kierkegaard mentions that according to Descartes man finds
himself as a thinking being only after doubting everything.
From that point man is led necessarily to accepting the existence of God; God becomes a guarantee that men can apprehend truth with the help of the implanted ideas. However, man can make a mistake in cognition because in his
freedom he can go farther than thought allows. By taking
this stand Kierkegaard believes that Descartes, at least in
one passage in his *Meditations*, has admitted that "freedom
in man is superior to thought," and yet in general Descartes
"has construed thought, not freedom, as the absolute." In
the next sentences Kierkegaard declares, as did "the elder
Fichte" also, that for him freedom, action, and existence are
higher than thought and, on this basis, seeks to show the
inadequacy of Descartes's formulation: *Cogito ergo sum.* If
by *cogito* is meant the activity of thinking, according to
Kierkegaard this *cogito* is "something derived," for thinking always presupposes an existing subject who thinks.
Therefore one may say that *sum*, as a qualification of
being, stands higher than *cogito*, which represents thinking. Thus the proof from *cogito* to *sum* is inadequate, because what is to be proved is presupposed. If, however, this
cogito is made "identical" with activity, the priority of freedom over thought is acknowledged. The formula *cogito
ergo sum* is therefore unsatisfactory, because it does not
permit the relation between thought and existence to become clearly manifest.

In an appended entry Kierkegaard shows how he considers the difficulties to be taken care of through a clear
separation of thought and freedom. This he does by a presentation of the so-called dialectical and pathos-filled transitions.[194] By way of these two essentially different series
of transitions, Kierkegaard is able to effect a sharp separation between the spheres of thought and of actuality. If

[193] IV C 11 (*J. and P.*, III, 2338). See Descartes, *Meditations*,
especially IV.
[194] IV C 12 (*J. and P.*, III, 2339).

"motion" or "change" takes place in a qualitatively different way within each of these two areas, there must also be a qualitative difference between the areas themselves. Kierkegaard's theory of dialectical and pathos-filled transitions comes to have crucial importance in the development of his method, and in discussing this method we will look at this theory in greater detail.

The third group of questions is concerned with border issues between metaphysics and ethics. For a clearer understanding of Kierkegaard's formulation of the problems, the following must be said first. As can be seen in one of his earliest journal entries,[195] Kierkegaard makes a distinction between a lower and a higher form of ethics. He uses the term "ethics" only for the higher form. This form of ethics is characterized by having incorporated the consciousness of the eternal, which as yet is not the case with the lower forms of ethics. To them belong all kinds of moral codes and social morality. According to Kierkegaard these forms still belong essentially to the esthetic and are thereby embraced by metaphysics, which forms a summarizing totality within the sphere of the esthetic.[196]

As early as 1834 Kierkegaard was considerably engrossed in ethics proper and neglected the lower forms, which include all the intermediate forms from the completely primitive human patterns up to man's comprehension of the eternally binding laws, a comprehension which in paganism first came with Socrates. The Socratic insight into the possibility of the eternal marks the boundary between the moral forms of ethics and essential ethics.

In 1842-43 Kierkegaard makes up for lost time with respect to morality or the lower forms of ethics, and during his exploration of these questions he quite logically places his observations under the rubric *"Philosophica"*; this is why they are discussed here and not in the section on ethics.

The best source for the study of morality or lower forms

195 See I A 221 (*J. and P.*, I, 852).
196 See pp. 45-47 above.

of ethics is Aristotle, who keeps this practical study within the confines of everyday life and has a certain aversion to the Platonic speculation on the good as an eternal and absolute determinant. Kierkegaard takes note of this in saying that Aristotle, in contrast to Socrates and Plato, "ends in a realistic [*realistisk*] contradiction."[197] We find many entries in this vein written while Kierkegaard was reading moral and political works in which Aristotle does in fact cite many examples of the moral and political situation in Greece. Aristotle places virtue as the goal for the individual's life, but virtue is quite consistently conceived as an esthetic qualification. Kierkegaard notes the following on the close connection of this kind of virtue to esthetics: "The identity of virtue and beauty is also seen by Aristotle (3:10): φοβησεται μεν ουν και τα τοιαυτα, ως δει δε και ως ο λογος υπομενει του καλου ενεκα· τουτο γαρ τελος της αρετης."[198]

In several entries Kierkegaard dwells on the difficulties which he believes are entailed by Aristotle's understanding of the relationship between action and the voluntary, such as IV C 16-20 (*J. and P.*, I, 892, 893, 112; III, 3784).

Kierkegaard is also aware that Aristotle works with three kinds of virtue, namely "moral virtues,"[199] "intellectual virtues," and "political virtues,"[200] a division which with appropriate modifications Kierkegaard finds again on a higher plane and which he later uses in his authorship.[201]

In his account of Aristotle's views on self-love, Kierkegaard makes several observations which clearly state the reasons why, on the whole, he must regard Aristotle's eth-

[197] IV C 21 (*J. and P.*, I, 113).

[198] IV C 22 (*J. and P.*, V). *Nicomachean Ethics*, 1115, 11ff. "Hence although he will sometimes fear even terrors not beyond a man's endurance, he will do so in the right way, and he will endure them as principle dictates, for the sake of what is noble; for that is the end at which virtue aims."

[199] IV C 25 (*J. and P.*, III, 3292).

[200] IV C 27 (*J. and P.*, I, 114).

[201] Judge William, for example, calls them "the personal, the civic, the religious virtues." *Either/Or*, II, p. 266.

ical views as being on a lower plane: "Aristotle has not
perceived the qualification of spirit. Therefore he recommends even external goods, although only as an accom-
paniment, a drapery, but at this point he lacks the category
for making a consummating movement."[202] Kierkegaard's
claim that "the Greek mentality [Græciteten] was unable
to comprehend marriage"[203] must be regarded as consistent
with this judgment of Aristotle's view of ethics. Kierkegaard advances this opinion in an entry in which he also
makes a note of the main points in his reading of Aristotle's
Politics.

Kierkegaard concludes his notations in *"Philosophica"*
on the boundary problems of ethics with an outline which
points to his own way of resolving the ethical issues. However, he also mentions in *"Philosophica"* the connecting
links between Aristotle's political and social philosophy
and his own ethical views, which first and foremost place
the individual's eternal worth squarely in the center.

The first step on the way to an ethic which is higher than
Aristotle's is, according to Kierkegaard, the Socratic-Pla-
tonic teaching about the good in and for itself. But something abstract still clings to the good in and for itself as
the norm for the ethical, and Kierkegaard, prompted by his
reading of Leibniz, asks how this good relates to God as a
personal power. His question, which he underlines, reads:
*"Is the good good because God wills it, or is it good in and
for itself?"*[204] For Kierkegaard the answer is already given
in the formulated question, since the good as a purely
abstract idea cannot be the final or the highest authority
for him.

With a turn toward the anthropological, Kierkegaard en-
titles his outline *"Interested Knowing and Its Forms."*[205] In
it he first of all lays the foundation for his specific under-

[202] IV C 26 (*J. and P.,* IV).
[203] IV C 28 (*J. and P.,* III, 2590).
[204] IV C 72 (*J. and P.,* I, 894).
[205] IV C 99 (*J. and P.,* II, 2283).

standing of the concept of the interesting, which to him is a *"border category, a boundary between esthetics and ethics."*[206] In the same outline he also characterizes the next step as the kind of ethics in which the good becomes a determining force in the human personality. When Kierkegaard next points out that "interested knowledge enters with Christianity," this is to be understood in the sense that only Christianity provides an example of an absolute unity of the eternal and the personal. In the light of this example, "interested knowledge" acquires a new qualitative definition.

In his little outline Kierkegaard goes on to mention the contrasting positions of doubt and of faith. In an earlier entry not included in *"Philosophica"* he considers the manner in which doubt can be conquered and the leaps to the ethical and to faith can be made. "What the skeptics should really be caught in is the ethical. Since Descartes they have all thought that during the period in which they doubted they dared not express anything definite with regard to knowledge, but on the other hand they dared to act, because in this respect they could be satisfied with probability. What an enormous contradiction! As if it were not far more dreadful to do something about which one is doubtful (thereby incurring responsibility) than to make a statement. Or was it because the ethical is in itself certain? But then there was something which doubt could not reach."[207] Kierkegaard says somewhat the same thing in two entries included in *"Philosophica."* "It is most remarkable that almost all the skeptics have always left the reality of the will uncontested. Thereby they would actually arrive at the point they should reach, for recovery takes place through the will."[208] "Doubt is certainly not halted by the necessity of knowledge (that there is something one must acknowledge) but by the categorical imperative of the will, that there is something one cannot will. This is the will's con-

[206] *Fear and Trembling*, p. 92.
[207] IV A 72 (*J. and P.*, I, 774).
[208] IV C 56 (*J. and P.*, II, 1243).

cretion in itself, by which it shows itself to be something other than an ethical phantom."209

To this it must be added that Kierkegaard, as various entries show, is speaking out of careful reflection when he writes of will in relation to knowledge and the significance of the will when it is a matter of halting doubt in order to arrive at the ethical. His thoughts on the role of the will and of knowledge are undergirded by his penetrating investigation of the interplay between the three transactional links in the human subject—namely, feeling, cognition, and will.210

As shown by "*Philosophica*," Kierkegaard's concentration on philosophical problems made it possible for him ultimately to clear up the central questions related to ontology, freedom, and the border areas of ethics.

For the most part, the later journal entries in the realm of philosophy provide only a more elaborate statement of the problems on which Kierkegaard had already become clear. After 1843 these entries gradually become more and more infrequent and finally appear only sporadically.

In a journal entry from 1844 Kierkegaard amplifies the idea of the principle of identity,211 which he touched on in 1839.212 In a few other entries he treats "the dialectic of beginning,"213 which again is only a development of the thought he had advanced in his polemic against Hegel's insistence on a presuppositionless beginning.214

In a whole group of entries in 1844215 Kierkegaard continues to devote himself to this doctrine of dialectical and pathos-filled transitions, which he now summarizes in the phrase "my theory of the leap."216 In this cluster of entries

209 IV C 60 (*J. and P.*, II, 1244).

210 See the important points and references in IV C 78 (*J. and P.*, IV, 3657).

211 V A 68 (*J. and P.*, I, 705).

212 II A 496 (*J. and P.*, I, 2) and A 454 (*J. and P.*, II, 1578).

213 V A 70 (*J. and P.*, I, 768) and A 72 (*J. and P.*, I, 912).

214 See p. 63 above.

215 V C 1-9 (*J. and P.*, III, 2345-51).

216 V C 12 (*J. and P.*, III, 2352).

he seeks to work out all the special forms of the leap and all the transitions between the various areas where the leap is used. At the same time Kierkegaard notes that other philosophers seldom pay any attention to the reality of the leap, neither in thinking nor in existence. In one particular entry he also considers the leap in relation to logical principles.[217]

In 1844 Kierkegaard read Trendelenburg's *Elementa logices Aristotelicae*,[218] from which he copied a number of Greek quotations. His continued interest in Aristotle centered upon psychology and especially upon rhetoric, because of its connections with his own inquiry into the question of the art of communication.

As for Kierkegaard's extensive study of Spinoza in 1846,[219] it may be said that, aside from his philosophical viewpoints, his primary interest was to criticize sharply Spinoza's rejection of theology in the course of the world and in the life of the individual. Kierkegaard attempts to prove with examples from Spinoza's works that he, in Kierkegaard's opinion, could not get around "the dialectic of theology"[220] in his thinking. Kierkegaard believes that Spinoza also falls short in his concept of motion. Of the several critical remarks against Spinoza, only this one, directed particularly to Spinoza's principal work, *Ethics*, is quoted here: "The question is only whether his whole ethics is not to be charged with a duplicity, that he simultaneously (in order to do away with theology) contemplates everything at rest and then also (by virtue of the defini-

---

[217] V A 74 (*J. and P.*, III, 2341).

[218] F. A. Trendelenburg, *Elementa logices Aristotelicae* (Berlin, 1842).

[219] See especially VII[1] A 31 (*J. and P.*, II, 2291) and C 1-4 (*J. and P.*, IV); Kierkegaard, however, mentions Spinoza several times prior to 1846, for example in III B 179:63 (*J. and P.*, I, 911); IV B 1, p. 103 (*Johannes Climacus, or De omnibus dubitandum est*, p. 99); and IV A 190 (*J. and P.*, II, 1333). In the last of these entries Kierkegaard turns on Spinoza severely, because he "continually objects to miracles and revelation."

[220] VII[1] A 35 (*J. and P.*, IV).

tion's *suum esse conservare*) gets finitude in process: that is, the concept of motion is lacking here."[221]

It is only natural to conclude the discussion of Kierkegaard's work with philosophical problems by saying something about the enthusiasm which Trendelenburg's book *Geschichte der Kategorienlehre*,[222] published at the end of 1846, awakened in him. He writes: "There is no modern philosopher from whom I have profited so much as from Trendlenburg. At the time I wrote *Repetition* I had not yet read him—and now that I have read him, how much clearer and explicit everything is to me. My relationship to him is very strange. A part of what has engrossed me for a long time is the whole doctrine of categories (the problems pertaining to this are found in my older notes, on a quarto piece of paper [i.e., IV C 87-96]). And now Trendlenburg has written two treatises about the doctrine of categories, which I am reading with the greatest interest."[223]

It is worth nothing that Kierkegaard here refers explicitly to his entries in *"Philosophica"* in 1842-43 (the period in which he did his crucial work on philosophical problems).

Trendelenburg does not give Kierkegaard anything new but helps him to greater clarity. This, too, is expressed in the following comment: "What I have profited from Trendlenburg is unbelievable; now I have the apparatus for what I had thought out years before."[224]

In the discussion of *"Philosophica"* it was pointed out that Kierkegaard makes an important distinction between moral and social theory on the one hand and ethics, properly understood, on the other. According to Kierkegaard, each of these two forms of ethics has its own totality, since

---

[221] VII¹ C 1 (*J. and P.*, IV).

[222] F. A. Trendelenburg, *Geschichte der Kategorienlehre* (Berlin, 1846).

[223] VIII¹ A 18 (*J. and P.*, V). For IV C 87-96, see collation of entries at end of *J. and P.*, I, III, and IV. Kierkegaard consistently omitted the second "e" in Trendelenburg's name.

[224] VIII² C 1 (*J. and P.*, V).

a distinction can be made between the two on the basis of an ontological qualification.

Ethics as moral and social theory has its goal within temporality; it establishes laws and rules for external social relations among men. As such it is part of philosophy, the discipline which attempts to give a comprehensive survey over finitude's empirical world and thereby also over the human relationships within this finitude. Through its synthesizing activity philosophy arrives at a few final abstract definitions or ideas which rank above empirical actuality. With this description of the world as a coherent totality philosophy reaches its boundary.

In continuation of Platonic thought, Kierkegaard defines the being to which philosophy principally devotes itself in its exploration of empirical actuality as a nothingness, since everything in this actuality is only of transitional character. Only ideas about this world seem to have an eternal continuance, but since they are merely abstractions, their being also falls essentially into the sphere of nothingness. To Kierkegaard the possibilities of philosophy —from an ontological point of view—are exhausted with these definitions.[225]

But one may ask whether there is not the possibility of a being which can be said to stand in contrast to nothingness. Kierkegaard answers this question affirmatively and points to another and higher totality than that which metaphysics knows. This higher totality has its beginning in genuine ethics. The first journal entry in which Kierkegaard puts this on record is from 1839, and it reads: "All relative contrasts can be mediated; we do not really need Hegel for this, inasmuch as the ancients point out that they can be distinguished. Personality will for all eternity protest against the idea that absolute contrasts can be mediated

[225] Since philosophy's intrinsic interest lies within finitude, its knowledge about reality ends, according to Kierkegaard, in a negativity. Only knowledge of the infinite yields a positivity, for "Positive knowledge is infinite knowledge; negative knowledge is finite knowledge." IV C 74 (*J. and P.*, II, 2282).

(and this protest is incommensurable with the assertion of mediation); for all eternity it will repeat its *immortal* dilemma: to be or not to be—that is the question (Hamlet)."[226]

In this entry Kierkegaard acknowledges in the first place that philosophy justifiably mediates between the contrasts of finitude, inasmuch as philosophy's area of exploration lies within the confines of finitude, where contrasts are only relative. In the second place Kierkegaard shows that there is an area where philosophy's attempt to mediate is unjustified, namely, where it is a matter of absolute contrasts. He thereby points to a new form for being which is especially characterized by its absolute contrasts, which cannot be mediated. This new form of being is to be found only within the personality, the only possible place for absolute contrasts. There is—and everyone must acknowledge this—nothing absolute and eternal within the empirical world. Here Heraclitus's statement applies: "παντα χωρει και οὐδὲν μενει."[227] The only place where the possibility of the eternal can conceivably be present is man himself. Kierkegaard's presupposition is that man, besides being qualified as a temporal being, also has within him the possibility of the eternal. Therefore he is obliged to protest against the extension of mediation to the whole human personality. Since man thus is composed of two qualitatively different components, he stands in his ethical choice before an either/or which cannot be mediated.

This assumption, which means that the personality becomes the focus of a new ontological qualification, forms the basis for Kierkegaard's reflections on ethics. This point of departure acquires further significance for him in that only man, according to Kierkegaard's conception, can be addressed by a transcendent power, because man alone has within himself the possibility of the eternal. (A stone, a tree cannot be addressed.) The implications of these

[226] II A 454 (*J. and P.*, II, 1578).
[227] See Heinrich Quiring, *Heraklit* (Berlin, 1959), p. 82.

lines of thought will be dealt with when Kierkegaard's works are considered separately.

Accordingly, with his affirmation of the eternal in man, Kierkegaard has laid the foundation for a specific new ontology within a totality which is higher than metaphysics.[228] In the section on philosophy of religion it will be shown how this new totality gets its finite support from dogmatics, but it begins with ethics, which presupposes the presence in man of two qualitatively different opposites.

After these prefatory remarks on the separation of metaphysics and ethics as belonging in two different ontological realms, we can look more closely at the specific stages of Kierkegaard's work in elucidating the concept of the ethical.

Kierkegaard's first journal· entry on ethical issues may suggest that he understands his own inner conflicts as an exception. In this entry he considers the question of the extent to which a great man may permit himself to break ethical laws. Kierkegaard writes: "Should a great man be judged according to principles different from those used for every other man? The question has often been answered with 'Yes,' but my opinion is 'No.' A great man is great simply because he is a chosen instrument in the hands of God. But the moment he fancies that it is he himself who acts, that *he* can look out over the future, and on that basis he lets the end justify the means—then he is small. Right and duty are valid for everybody, and trespassing against them is no more to be excused in the great man than in governments, where people nevertheless imagine that politics has permission to do wrong. To be sure, such a wrong may often have a beneficial result, but for this we are not to thank that man or the state but providence."[229]

Here for the first time in Kierkegaard we confront the

[228] A precise separation of the two totalities is given later by Vigilius Haufniensis; see *The Concept of Anxiety* [*Dread*], pp. 23-27.
[229] I A 42 (*J. and P.*, IV).

question of the defensibility of a suspension of the ethical. Here Kierkegaard opposes the superficial view which is sympathetic to the great man's breaking of the laws of ethics and duty. As far as I can see, Kierkegaard's question is motivated by his own similar conflict when he as a "master-thief" wanted to help his father by rooting out the reason for his melancholy. Was it not reprehensible to want to wrest another man's secret from him against his will, even if it was done out of love?[230]

But however this may be, Kierkegaard in the cited entry has clearly stated that a frivolous suspension of the ethical is reprehensible, no matter who does it. Whether there can be a teleological suspension of the ethical, which, it is well to note, always will bring strife and suffering for the one who acts, is a matter Kierkegaard leaves in abeyance for the time being.

In presenting the different forms of ethics, Kierkegaard in the next few entries follows an ascending line.

In discussing the difference between the classical and the romantic, Kierkegaard makes a clear distinction between the goals of action which lie within temporality and those which point beyond empirical actuality. Kierkegaard simply will not bestow the name ideals on goals which are confined to finitude, declaring that "an ideal attainable in this world" is "no ideal."[231]

Kierkegaard's dim view of ideals contained within temporal actuality goes together with his views on the inadequacy of a morality limited to the shifting forms of inter-human association. The following sentence clearly brings out this dim view: "The esthetic ideal is replaced by national taste, yes, town-and-class taste, and the most correct copy of it."[232]

Kierkegaard goes on to show how the ethical requirement takes shape on the basis of the idea of the eternal norms in man. Only with these norms as a starting point

---

[230] See pp. 26-27 above.
[231] I A 221 (*J. and P.*, I, 852); see also pp. 54-55 above.
[232] I A 222 (*J. and P.*, I, 853).

can there be any question of the ethical in the proper sense, an ethic which is well grounded and can enter into relation with external actuality. In an important journal entry from 1840 Kierkegaard explores how initially the personality, having this consciousness of the eternal in man, can and ought to act in the world of time. Among other things he says: "I become conscious simultaneously in my eternal validity, in, so to speak, my divine necessity, and in my accidental finitude (that I am this particular being, born in this country at this time, throughout all the various influences of changing conditions). This latter aspect must not be overlooked or rejected. On the contrary, the true life of the individual is its apotheosis, which does not mean that this empty, contentless *I* steals, as it were, out of this finitude, in order to become volatilized and diffused in its heavenward emigration, but rather that the divine inhabits and tolerates the finite."[233]

In an entry quite closely related to the one just quoted, Kierkegaard emphasizes the point that Plato's belief that man has the truth within himself is "a thought just as beautiful as profound and sound,"[234] and goes on to speak of the task of actualizing this truth in one's life. With that Kierkegaard specifies the step in ethical development which later culminates in the formulation: Subjectivity is truth. But as will be seen, it was also transparent to Kierkegaard that this position was only a step on the way to the deeper experience which comes when man encounters Christianity.

These reflections on the ethical are abstract, but Kierkegaard continually works concurrently at presenting his ethical views by means of historical or fictitious characters. The latter method of working with ethical issues may be said to be quite characteristic.

In Socrates's irony Kierkegaard finds an example of a transition from using relative goals to an ethic grounded

[233] III A 1 (*J. and P.*, II, 1587).
[234] III A 5 (*J. and P.*, II, 2274).

on individual existential consciousness of the infinite. In this way Socrates furnishes the first concrete example of "the movement of infinity," a concept which plays an important role in Kierkegaard's ethics.[235]

Up until 1843 Kierkegaard in his journals interprets Socrates primarily as an ironist; not until *Either/Or* is Socrates mentioned as an ethicist as well. In *The Concept of Irony* Socrates is accordingly portrayed as an ironist.

For the reasons stated, the point of view of irony comes to be regarded as a transition stage between ethics on the lower plane and ethics in the proper, genuine sense. Individual ethical development thus has its beginning in irony, which neutralizes the relative ethical viewpoints. This development, in which the ethical requirement for the individual is continually intensified, approaches its boundary at the level of humor, which also is synonymous with the boundary for the human capacity. For this final stage Kierkegaard finds a representative in Hamann.

From this time on, Socrates and Hamann stand as representatives of irony and humor and are, to use Kierkegaard's image, at "the two opposite ends of a teeter-totter (wave motions)."[236] These "two opposite ends" indicate the two extremities in man's ethical development when it comes under the requirement of the eternal. Between these extremities lie man's experiences of willing to actualize the ethical by means of his own abilities. Continuing with the ethical beyond irony, man, by means of the position of humor, experiences "himself in his nothingness"[237] and inadequacy.

Kierkegaard gives definite reasons why he chooses Hamann as the representative for humor, concluding with the comment: "Thus one can truthfully say that Hamann is the greatest humorist in Christianity (meaning the greatest humorist in the view of life which itself is the most

[235] See p. 21 above.
[236] I A 154 (*J. and P.*, II, 1671).
[237] II A 627 (*J. and P.*, II, 1688).

humorous view of life in world-history—therefore the greatest humorist in the world)."[238]

The close connection of humor with Christianity, which Kierkegaard speaks of in many of his entries,[239] places humor on a higher plane than irony, a view Kierkegaard expresses in these words: "Some say that irony and humor are basically the same with only a degree of difference. I will answer with Paul, where he talks about the relationship of Christianity to Judaism: *Everything is new in Christ.*

"The Christian humorist is like a plant of which only the roots are visible, whose flower unfolds for a loftier sun."[240]

Irony and humor are alike in that they both still reside in the province of the human, but humor is closer to Christianity than irony. Kierkegaard arrives at his clarified viewpoint on irony and humor at about the same time. Yet he writes a treatise only on the concept of irony. The fact that he did not also write a treatise on humor with Hamann as its representative is no doubt due, as we shall soon see, to his own penetrating experiments as a humorist, which provided him with experiences that made him personally the representative of humor in his own life as well as in his authorship.

In his "study of irony and humor,"[241] Kierkegaard also takes into consideration their negative forms. Many examples of negative irony were already to be found in the romantic movement in its day, which used irony in an unwarrantable way—something Kierkegaard knew from his own existential experience. In *The Concept of Irony* Kierkegaard shows how the freedom irony gives from narrow bourgeois bonds can be misused for egotistical ends. If

[238] II A 75 (*J. and P.*, II, 1681).

[239] See especially II A 78 (*J. and P.*, II, 1682), A 84 (*J. and P.*, II, 1686), A 102 (*J. and P.*, 1690), A 146 (*J. and P.*, II, 1704), A 147 (*J. and P.*, II, 1705).

[240] II A 102 (*J. and P.*, II, 1690).

[241] II A 186 (*J. and P.*, IV).

this negativity goes so far that it takes up a consciously un-sympathetic posture toward Christianity, it is no longer irony but a negative form of humor.

Kierkegaard cites Heine as an example of this negative humor. In one entry Kierkegaard tries to explain more precisely how humor in Heine "developed as diabolical humor." This happened primarily because Christianity became to him "an offense."[242]

Kierkegaard defines the two opposite poles implicit in humor: "Humor can be either religious or demonic (in relation to the two mysteries)."[243]

In his earliest journals Kierkegaard names as examples of the negative posture toward Christianity three types who move in the direction of demonic humor. They are the three characters who interested him so much later: Don Juan, Faust, and Ahasuerus. Among other comments on these three Kierkegaard says: "Representing life in its three tendencies, as it were, outside of religion, there are three great ideas (Don Juan, Faust, and the Wandering Jew), and not until these ideas are mediated and embraced in life by the single individual, not until then do the moral and the religious appear. In relation to my position in dogmatics, this is the way I view these three ideas."[244]

In relation to demonic humor these three figures may be stationed as follows: Don Juan stands on the lowest plane since his doubt, which is the mark of demonic humor, is as yet unconscious. In the middle is Faust; his doubt is merely intellectual. Not until Ahasuerus do we have an existential doubt, and there we also have negative humor in its distinctly demonic form.

Kierkegaard's extensive use of individualities as repre-

[242] II A 142 (*J. and P.*, II, 1622).

[243] III A 46 (*J. and P.*, II, 1721). What Kierkegaard understands by "the two mysteries" is illuminated in II A 767 (*J. and P.*, I, 292): "The divine and the diabolic are the only genuine mysteries, but the mystery of God is revealed in Christ—whereas the mystery of the devil (*mysterium impietatus*) will first become visible in a corresponding manifestation: the anti-Christ."

[244] I A 150 (*J. and P.*, I, 795).

sentatives of the ethical philosophies of life rests on his urge to attach his ethics closely to actuality. By means of individualities he can give a kind of presence to abstract ethical qualities in positive as well as in negative forms; the abstract laws are brought closer by the concrete examples.

This propensity in Kierkegaard is further encouraged later by the stress upon "interested knowledge,"[245] which is made principally through individual representatives. But in the imaginative actualizing of abstract ethical laws there is also to be found the essential origin of Kierkegaard's concept of contemporaneity, because through actualization man becomes existentially contemporary with the eternal. This concept can be used and is used by Kierkegaard on all levels of the ethical, but it acquires primary importance only in relation to Christianity. Although Kierkegaard encounters the question of *"Christ's appearance"* to "his *own age*"[246] as early as 1843, it is understandable that Kierkegaard does not want to actualize imaginatively this highest instance of contemporaneity prior to an exhaustive treatment of the human forms of contemporaneity and prior to an approach to specifically Christian problems.

Since Kierkegaard's ethical-religious experiences stretch through his whole lifetime, it is of course not to be expected that in the beginning of his authorship proper he already had insight into all the possible existential consequences and collisions implicit in his ethical and religious viewpoints prior to 1843. But in that time he did achieve a clear demarcation between the specifically Christian forms and those contained within the sphere of the human.

In going through his authorship we will see how his new experiences influenced certain aspects of his views on Christianity's ethical requirement and its offer of reconciliation to man.

[245] See p. 80 above.
[246] IV A 47 (*J. and P.*, III, 3075).

The most important aspect of Kierkegaard's work with philosophy of religion may be said to be his efforts to point out the essential difference between all human approaches and all religions on the one hand and Christianity on the other. At first Kierkegaard no doubt was prompted in these efforts by Hegel's blending of philosophy and theology, but he expands and deepens the issue of the difference between philosophy and theology to embrace all religions and philosophies of life outside of Christianity.

Kierkegaard's treatment of the difference between philosophy and theology has already been discussed; therefore the special focus now will be on the relationship between Christianity and other religions.

Apparently he first became absorbed in this question through the reading of two treatises: Karl Rosenkranz, *Eine Parallele zur Religionsphilosophie*, and Carl Daub, *Die Form der christlichen Dogmen- und Kirchen-Historie*.[247]

During this reading Kierkegaard first jots down in brief notes some ideas on the Jews' concept of God and then the observation that within "polytheism" "monotheism" always lies hidden and vice versa, since even in the out-and-out monotheism of the Jews there is a connection with polytheism. Kierkegaard voices this in the following entry: "Monotheism always lies concealed in polytheism, without therefore hovering everywhere as an abstract possibility, as with the Greeks ('the unknown God')." And "On the other hand, abstract polytheism is found in the Jews' *plural* expression 'Elohim,' without either a collective or a distributive predicate."[248]

In connection with these reflections on philosophy of religion Kierkegaard tries to define more closely Mohammedanism's position regarding polytheism and monotheism and in relation to Christianity. In his most detailed

[247] II A 71 (*J. and P.*, II, 2211) and references. Both treatises appeared in *Zeitschrift für spekulative Theologie*, ed. Bruno Bauer, I-III (Berlin, 1835-38).

[248] II A 73 (*J. and P.*, II 1306).

entry on Mohammedanism Kierkegaard summarizes his
views thus: "No prophet, no historian could find a more
descriptive expression for Mohammedanism than the one
Mohammed himself has given in the suspension of his
sacred tomb between two magnets,* that is, between the
divine which did not become human (incarnation) and
the human which did not become divine ("brothers and
co-heirs in Christ"). It is neither individualized polytheism
nor concretized monotheism (Jehovah), but abstract monotheism—'God is one'—in which it is specifically the number which must be *affirmed*, not like the Jewish God who
to a certain degree was unpredicated, yet still more concretized: 'I am who I am.'[*] Here there is no incarnation
(the Messiah), not merely a prophet (like Moses), for there
were many prophets among the Jews without any difference in power even though with a difference in degree,
but Mohammed demanded a specific superiority (approximating an incarnation, but, of course, like everything else
in Mohammedanism, stopping at the half-way point)."[249]

In a copious entry Kierkegaard copies Rosenkranz's
outline, which is an attempt to reduce the different religions "to the simplest terms"[250] by laying down the following three propositions:

> "1) *der Mensch ist Gott*
> 2) *Gott ist Gott*
> 3) *Gott ist Mensch.*"

These three propositions, according to Rosenkranz, encompass in an abstract way the essential elements in polytheism, monotheism, and Christianity. Kierkegaard next
gives historical examples of the positions represented in
these abstract propositions. The first proposition comprises
the ancient Indian religions, the Greek *"religion of art,"*
and the Romans' practical religion. The second proposition
represents monotheism, three forms of which are cited:

[249] II A 86 (*J. and P.*, III 2734); see also II A 87-89 (*J. and
P.*, III, 2735-37) to which the asterisks refer.
[250] II A 92 (*J. and P.*, V).

Judaism, Mohammedanism, and "the more isolated Deism."

Interestingly enough, Kierkegaard makes a note on the Old Testament development of the Jewish religious outlook (as Rosenkranz sees it). We read: "Judaism develops in the first books, where God appears in his omnipotence as lawgiver [p. 13] (Moses stays completely in the background); then in Job the detached individuality appears in a kind of opposition to God, and [p. 14] in the Psalms sets his mind at rest by [acknowledging] that God is God, the Almighty, against whom man must not strive."[251]

In this connection Mohammedanism is touched upon only briefly, possibly because Kierkegaard had already expressed his thoughts on it in the entries above. Concerning deism he says, "Deism basically reverses the relationship, for while monotheism as such presupposes that God is God and therefore man is man, it presupposes that man is man and therefore God is God (as a necessary accessory to realizing man's deserved bliss)."

In closing, Kierkegaard refers to Rosenkranz's comparison of Christianity with polytheism, monotheism, and deism, respectively. Rosenkranz, emphasizing the superiority of Christianity to other principal forms of religion, comes to the following conclusion, as Kierkegaard reads it: "Therefore Christianity contains the most glorious lifeview."

Kierkegaard's reading of Daub provides an example of Kierkegaard's creative method of working—for example, when he supplements Daub's thoughts on the life of Christ with his own. Kierkegaard writes: "It is certainly true, as Daub says (Bauer's periodical), that the whole story of Christ's life is contained in three statements: Did you not know that I must be in my Father's house? I must work the works of him who sent me, while it is day; night comes

251 See also Kierkegaard's observations on Judaism's relation to the historical in II A 352 (*J. and P.*, II, 2212) and the distance between Judaism and Christianity II A 355 (*J. and P.*, II, 2213).

when no one can work. It is finished. But one should not forget three others: And the child grew and became strong, filled with wisdom (Luke 2:40). He is tempted. My God, my God, why have you forsaken me?"[252]

The qualitative difference between Christianity and all other religions is the primary presupposition for Kierkegaard's views on the relation between Christianity and all other philosophical and religious positions. An early entry reads: "All other religions are oblique; the founder steps aside and introduces another who speaks; therefore, they themselves belong under the religion—Christianity alone is direct address (I am the truth)."[253]

By stressing Christ's claim "I am the truth" as central to Christianity, Kierkegaard wants to point out that Christianity's truth is the one and only concrete truth. Truth in all other religions than Christianity, and in philosophy as well, has an abstract character. Thus truth is always distinct from the person who sets it forth. A founder of a religion may claim that he has the truth, or that it has been revealed to him; the philosopher may also say that he knows the truth. In all these instances the person and the truth stand as two spheres, distinct and separate from each another. Only Christ has identified himself as the person with the truth. He does not have the truth but *is* himself the truth. In Christ the truth and the person are fused in an absolute unity. The most that can be said in all other philosophies of life than Christianity is that the individual should try to actualize the truth in his life.

Another consequence of the statement "I am the truth" is that the historical element is accentuated essentially, and historical reports about Christ thereby have a significance qualitatively different from reports about other men's lives, even the prophets. That is to say (and this applies to all men except Christ), where there is a separation between the person and truth the historical element is unimportant in relation to the truth itself. The essen-

[252] II A 97 (*J. and P.*, I, 279).
[253] II A 184 (*J. and P.*, I, 427).

tial point is the truth itself, not who has it or by whom it is set forth.

Before proceeding, we must pause at still another sentence in this focal entry on Christianity, one which seems to be in sharp contradiction to later statements: "Christianity alone is direct address." It is well known that Kierkegaard later strongly emphasized that Christ could never communicate himself directly.[254] This apparent contradiction is explained by the fact that Kierkegaard later regards the connection between the person of Christ and his words from the point of view of his well-grounded dialectic of communication. Looked at from this position, the statement "I am the truth," spoken by an individual man, very logically becomes indirect address.

Scarcely a month after writing in entry II A 184 about the essential difference between Christianity and the other religions, Kierkegaard, while reading J. E. Erdmann's *Vorlesungen über Glauben und Wissen*, becomes aware that Erdmann also "heroically maintains faith in its purely historical aspect as not being outside Christianity. . . ."[255] Kierkegaard however takes note that Erdmann does not apply the historical viewpoint to tradition.

As previously stated,[256] Kierkegaard emphasizes later in *"Philosophica"* that "it is the historical which is the essential" for Christianity. This is found partly in the polemic against Leibniz, in which Kierkegaard cites the passage from Leibniz's *Theodicy*[257] stressing eternal abstract truths in contrast to the historical.[258] Kierkegaard then asks: "But Christianity is an historical truth; how then can it be the absolute? If it is historical truth, it has appeared

[254] But already in 1842-43 the idea of Christ as the *"absolute paradox"* (IV C 84 [*J. and P.*, III, 3074]) prepares the way to an understanding of Christ's incognito, consequently the impossibility of a direct communication.

[255] II C 44 (*J. and P.*, II, 2250).

[256] See p. 75 above.

[257] See IV C 35 (*J. and P.*, II, 1635) with editors' references.

[258] See also Niels Thulstrup's Introduction to *Philosophical Fragments*, pp. xlvii-lii.

at a certain time and a certain place and consequently it is relevant to a certain time and place." With the concluding comment on Christianity—"it is precisely the historical which is the essential; whereas with other ideas this is incidental"—Kierkegaard stresses the historical side of Christianity without, however, attempting to answer the question of how, in spite of its historicity, one can attribute absolute character to it. That this cannot be achieved along the road of knowledge but only by the leap of faith was familiar to Kierkegaard earlier when he noted that "an a priori certainty"[259] with respect to Christianity exists only for faith.

In his treatise *Johannes Climacus, or De omnibus dubitandum est* Kierkegaard also mentions the fusing together of the two essential elements in Christianity implicit in the statement "I am the truth," that is *the person*, which points to the historical, and the truth, which means eternal truth. It is to these two elements that Kierkegaard refers when he says that "great difficulty must have been caused to philosophy, because Christianity said that *it* had come into the world by a new beginning, and this beginning was at once historical and eternal. . . ."[260]

Of other special attributes of Christianity which accentuate this exceptional character Kierkegaard cites the following: only with Christianity does the individual life get a new and imperishable reality. He says: "According to Christian doctrine man is not to merge in God through a pantheistic fading away or in the divine ocean through the blotting out of all individual characteristics, but in an intensified consciousness 'a person must render account for every careless word he has uttered,' and even if grace blots out sin, the union with God still takes place in the personality clarified through this whole process."[261]

---

[259] I A 316 (*J. and P.*, I, 252); see also, for example, III A 211 (*J. and P.*, II, 2277) and A 216 (*J. and P.*, II, 1101).

[260] IV B 1, p. 117 (*Johannes Climacus, or De omnibus dubitandum est*, p. 119).

[261] II A 248 (*J. and P.*, IV).

The comprehensive nature of Christianity is pointed to in the following journal entry: "Christianity's universal character is discernible also in this—that with Christianity all national distinctions cease as transcended elements. The only distinction which might seem to remain is that between the Orient and the Occident, although this is on a far greater scale and is based essentially on contrasts of dogma as such, whereas the other distinctions were only secondary and were based on national contrasts. The remaining contrasts (Catholic—Protestant, etc.) are often within national similarities and *simply* are based upon the objective qualifications of the idea."[262]

Kierkegaard goes on to say in another entry that Christianity upon entering the world has taken first place and has brought all other relationships down to a lower plane: "In Christianity everything has dropped to a lower level because a higher factor has entered in."[263] Later this thought proves to have wide implications in Kierkegaard's structuring of his authorship.

Kierkegaard further illustrates Christianity's unique position in relation to other religions by saying: "When one views the historical roles of the religions on their journey through the world, the relationship is as follows: Christianity is the actual proprietor who sits in the carriage; Judaism is the coachman; Mohammedanism is a groom who does not sit with the coachman but behind."[264]

In conclusion, mention must be made of the concept of offense, which later becomes an important diagnostic term in Kierkegaard's description of Christianity. "When a person first begins to reflect upon Christianity, it undoubtedly is at first a cause of offense before he enters into it; yes, he may have wished that it had never come into the world, or at least that the question about it had never arisen in his consciousness. Therefore it is nauseating to hear all this talk by meddlesome, intervening intermediaries about

[262] II A 249 (*J. and P.*, I, 431).
[263] II A 379 (*J. and P.*, III, 2858).
[264] II A 499 (*J. and P.*, I, 447).

Christ as the greatest of heroes. A humorous view is far preferable."[265]

In order to emphasize Christianity's unique position with respect to the other religions and philosophy, Kierkegaard subsequently and continually lays stress on Christianity's most central thought, the presupposition for the entire content of Christianity—the claim of the incarnation of the eternal, which finds its adequate expression in the words: "I am the truth." Nevertheless, in considering this question he seldom mentions the sentence "I am the truth" itself, which probably is related to Kierkegaard's perception that the statement could be attacked by historical criticism.[266] On the other hand, not even the most radical critic of Christianity could deny that Christianity's uniqueness as a religion is its claim that God has revealed himself in history as a specific individual human being.

With Kierkegaard's emphasis on the fusing together of time and eternity as essential for Christianity, the dogma of the Incarnation was bound to come to the fore. From now on we see that Kierkegaard's primary concern is to stress all the difficulties which faith in God's Incarnation brings about. He is less concerned with the doctrines of the Resurrection and Ascension; these dogmas are reality only to the person who is already within the sphere of faith. Consequently Kierkegaard has to reject the use of the two dogmas for the purpose of apologetics, thus as proofs for the truth of Christianity.

A line can be drawn from the dogma of the Incarnation to Kierkegaard's structuring of an ontology which stands on a plane above the ontology basic to philosophy. Ethics has already broached the question of such an ontology. But this higher form of ontology gets its decisive foundation in Christianity's claim of an eternal being.[267] This

[265] II A 596 (*J. and P.*, II, 1710).

[266] See Fr. Strauss, *Das Leben Jesu* (Tübingen, 1835) and *Die christliche Glaubenslehre*, I-II (Tübingen, Stuttgart, 1840-41).

[267] In the journal entry II A 248 (*J. and P.*, IV) about an

eternal being is in contrast to the being with which philosophy is concerned and which in the first analysis is shown to be identical with nothingness. On the other hand, ethics, which according to Kierkegaard represents the possibility of the eternal, now gets its corresponding ontological foundation through Christianity's claim of eternity as a reality.

With this Kierkegaard completes the task undertaken in the area of the philosophy of religion: to draw a clear and decisive boundary between metaphysics and dogmatics as two completely different totalities.

Kierkegaard's additional work in the philosophy of religion as well as the theology involved in the central issues of Christianity will be treated in the survey of his works.

Finally we must mention the writing that was most important to Kierkegaard and which was done concurrently with work in various areas—namely, the upbuilding or edifying entries. Understandably they first begin with the breakthrough in May 1838, and they intimately and personally reproduce his inner struggles and religious development. These entries may at the same time be regarded as a preparatory step to the rich upbuilding literature which constitutes the most important portion of Kierkegaard's writings.

It should also be noted that after 1843 much space is given in Kierkegaard's journals to comments on his own works and to discussion of his methodical procedure in the authorship.

"intensified consciousness" which Christianity gives man there is a thought about an eternal being as an ontological qualification. Kierkegaard uses this idea later in *Philosophical Fragments* (title page), where he poses the question about the possibility of "an eternal consciousness" through relationship to Christianity as something historical.

II Kierkegaard's Dialectical Method

Concurrently with his concentration on the previously discussed subjects, Kierkegaard seeks to work out a method which he can use to develop a comprehensive view of life's manifold forms,[1] especially of human existence, with an emphasis on subjective actuality and its relationship to Christianity as the base.

The central and determining concept for Kierkegaard in the structuring of this method becomes the concept of *consistency*. The rigorously thorough application of this concept in all of Kierkegaard's processes of thought signifies that he is attempting to deal with the issues which are central for him according to a scholarly-scientific method.

How this is done and what the results are will become evident through an examination of the developmental stages of the method, its structural coherence and, moreover, the application of the method to the different forms of actuality; but first a few remarks on the concept of consistency.

The ideal in all spheres of scholarship is to reach a scientifically and scholarly correct treatment of the subjects investigated—an ideal achieved only by way of thorough consistency. The two auxiliary disciplines which must be considered in this connection are logic and mathematics, the whole structure of which rests on the principle of consistency. Consistency, or more accurately, consistent thinking, is the implicit but indispensable premise for these two disciplines; consequently they become the norms

[1] On this see in particular Johannes Sløk, *Die Anthropologie Kierkegaards* (Copenhagen, 1954) and Hermann Diem, *Kierkegaard's Dialectic of Existence*, tr. Harold Knight (Edinburgh and London, Oliver and Boyd, 1959).

for a consistent and thereby scholarly treatment of other areas of scholarship. The significance of consistency in these two disciplines is therefore a matter of course, but when, just as in logic, rules for consistent conclusions are formulated by means of hypothetical judgments, it is done to insure that these particular judgments are also encompassed by the strict law of consistency. In this connection it may be said that indirect argument, which is closely related to the doctrine of hypothetical judgments, is also entirely built upon the principle of consistency. From this it appears that all argumentation, be it direct or indirect, must follow the strict demands of consistency if it is to deserve the name of scholarship.

However, despite the fact that consistency is a fundamental principle in all scholarly research, an error of judgment arises if this principle is defined too narrowly and is then applied to all the spheres of existence. Examples of such an expanded and unjustified application of this concept can be found in the attempts to treat mental-spiritual phenomena on the basis of a narrow, mathematical concept of consistency as in the natural sciences. It is understandable that the great results achieved by applying mathematical-quantitative consistency in the sphere of the natural sciences are a temptation to an extension of the same method to other areas. There are examples in philosophy of attempts to prove the correctness of a line of thought by appealing to narrow, mathematical consistency without any particular consideration of the various manifestations of actuality. Spinoza provides a striking example of this in his *"Ethica, ordine geometrico demonstrata,"* where the mathematical-geometrical argument is supposed to be a guarantee of the reliability, of the conclusions, even when the argument concerns the higher forms of mental-spiritual life.[2] Examples from Spinoza—and many could

[2] Thus in journal entry VII[1] A 35 (*J. and P.*, I, 931) Kierkegaard criticizes Spinoza for treating problems which belong under "teleological dialectic" and thereby under freedom within

be cited here—show that if the concept of consistency is not modified in its application to the different spheres of actuality, this concept, which is the ideal for all scientific scholarship, can be applied in an inconsistent and, from the point of view of scientific scholarship, inadequate manner.

As far as can be seen, it was through F. C. Sibbern that Kierkegaard, during his work with the issue of scientific scholarship, became aware of the significance of the concept of consistency. In his methodological expositions, which fill a great part of his logical works,[3] Sibbern uses the expression "consistency" an astounding number of times. We find several analogies to Sibbern in Kierkegaard's use of the concept of consistency, but despite repeated approaches to an extended application of the concept of consistency, Sibbern remained at the half-way mark and did not manage to collect his dispersed thoughts on this concept into a general viewpoint. It is in Kierkegaard that we first encounter an attempt to formulate a thoroughly reflected resolution of the problem of consistency and the modifications of this concept in dealing with the different forms of actuality. Sibbern's permanently valuable book *Om Erkjendelse og Granskning (On Knowledge and Research)*,[4] also aided Kierkegaard in his work on evolving "the method." Thus Sibbern must be acknowledged to have shared unwittingly in Kierkegaard's work in this special field. Particular references to this will be given later.

Kierkegaard's use of the principle of consistency is already traceable in his treatment of the traditional subjects; his application of it advances in three stages:

"an immanental view," where the leap as a category of transition cannot come into view.

[3] Chiefly *Logik som Tænkelære* of 1827. *Logik som Tænkelære* of 1835 does not make any great changes on this point. Kierkegaard audited Sibbern's lectures on logic during the second semester of 1830-31.

[4] F. C. Sibbern, *Om Erkjendelse og Granskning* (Copenhagen, 1822).

(a) Kierkegaard pursues in all their consistent implications previously given resolutions of problems within the various disciplines and arrives either at a verification or a rejection of each one;

(b) he constructs his own new viewpoints on the different spheres and by giving full consideration to all their consistent implications attempts to establish the correctness of these viewpoints;

(c) finally he is able to place the subjects into the new context created by his dialectical method.

The following account of Kierkegaard's structuring of a method falls into two parts: first, the elements Kierkegaard uses to form his dialectical method; next, how Kierkegaard tries to unify these elements into wholes which can be used to resolve the task he has assigned himself—namely, to provide a coherent description of human existence in all its relationships and all its forms.

The very first entry in category A of the papers (April 15, 1834) may be grouped with the entries concerning "the method." It reads: "In order to see one light determinately we always need another light. For if we imagined ourselves in total darkness and then a single spot of light appeared, we would be unable to determine what it is, since we cannot determine spatial proportions in darkness. Only when there is another light is it possible to determine the position of the first in relation to the other."[5] This entry can no doubt be interpreted to mean that Kierkegaard has perceived that no position or viewpoint can ever be determined solely by itself; it can be more explicitly determined only in relation to another position or another viewpoint. Despite its metaphorical form, this abstract observation will later be seen to play an important role in Kierkegaard's reflections on method.

The next entry on "the method" is found in I A 8 (*J. and P.*, I, 117) of the *Papirer*. Kierkegaard probably wrote it while reading *Om Erkjendelse og Granskning*.[6] Sibbern

[5] I A 1 (*J. and P.*, II, 2240).

deals with the same issue Kierkegaard comes to grips with in his note—namely, the question of the significance of the "a priori construction" in the knowledge of the physical world and in the understanding of an author's works. For the most part Kierkegaard agrees with Sibbern regarding penetration of an author's work but is more guarded when it comes to knowledge of the physical world. Of this he writes: "The reason I cannot really say that I positively enjoy *nature* is that I do not quite realize *what* it is that I enjoy. A work of art, on the other hand, I can grasp. I can —if I may put it this way—find that Archimedean point, and as soon as I have found it, everything is readily clear for me. Then I am able to pursue this one main idea and see how all the details serve to illuminate it. I see the author's whole individuality as if it were the sea, in which every single detail is reflected. The author's spirit is kindred to me; he is very probably far superior to me, I am sure, but yet he is as limited as I am. The works of the deity are too great for me; I always get lost in the details."

This journal entry is important because it so early indicates agreement and disagreement between Kierkegaard and Hegel on a crucial point in "the method." They agree in that both are interested in finding a dominating thought (Hegel would say an idea) from which all content may thereafter be derived. The decisive difference is that Kierkegaard believes (together with Sibbern) that the derivation of the concrete content of the "great thought" does not take place by an inevitable process—as Hegel believes—but by the intellectual process of explicating the implications contained in the "great thought."

Kierkegaard cites at the end of this entry—where he in part comes close to Sibbern's position on knowledge of the physical world—an example of how in certain limited fields this knowledge can advance along deductive paths. He writes: "How remarkable that one of the best, yes, the very best writer about bees was blind from early youth. It seems to indicate that however much one believes in the importance of the observation of externals, he had found that [Archimedean] point and now by a purely intellectual activity had deduced from all this the details and had reconstructed them analogously to nature."

The way to find this Archimedean point is through "an inner intuition,"[7] another concept which is found in Sibbern and which subsequently plays an important role in Kierkegaard's thinking.

In the entry just cited, attention is called to the possibility of deductively deriving from a higher concept the links contained therein. In this procedure analysis is primary. The next entry on method describes the movement in the opposite direction. Here the point is to collect the different elements into an organic whole. Kierkegaard notes: "It seems to me that the difference between an author who picks up his material everywhere but does not work it up into an organic whole is the same as the difference between the mock turtle and the real turtle. Some portions of the real turtle's meat tastes like veal, others like chicken, but the whole is formed in one organism. All these various kinds of meat are found in the mock turtle, but that which binds the separate parts is a sauce, which still is often more nourishing than the jargon which goes into a lot of writing."[8] Kierkegaard supposedly wrote this note, too, on reading *Om Erkjendelse og Granskning.* Sibbern speaks in this book of an organic summing-up of various qualifications in one organic whole, and he contrasts this synthesis with that which comes out of mathematical processes of thought, where the isolated elements are dominant.[9]

It is sufficiently clear that Sibbern's expression "an organic whole"[10] also refers to the actuality of the subject. But Sibbern's confusion is that in *Om Erkjendelse og*

[7] I A 8 (*J. and P.,* I, 117); Sibbern treats this question in great detail in *Philosophiskt Archiv,* 1829, pp. 97ff; see further *Erkjendelse og Granskning,* pp. 88ff., and *Logik,* 1835, pp. 77ff.

[8] I A 32 (*J. and P.,* V).

[9] *Erkjendelse og Granskning,* pp. 126ff.

[10] Ibid., p. 142.

Granskning, probably influenced by Hegel's philosophical terminology, he uses the term "system"[11] for the organic unity. From the time he wrote this note on the organic, the goal for all Kierkegaard's dialectical efforts—as far as we can see—is simply and solely organic unity and not systematic unity. From now on the organic and the dialectic stand in intimate relation to each other, and later Kierkegaard very decisively affirms the unqualified relation between those two.[12]

After finding in the idea of organic coherence the goal for his dialectical work, Kierkegaard then seeks to gather together all the elements and definitions which were to form the foundation for his dialectical method.

Kierkegaard's next step in working out this method is to explain the concept of consistency. This is introduced with the following apparently insignificant entry which, however, opens new perspectives for using this concept in structuring the method: "The same thing is done with the concept 'orthodoxy' as with the concept 'consistency.' Many think that being consistent means always doing the same thing and presumably would have us go around with umbrellas in sunny weather because we use them in rainy weather."[13]

This journal entry expresses the view that the concept of consistency must not be used in a one-sided and schematic manner; this concept must be closely correlated with the form of actuality to which it is applied. This realization opens the way to seeing that the concept of consistency has more dimensions and that its structure is more complicated than is usually assumed. It now becomes Kierkegaard's task to think through the possible modifications in the application of this concept to the theoretical disciplines and to concrete actuality. From now on the idea of a modi-

[11] Ibid., p. 82. Sibbern commends "Hegel's profound and at the same time sharply perceptive logic."
[12] *Authority and Revelation*, p. 58n.
[13] I A 45 (*J. and P.*, III, 3045).

fication of the concept in relation to the various forms of actuality becomes especially significant and also influences his concepts of existence.

It is interesting to note that Kierkegaard now, after the first entry about the concept of consistency in the beginning of 1835, and for many months thereafter, uses the expression "consistency" and "consistent" in his journal entries more often than at any other time. One gets the definite impression that Kierkegaard at this time (after having achieved a new perspective on it) is "practicing" the various possible applications of this concept.

It is not possible to establish clearly how quickly Kierkegaard arrives at a full perception of the equivalent modifications of this concept in applying it to the various spheres of actuality; on the other hand it is possible to ascertain that he very soon centers his attention on applying consistent thinking to the actuality of the person as subject.

We will first give particular examples of Kierkegaard's application of the concept of consistency and thereafter follow his movement toward the actuality of the subject as the ultimate goal.

When Kierkegaard early in 1835 applies the concept of consistency the first time, he does so by utilizing indirect proof, in which consistency plays a special role. This form of proof is used primarily in a way that seeks to show the weak sides of a claim or a theory by thinking through its consequences. Trendelenburg, of great interest to Kierkegaard later, makes the statement in his *Logische Untersuchungen* with regard to consistency in relation to indirect argument: "The force of indirect evidence is always consistency in concepts."[14] Trendelenburg, moreover, says of this argument: "We marvel at the degree of its cold-blooded, penetrating acuteness, that the embryo of the foreign thought is impregnated from all sides, so as to reveal its misformed being."[15] Trendelenburg also cites in his

[14] F. A. Trendelenburg, *Logische Untersuchungen*, I-II (Berlin, 1840), II, p. 323 (ed. tr.).
[15] Ibid., pp. 323-24 (ed. tr.).

books many instructive examples of the application of indirect proof from the history of philosophy.

The philosophical and theological situation in Kierkegaard's day provided a rich opportunity for him to test the cogency of thought by means of indirect proof. Hegel's speculative thinking as well as Grundtvig's theories of the Church were good subjects for thorough testing by means of such an argument. Kierkegaard's first recorded attempt at thinking through the consequences to uncover possible errors in a propounded claim is aimed at Grundtvig's theories of the Church.[16] Kierkegaard seems to have deliberated upon the issues implicit in the theory of the Church with such thoroughness that eleven years later he could use almost without change his critical observations in his treatment of this theory in *Concluding Unscientific Postscript*.[17]

Presumably prompted in part by the commotion occasioned by Grundtvig's theories of the Church, Kierkegaard again makes use of consistency in indirect argument pertaining to Christianity's various historical formations. Kierkegaard's critical attitude at the time toward the historical forms of Christianity is clearly evident in his letter to Peter Wilhelm Lund: "As you will know, I grew up in orthodoxy, so to speak, but as soon as I began to think for myself the enormous colossus gradually began to totter. I call it an enormous colossus deliberately, for taken on the whole it actually is very consistent and through the many centuries the separate parts have fused together so tightly that it is difficult to get at it. Now I could very well accept particular parts of it, but then these would prove to be comparable to the seedlings often found in rock fissures. On the other hand, I could probably also see the distortions in many separate points, but for a time I was obliged to let the main foundation stand *in dubio*."[18]

This indirect argument, initiated so early against particular modes of Christianity, continues to be part and parcel

[16] I A 60-62 (*J. and P.*, V).   [17] *Postscript*, pp. 36-41.
[18] I A 72 (*J. and P.*, V).

of Kierkegaard's thinking thereafter and forms the basis of his criticism of "Christendom."

In the application of the method of indirect argument to various philosophical systems, Kierkegaard concentrates exclusively on a sweeping criticism of Hegel and does not go into the other systems more deeply because his primary concern is a thorough penetration of the problems dealing with subjective actuality. His attitude is clearly expressed in these words written during a summer sojourn at Gilleleje in 1835: "What matters is to find a purpose, to see what it really is that God wills that *I* shall do; the crucial thing is to find a truth which is truth *for me*, to find *the idea for which I am willing to live and die.* Of what use would it be to me to discover a so-called objective truth, to work through the philosophical systems so that I could, if asked, make critical judgments about them, could point out the fallacies in each system; of what use would it be to me to be able to develop a theory of the state, getting details from various sources and combining them into a whole, and constructing a world which I did not live in but merely held up for others to see; of what use would it be to me to be able to formulate the meaning of Christianity, to be able to explain many specific points—if it had no deeper meaning *for me and for my life?*"[19]

In indirect argument Kierkegaard uses consistency primarily with a negative purpose, to expose the weaknesses in certain positions. Consistency plays an essentially positive role for Kierkegaard in the propounding of new points of view and in the structuring of new theories, since the scholarly tenability of these theories depends upon a painstaking extraction of all their implications. This deductive way of arriving at conclusions gradually acquires great

[19] I A 75, p. 53 (*J. and P.*, V). The words "live and die" in the quotation may sound like an echo of similar reflections in Sibbern, where the two words are also underlined: "There must be something of which man is so convinced, as of his own existence, that he will *live and die upon its truth.*" See Sibbern, *Erkjendelse og Granskning*, p. 178.

significance for Kierkegaard. Entry I A 8, cited previously (p. 110), suggests one possible way of using it, the deduction of particular details in an author's work from his "great thoughts." This venture opens up wider ranges for him in the future. Since his interest is turning in the direction of the actuality of the individual, he sees his task to be a thoroughly concrete characterization of the mental-spiritual structure of the individual in order not only to derive from this foundation consistent conclusions with respect to his own existential position but also to be able to depict the life-positions of other men by means of "the consistent development."[20] In this way Kierkegaard is led to a more explicit definition of the basic elements of concrete individual existence and in a wider sense to a perception of how these elements form an organic unity in the life of the individual.

After arriving at this profound insight into the concept of consistency and its modifications, which is the primary presupposition for the structuring of his dialectical method, Kierkegaard is able to carry through his project with greater methodical assurance.

A more systematic work with issues of method begins in 1836. At this time Kierkegaard also undertakes to go his own way by removing himself from home influences and also by breaking off his studies at the University. His intention now is to concentrate in scholarly and existential ways upon certain currents of intellectual life, primarily upon romanticism, which leads him to a more specific study of irony and humor. At the same time he wants to investigate more closely the three great ideas which for him are embodied in the figures of Don Juan, Faust, and Ahasuerus.

During these studies Kierkegaard is less engrossed in personal rumination and tries rather to enter with sympathetic insight an unfamiliar world in order to explore it experimentally. Not until two years later does Kierkegaard,

[20] I C 85 (*J. and P.*, V).

enriched by new experiences, return to an intense concern for his own subjective actuality and to reflections on the fundamental components of this actuality.

The progress of this development, beginning with an interest in and a penetration of his environment and finally leading him back to personal issues, can be closely followed in the journal entries of 1836-38. During the first stage of this development Kierkegaard gets a good deal of practice in psychological experimentation by identifying with the psychic life of others.

The earliest experiments have already been discussed in the section on Kierkegaard's study of psychology, but the subject of Kierkegaard as an experimenting psychologist is so vast that it can only be touched upon partially here.[21]

Kierkegaard's first journal entry in 1836 is on the dialectical method for knowledge of actuality, and it reads: "Actually, the important thing in reasoning is the ability to see the part within the whole. Most people never actually enjoy a tragedy; it falls into separate pieces for them—nothing but monologues—and an opera into arias, etc. The same sort of thing happens in the physical world when, for example, I walk along a road parallel to two other roads with interspersed strips of ground; most people would only see the road, the strip of ground, and then the road, but would be unable to see the whole as being like a piece of striped cloth."[22]

Before any discussion of the many themes implicit in this entry, it should be noted that Kierkegaard credits himself with the condition for all dialectical cognition and thinking, the ability "to see the part within the whole" or, what amounts to the same thing, to see the separate parts as "an organic whole," something with which Kierkegaard

---

[21] See G. Malantschuk, "Søren Kierkegaard som eksperimenterende Psykolog," and Arild Christensen, "Om Indlevelsens Grundlag hos Søren Kierkegaard," *Meddelelser fra Søren Kierkegaard Selskabet*, IV, 2 and 3, 1953.

[22] I A 111 (*J. and P.*, II, 2245); compare with *Either/Or*, I, pp. 121-22n.

was already familiar. As a methodological principle of cognition, but on a higher plane, this thought is mentioned by Plato in the following words: "ὁ μὲν γάρ συνοπτικὸς διαλεκτικός" ("He who sees things in their connexion is a dialectician").[23] Kierkegaard's point of departure for this journal entry is the idea of integrative cognition; whether he encountered this thought in reading Plato or Sibbern or some other intermediary is difficult to ascertain. In any case it means various things to Kierkegaard. The entry just quoted speaks of the use of this ability of synthesizing cognition on the—from Kierkegaard's epistemological point of view—lowest level. On this level is the kind of actuality Kierkegaard calls the "purely physical."[24] But the use of this epistemological principle also entails modifications. Kierkegaard's earlier treatment of the concept of consistency taught him the possibility of modifications in a principle when it is applied to different forms of actuality. Kierkegaard could learn about the various modifications of this epistemological principle in relation to actuality also from Plato, who applies the principle to a higher kind of actuality.[25]

Kierkegaard is not through after applying the principle to a lower plane of actuality. The very next entry shows that he is seeking analogies to such an integrative cognition in other areas, in this case in "the sphere of emotions." Just as it is difficult "to encompass the mass of empirical data"[26] on the physical plane as a unity, so also, according to Kierkegaard, it is difficult in "the sphere of emotions" to form a basic mood from diverse emotional qualities. On this same occasion it is pointed out that it is impossible to achieve this basic mood when it has no frame of reference in a limited concrete occurrence but is lost in an unlimited

[23] Plato, *Republic*, 537 C.

[24] See *Either/Or*, I, pp. 121ff.

[25] It should be noted that the word συνοπτικὸς in its original meaning points to a visible actuality.

[26] I A 112 (*J. and P.*, II, 2246). See repetition of the entry in *Either/Or*, I, pp. 121f.

context, as when the feeling is toward a countless number of men or mankind as such.[27]

The next expansion of the principle of the integration of parts into a whole is on the plane of cognition, but Kierkegaard thereafter extends this principle to include also the existential situation and his dialectic of communication. If this line of development is seen from the angles of time-space, it may be said that whereas the spatial relations are accentuated in Kierkegaard's first journal entry about the ability to comprehend, time comes to the fore in other ways of using this ability.

This line of development shows that Kierkegaard is moving in the direction of subjective actuality, inasmuch as time, to use Kant's expression, is "die Form des innern Sinnes"[28] in contrast to space, which designates externality.

In Kierkegaard's intensive work with the idea of an integrating capacity, certain levels (on an ascending scale) and possible uses of the idea are discernible. The following outline may provide a helpful comprehensive view.

(1) The first step is given in journal entry I A 111 (*J. and P.*, II, 2245) and concerns an integration of parts on a purely physical level. To put it briefly, this level is one of *seeing* things together as a unity.

Parallel to level 1 is the previously mentioned analogy to cognition's integrating ability in the sphere of emotions. At the same time it may be said that this analogy has a certain relation to level 4.

(2) The next level is the ability to form a unity of the elements apprehended through hearing. Here the succession of time-factors plays a role. Kierkegaard's use of this form of cognition concerns actuality in the world of sound

[27] There is here a trace of Kierkegaard's later pronounced negative attitude to the kind of "emotion" which is oriented toward abstractions such as the nation, humanity, etc.

[28] Immanuel Kant, *Critik der reinen Vernunft* (Riga, 4th ed., 1794), p. 49; *Immanuel Kant's Critique of Pure Reason*, tr. Norman Kemp Smith (London, Macmillan, 1950), p. 77: "the form of inner sense."

where such unities might be found, as in music. He experiences a special use of this form of cognition while listening to Mozart's music.[29]

(3) The third level is in the sphere of thought where the dialectician must seek to hold various contents of thought "thinking together." This is the most advanced form of the integrating ability, the foundation for all dialectics, and corresponds to the activity of Plato's ideal dialectician.

(4) Through intensified concentration on the actuality of the subject, Kierkegaard discovers that the sphere of existence also requires positing the basic principle that the particular elements in existence may be joined in a unity in contemporaneity. In this way Kierkegaard approaches the concept of contemporaneity from the side of cognition, but, as will be seen, this concept is given a different and deeper foundation.

(5) Finally, mention must be made of the significance of the ability to unite elements in contemporaneity in receiving and communicating a thought content. As we have seen, all of Kierkegaard's work in penetrating various disciplines is marked by a parallel activity with many subjects contemporaneously. In the works, too, Kierkegaard deals with different subjects in many parallel "layers." This method of integrating contemporaneously many elements into a unity also pervades Kierkegaard's dialectic of communication. That Kierkegaard also thought of using the same procedure in eventual lectures is evident in the following statement from a later time: "The lecture will try as far as possible to make everything *present*, if possible, to convey the impression to you that at one and the same time you have the most contradictory thoughts. Therefore it will not have the simplicity of the more strictly academic lecture, which has a definite place for the discussion of each particular point, about which there is no discussion either before or after. No, the lecture will constantly, if I dare say so, be haunted by the memory of what was said

[29] See entries (1835-36) I A 64 (*J. and P.*, V) and I C 125 (*J. and P.*, IV).

on other points; the reflections will constantly traverse the points at issue in order to call to mind the past and the future, in order to maintain, if possible, the impression that everything is present at one and the same time. . . ."[30]

But it is not solely through reflecting on theory of knowledge that Kierkegaard is steadily led into a more intense concentration upon subjective actuality and the working out of its patterns of possibility. No less significant are the existential incentives which will now be examined more closely in order to show how Kierkegaard seeks to embrace the total actuality of the subject within ever new perspectives until he finds an exhaustive interpretation of all the issues related to this actuality.

The most important of the existential foundations is in the sphere of religion. After the spring of 1838, Kierkegaard, most likely because of his friend P. M. Møller's death, is prompted to turn back to his own personal problems. In May of 1838 he has the experience already referred to, an experience which, following Paul (Philippians 4:4), he describes as *"an indescribable joy"*;[31] this joy, given to him "inexplicably" and "for no apparent reason," is the beginning of a new positive attitude toward Christianity. Reconciliation with his father further strengthens in a concrete way this new attitude. His father's death in the summer of 1838 could only fortify this return to the original religious position, but on a higher plane.

For Kierkegaard this transition is marked by the fact that from now on Christianity to him is no longer a subject which concerns him only objectively, but it is something which touches his personal life in a crucial way and concerns his whole existence. The first journal entry that says anything about this transition from an objective spectator-relation to Christianity to a subjectively interested relation is this: "I am going to work toward a far more inward relation to Christianity, for up until now I have in a way been standing completely outside of it while fighting for its

30 VIII² B 88, p. 180 (*J. and P.*, I, 656).
31 II A 228 (*J. and P.*, V). See also pp. 35 and 101 above.

truth; like Simon of Cyrene (Luke 23:26), I have carried
Christ's cross in a purely external way."[32] It is worth noting
that this was written scarcely a month after the note about
an indescribable joy." This new attitude is given expression in many subsequent entries. A few examples are given
here.

An entry already referred to (II A 377 [*J. and P.*, 3377])
says, among other things: "Let us never forget that all
Christianity is a life-course."[33] Entry II A 392 (*J. and P.*,
II, 1313) gives the impression that Kierkegaard, in saying
enthusiastically that Paul (Romans 11:33) gave "one of
the most profound expositions the world has ever heard,"
is himself caught up in this same question, and is led further to his own subjective actuality, which at the conclusion of the entry he characterizes by saying that "God is in
truth no less in the unique life of the individual than he is
in the noise of the complications of the world. . . ."

This new situation of the subjective appropriation of
Christianity is eloquently described in another entry in
which Kierkegaard points to the consequences for the individual of such an appropriation. "Only when a life-view
is no longer a thought-experiment among other thought-
experiments, but rather an outlook which precisely by being this has a *drive* (an inner, immanental power) requir-
ing actualization and because of this posits itself at every
moment, only then does the true cleavage in a man appear. . . ."[34] Here it is clearly expressed that the stage for
a man's action has moved into the sphere of inner actuality. This is significant for Kierkegaard's interpretation of
the ethical as an eternal commitment which is superior to
all merely external stipulations and laws. This understanding distinctly lays weight on subjectivity, which alone contains the possibility of the eternal and thereby the possibility of being addressed by the eternal. A few examples will
show how Kierkegaard's ethical views are an obvious consequence of his new religious direction.

[32] II A 232 (*J. and P.*, V).   [33] See p. 18 above.
[34] II A 430 (*J. and P.*, I, 868).

On this basis Kierkegaard protests regarding the human personality under the determinants of relativity, as is the case in Hegel's system.[35] The eternal in man, the basis of the religious relationship, excludes the possibility of a mediation.

In another entry[36] Kierkegaard considers that his ethical position, according to which the individual seeks to actualize the eternal requirement, justifies his use of the word "transcendence," which Kant would repudiate in both ethics and epistemology. This example shows that Kierkegaard believes there is access to the transcendent from the side of ethics as well.

A more detailed discussion of these relations requires a tracing of the fundamental categories of subjective actuality. Kierkegaard is led by the above elements in his new view of Christianity and ethics to the task of thinking through the a priori concepts and their function in the subject.

It sounds like a dismissal of the purely empirical sciences when Kierkegaard writes: "Empiricism is a perpetually self-repeating false sorites, both in the progressive and the regressive sense."[37] With this statement Kierkegaard acknowledges that "empiricism," with its chains of data and reasoning ("sorites"), does not arrive at what is the most important, namely the reality of the eternal.

In his work on the question of a priori concepts as basic elements for subjective actuality, Kierkegaard seems to have received suggestions and hints from Sibbern, as the relevant passages will indicate.

Kierkegaard's method of treating a priori concepts can best be illuminated by comparison with Kant's classical attempt to deal with truths a priori. The following dissimilarities between Kant and Kierkegaard may be noted:

(a) Kant's attempt to justify truths as a priori applies to

---

[35] II A 457 (*J. and P.*, II, 1578).
[36] II A 486 (*J. and P.*, II, 2234).
[37] II A 247 (*J. and P.*, II, 2254).

metaphysics, to which he would attribute the same cogency already possessed by mathematics and physics. In his work with the a priori concepts Kierkegaard is interested in defining the basic relationships which have essential significance for subjective existence.

(b) Kant seeks to find the rules for the possibility of synthetic a priori judgments. For Kierkegaard the synthesis of the factors in the subject are of crucial importance.

(c) Kant wants to find his categories through a deductive procedure, which is already patterned in the logical structure of judgments. Kierkegaard wants to achieve clarity about the "a priori basic concepts" by concentrating on them. He says: ". . . thus there is no deductive development of concepts or what one could call that which has some constitutive power—man can only concentrate upon it. . . ."[38]

(d) Kierkegaard upbraids Kant for bringing the categories nearer to the absolutely true but then, on the other hand, removing the categories from this position by his claim that approximation to this truth must be understood as an infinite process. Kierkegaard writes of this: "Philosophers usually give with one hand and take away with the other. So it is with Kant, who indeed taught us something about the approximation of the categories to the genuinely true (νοούμενα), but by making it infinite he thereby took it all back. Generally this use of the word *infinite* plays a great role in philosophy."[39] This remark belongs together with Kierkegaard's later ironic observation: "Categories are the shewbread of our modern age—digestible only for the clergy."[40]

For Kierkegaard, categories, which he puts into close relationship to ethics, have genuine significance for actuality. By one's actualizing them in individual existence, the transcendent can be achieved, contrary to Kant's claim. For Kierkegaard there is not in this respect *"ein Ding an sich"*; a higher form of this may be found in Kierkegaard's cate-

[38] II A 301 (*J. and P.*, II, 2257).
[39] II A 47 (*J. and P.*, II, 2087).
[40] II A 398 (*J. and P.*, V).

gory of the paradox, which is "an ontological qualification which expresses the relation between an existing cognitive spirit and the eternal truth."[41]

How closely Kierkegaard links his categories to the ethical can also be seen in the following entry: ". . .—so also in spiritual things all receptivity is productivity."[42] This statement presupposes the re-creative power of the subject, a presupposition which is characteristic of Kierkegaard's understanding of the ethical. Thus Climacus later uses this statement word-for-word in *Concluding Unscientific Postscript*, where he gives examples of the subject's movement in the direction of bringing about ethical-existential actuality.[43]

Kierkegaard's observation that one discovers categories by concentrating on his subjective actuality must not be misinterpreted to mean that in the last analysis the basic categorical qualifications are to be conceived simply as anthropologically grounded in subjectivity. Kierkegaard's final premise is religious-theological in nature, which is understandable in view of his whole relation to the religious. Therefore he thinks that the provision of a solid basis for deriving and adducing categories requires more than the claim that deriving and adducing are undertaken not in relation to a particular subject but to all mankind as a superior subject. Kierkegaard comments ironically on the philosophers who ground their categorical qualifications this way, forgetting that "there is something higher than *the atmosphere*." Kierkegaard's entry on this reads: "The philosophers think that all knowledge, yes, even the existence of the deity, is something man himself produces and that revelation can be referred to only in a figurative sense, in somewhat the same sense as one may say the rain falls down from heaven, although the rain is nothing but an earth-produced mist; but they forget, to keep the metaphor, that in the beginning God separated

---

[41] VIII¹ A 11 (*J. and P.*, III, 3089).
[42] II A 536 (*J. and P.*, I, 878).
[43] *Postscript*, p. 72.

the waters of the heaven and of the earth and that there is something higher than *the atmosphere*."[44]

The very next entries show that Kierkegaard fully appreciates purely "human knowledge"[45] and its objective reality, but through his concentration on the subject he has arrived at a different and, in his opinion, a higher kind of knowledge than that of the objective sciences.

With respect to the relation between categories and actuality, Kierkegaard could agree with the view which he heard Sibbern present (December 17, 1838). Kierkegaard gives the following account: "In his lecture today Sibbern made a very good observation about how one must assume a real ideal being, which in itself has being before its expression in actual being, something one can discern in the fact that in speaking of eternal truths one would not say that they now come to be but that they are now revealed, i.e., in the fullness of time."[46]

Kierkegaard's previously mentioned return to preoccupation with subjective actuality and with its a priori elements leads him on to a more precise determination of the content of these elements. The first reference to this question is found in the following brief comment: "It is obvious that there is a cognitive unity of two elements, one of which is not coordinate with the other but subordinate, as when the girl gives up her *name* in marriage (*nomen dare alicui*, precisely in order to take his name)."[47] This statement, dated June 26, 1839, has many immediate forerunners[48] which speak of the conflicting elements within subjective actuality, but not until entry II A 461 (*J. and P.*, II, 2265) does Kierkegaard clearly state that these elements are not coordinate but one is superior to the other.

[44] II A 523 (*J. and P.*, II, 2266).
[45] II A 526 (*J. and P.*, II, 2269).
[46] II A 305 (*J. and P.*, I, 194).
[47] II A 461 (*J. and P.*, II, 2265).
[48] Compare this to the two closest journal entries, II A 430 (*J. and P.*, I, 868) and II A 454 (*J. and P.*, II, 1578), in which Kierkegaard points to the state of conflict in the subject.

We also note that Kierkegaard uses the expression "unity" to express the relation between the two elements, but later he uses the synonym "synthesis" for such a unity. It can therefore be said that in the entry about this "unity" we have the first suggestion of his important concept of synthesis, which always embraces two (or more) elements, one of which must be subordinate to the other, for example, the temporal subordinate to the eternal.

In this first outline Kierkegaard lays the groundwork for further reflections on the fundamental elements in subjective actuality. Kierkegaard fills in the outline with many conceptual pairs representing analogies to "the cognitive unity of two elements." While working on the enlargement of this outline, Kierkegaard finds Sibbern's concept of "the collateral" to be helpful.

Since the expression "the collateral" from Sibbern's philosophical terminology plays an especially important role in Kierkegaard's continued exploration of the existential factors of the subject, we must briefly refer to its position in Sibbern's philosophy. The fullest explanation of this concept is in his book *Bemærkninger og Undersøgelser, fornemmelig betræffende Hegels Philosophi, betraget i Forhold til vor Tid (Observations and Investigations Particularly on Hegel's Philosophy Seen in Relation to Our Time*; 1838).[49]

By the concept of "the collateral" Sibbern means that the development of mental-spiritual content in the realms of both external and internal actuality takes place simultaneously along many lines. All mental-spiritual activity is always shared by a multiplicity of parallel factors—thus the expression "collateral" or parallel. In Sibbern the collateral is most strongly stressed in his criticism of Hegel's system. On the basis of his understanding of the collateral, Sibbern must protest against Hegel's philosophy, mainly on the following points:

[49] Appended to the title: "Special Reprint of a Review of Professor Heiberg's *Perseus*, No. 1," in *Maanedsskrift for Litteratur*, X, 1838.

(a) Against Hegel's method, for its "merely linear course"[50] in which movement takes place along a single line since the one concept passes over into the other, etc.

(b) Against "Hegel's moral philosophy," which Sibbern also criticizes on the basis of his view of the collateral, saying among other things: "Here is apparent Hegel's lack of adequate attention to what I call the organizing idea and to the collateral."[51]

(c) On the question of the relation of thinking to feeling and willing Hegel gives thought "excessive significance."[52] Concerning this Sibbern says: "Everyone who observes must acknowledge that thought can be only one main element in existence [*Existentsen*] *alongside* others which stand with it on equal footing. But here again we see Hegel's great lack of attentiveness to the collateral in existence [*Tilværelsen*] and to the genuine organizing idea or to the kind of organization to which the collateral essentially belongs." And further: "No wonder, therefore, that we do not find in Hegel the well-known triad: cognition, feeling, and will, which everyone who has looked into the inner life of man properly and thoroughly must surely acknowledge to lie as the base of man's mental-spiritual existence, and which, after Kant formulated it, although in another way, has made a strong claim and has found a rather universal recognition and acceptance."[53]

Sibbern wonders that "men with free passage in the world of ideas"[54] could not see these and other errors in Hegel's philosophy.

Among the collateral concepts attributed to the subject as parallel series of qualifications there are, according to Sibbern: "*The genuine synthetic unities* in a special sense or the *genuine* synthetic combinations of two forming a

[50] Sibbern, *Observations and Investigations*, p. 130; see also p. 125: "in its linear, although epicyclic (or, better, spiral), ascending course. . . ."
[51] Ibid., pp. 40-41.   [52] Ibid., p. 93.
[53] Ibid., pp. 95-96.   [54] Ibid., p. 30.

third . . ."[55] and "such triads as we have, for example in *cognition, feeling,* and *will.*"[56]

These quotations from Sibbern show that by the concept of the collateral he meant to express the fullness and exuberance of existence. This also emerges in his book in appreciative references to P. M. Møller's paper "On Immortality"; at the same time he is critical of philosophical views, Hegelian philosophy in particular, which are not concerned sufficiently with the question of immortality: "But this holds true particularly of a philosophy which, both in its philosophy of nature and philosophy of mind, makes a particular point of going through the ascending levels and stages of existence [*Tilværelsens*] and then partly forgets and partly neglects the most important considerations regarding that which in a collateral way and in collateral respects manifests itself in life and existence [*Tilvær*]."[57]

It is these thoughts of Sibbern on the collateral relationship that Kierkegaard incorporates in his expansion of the pattern of unity of two elements.

It must, however, be pointed out here that with respect to the essential structure of the outline Kierkegaard is already beyond Sibbern in the comprehension of "synthetic unities." Sibbern thinks of the two concepts which enter into conjunction as standing on equal footing[58] with each other; whereas Kierkegaard clearly states that one component takes the lead and the other is subordinate. Whether Kierkegaard derived the idea for his pattern from Sibbern's use of combinations such as "relative absoluteness"[59] is difficult to determine. With respect to the "triad" of determinants—cognition, feeling, and will—Kierkegaard, like Sibbern, acknowledges their equality of status.

Kierkegaard, as stated, completely concurs with Sibbern's idea of the collateral, according to which there are

[55] Ibid., p. 130.   [56] Ibid., p. 131.   [57] Ibid., p. 12.
[58] Ibid., p. 95, but especially p. 125.
[59] Sibbern, *Logik som Tænkelære* (Copenhagen, 1830), pp. 205f., also the section on "*Høiere og lavere Begreber*," p. 235.

parallel series of qualifications in the subject. A month after sketching the unity of the two components he clearly articulates his concurrence with Sibbern when he discovers in reading I. H. Fichte's treatise *Aphorismen über die Zukunft der Theologie, in ihrem Verhältnisse zu Spekulation und Mythologie*[60] that Fichte also had the same objection to Hegel's method as Sibbern—namely, that according to this method everything proceeds along one single line of thought or, as Sibbern would say, "only linearly."[61] Kierkegaard writes of this and gives the page number in the journal containing the treatise:

On page 252 Fichte also expresses himself in opposition to the current method of regarding the one as proceeding from the other in a dialectical process. And this vindicates the significance of what Sibbern calls the collateral.[62]

The next step for Kierkegaard is to work out the parallel series of qualifications of subjective actuality by "concentratedly deliberating upon it,"[63] that is, by observing existence and by thinking consistently. Since, unlike Kant, he does not think they can be deduced from a previously posited pattern, their number cannot be precisely determined, and the groupings do not have the same architectonic structure, as in Kant's thought.

The interdependent concepts most used by Kierkegaard are: temporal-eternal, necessity-freedom, finite-infinite, body-mind-spirit. These coupled-concepts can be supplemented by many more, but it should be noted that they express the same fundamental relation. Thus up to a point many series of coupled concepts can be drawn—such as being-essence, quantity-quality; Kierkegaard also uses these determinants at times. The important aspect of this arrangement of coupled concepts is that, together with the triad of cognition, feeling, and will, they reproduce

[60] In *Zeitschift für Philosophie und spekulative Theologie,* ed. I. H. Fichte (Bonn, 1839), III.
[61] Sibbern, *Hegels Philosophie,* p. 125.
[62] II A 519 (*J. and P.,* III, 3277).
[63] II A 301 (*J. and P.,* II, 2257).

man's basic existential structure as seen from different angles.

In this way there is corroboration of the insight that in thought and in existence there are many factors which must be considered at the same time; when thought and existence are developed properly, they both move along many lines and are not one-track and merely "linear." With this we have arrived at the central point of departure for Kierkegaard's whole dialectic, which presupposes many simultaneous parts in the subject and takes this as a hard fact in dealing with subjective actuality.

After defining the subject in its "breadth," so to speak, embracing possible parallel lines, Kierkegaard's next task is to describe it in its "length," its possible development or movement on the basis of the given presuppositions. This task he did not complete until 1842, but since he had the principal categories for finishing the task and since he had also established the content of the concept of synthesis, he was able to work, even then, on defining the subject "longitudinally," that is, in terms of stages.[64]

The following comment, however, must be made at this point: It was clear to Kierkegaard that if rules are to be established for the direction of the individual's life, there must be a criterion by which the direction can be judged. Kierkegaard believed that it is permissible to reject norms and standards only in a theoretical thought-experiment, if he wanted to do so. In existence it is impossible to do this.[65] In existence everyone must have a criterion of some kind for his life. Existence itself presupposes an evaluation, and a consistent nihilism in practice would mean suicide.

Kierkegaard finds this criterion for a man's spiritual development in Christianity. It is also interesting to see that Kierkegaard's reference to "the collateral," which helped him to delineate the structure of the subject and

[64] See I A 248 (*J. and P.*, II, 1966); I A 101 (*J. and P.*, I, 29); and II A 5 (*J. and P.*, I, 783); see also pp. 143-50 below.

[65] See IV A 72 (*J. and P.*, I, 774); IV C 56 (*J. and P.*, II, 1243); IV C 60 (*J. and P.*, II, 1244).

form the basis for a satisfactory account of the development of the subject, comes at the same time as his claim that only Christianity "explains the world" and thereby also the most important occurrence, human existence. Kierkegaard further emphasizes as strongly as possible that "common human existence" does not, however, explain Christianity. Finally, it is pointed out in the same entry that Christianity is on a qualitatively new level. He says of Christianity: "It contains not only something which men have not themselves given, but something which has never occurred to the mind of any man even as a wish, an ideal, or anything else."[66]

Therefore Kierkegaard wants to use Christianity as the primary principle in his work of understanding existence [Tilværelsen] and man, and he says of those philosophers who adhere to Christian doctrines only insofar as these doctrines agree with their own philosophical speculation: "Philosophers treat dogmas, the sacred affirmations of Scripture, in short, the whole sacred consciousness, the way Appius Pulcher treated the sacred hens. One consults them, and if they predict something bad, then like the general one says: If the sacred hens won't eat, then let them drink—and thereupon casts them overboard."[67]

Christianity is the orienting principle in the longitudinal structuring of the dialectical method. From now on the method consists of delineating human existence, with all its given presuppositions and its variety of existential factors, as it moves steadily forward to higher and higher levels and finally to a confrontation by Christianity. This ascending line is touched upon by Kierkegaard in an early journal entry.[68]

[66] II A 517 (J. and P., III, 3275).

[67] II A 529 (J. and P., III, 3278). According to Livy, Appius Claudius Pulcher, son of Appius Claudius, lost the battle of Drepana in 249 because he treated the augur's warning in this way.

[68] II A 24 (J. and P., II, 2380).

The "longitudinal" structuring of the dialectic takes three lines:

(1) First of all Kierkegaard seeks to clarify the changes ("modifications")[69] (the particular qualifications as well as their relationship to each other) which emerge during the subject's movement through the different levels and positions toward Christianity, which thereafter gives all these qualifications a qualitatively new meaning. Kierkegaard gives many examples of these modifications in his works; therefore they will be discussed in some detail in the survey of his published writings.

(2) Second, Kierkegaard works out his "theory of the leap"[70] and on the basis of this arrives at a precise demarcation of the different phases of individual development. The most important boundary line for him comes between the purely human life-sphere and Christianity. As early as 1835 Kierkegaard uses the term "the despairing leap"[71] to denote the transition from the human to the Christian and the cleft between. From now on Kierkegaard makes this view of the significance of the leap in dialectics and in existence the basis on which he develops his theory of the leap. He completes the work on this theory before beginning his authorship proper—thus the most important information on this also appears in his journals and papers.

After establishing the need of positing this leap, which he calls the qualitative leap because it leads from the quantitative situation of human life to something qualitatively new, Kierkegaard is led to assume many less decisive leaps in man's mental-spiritual development.

From now on Kierkegaard considers this development from the double point of view of thought and of existence,

[69] For Sibbern's use of modifications see *Logik som Tænkelære*, p. 233 and references.

[70] The expression itself, "my theory of the leap," is first mentioned by Kierkegaard in 1844 in entry V C 12 (*J. and P.*, III, 2352).

[71] I A 99 (*J. and P.*, III, 3247).

and he makes a sharp distinction between the two spheres. As a consequence of this he gets two series of transitions: dialectical leaps and pathos-filled leaps, with the emphasis falling particularly on pathos-filled leaps.[72]

On the basis of the aspects of the leap mentioned here Kierkegaard arrives at the following outline, which eventually embraces all the varieties of leaps and provides the structure for his theory of the leap:

(a) First of all there is the series of dialectical leaps which is discovered when through consistent thought one seeks to characterize the path of the subject's mental-spiritual development.

(b) The next series, pathos-filled leaps, is not a movement within thought but denotes the actual leaps which are made within the sphere of existence itself.[73]

(c) The leap from possibility to actuality. Although Kierkegaard makes a sharp distinction between the spheres of thought and of existence, he knows that transitions from thought to actuality and the reverse are always taking place. From his own position Kierkegaard is most interested in transitions from the medium of thought to existence. He therefore places a special emphasis upon Aristotle's references to precisely these transitions.[74] For Kierkegaard this kind of a leap signifies a returning to this existence after reflection has become attentive to existence in the form of possibility. Since Kierkegaard as a dialectician sees his primary task to be the presentation of existential possibilities, he calls special attention to the transitions from these possibilities to existence itself.

(d) Finally there are the previously mentioned transitions from actuality to possibility. These transitions can only figuratively be called leaps. This is apparent from the fact that the transition from possibility to actuality requires an actual movement, whereas the transition from actual-

[72] IV C 12 (*J. and P.*, II, 2339); VI A 33 (*J. and P.*, III, 2553).
[73] As such the leap belongs to "existence-categories" (V B 150:21 [*J. and P.*, V]).
[74] For example, in IV C 47 (*J. and P.*, I, 258).

ity to possibility is a turn to the medium of thought, consequently to the mere possibility of actuality. This transition can best be designated as an act of abstraction, since thought by this means gets an abbreviation of actuality and in its medium seeks to reproduce actual conditions.

By means of this structure Kierkegaard is able to maintain a clear overview of all the discontinuities in the domains of reflection and of existence. The concept of consistency is particularly useful to him both in working out and applying his theory of the leap. With his passion for "distinction" he works out all the boundary-transitions and points of separation between the different spheres. In this way he is able also to overcome completely the confusion promoted especially by Hegel's philosophy because of a blending of the different spheres. This philosophy did its best to mediate the difference between Christianity and speculation, with the result, however, that a confusion of thought and actuality took place.

One more observation should be made in connection with Kierkegaard's theory of the leap. Kierkegaard's work with the question of the leap prompts him to determine also the relationship of the forms of logical inference to the leap. His first observation on this concerns inductive inference, which he believes always results in a leap if "a law"[75] is to be framed from particular experiences. Kierkegaard gets deeper insight on this point by reading Trendelenburg's works.[76] Even though, according to Kierkegaard, Trendelenburg was not aware of the problem of the leap, in his account of other philosophers' views on indirect argument he was close to Kierkegaard's thinking about the leap and also to his view of first principles in logic and

[75] IV C 75 (*J. and P.*, I, 1072). See Sibbern, *Philosophiskt Archiv*, p. 100: "From the sensible perception of sensible givens to intellectual penetration of them, which brings the light of reason to bear upon the assembled data, there can be no transition except *per saltum*, for sensible perception does not pass over little by little into insight and intelligibility."

[76] See V A 74 (*J. and P.*, III, 2341); V C 11 (*J. and P.*, V); and V C 12 (*J. and P.*, III, 2352).

metaphysics. Kierkegaard accepts Trendelenburg's view that there can be no direct proof for first principles. To Kierkegaard this means that they are acquired only by the leap of intuition and that they are self-evident.[77]

The indirect proof for these principles consists in a demonstration of their justification through being applied in appropriate areas of actuality. Kierkegaard writes as follows about the logical conclusions: "By analogy and induction the conclusion can be reached only by a LEAP.

"All other conclusions are essentially tautological."[78]

Kierkegaard gradually discovers that not only Hegel but also many other thinkers lacked logical stringency in their thought, since they could perceive the presence of the leap but did not try to draw out its implications. "Basically all acknowledge the leap and use it in psychological and ethical formulations but explain it away in logic."[79]

(3) Point three in the development of the longitudinal perspective may be called (to use Kierkegaard's own terminology) the law of repetition, which is also related to Kierkegaard's concept of the leap. This can be defined more explicitly as follows: as each new and higher viewpoint enters into existence, the earlier evaluations lose their significance and everything must be seen in the new light. On the one hand this law is directed against Hegel who, according to Kierkegaard's interpretation of him, maintains that the new, opposing element first of all wipes out the preceding one. This happens when a concept in dialectical movement goes over into its opposite. With a certain irony Kierkegaard comments on Hegel's assumption: "Hegel's subsequent position swallows up the previous one, not as one stage of life swallows another, with each still

[77] While reading Trendelenburg's *Elementa logices Aristotelicae*, Kierkegaard notes that according to Aristotle there are two forms of "the immediate," namely, sense perception and first principles. Both these forms carry immediate certainty within themselves. See V A 75 (*J. and P.*, II, 1941) with references.

[78] V A 74 (*J. and P.*, III, 2341).

[79] V C 8 (*J. and P.*, III, 2350).

retaining its validity, but as a higher title or rank swallows up a lower title.—"[80]

As Kierkegaard sees it, the content of the subject's previous experience is fully retained when a new factor enters or when a new stage begins, but each time the total content is seen in a new perspective. Kierkegaard very likely got the idea for this viewpoint from Christianity. His first remark on this reads: "In Christianity everything is one level lower, because a higher element has entered in."[81] A later comment on the law of repetition reads: "The threshold of consciousness or, as it were, the key, is continually being raised, but within each key the same thing is repeated."[82] This law plays an important role, as will be seen, in the development of the structure of the authorship.

Up to this point we have been concerned exclusively with Kierkegaard's delineation of the subject's actuality in latitudinal and longitudinal perspectives. But in addition to these two, Kierkegaard has another perspective, which, to continue the metaphor, could well be called a depth perspective, expressed in this way: "The trouble with philosophers in respect to Christianity is that they use continental maps when they ought to use special large-scale maps, *for every dogma is nothing but a concrete extension of the universally human consciousness.*"[83]

By this Kierkegaard wishes to say that development in the individual life consists of a steadily deeper and more concrete knowledge of oneself. One is not to look at himself abstractly but "ought to use a special map" and thereby clearly recognize the numerous unique factors and motivations in his life. Kierkegaard believes that by taking this path a person can obtain, on the human level, an insight into his own inadequacy. Christianity later reinforces this perception in a qualitatively new and decisive way. In *Concluding Unscientific Postscript*, for example, Climacus

[80] II A 49 (*J. and P.*, II, 1569).
[81] II A 379 (*J. and P.*, III 2858).
[82] V A 96 (*J. and P.*, IV).
[83] II A 440 (*J. and P.*, III, 3272); see pp. 19-20 above.

makes a thorough application of this viewpoint. Both depth-perspective and longitudinal-perspective outline the path of man's inward deepening or actualization of inwardness.

By elucidating the various aspects of subjective actuality Kierkegaard arrives at a whole view of man. The relatedness of the different expressions of spirit in man constitutes, by analogy to the numerous functions of physical man, a living organism regarded as an organic whole. Kierkegaard's original point of departure, the gathering together of material and working it up into "an organic whole,"[84] takes on a new and comprehensive meaning through application to the knowing and existing subject himself.

Concerning the importance for a dialectician to have such a penetrating knowledge of his own subjective actuality as a coherent totality, Kierkegaard states: "Modern theorizers are so foolishly objective that they completely forget that the thinker himself is like the flutist's instrument and that it is of utmost importance to know one's instrument (here is psychology), yes, of a quite different kind of importance, for the thinker has a relation of infinite inwardness to his object such as no flutist has to his instrument."[85]

A dialectician, according to the entry, must know his instrument even better than the flutist, for the instrument is his own interior actuality, and the dialectician must stand "in an infinitely inward relation" to his own actuality. In this statement Kierkegaard describes his own ideal "thinker." According to this, the subject must also learn to know himself, since this is the first condition for being able to realize oneself.

As Kierkegaard understands it, insight into the subject's organic coherence is the most adequate expression for the essence of dialectic. But as we shall see next, Kierkegaard also tries to formulate coherent views of subjective actual-

[84] I A 32 (*J. and P.*, V).   [85] VI A 63 (*J. and P.*, IV).

ity from points of view other than the organic. We will attempt to name all of them before dealing with the question which is already pressing in, namely: is Kierkegaard, with his combinative views, on the way to building what he otherwise so vigorously fought—"a system"?

The conception of the dialectical as the organic[86] is but one of several points of view from which Kierkegaard tries to integrate the numerous factors of the subject into a coherent whole. We find in his writings many forms of summation carefully thought through, each of which describes the actuality of the subject from a particular angle. All these various combinative views have a collateral relation to each other. In our survey of them attention will be given to their temporal sequence insofar as this can be established, but it should be noted from the outset that Kierkegaard uses his own unique method in working them out— many themes simultaneously parallel. Inasmuch as Kierkegaard, from the initial adoption of methodological points of view on actuality in conscious opposition to the traditional objective sciences, stresses the central significance of the subject's structural composition, we assign to first place a discussion of Kierkegaard's transition from an objective to a subjective way of looking at man.

It has been pointed out many times that Kierkegaard, contrary to the traditional objective approach to the subjects of interest to him, looks for the elements which can be related to the existential life of the subject. In the discussion of these areas in Part I this movement was described in some detail and with copious use of Kierkegaard's own words in order to show how this very important realignment took place. In dealing further with the tension between the objective and the subjective present in the development of his own special views, we must touch on particular central issues involved in the relationship.

According to Kierkegaard, the traditional disciplines pre-

[86] VII² B 235, p. 76 (*Authority and Revelation*, p. 58).

suppose that the ideal is to give as objectively correct a description of phenomena as possible. This line is quite justifiable for many branches of science but inadequate for the area most important to Kierkegaard—man's existential situation and task, which are not directly accessible to external empirical scrutiny.

Kierkegaard's argument regarding the relation of the different disciplines to the concept objective-subjective goes like this. The relation between the objective and the subjective is closely connected to the relation between thinking and being. Emphasis on thinking means emphasis upon objectivity; if being is in the foreground, the subjective is more prominent. The subjective, however, must never be confused with the arbitrary. Applied to the various sciences this means that logic and mathematics are the most objective sciences, since they are concerned with pure thought-objects. Next come the natural sciences, which propose to describe external or objective empirical actuality. Thereafter come the sciences which have the investigation of human existence as their object. But here the subjective element begins to assert itself, for here the point is not merely an objective knowledge of man but also man's appropriation of this knowledge, consequently a subjective process. Here thinking passes over to a concern with the problem of being.

Among the disciplines which have man's existence as their object Kierkegaard includes the subjects discussed in the first part of this book—mythology, psychology, esthetics, philosophy, ethics, dogmatics, and philosophy of religion. From now on, however, Kierkegaard divides these disciplines into sharply distinct groups: the first group embraces mythology, psychology in the general sense, esthetics, and ethics as morality and moral philosophy; to the second group belong ethics in Kierkegaard's sense of the word, dogmatics, and the psychology which describes man's states and situations occasioned by his encounter with the eternal and then with Christianity. Philosophy concludes the first group, and the task of philosophy as

Kierkegaard sees it is to provide an objective, coherent view of existence [*Tilværelsen*] in the sphere of temporality; all the disciplines in the first group together with the natural sciences fall within the synoptic task of philosophy. In short, confining itself to areas which thought can master, philosophy attempts to deliver an objective and total view of existence [*Tilværelsen*].

As far as the first group is concerned, it is objectivity which has the last word. In the second group, however (that is, in the areas which Kierkegaard regards as most fundamental for man), the subjective attitude, therefore subjectivity, is decisive, which means that these areas are incommensurable with science in the elemental sense. The difference between the two groups can also be seen in the way in which the objective disciplines are preoccupied with finite and quantitative relations and dimensions, whereas the disciplines in the second sphere proceed upon the pre-supposition that for the human subject there can be existential factors and decisions of infinite significance which because of their nature cannot be expressed in a direct and objective manner. Here the main stress is not on thought but on being. Kierkegaard holds that only dogmatics, which operates with the concept of faith as opposed to objective knowledge, can provide coherence in the second sphere.

It must be stated, however, that strictly speaking there is no objectivity without some connection with subjectivity, and neither is there any subjectivity without an indirect objective aspect. As we have seen, according to Kierkegaard's view of the objective-subjective, there is an ascending scale from the predominantly objective disciplines to those in which the subjective prevails. In this way every discipline gets its proper place, and confusion arises if this stationing is not respected.

The greatest confusion to arise because of the lack of clear distinctions between the objective and the subjective, between thought and being in the widest sense, is, in Kierkegaard's opinion, the one Hegel was guilty of in trying to make Christianity commensurable with his speculative thought.

Kierkegaard finds in the modern natural sciences another, less familiar, example of how confusion arises when objective scrutiny illegitimately tries to extend its competence to all areas of life.

The proper task for these disciplines is to investigate external objective actuality, but they try also to make claims in areas where narrow, limited, natural-scientific investigation must fall short. This explains why Kierkegaard, who initially was well disposed toward natural-scientific inquiry, later turned against it. Kierkegaard's sharp rejection of the natural sciences' illegitimate encroachment, according to his view, is specifically related to his basic views on the objective-subjective relationship. Subjective truths are of higher value to man than all the dazzling results of external, objective research. Kierkegaard thus links the subjective-objective point of view to an ethical consideration, with the result that he fears that the natural sciences, encouraged by great results in their research with empirical actuality, will go so far as to deny facts other than these which can be established by external, objective methods. By this procedure the idea of transcendence and of the presence of eternally binding ethical laws would be denied, which would lead to the relativizing of all values. Kierkegaard says of this: "Finally, just as metaphysics has supplanted theology, it will end with physics supplanting ethics. The whole modern statistical approach to morality contributes to this."[87] And a little later: "In our time it is the natural sciences which are especially dangerous. Physiology[88] will ultimately extend itself to the point of embracing ethics. There are already sufficient clues of a new endeavor—to treat ethics as physics, whereby all of ethics becomes illusory and ethics in the race is treated statistically

[87] VII[1] A 15 (*J. and P.*, I, 927).
[88] "Physiology," which Kierkegaard names, would correspond to "biology" in current usage.

by averages or is calculated as one calculates vibrations in laws of nature."[89] Another of Kierkegaard's principal objections to using only a biological base for his knowledge of man reads thus: "Think of a brilliant physiologist (those mere butcher-apprentices who think they can explain everything with a knife and with a microscope are an abomination to me)—what does he do? First and foremost he grants that every transition is a leap, that he cannot explain how a consciousness comes into existence [*bliver til*] or how a consciousness of the environment becomes self-consciousness or God-consciousness; he concedes that no matter how much he explains the nervous system he cannot explain the essentially constitutive, the idea. A brilliant physiologist admits that there is no analogy."[90]

Having affirmed the primacy of truths related to the subject and the secondary significance of empirical, objective thought and having always had respect for consistent, logical thinking, which prohibits a superficial erasure of the differences and transitions between spheres, Kierkegaard is obliged to warn against possible encroachment from the natural sciences in this way.

While Kierkegaard is thus on guard against the natural sciences' illegitimate extension of the principle of objectivity, it is worth noting that he takes a very positive attitude toward the direct experience of the world of nature when it is linked to ethical and religious factors, that is, when it touches the subjective aspect of man. The impression of nature's vastness[91] which he experiences during his stay in Gilleleje in 1835 could be mentioned here. This impression is promptly related to his whole religious focus. From his observation of nature Kierkegaard also draws numerous metaphors, symbols, and analogies, not only in his journals but particularly in his works in descriptions of man's actuality.

For Kierkegaard the nature of the subjective viewpoint

[89] VII¹ A 182, p. 119 (*J. and P.*, III, 2807).
[90] VII¹ A 182, pp. 119f. (*J. and P.*, III, 2807).
[91] I A 68 (*J. and P.*, V).

is primarily directive and directional, pointing toward the area of his primary interest. We stress this viewpoint because it is the connecting link which leads Kierkegaard from the traditional disciplines to a central reorientation which puts things in place according to a new principle. With a view to such a realignment of the disciplines, he writes: "Usually a single science is treated by itself. Then one has much to say and gives no thought to the possibility of everything suddenly being dissolved if the presupposition must be altered."[92] When Kierkegaard continues and says, "This is especially true of esthetics, which has always been assiduously cultivated but almost always in isolation," and in the next entry notes "the relation between esthetics and ethics" and "a qualitatively different dialectic," it is clear that his realignment of the disciplines is due to the increasing role granted to subjectivity. It is particularly ethics in the Kierkegaardian meaning of the term which emphasizes subjectivity and supersedes the areas with an esthetic focus.

It is characteristic of Kierkegaard's method of working that within two weeks he made two drafts of the theory of the stages: one from a dogmatic and one from a phenomenological point of view. After this these two views intercross until Kierkegaard works them together into a coherent whole. Since these two viewpoints arise from totally different points of departure, they will be treated separately.

(1) The dogmatic view. Kierkegaard appends to one of the few journal entries critical of Christianity (all written in the autumn of 1835) a note (dated January 14, 1837) in which he stresses the contrast between Augustine's view of man according to Christian dogmatics and Pelagius's optimistic view of man's moral and religious qualifications. Kierkegaard's endorsement of Augustine's view is unmistakable. During the years 1835-37 Kierkegaard probably had experiences which made quite clear the inadequacy of

[92] IV C 104 (*J. and P.*, I, 143).

the merely human. "There is a contrast of primary significance between Augustine and Pelagius. The former
crushes everything in order to rebuild it again. The other
addresses himself to man as he is. The first system, therefore, in respect to Christianity, falls into three stages: creation—the fall and a consequent condition of death and impotence; a new creation—whereby man is placed in a position where he can choose; and then, if he chooses—Christianity. —The other system addresses itself to man as he is
(Christianity fits into the world)."[93]

Augustine outlines the three positions of man in relation
to Christianity: (1) the condition of innocence (*"posse non
peccare"*), (2) man's slavery under sin (*"non posse non
peccare"*), and (3) man's regeneration through Christianity (*"non posse peccare"*). Kierkegaard incorporates this
as the central methodological point of view in his work of
characterizing the steps and stages in man's spiritual development. Thus for Kierkegaard the conflict between
Augustine and Pelagius is not merely an historical event
but the continuing current battle about the proper understanding of man's abilities and capacities, including Christianity's view of them. While Kierkegaard himself represents Augustine's position, he feels that Hegel's system in
particular represents Pelagius's optimistic view of man.
When Kierkegaard says of Pelagius that his "system addresses itself to man as he is (Christianity fits into the
world)," Hegel's name could very well be substituted for
Pelagius, for he also sought to make Christianity conform
to the world.

In any case Kierkegaard finds in Augustine's "system" the
initial contours of his outline of the stages. This abstract
outline now needs to be filled out with concrete qualifications drawn from the many levels through which subjectivity develops.

(2) This is done according to the next point of view,
which can best be characterized as the phenomenological

[93] I A 101 (*J. and P.*, I, 29).

position, since attention here is concentrated particularly upon depicting the appearance of the different levels of development in man. Presumably Kierkegaard received an impetus to work with the phenomenological from his teachers F. C. Sibbern and Paul M. Møller. Kierkegaard could have found promptings to work with the different levels of conscious life of the individual in Sibbern's book *On Knowledge and Research*. In this book Sibbern writes: "There is also in the inner life of consciousness, where we should grow in insight and cognition, a self-operating working and becoming ($\phi\acute{v}\sigma\iota\varsigma$) to which our own work refers, and through which then, *all by itself, a light must go on for us*. But this independently working life in us requires its time and has its stages, likewise its crises."[94] Sibbern's statement conceivably might have drawn Kierkegaard's attention to his subsequent sphere of interest, the stages. It is more probable, however, that Kierkegaard was stimulated by P. M. Møller to his work with the stages as the developmental levels of the subject. We have many written evidences of this, and although at this time Kierkegaard could not have gotten his impulse from P. M. Møller's books, he certainly was familiar with these views from conversations with him or through his lectures.

It should be noted that P. M. Møller uses the word "stages" for the first time in his lectures in 1834 on "The History of Ancient Philosophy" to designate the levels of "the powers of the mind"[95] in Aristotelean psychology. In the winter semester of 1837, P. M. Møller lectured on "Ontology or the System of Categories," and in the published portions of the lectures he mentions the significance of a phenomenological presentation of the developmental levels of the human consciousness, precisely the task Kierkegaard is working on during these years. P. M. Møller makes it clear that Hegel in his *Phenomenology of Mind* was one of those who attempted to complete this task. He says: "The

[94] Sibbern, *Erkjendelse og Granskning*, pp. 190-91.
[95] Paul Martin Møller, *Efterladte Skrifter*, I-VI (Copenhagen, 3rd ed., 1855-56), IV, p. 235.

introduction to metaphysics, in the proper meaning of the work, is a unique philosophical discipline which develops the various stages which the human consciousness goes through from its immediate form to its cultivated level where metaphysics begins. Hegel has provided such a philosophical propaedeutic in his *Phenomenology of Mind*, but this work by its multiplicity of content goes far beyond the boundaries stipulated by this definition and in addition presupposes readers who have knowledge of the history of philosophy."[96]

The same estimate is expressed in P. M. Møller's *Strøt-anker (Random Thoughts*; 1826-37): "The study of philosophy must be in part a historical study, but the history of philosophy is not in the least a philosophical discipline if it presents the systems in their own external, arbitrary, or historically conditioned forms. It is quite another matter to present the path of the human mind's necessary development along the various stations it must pass through (as Hegel's *Phenomenology of Mind*); but then one does not have to enumerate names, dates, and other details."[97]

For his working out of the stages from a phenomenological position Kierkegaard may have found suggestions in Sibbern, but very likely his most important inspiration came from P. M. Møller. As far as the latter is concerned, many things other than those mentioned here point to his having influenced and advanced Kierkegaard's efforts to concretize his material in developing the stages. Here we find also what to my mind is a unique tendency in Danish philosophical thought: not to lose sight of the concrete while preoccupied with abstract concepts.

In connection with the stages it may be illuminating to mention H. L. Martensen's attempt to mediate between a dogmatic and a phenomenological view of the stages in his licentiate thesis, *"De autonomia conscientiae sui humanae, in theologiam dogmaticam nostri temporis introducta"* (1837). Martensen summarizes Schleiermacher's

[96] Ibid., III, p. 189.   [97] Ibid., III, p. 78.

dogmatic view of Christianity's relationship to man under *"stadia tria."*[98] This view, which he calls subjective and regards as influenced by Kant, is compared with Hegel's formulation of three stages, which in contrast to Schleiermacher's subjective stages are called objective. In this way Martensen brings out an opposition between Schleiermacher and Hegel which is almost analogous to the one we find in Kierkegaard between Augustine and Pelagius. For Martensen the conflict he presents has no further significance; whereas Kierkegaard develops it and fills out Augustine's abstract sketch with concrete material.

Kierkegaard makes the first attempt to achieve a combinative conception of the stages from the phenomenological position in a lengthy journal entry dated January 27, 1837, and titled: *Something About Life's Four Stages*, also with reference to mythology.[99] From the phenomenological viewpoint, Kierkegaard wants to indicate more concretely, without, however, "enumerating names, dates, and other details," the basic tendencies of the different periods as they express themselves in life. On the basis of such basic tendencies one can then trace all life's phenomena in a given period and understand them in their interrelationship.

It is worth noting that Kierkegaard, referring to the individual, mentions specific age levels, which (in the early draft) correspond to the two first stages representing mythology's great span of years in the history of the race:[100] "The first is the stage where the child has not separated himself from his surroundings ('me'). The I is not given, but the possibility of it exists and to that extent is a conflict." "As far as I know mythology, this stage corresponds to the oriental mythologies." And further, with regard to the next stage, which does not have the restlessness of the first stage: "But after this turmoil comes a peace, an idyllic well-being. It is the youth's satisfaction in family

[98] Pp. 128ff. [99] I C 126 (*J. and P.*, IV).
[100] See p. 24 above.

and school (Church and State), it is the second stage: Greek mythology."

It is easy to show that development in race and individual parallels periods of mythology. It is more difficult to establish the same parallel scheme when it comes to the more intellectually developed period in the history of man. Kierkegaard tries to take care of these difficulties in a new way, which will be discussed in dealing with the next combinative point of view.

The fact that Kierkegaard in his work from a phenomenological position assumes "four stages" compared to Augustine's formulation with three stages is connected with Kierkegaard's high regard for the mythological periods, which for him constituted two stages. The first of the two next stages could be called a forerunner of Kierkegaard's ethical stage, expressed by the term "the romantic": with "the romantic arises a question about beyond-the-world satisfaction." The last stage is Christianity.

When Kierkegaard wrote the early draft on the four stages, he was completely clear about the first two, and their structure remains unchanged;[101] the only change is in their placement with respect to the two next stages. But in the beginning of 1837 Kierkegaard is still unclear about the complete structuring of the ethical and religious stages. He continues to work on the formulation of these two stages and gathers memoranda to this end, as appears in the following sentence: "N. B. Observations about the two last stages are to be found among my papers."

Kierkegaard's movement toward a conclusion, the three stages, can be approached first by comparing, as he himself does, his four stages with Hegel's three and then by noting how Kierkegaard's final conception of the stages is related to Hegel's stages.

Kierkegaard makes the following two comments on the relation between his four stages to Hegel's three: "Note:

[101] On pp. 24-25 above his use of the two stages in *Either/Or* is discussed, but he uses a modification of them as early as in *The Concept of Irony*, p. 102.

the System has only 3 stages—immediacy, reflection, and unity. Life has 4.

"*Note*: to what extent does Hegel include my two first stages, since his first stage (the immediate) as pure abstraction actually is a nothing, and all philosophy within its systematic retrograde crab-movement must begin with conflict, which in the first stage he perhaps sees as the conflict between the 'I' and the world, and his peace is not Grecian, which can only correspond to such a prior stage as my first one; but the last."

In the first note we see that Kierkegaard assumes life has four stages in contrast to Hegel's abstract formulation of three stages. In this way Kierkegaard also stresses the significance of the subjective elements in the development of his stages.

In the second note Kierkegaard explains more explicitly how Hegel, simply because of his abstract philosophical point of departure, is prevented from being aware of the two stages which Kierkegaard names as the first two. Furthermore, since Hegel's first stage is "a nothing," he actually has only two stages: that of reflection and that of unity.

This criticism reveals that Kierkegaard at the time still has not discovered the basic weakness in Hegel's three stages. He does not find it until he himself arrives at three stages by arranging the wealth of experiences acquired while working with the phenomenological position under the dogmatic point of view in such a way that his perspective of the stages is now in line with Augustine's.

The synthesis of these two viewpoints occurs for a number of reasons. Kierkegaard perceives that the difference between the philosophies of life in Oriental and Greek mythology, between them and certain esthetic humanistic philosophies of life as well, is not as great as the difference between these three positions and the position which arises when the eternal shapes existence. Therefore he later combines the three first positions in the esthetic stage, which is bounded by irony. The essential distance is first of all between the esthetic and the ethical. With this interpretation, conditioned primarily by the dogmatic view, the two first stages, together with substantial contributions from the higher humanistic positions, become one stage.

The ethical stage is established on the basis of experience provided in the encounter with eternal demands. This stage eventually embraces various subdivisions climaxing in humor as the final position of the ethical. The concluding position, Christianity, the qualitatively new, has its own levels and possibilities for intensification.

Thus Kierkegaard finally ends with three stages, the same number as Hegel, but the new grouping of elements, with particular attention to existence, has the astonishing result that Hegel's three or, more correctly, two stages (seen from Kierkegaard's final position) shrink into one stage. All his "three" stages have to be placed within Kierkegaard's esthetic stage. According to Kierkegaard's conception, Hegel simply does not arrive at the ethical stage, to say nothing of the religious. With his process of thought he stops in the domain of the esthetic. Hegel's supreme intellectual principle is the principle of identity, which combines all the dialectical factors into a unity, but according to Kierkegaard it is the acknowledgment of the unconditional validity of the principle of contradiction which leads from the esthetic stage to the next stage—the ethical.

Kierkegaard places so much emphasis on the establishment of the stages because the standpoint of the stages lends itself to determining the periods in the development of subjective actuality.

On September 20, 1837, Kierkegaard wrote this methodologically significant entry: "It would be interesting to follow the development of human nature (in the individual man—that is, the various ages of man) by showing what one laughs at on the different age levels, in part by making these experiments with one and the same author, for example, our literary fountainhead, Holberg, and in

part by way of the different kinds of comedy. It would—
together with research and experiments concerning the
age level at which tragedy is most appreciated and with
other psychological observations about the relation between comedy and tragedy, why, for example, one reads
tragedy alone by himself and comedy together with others
—contribute to the work I believe ought to be written—
namely, the history of the human soul (as it is in an ordinary human being) in the continuity of the state of the
soul (not in the concept) consolidating itself in particular
mountain-clusters (that is, noteworthy world-historical representatives of life-views)."[102]

The last four lines, which intentionally sound like an
expanded title of a book, epitomize precisely the connection
between the three points of view—the psychological, the
esthetic, and the paradigmatic, while the preceding text
explains how the connection is to be understood. Following Kierkegaard's own procedure, closer examination of
these points of view will show how the first standpoint
provides the foundation for the second, and that again
for the third.

(1) The psychological standpoint is articulated in the
phrase: ". . . the history of the human soul (as it is in an
ordinary human being). . . ." The section on psychology
in this book stresses the central role of psychology and
philosophical anthropology in Kierkegaard's own life and
in his thinking. In this journal entry we hear how Kierkegaard intends to utilize methodically his knowledge of
psychology in forming inclusive concepts. When we consider his earlier draft on the stages, we see that the
methodological movement is now in the direction of connecting the psychological standpoint to the phenomenological precisely at the point where the latter point of view
proves to be inadequate to a description of individual actuality, especially if one intends to collate the different
periods in the development of mental-spiritual life with

[102] II A 163 (*J. and P.*, IV).

specific age levels in individual development. Strictly speaking, this could be carried through with some precision only for the two mythological periods, corresponding to "childhood" and "youth." In characterizing these periods Kierkegaard also uses "the Page" and "Papageno" from Mozart's operas and shows that here one could be satisfied with "mythical" representatives of the age levels referred to.[103] By establishing the psychological point of view first of all, Kierkegaard thinks it will be possible to cover all the levels of man's development. As a methodological aid in carrying through this task he intends to use ". . . investigations and experiments concerning the age when tragedy is most appreciated and other psychological observations on the relationship between comedy and tragedy. . . ." With this Kierkegaard points toward the second point of view, the esthetic, which together with the psychological (in the empirical sense of the word) forms the boundary for the phenomenological. We become aware, however, that all these investigations in the first series should embrace the expressions of ordinary psychic life and not its aberrations.

(2) Thus it becomes apparent that to implement the psychological point of view, which is an elaboration of the phenomenological point of view, the assistance of a new departure point is needed—namely the esthetic. It is abundantly clear that this help from the esthetic is available in its most distinguished area, which to Kierkegaard is the dramatic.

In other words, in his study of the psychological aspects of man, Kierkegaard now intends to put more weight on the individual's inner conflicts, intimations of which, at least to begin with, are supplied by the antitheses in drama: tragedy-comedy. Already in his first note about the dramatic Kierkegaard anticipates an ascending scale of conflict situations which ultimately must pass beyond the esthetic domain[104] and thus beyond the phenomenological.

[103] See *Either/Or*, I, pp. 74-82; and pp. 24-25 above.
[104] See pp. 46-48, above.

By the phrase "in the continuity of the state of the soul (not in the concepts)" Kierkegaard intends to emphasize more strongly that in dealing with the history of the human soul the stress will be on emotions, will, and mood, and not on explaining concepts and on analyses. This is in harmony with his interest in tragedy and inner conflicts.

(3) This history of the soul with primary emphasis on man's subjective condition now flows into the paradigmatic point of view, articulated in the words: ". . . particular mountain-clusters (that is, noteworthy world-historical representatives of life-views)." With the phrase "mountain-clusters" Kierkegaard unambiguously expresses that the "consolidating" factor in them is their stamina in maintaining continuity in a basic outlook which characterizes cognition, feeling, and will.

Originating in a psychological and esthetic approach, the presentation of these "noteworthy . . . representatives of life-views" marks a step forward from the first draft on the stages with its center of gravity in the phenomeno-logical point of view. Kierkegaard is now gaining the new insight that the numerous forms and levels of mind and spirit cannot be assigned automatically to specific age levels, but that the great differences necessitate the choosing of historical paradigms who can then have meaning for the individual according to his mental-spiritual maturity and willingness to let himself be instructed by them.

The idea of "mountain-clusters" provides Kierkegaard with a broad choice of representatives for the different philosophies of life (also negative, such as Don Juan, Faust, Ahasuerus, who, incidentally, may be considered as background for the positive philosophies of life), which from now on he can place into relation with each other and incorporate into the larger coherence of mental-spiritual development.

Three observations may be added regarding Kierkegaard's attempt to present these three representatives. In the first place, using these representatives enables Kierkegaard to reflect on the incommensurability of the individ-

ual's external and internal life. As long as the phenomenological point of view is in the foreground such a consideration is precluded. It is interesting that the very same day
Kierkegaard wrote the entry under consideration he also
wrote: "Unfortunaely my real spirit frequently is present
in me only κατα κρυψιν."[105] Here the reference is particularly
to the hiddenness in the individual who is not revealed.
This entry may be regarded as the very beginning of
Kierkegaard's study of the individual's hidden life and its
incommensurability with external phenomenological expression.

In the second place, as far as I can see, the motivation
for grouping together two of the most important of these
representatives, Socrates and Christ, must be sought in
Kierkegaard's interest in "noteworthy world-historical representatives of life-views." This antithesis, later clearly
expressed in the first thesis in *The Concept of Irony*, comes
to dominate the whole structure of his authorship in a
remarkable way.

In the third place, it ought to be said that for Kierkegaard there is a difference between these "historical" representatives who are used as paradigms and the life-view
representatives we meet in the various pseudonymous
writers, who do not all need to have the character of paradigms. Kierkegaard considers that Job, Abraham, Socrates,
and Hamann must be included among these historical
paradigms. Of the pseudonymous writers only Johannes
Climacus has any connection with a historical person.

Some of the entries following II A 163 (*J. and P.*, IV),
including II A 164 just mentioned, indicate that Kierkegaard promptly lays out certain aspects of the task he
assigns himself in this significant journal entry bearing
on method. For instance, he writes that he now has the
idea for his doctoral dissertation. "Now I know a suitable
subject for a dissertation: concerning the concept of satire
among the ancients, the reciprocal relation of the various

[105] II A 164 (*J. and P.*, V); in the form of concealment.

Roman satirists to each other."[106] The concept of satire which Kierkegaard considers treating bears on the relationship of tragedy and comedy. That Kierkegaard in dealing with such a subject cannot confine himself simply to an exposition of conceptual structures but chooses to use the procedure described in the methodological journal entries above is shown by his later choice of Socrates as the representative in his doctoral dissertation on a theme related to satire.

In the next entry, II A 167 (*J. and P.*, V), Kierkegaard refers to Holberg, as he does in II A 163, and in using an example from his works to illustrate the fluctuation between the comic and the tragic he goes back to his own reflections on that point in 1834-35.[107] "Holberg's *E. Montanus* remains a comedy (although in so many other respects it is a tragedy), because in the end madness wins by laying a punishment upon E. and *forcing* him to *knowledge of the truth* by a means (beating him) which is more demented than all the rest of their madness."[108]

With the paradigmatic viewpoint Kierkegaard has found a way to give his ethical-religious intentions concrete and individual character.

The last entry bearing on method prior to the writing of the works to be published reads as follows:
"*Concerning the Concepts* ESSE *and* INTER-ESSE
A methodological attempt.
The different sciences ought to be ordered according to the different ways in which they accent being and how the relationship to being provides reciprocal advantage.

	The certainty of these is
Ontology	absolute—here thought and being
Mathematics	are one, but by the same token
	these sciences are hypothetical.

Existential science. [*Existentiel Videnskab*]."[109]

---

[106] II A 166 (*J. and P.*, V).   [107] I A 34 (*J. and P.*, IV).
[108] II A 167 (*J. and P.*, V).
[109] IV C 100 (*J. and P.*, I, 197); compare with various

The central point here, as the title indicates, is to determine the relation between essence ("ESSE") and being ("INTER-ESSE"). Essence is dominant in the disciplines which have as their goal the investigation of objective actuality; whereas being is decisive in the areas where the subjective and the existential are to be emphasized.

The viewpoint expressed in this methodological entry is the most inclusive of all the positions Kierkegaard establishes. While the points of view considered up until now completely ignore certain subjects within the objective domain, it is possible on the basis of this last position to establish a framework which embraces all the areas of scientific scholarship and existence.

Moreover, by means of this methodological entry, the dimensions of the concepts "objective" and "subjective" and the relations between them, as well as the relations between essence and being, touched on in our discussion of the subjective standpoint, can finally be delineated.

Kierkegaard's primary objective in this final methodological synthesis is to provide a short but adequate formulation by which he can unequivocally and consistently define the boundaries between knowledge and existence and locate the separate disciplines accordingly. When this demarcation and placement are completed, Kierkegaard can also give the concepts "necessity" and "freedom" as well as the concept "consistency" their final and concluding elaboration.

The question of marking the boundaries of the two primary areas, knowledge and existence, can best be treated by considering two other entries closely connected to IV C 100 (*J. and P.*, I, 197), namely, IV C 99 (*J. and P.*, II, 2283) and IV C 101 (*J. and P.*, V). The first of these indicates the path which leads beyond the immanent domain

---

portions in Sibbern's *Erkjendelse og Granskning*, especially pp. 131ff., and Paul M. Møller's statement about "mathematical and ontological" thought as "disinterested knowledge" (*Efterladte Skrifter*, V, p. 82).

of knowledge to transcendent reality. The second entry is like a last look at Hegel's system and, in a wider sense, at all attempts to give an exhaustive and inclusive immanently based description of all the relations of existence [*Tilværelsens*].

Entry VI C 101 (in German in the *Papirer*) consists of a heading in Hegel's *Logik*:

A.
ESSENCE AS THE GROUND OF EXISTENCE
a) *The Determinations of Pure Reflection.*
    (α) Identity   (β) Difference   (γ) Ground.
b) *Existence.*
c) *The Thing.*

B.
APPEARANCE
a) *The World of Appearance.*
b) *Content and Form.*
c) *The Relation.*

C.
ACTUALITY[110]

Kierkegaard's intention in transcribing these headings from Hegel's *Logik* is clear. The Kierkegaard who already has arrived at a satisfactory insight into the fundamental categories of existence [*Tilværelsens*], especially with regard to the determination of the concept "actuality" ("being"), wants to take one more look at Hegel's determination of the categories which group themselves around his concept "actuality," and also at the concept itself. If one scrutinizes more closely the pages in Hegel's *Logik* from which Kierkegaard has noted the headings, one understands that it must be right here that Kierkegaard could find illumination about the two central concepts in his last

[110] IV C 101 (*J. and P.*, V). Entry is from G.F.W. Hegel, *Encyclopädie der philosophischen Wissenschaften im Grundrisse*, I-III (Berlin, 1840), I, *Die Logik, Inhalts-Anzeige* (*Table of Contents*). See *The Logic of Hegel* (Vol. I, of *Encyclopädie*), tr. William Wallace, 2nd ed. (London, Oxford University Press, 1931), headings on pp. 212-57.

methodological entries: essence and being. Prior to the headings Kierkegaard transcribes, Hegel discusses in detail the principle of his dialectical method in relation to other dialectical methods. There again Kierkegaard could find material to convince him of the difference between the course of his own dialectical efforts and Hegel's.

While reading Hegel's discussion, Kierkegaard is also able to see that Hegel's views on actuality are substantially different from his own. Hegel's concept of actuality is completely encircled by reflection and no place is left for the actuality which might lie outside reflection's immanental domain and has transcendence as its hallmark. For Hegel, therefore, such concepts as essence and being, form and content, external and internal, etc., must be regarded as identical. Directly preceding the heading "*C. Die Wirklichkeit*," Hegel gives a definition of actuality in which he speaks of the identity of internal and external as two components of actuality: "By the manifestation of force the inward is put into existence, but this putting is the mediation by empty abstractions. In its own self the intermediating process vanishes to the immediacy, in which the inward and outward are absolutely identical and their difference is distinctly no more than assumed and imposed. This identity is Actuality."[111]

It is interesting to see that Kierkegaard's first pseudonymous book, *Either/Or*, begins[112] with this very criticism of Hegel, that his concept of actuality builds upon the identity of external and internal. Thus in the authorship proper Kierkegaard begins his criticism of Hegel in direct continuation with the last lines written in entry IV C 101.

Kierkegaard's criticism of Hegel's concept of actuality is basically equivalent to criticism of Hegel's dialectical method, since Hegel's concept of actuality is indissolubly linked to his method. It is his dialectical method which in its logically necessary course unfolds all the factors of actuality. This is confirmed by Hegel's statement: "If the

[111] Ibid., p. 257.   [112] *Either/Or*, I, p. 3.

logical forms of the notion were really dead and inert re-
ceptacles of conceptions and thoughts, careless of what
they contained, knowledge about them would be an idle
curiosity which the truth might dispense with. On the
contrary they really are, as forms of the notion, the vital
spirit of the actual world. That only is true of the actual
which is true in virtue of these forms, through them and
in them. As yet, however, the truth of these forms has
never been considered or examined on their own account
any more than their necessary interconnexion."[113]

For Kierkegaard Hegel is a striking example of philosophy's efforts to penetrate actuality ("being") with logical
thought and to bring all the factors of existence together
in one formula for which the identity of these factors is
the proper premise. But Kierkegaard's study of philosophical and theological problems taught him rather—and many
passages witness to this—that dualism comprehends existence in a truer and more profound manner than monism.
He formulates this thought very clearly in an entry from
1844: "The view which sees life's doubleness (dualism) is
higher and deeper than that which seeks unity or 'pursues
studies toward unity' (an expression from Hegel about all
the endeavors of philosophy); the view which sees the eter-
nal as $\tau\epsilon\lambda o\varsigma$, and the teleological view in general, is higher
than all immanence or all talk about *causa sufficiens*. The
passion which saw paganism as sin and assumed eternal
torment in hell is greater than the *summa summarum* of
the thoughtlessness (which is disheveled) which sees
everything within immanence."[114]

Kierkegaard then drafts (IV C 99 [*J. and P.*, II, 2283])
an interpretation which does not stop at "the philosophical
endeavor" for a monism and for an immanental interpretation of the concept "actuality," but which contains elements pointing toward a transcendence.

[113] *The Logic of Hegel* (Vol. I of *Encyclopädie*), tr. William
Wallace, para. 162, p. 291.
[114] IV A 192 (*J. and P.*, I, 704).

> "Interested Knowing and Its Forms
> What is knowing without interest?
> It has its interest in a third (for example,
> beauty, truth, etc.) which is not myself,
> therefore has no continuity.
> Interested knowing enters with Christianity.
> The question of authority.
> of historical continuity.
> of doubt.
> of faith.
> Is knowledge higher than faith? By no means."

In opposition to Hegel's claim of the commensurability of external and internal, Kierkegaard advances his category of *"interested knowing* and its forms,"[115] a knowing which is especially concerned with personality, for only within personality can there arise incommensurability between actuality and thought or between two opposing positions. This happens when the individual is placed before the absolute "either/or" of the ethical. In such a case the objective position of "the system" is penetrated by a personal interest in an actuality which lies outside the boundaries of immanental thinking. By advancing the category of "interested knowing," Kierkegaard would emphasize that man's essential task is on the other side of all objective and systematic reproduction of actuality.

The next level in the movement toward transcendent actuality consists of conquering doubt—or, more correctly, despair—the possibility of which crops up when man is placed before the requirement of the eternal. In the following significant remarks taken from *Johannes Climacus, or De omnibus dubitandum est* (written at the same time as entry IV C 99), Kierkegaard characterizes this new position in relation to "the system" and all objective knowledge. Among other things, Climacus says of the relationship between objective knowledge and the transition to a higher position: "All knowledge, therefore, which is disinterested (mathematical, esthetic, metaphysical) is merely the pre-

[115] Of the relation of this knowing to Kant's view of the esthetic, see p. 47 above.

supposition of doubt [i.e., it belongs merely to the sphere
of reflection, which brings two oppositions together, but
has itself no concern with, or interest in, the knower.] But
whenever personal interest is thus removed, doubt is not
overcome [in the way that philosophy proposes to overcome it by certainty and religion by faith]; it is merely
rendered null and void, neutralized, excluded; and all such
knowledge is but a retrogression. If anybody, therefore, by
any so-called objective thinking, imagines he can conquer
doubt, he is mistaken. For doubt is a higher form than all
objective thinking, because it presupposes objective thinking, but has a third thing, viz. Interest or Consciousness,
pertaining to it. In this respect the behaviour of the Greek
Sceptics seemed to J. C. far more consistent than the
modern way of overcoming doubt. The Sceptics realized
quite well that doubt is due to interest, and so they thought,
quite consistently, that they could annul doubt by changing interest into apathy. This procedure was consistent,
whereas it is an inconsistency which has moved modern
philosophy to try to overcome doubt methodically by the
System. The illogicality seems to be based on ignorance of
what doubt is. Even if the System were absolutely complete, even if actuality exceeded expectations, still doubt
would not be vanquished. It begins first. For doubt is due
to interest, and all systematic knowledge is disinterested.
You can see from this that doubt is the beginning of the
highest form of existence, because it can have everything
else as its presupposition."[116]

Through an understanding of the complex of problems
related to philosophy's objective, comprehensive knowledge
and personality's listening to and interest in the ethical
demands, the transition leading from doubt to faith is
initiated. Kierkegaard thinks that these higher forms of
man's understanding of his situation, reaching their climax in the encounter with Christianity, must be regarded
as "existential knowledge." It is upon this kind of knowl-

[116] IV B 1, pp. 148-49 (*Johannes Climacus, or De omnibus
dubitandum est*, pp. 152-53).

edge that he concentrates his very considerable insight into both method and substance.

By his formula to the effect that accentuating being "makes for reciprocal advantage," he is able to make a clear distinction between the areas of philosophy and of faith and at the same time unambiguously relate the appropriate disciplines within each of these two areas.

Furthermore, this clear demarcation of the area of knowledge from the area of faith, together with a stipulation of the relation between the concepts "essence" and "being," forms the basis for Kierkegaard's cogent delineation of the relation between necessity and freedom and gives him additional grounding for the final formulation of the concept "consistency."

The deepened perspective on the concepts "necessity," "freedom," and "consistency" and the resultant possibility of using them more extensively in characterizing the existential situation appear as early as *Either/Or*, consequently very near the time entries IV C 99-101 were written.

It must first be noted that in entry IV C 100 (*J. and P.*, I, 197) on method there is the consciously assimilated thought of the synthesis of two contrasting elements; this is expressed in the possibility of a conflict between "thought and being." As we already know, the opposites embodied in the synthesis can appear as several parallel conceptual pairs which are completely dependent upon whatever aspect of actuality is the object of attention. Thus all these pairs of opposites are simply different aspects of perspectives upon the same fundamental relation. The contrasting pair "essence-being" can be replaced with "necessity-freedom," the synthesis of which pertains particularly to historical development. The contrasting pair "necessity-freedom" (in place of "essence-being") is used in *Either/Or*, because historical actuality is the concern there. We see that Judge William, entirely in line with the pattern for grouping disciplines according to greater or lesser accent on "being," speaks first of the "spheres with which philosophy properly deals, which properly are the spheres for thought," consequently first and foremost "logic, nature, and history."[117] In these spheres "necessity" rules. But thereafter he shows that the second element, "freedom," already begins to assert itself in history. Instead of saying that "being" gradually is stressed more and more in history, he speaks of the increasing significance of freedom in the historical development of the individual.

The basis for this concept, therefore, is the outline in journal entry IV C 100 (*J. and P.*, I, 197), but with different contrasting pairs. Through Judge William's various expositions we get a description of how the relation "necessity-freedom" ranges a scale in which being, and thereby freedom, is stressed more and more.

From the new insight into the relation between necessity and freedom Kierkegaard is led further to a significant elaboration of his view of the different forms of the concept "consistency." As already stated, Kierkegaard previously worked very much with this concept, and it will now be shown how he uses it in developing the combinative points of view.

When Kierkegaard began his methodological project, it was his aim to fulfill the strict requirements of consistency throughout all his intellectual operations. It later became clear to him that there are many forms of consistency, depending on the area in which it is to be applied.

This extended application of the concept of consistency reaches its climax when Kierkegaard, in *The Concept of Irony*, relates the concept to the manifestations of freedom which characterize the standpoint of irony. In his exposition of Socrates's position Kierkegaard uses such phrases as "the very consistency of vice,"[118] "the internal self-consistency of ideal infinity itself,"[119] "the *infinite self consistency* of the good,"[120] and "sin is *inconsistency*."[121]

---

[117] *Either/Or*, II, p. 178.
[118] *The Concept of Irony*, p. 64.
[119] Ibid., p. 233.   [120] Ibid., p. 250.
[121] Ibid.

In all these expressions consistency is related to both the positive and negative forms of the freedom inherent in Socrates's irony. Of the freedom of irony itself in Socrates Kierkegaard declares: "What we see in Socrates is the infinitely exuberant freedom of subjectivity, that is, irony."[122]

Furthermore, by saying in *The Concept of Irony*, "the idea of consistency, the law upon which rests the realm of knowledge,"[123] Kierkegaard alludes to the significance consistency can have in the area of knowledge, something Socrates did not perceive since he was interested only in the knowledge which is linked to existence.

From the expressions (1841) quoted above, it is apparent that only a keystone was needed in order to construct a comprehensive view of the application of consistency in all the areas of knowledge and existence. The completion of this development parallels the working out of the dialectical method. The overshadowing significance consistency had upon Kierkegaard's work with this dialectical structuring is clearly stated in a familiar sentence from *Johannes Climacus, or De omnibus dubitandum est.* Climacus declares that "For him consistency was a *scala paradisi.*"[124] As far as I understand the next part, Kierkegaard is alluding to his efforts to work the dialectical points of view into an inclusive whole through the use of consistent thinking.

This applies, for example, to the account of how Climacus-Kierkegaard tries, "from a single thought," "to climb up step by step to a higher thought" "on the path of consistency" and then from this thought to return by consistent thinking to the point of departure. But it is very important to note Climacus's use of "links in consistent thinking." It is stated that in the dialectical movements of thought on each level these links are interrupted by just as "many bumps as there were links in the sequence of

---

[122] Ibid., p. 233.   [123] Ibid., p. 242.
[124] IV B 1, p. 105 (ed. tr.); see *Johannes Climacus, or De omnibus dubitandum est*, p. 104.

consistent thought." If the links symbolize movement in individual development, this explanation must be taken as an expression of the idea that each link involves a leap (a break). Therefore it seems clear that these "bumps" mean breaks in the existential links in the development of a person toward Christianity, but then Christianity completely breaks the continuity with what precedes in order to place him in a higher position.

The next lines indicate how Climacus keeps trying to gather the already consistently worked out themes into a unity and how he intends everything to fall into proper place: "As long as he was working to climb up, as long as consistent thinking had not yet been able to make its way, he would be oppressed, for he was afraid of losing the numerous conclusions which he had already formulated but which still had not become entirely clear to him and necessary. When we see a person carrying a great number of breakable articles stacked one upon the other, we are not surprised that he walks unsteadily and continually tries to keep his balance. But if we do not see the stack, we smile, just as many people smiled at J. Climacus without suspecting that he was carrying a much higher stack than generally needed to occasion surprise, and that his soul was uneasy lest a single one of the logical inferences [consistencies] should drop out, and the whole pile fall to pieces."

This entry shows the fundamental importance of the concept of consistency to Kierkegaard in his search for a coherent perspective of existence. While engaged in this task, Kierkegaard at the same time arrived at an understanding of the forms of consistency relevant to existence.

When Kierkegaard arrived at his synoptic formula in journal entry IV C 100 (*J. and P.*, I, 197), he essentially had found the keystone for the final form of the concept of consistency. This happened, as has been pointed out, in connection with his deeper understanding of the relation between necessity and freedom, which is used in *Either/ Or*. We see there that Kierkegaard's pseudonymous writers join the concept of consistency closely together with the twin concepts "necessity-freedom." Kierkegaard's pseudonyms transfer the elaborated understanding of the relation between necessity and freedom to the understanding of the forms of consistency. Here also there is an ascending scale, beginning with the level where consistency is determined by necessity, to a higher level where it is freedom which defines consistency. On the lower levels, therefore, one can speak only of the consistency of necessity. Nature is constantly dominated by necessity, and because of natural laws we therefore have the "consistency of nature."[125] Nature's necessity is equivalent to "the consistency of nature."

With this point of departure the way is now open to the understanding that where freedom is predominant, that is, in man's historical development, consistency is defined by freedom and not by necessity. With this we come to the view "the consistency of freedom,"[126] containing a whole scale of expressions for a consistency which is modified in relation to the numerous manifestations and forms of freedom.

With this turn the whole range of existence is brought under consistent reflection. How decisive the concept of consistency becomes for Kierkegaard can be seen from the use he makes of the concept from now on. The claim can justifiably be made that from this point on he considers all concepts and all conceptual content from the point of view of consistency. But of course he is primarily interested in the consequences as they concern existential concepts and their relations. His whole authorship testifies to this. At present we will be content to name a few central concepts of existence to which the concept of consistency is brought into relationship: "Consequence of the moment,"[127] "explains original sin by its consequences,"[128] "consequence

---

[125] *Either/Or*, I, p. 157.   [126] *Repetition*, p. 44.
[127] *Philosophical Fragments*, p. 72.
[128] *The Concept of Anxiety* [Dread], p. 24.

of sin,"[129] "consequence of offense,"[130] "consequence of the Deity's presence in time."[131]

Just these few examples manifestly justify the claim that the concept of consistency is the nerve in Kierkegaard's dialectic. From now on Kierkegaard evaluates the worth of other authors' performances on the basis of their consistency. This is clearly articulated in his polemic against Adler, when he says: ". . . explanation and understanding are what I desire; consistency is all I demand. . . ."[132] A dialectician must be consistent in his thinking. In a clear allusion to himself Kierkegaard says later in connection with Adler: "When an eminent thinker with the idea of consistency tightens the reins of thought to the uttermost, only very few will understand him. And the majority will be repelled. If, however, he relaxes the dialectic, talks nonsense once in a while, many will understand him."[133] From the very beginning of his authorship Kierkegaard practices in his dialectic this tightening of reflection with "the idea of consistency," and in this way his dialectic has an indissoluble connection with the concept of consistency.

Since, then, every concept, every philosophy of life, and also the passions which make up these attitudes, must be looked at from the standpoint of consistency, the implication is that all these qualifications have a corresponding dialectic—that is, inherent in them are certain consequences. Again for Kierkegaard the most important of these qualifications are those concerned with existence. Likewise, then, every concept of existence has its own dialectic. With respect to the concrete side of existence it

[129] Ibid., p. 101.   [130] Ibid., p. 129.
[131] *Postscript*, p. 517.
[132] VII² B 235, p. 20 (omitted in *On Authority and Revelation*, pp. 11-12).
[133] VII² B 235, p. 75 (omitted in *On Authority and Revelation*, pp. 57-58).

may also be said that "almost every passion has its own"[134] dialectic, that is, involves very definite consequences.

But the dialectic must simultaneously have an overview of the various spheres of existence. Kierkegaard attains this through his combinative points of view. A good many of these viewpoints allow him to examine this actuality from many angles.

It must be noted here that the viewpoint that man is a synthesis of two contrasting qualities is the simplest in formulation and the essential basis of all the other points of view. We have treated in some detail the close relation between simple perspectives and the organismic view, as well as the scientific and the existential points of view. Such a close relation between the above points of view can also be pointed out.[135]

Kierkegaard uses all these viewpoints in the development of his authorship and it is precisely this dialectical method which allows him to play on many strings at one time. Therefore Kierkegaard, unlike Hegel, for example, is not obliged to postulate unilaterally and in all areas one and the same movement through "the logical trinity"[136] with no regard to whether the method is appropriate to the respective aspects of actuality. Kierkegaard, on the contrary, despite the a priori elements in his method, develops it on the basis of experience in the arena of actuality to which his dialectic applies. This he does in conscious opposition to the philosophical systems of his day, especially to the Hegelian system, which lacks serious consideration of actuality.

Kierkegaard's own goal in this regard is clearly indicated in this journal entry from 1840: "Si philosophi hujus ævi jure contenderint, disputationes ipsorum et magna eorun-

---

[134] *Either/Or*, I, p. 157.

[135] In my little *Kierkegaard's Way to the Truth* (Minneapolis, Augsburg, 1963) I have tried to show how the whole doctrine of the stages can be built on the basis of the postulate of the synthesis.

[136] I A 317 (*J. and P.*, II, 1567).

dem de ph. merita ignorare immo non in succum et san-
guinem convertere non impunite licere, equidem non neg-
averim mihi persuasum esse, melius veritati consultum
iri, si illorum vestigia non secuti non vitam ex systemate
disponere et interpretari, sed systema tandem ex experien-
tia evadere atque prodire conamur ab utrimque enim pug-
nandum est—".[137]

In this entry Kierkegaard criticizes the philosopher who
interprets life solely *ex systemate*, and he emphasizes that
the system ought to be built on the basis of experience
while at the same time continually taking ideality into consideration.

In developing his dialectical points of view according to
this entry, Kierkegaard does not neglect absorption in the
numerous vicissitudes of life, and by his experiments he
draws forth life's hidden aspects. At the same time, however, he tries to order the material thus acquired according
to the lines provided by the ideal and a priori elements of
the subject. In this way both actuality and ideality have
their proper expressions.

We also see here that in order to indicate the goal for
his efforts Kierkegaard uses—the only time, I dare say—
the term *systema*. This is the appropriate time and place
to ask whether Kierkegaard, with his consciously sought
comprehensive view and his subsequently claimed "comprehensive design in the whole"[138] did not create "a sys-

[137] III A 24 (*J. and P.*, III, 3281). "If contemporary philosophers would have disputed in a just manner, I would at any rate
not have denied that they could be at liberty with impunity to
devote themselves vigorously even to their disputations and to
the deep-seated questions of importance in the field of philosophy, ignorant of the involvements; I say I would not have
denied that they had persuaded me that it would have been
better to look to the truth in such matters; if upon following
those of earlier days we try not to systematize life and to interpret it from that point of view but nevertheless to obviate
the systematic make an experimental approach, we thereby
betray life. Both of these approaches ought to be avoided—."
[138] X¹ A 116, p. 87 (*J. and P.*, V).

tem," something he usually opposed strongly, especially in its Hegelian form.

To show that there is no conflict in Kierkegaard between his continual battle against "the system" on the one hand and his claim to have created in his authorship a unity consistently and thoroughly thought through, I shall indicate the fundamental differences between "the system"— thinking particularly of Hegel's philosophy—and Kierkegaard's claim of a unity in his authorship.

(a) Inasmuch as method has basic significance both for Hegel and for Kierkegaard in the development of their views of existence [*Tilværelsen*], it is important to distinguish between the primary purposes of their methods. Of Hegel's method it may at once be said that from the very beginning it aimed at bringing about a finalized unity of all the elements, since Hegel's method, according to his own conception, *reproduces* the necessary course of the Idea in the unfolding of its whole content. Therefore it can be said that actuality itself is created by the method, since the "logical triad" essentially expresses the movement of actuality itself. Since, then, all the links in the movement of the method are necessary, their mutual connection can be stated, but in this way the contents of the idea and of actuality are emptied. In other words, the method tends toward creating a "system of existence."[139]

For Kierkegaard, however, the method is an instrument which is thoroughly tested in the situation of actuality and is therefore applicable to it, but it can never itself produce actuality. Strictly speaking, it can be said that Kierkegaard's dialectic is concerned only with the possibilities of actuality; actuality itself cannot be created by the dialectic but must come in another way, for example, through the individual's conversion of possibility into actuality through his own action. Therefore Kierkegaard's dialectical method never presumes to be a movement within actuality itself. For Kierkegaard the dialectical method is an instrument of

[139] *Postscript*, p. 99.

thought, but according to his view actuality in the medium of thought is always changed into possibility. In his authorship Kierkegaard embodies the full implication of this insight. As an existential thinker he always operates with the various forms of possibility, and his closest approximation to actuality during his reflective operations is the placing of contrasting possibilities over against each other, only one of which, by means of choice, can become actuality.[140]

(b) Furthermore, in Hegel it appears as if it were the idea or the concept which of necessity switches around and produces actuality and its forms.[141] In Kierkegaard it is the person who with his methodological insight tries to bring order in conceptual relations. As a result of Hegel's conception of method, concept and actuality are congruent for him. Kierkegaard, however, maintains a strict separation between them. It is impossible to reach actuality from

[140] Kierkegaard's reflections on the relation between indicative and subjunctive (see II A 159 [*J. and P.*, III, 2313] and especially II A 161 [*J. and P.*, III, 2315]) contain the beginnings of his use of possibility as a category in representing individual actuality. Later this train of thought is clearly formulated by Climacus as follows: "In the form of a possibility it becomes a requirement. Instead of presenting an account of the good in the form of actuality, as is usually done, instead of insisting that such and such a person has actually lived and has really done this or that, by which the reader is transformed into an admiring spectator, a critical connoisseur, the good should be presented in the form of a possibility. This will bring home to the reader, as closely as is possible, whether he will resolve to exist in it" (*Postscript*, pp. 320-21).

[141] Paul M. Møller had been critical of "the concept's own self-movement" (*Efterladte Papirer*, V, 69). In the following entry Kierkegaard concentrates his criticism on this point: "It had already been noted in the Platonic dialectic that the concepts switch around ($\mu\epsilon\tau\alpha\beta o\lambda\eta$, $\mu\epsilon\tau\alpha\beta\alpha\lambda\lambda\epsilon\iota\nu$ $\epsilon\iota s$ $\tauo$ $\epsilon\nu\alpha\nu\tau\iota o\nu$). In Hegel's thought the matter is confused by the use of his immense authority to force upon men, as it were, the illusion, to oblige man to believe, that it is the concept *itself* which switches around by an immanent necessity" (VII[2] B 235, p. 159, omitted in *Authority and Revelation*, p. 126). See also XI[2] A 212 (*J. and P.*, III, 3102).

a concept without the leap, since ideality and actuality lie on essentially different planes.

(c) Moreover, Hegel's "system" and Kierkegaard's combinative viewpoints differ in that Hegel wants to explain all world history and thereby provide through his speculations a "system" embracing and exhausting all existence [*Tilværelsen*]. All the links in this system are identical and by necessity bound to each other. In this view, then, the principle of identity must be the dominant principle.

Here, too, Kierkegaard's endeavors take the opposite direction. He absorbs himself primarily in the states of individual actuality, as apprehended in the form of possibility. He cannot establish a "system of existence" by his method, because, by pointing rather to a step-by-step ascending scale of contrasting possibilities within individual existence, he expresses the presence of two opposite spheres of actuality (the actuality of the good and of the evil), which qualitatively exclude each other. By this procedure the principle of contradiction acquires continually greater significance in his dialectical operations. But this also establishes the impossibility of arriving at a final view of world-historical development.

A more exhaustive comparison of Hegel's and Kierkegaard's methods would show how Hegel's propensity for a systematic finality is broken at every point by Kierkegaard's maintenance of ethical and religious possibilities in the individual, possibilities which contain a task for the future and always will preclude a finalized view of existence [*Tilværelsen*] and world events.

By 1842-43 Kierkegaard had completed the development of his dialectical method. Now he has the basis for coordinating the material at his disposal according to the various dialectical points of view. His next task is to gain clarity on the way to present this to the reader.[142] Before we describe the interplay between his dialectical method and

[142] See F. J. Billeskov Jansen, *Studier i Søren Kierkegaards litterære Kunst* (Copenhagen, 1951).

his dialectic of communication in the development of his authorship, we will first look more closely at the material and the existential experiences at his disposal in the beginning of his authorship.

This material may be divided into three groups: the personal factors, the work in various subject areas, the consequences of his idea to become a pastor.

Among the personal factors belong: Kierkegaard's relationship to his father, his own existential experiences, the relationship to Regine.

As far as his relationship to his father is concerned, from all the evidence given by Kierkegaard there can be no doubt that during Kierkegaard's adolescence this relationship was decisive in prompting him either to acceptance or to protest and thus influenced his choice of life-orientation and also of the areas in which he became absorbed. Very likely Kierkegaard's feeling of belonging to $"\pi\alpha\rho\alpha\nu\epsilon\kappa\rho\omega"$ is also indirectly due to his father's influence. Kierkegaard writes about this state of mind in an entry dated January 9, 1838: "I was just searching for an expression to designate the kind of people I would like to write for, convinced that they would share my views, and now I find it in Lucian: $\pi\alpha\rho\alpha\nu\epsilon\kappa\rho\omega$ (one who like me is dead), and I would like to issue a publication for $\pi\alpha\rho\alpha\nu\epsilon\kappa\rho\omega$."[143] In this phrase Kierkegaard indicates the loss of the first spontaneity; this state of mind becomes an essential motif in his authorship.

Kierkegaard's independent experimentation with existential issues, initiated in the autumn of 1835 in protest against his father, gives him first and foremost an insight into the spheres of existence characterized by opposition to Christianity (Don Juan, Faust, Ahasuerus). But in all this experimenting he himself remains the most important object of his scrutiny. His ruthless self-ransacking and self-examination provide the stuff of knowledge about him-

[143] II A 690 (J. and P., V). Kierkegaard's reflection in this entry perhaps led to the choice of the title of his first book: *From the Papers of One Still Living*, S. V., XIII.

self and give an additional basis for his knowledge of man.[144]

Because of his engagement to Regine and its unhappy outcome, Kierkegaard is forced into experiences in a completely new sphere. Not only does he have to think through his own particular situation which led to the break, but he must also make a purely theoretical study of the whole idea of marriage and the relationship between man and woman, in order thereby to enable himself to define his own position and its problems.[145] The many-sided approach to all the factors connected with his engagement provide abundant material which can be used in the authorship.

The experiences provided by these three existential situations lead Kierkegaard to hold changing existential positions. These positions up to the beginning of his writing can be placed in a historical order which, as we will see, comes to have crucial importance for the design of the authorship.

These positions are:

(1) The break with his father's authority in 1835 introduced Kierkegaard's romantic period. The annihilating power of irony takes him deep into despair. This experience is utilized especially in *The Concept of Irony*.

(2) A return to his father's universally human, ethical philosophy of life, begun toward the end of 1837 and reinforced by the experience of *"an indescribable joy"*[146] and by reconciliation with his father in May, 1838. From the summer of 1838 until about September 10, 1840, Kierkegaard lives within the sphere of the ethical-humane, a position he later depicts in its ideal form through Judge

---

[144] Compare this to his later remark through a pseudonymous writer about the "mere thought of taking time upon one's conscience, of giving it time to explore with its sleepless vigilance every secret thought . . ." (*Fear and Trembling*, p. 110) and the saying *"Unum noris omnes"* (*The Concept of Anxiety* [*Dread*], p. 71).

[145] See X¹ A 476 (*J. and P.*, V).

[146] II A 228 (*J. and P.*, V).

William. With this position as the point of departure he moves into a positive approach to life's tasks: he completes his studies so that he has a basis for a career, and he is drawn closer to Regine, which leads to the engagement. During these two years Kierkegaard is on the way to preparing himself for a regular middle-class life as described later in the second part of *Either/Or*.

(3) This universally human ethical position breaks down for Kierkegaard immediately after the engagement: ". . . the next day I saw that I had made a mistake. Penitent that I was, my *vita ante acte*, my melancholy—that was sufficient."[147] He cannot realize marriage on a universally human, ethical basis, which presupposes the "equilibrium between the esthetic and the ethical."[148] Kierkegaard's παρανεκροι motif now plays a prominent role. He sees that life in its first spontaneity is all over for him; this situation is depicted in part I of *Either/Or*. The road to the second spontaneity may be long and difficult. It is particularly in this period and in this situation that Kierkegaard compares himself with those who also had experienced the breakdown of their immediate and natural desires. The figures of Antigone, Job, and Abraham enter Kierkegaard's field of vision right after the engagement. But for him they are only stages on the way to a deeper solution. For Kierkegaard the way to newness must go through penitence, which was not true of the characters just mentioned. Just after the engagement Kierkegaard struggles from the position of resignation through several intermediate stages to the experience of penitence and guilt, which must precede "the qualitative leap." The period after the engagement to the beginning of his authorship provides substance which he uses primarily in the pseudonymous books up to and

[147] X5 A 149:5, p. 161 (*J. and P.*, V). On the subject of Kierkegaard's penitence see Villads Christensen, *Søren Kierkegaard* (Copenhagen, 1963).
[148] *Either/Or*, II, pp. 159-338.

including *Concluding Unscientific Postscript*.[149] This will be treated in greater detail in the discussion of individual works up to and including *Concluding Unscientific Postscript*.

Kierkegaard relates the knowledge gained through working in various areas, such as esthetics, etc., to subjective actuality, and in this way he acquires substance he can use in his own dialectical activity. The objective truths and points of view do not become meaningful and significant for Kierkegaard until they illuminate actuality, his central concern: the actuality of the subject. How far Kierkegaard is able to go in using objective truths to clarify subjective actuality can best be seen in the way the basic principles of logic themselves, such as the principles of identity and of contradiction, are employed very consistently for a particular purpose, that of establishing the limits of the various areas within subjective actuality and of defining this actuality in relation to Christianity. Therefore Kierkegaard's work in the various disciplines, through this adaptation of the objective for use within the subjective point of view, yields rich material for the developing authorship.

Kierkegaard's university degree qualifies him for appointment as a pastor. The possibility of the ministry continues to be a matter of serious consideration for him. Although never ordained, Kierkegaard is prompted by the possibility of ordination to become an *"upbuilding"* [*opbyggende*] writer.[150] That his theological studies inevitably lead him to regard the "upbuilding" as central is due to his having an existential, not theoretical, interest in his fellow man. The central position of the upbuilding or edifying in his authorship is underscored further by the fact that this

[149] Here Kierkegaard follows the principle articulated in a journal entry: "Life can be interpreted only after it has been experienced, just as Christ did not begin to expound the Scriptures and show how they taught of him until after his Resurrection." II A 725 (*J. and P.*, I, 1025).

[150] More of this in my background essay "Poet or Pastor" in Søren Kierkegaard, *Armed Neutrality and An Open Letter*, pp. 3-24.

literature is under his own name or the pseudonym closest to him (Anti-Climacus).

Kierkegaard's dialectical proficiency together with his material was bound to have the result that he emerges in his writing as dialectician, psychologist, poet, and preacher. The dialectician takes precedence, since through his dialectical method[151] he has an overview of the developing structure of the authorship. In this connection it is interesting to note that even the preacher, who appears under Kierkegaard's own name, is judged according to the rigorous principles of the dialectician, who very carefully separates the different forms of the upbuilding material from one another and establishes their specific character, which gets the appellation "without authority."

The dialectician also has an overview of the psychologist and the poet. As for the psychologist, it must be said that he also occupies a central position in Kierkegaard's authorship. This is quite understandable if one considers Kierkegaard's assertion of the importance of "anthropological contemplation" and his persistent practice of experimental psychology.

The poet in Kierkegaard's authorship comes into being especially out of his relationship to Regine. Only the poet manages to identify himself with and describe the conflicts and their results, evoked by human passions, especially by the collision of human passions with the force represented by Christianity. But lest there be a confusion and blending of the spheres of existence in which the poet moves, the dialectician must give advice and direction here also.

In the next section on the dialectical structure of Kierkegaard's authorship, the chief emphasis in discussing the point of view in the individual works will be upon "arranging each individual work within the whole," that is, upon placing the individual works in relation to each other with-

[151] Compare with ". . . a balanced discernment despite a productivity that advanced by leaps and bounds. . . ." VII¹ B 75 (*J. and P.*, V).

in the authorship as a whole, and only secondarily will consideration be given to special treatment of "each part of the individual work."[152] If the latter task is to be carried out responsibly, each particular work must be dealt with from the standpoint of the dialectician.

[152] X⁵ B 168, p. 361 (*J. and P.*, V).

III

The Dialectic
Employed in the
Authorship

In our scrutiny of the dialectical structure of the authorship we will consider Kierkegaard's dialectic of communication, which plays a decisive role in the authorship because of Kierkegaard's extensive use of pseudonyms and
his very careful consideration given to the relations among
the various themes. Although Kierkegaard's dialectical
method was completely clear to him in 1842-43, his principles for a doctrine of communication were given their
final form only in the development of the authorship, at
the latest in 1846, after which Kierkegaard, early in 1846,
thought of "giving a course of 12 lectures on the dialectic
of communication."[1] At the beginning of his authorship
Kierkegaard already had arrived at a clear understanding
of the most important aspects of the art of communication.
Consideration of two kinds of dialectic—the dialectical
method and the dialectic of communication—from now on
dominate all the organizing work of developing the authorship. A clear understanding of the dialectical method, then,
was the first condition for the authorship, the dialectic of
communication the next. "My service through literature is
and will always be that I have set forth the decisive qualifications of the whole existential arena with a dialectical
acuteness and a primitivity not to be found in any other
literature, as far as I know, and I have had no books to
consult either. Secondly, my art of communication; its
form and its consistent execution. . . ."[2] When Kierkegaard

[1] VIII[1] A 82 (*J. and P.*, V). See the developed outline for the
lectures in VIII[2] B 79-89 (*J. and P.*, I, 648-57). For Kierkegaard's dialectic of communication see Lars Bejerholm's elaborated account, *Meddelelsens Dialektik* (Copenhagen, 1962).
[2] VII[1] A 127 (*J. and P.*, V). The word "secondly" clearly im-

later speaks of the "ingenuity of a major work"[3] and of the "exceedingly rigorous ordering"[4] involved in the planning of the authorship, this pertains primarily to his art of communication, the working out of which and the use of which assuredly cost him just as much effort as the development of the dialectical method itself.

A systematic progression in carrying out the authorship begins with *Either/Or*, but Kierkegaard's first two works, *From the Papers of One Still Living* and *The Concept of Irony*, point ahead to important subject matter and structural elements in the authorship to follow. We will look at these two works first, from the standpoints of the dialectic and the art of communication.

A characteristic feature of *From the Papers of One Still Living*[5] (a feature which, incidentally, marks Kierkegaard's whole production) is its polemical turn. The explanation for Kierkegaard's initial and continuing polemical quality lies in the dialectical method itself. Consistency is the nerve of the method, and it requires the working out of stringent positions, which always function polemically in the area where they are used, and this polemic becomes more forceful in proportion to the vagueness and muddledness in the area concerned. It is important to be clear on this point. Certainly Kierkegaard knew "that every man who in the proper sense is to fill out a period in history must always begin polemically";[6] yet he tried not to use polemics spuriously—it emerges as a natural result of his thinking, which carries a point of view to its logical con-

---

plies the importance of the art of communication as the second part in relation to the first, the dialectic, and this comment, written in 1846, also vindicates the claim that the dialectic of communication was used in its full dimensions at this time.

[3] VII² B 235, p. 72 (omitted in *Authority and Revelation*, p. 54).

[4] VII¹ A 104, p. 50 (*J. and P.*, V).

[5] An extensive study of the book *From the Papers of One Still Living* from other standpoints than these is found in E. Hirsch's *Kierkegaard-Studien* (Gütersloh, 1933), I, pp. 10ff.

[6] I A 340 (*J. and P.*, II, 1541).

clusion, which then becomes the standard for the area in question. Since in his entire authorship Kierkegaard stresses a consistent presentation of his standpoints, this polemical tendency, apparent already in his first book, is characteristic of his whole authorship.

The polemic is completely dependent upon the subject under discussion. In the book *From the Papers of One Still Living* the polemic is in the field of literature, and Kierkegaard leads off with a carefully reflected and well-grounded explanation of what is required of a poet who wants to work with epic material.

When Kierkegaard wrote *From the Papers of One Still Living*, he had reached a clear understanding of the relations among the three forms of poetry, lyric, epic, and dramatic, regarding their respective levels and also the necessary qualifications of the creative poet. His hierarchy —lyric, epic, dramatic—corresponds to the three transactional functions, feeling, cognition, and will, with feeling equivalent to lyric, cognition to the epic, and will to drama. Here Kierkegaard is simply following the structure of the stages, in which immediacy, which is essentially emotive, comes first, cognition second, and will as conflict-creating and thereby related to drama, third.

After correlating the three forms of poetry, Kierkegaard then runs through the possible positions of the lyrical poet, at the same time attempting to determine more specifically H. C. Andersen's place within lyrical poetry. Kierkegaard then presents his view of the epic poet. This is the central concern of the piece. Drawing many examples from the epic poetry of his day, Kierkegaard claims that the primary qualification of the epic poet is a solidly constructed philosophy of life as the background for his epic productions. This argument is aimed particularly and polemically at the poet H. C. Andersen, and Kierkegaard shows how H. C. Andersen, because he lacks a philosophy of life, does not manage in his works (of which Kierkegaard concentrates specifically on *Only a Fiddler*) to bring the epic material into a living, organic coherence. This can

only be done with the help of a thoroughly reflected philosophy of life. It is Kierkegaard's opinion that Andersen
has bypassed "the contemplation absolutely necessary for
all portrayal."[7] Of course, Kierkegaard's insistence on a
philosophy of life as a qualification for the epic poet must
not be considered to be directed at H. C. Andersen alone;
it applies to all epic writing. And as far as H. C. Andersen
is concerned it must not be forgotten that the polemic
against him is mitigated by the fact that Kierkegaard wants
to be maieutically helpful (to use a later expression of
Kierkegaard's) to H. C. Andersen and wishes his criticism
of him to be regarded as written "with sympathetic
ink. . . ."[8]

This sympathetic, helpful attitude toward H. C. Andersen on Kierkegaard's part is revealed in the fact that
Kierkegaard, just as he does in his later writing, confronts his reader, in this case H. C. Andersen, with the
possibility of choosing between certain major views of
life. That Kierkegaard as early as 1838 had a clear understanding of certain dialectical standpoints can be seen in
the way he counterpoints life-positions, which later return
again and again in elaborated and more complete forms.[9]
These two positions are "a merely human point of view,
Stoicism, for example" and "the religious," which Kierke-

[7] *S. V.*, XIII, p. 78.

[8] *S. V.*, XIII, p. 92. The expression in Danish denotes invisible
ink and here has the double meaning of the writer's attitude
and of the activity required of the reader if he is to read rightly
and fully.

[9] Two of the most important places where these opposite
positions are treated include *Concluding Unscientific Postscript*,
in which Johannes Climacus presents the two positions on the
basis of a positive ascending scale. The two positions come out
even more clearly in *The Sickness Unto Death*, in which the
Socratic human position in the first part of the book is placed
against the Christian view, but this time on a negative ascending scale. Significantly, Anti-Climacus uses the term "Stoicism"
for one of the final phases within the human position. Like
irony and humor, Stoicism also can be regarded with a positive
or a negative definition.

gaard qualifies more specifically as "the truly Christian conviction: that neither death, nor life, nor angels, nor principalities, nor things present, nor things to come, nor powers, nor height, nor depth, nor anything else in all creation, will be able to separate us from the love of god in Christ Jesus our Lord."[10]

Both these life-views require "the transubstantiation of experience," but the Christian view of life is built upon "a deeper empiricism" than the merely human. The defining of the boundaries between the purely human standpoint and the Christian, so very important to Kierkegaard's dialectic and which leads thereafter to the propounding of two forms of religiousness, Religion A and Religion B, appears here for the first time. Furthermore, concealed in this delineation of two views of life is the contrast on the personal plane between Socrates and Christ.

Kierkegaard's procedure to help Andersen find a view of life appears in many utterances pertaining to the dialectic as well as to the art of communication. On finding a philosophy of life Kierkegaard says: "If we ask how such a view of life comes to be, we answer that for him who does not allow his life to fizzle out completely but as far as possible seeks to turn its individual expressions inward again, there must of necessity come a moment in which a strange illumination spreads over life, without his needing in even the remotest manner to understand all possible particulars, for the subsequent understanding of which he now has the key; there must, I say, come a moment when, as Daub observes, life is understood backwards through the idea."[11]

Henceforth the life-view as "the key" has a double function (as Kierkegaard personally experienced): by means of "the key" we are helped to understand "backwards" what we have experienced. "The key" first of all creates the presuppositions for being able to recount past experience coherently; second, "the key" functions in the service

[10] S. V., XIII, p. 68; Romans 8:38-39.
[11] S. V., XIII, p. 69.

of communication. "Essentially a life-view plays the part of providence in the novel; it is the novel's deeper unity which provides it with an interior center of gravity; it frees the novel from becoming arbitrary or pointless, because the purpose is immanently present everywhere in the work of art."[12]

But to make clear how much is required in order to speak of a view of life, Kierkegaard declares "that the poet must first and foremost win for himself an authentic personality and that it is only such a dead and transfigured personality who is able to and ought to produce—not angular, earthly, palpable persons."[13] By "dead and transfigured personality" Kierkegaard cannot mean anything else than the view of life, be it human or Christian, which has as its presupposition what the pseudonymous writers call "the movement of infinity." In the domain of the human this movement assumes the form of irony or resignation; in the domain of the Christian it becomes "the movement of repentance." Only through this movement of infinity can the poet reach the level of spirit and from this level become the master of his material. Kierkegaard expresses it this way: "There must be an immortal spirit in the novel which outlives it all."[14]

Mention must also be made of what Kierkegaard says about the two forms of abortive attempts to arrive at a clarified view of life. He gives them the following names: "The first is ineffectual activity and the second a primitive passivity; the first is broken manliness, the second sustained womanliness."[15] These definitions, together with his thoughts on "*Superstition as a Substitute for True Poetry*,"[16] can be regarded as the first sprouting of Vigilius Haufniensis's later reflections on the nature of the demonic, which originates in man's failure to understand himself and in the consequences of this defect for existence.

[12] Ibid., p. 73.
[13] Ibid.,
[14] Ibid., p. 74.
[15] Ibid., p. 72.
[16] Ibid., p. 78.

The work contains also the following existential observations, which Kierkegaard later expands according to his dialectical method.

(1) An emphasis on the way "a profound and earnest embracing of a given actuality" can "have the highest significance for the individual."[17] With this statement Kierkegaard means that accepting a given actuality, as he himself had to accept his melancholy inheritance, can become meaningful to the individual. In these comments the category of the individual begins to emerge.

(2) In this work Kierkegaard also gives, publicly and unequivocally, his first criticism of the religious condition of his age, ". . . whose principle (*sit venia verbo*) is nothing but Protestantism's deep and inward life-view reduced *in absurdum zum Gebrauch für Jedermann.*"[18]

From the standpoint of the art of communication, *From the Papers of One Still Living* is also of interest because it introduces the splitting process within existential possibilities, which from now on becomes the point of departure for the pseudonymous apparatus.[19] In *From the Papers of One Still Living* this process embraces only two persons: Kierkegaard himself and his other *I*, his "alter ego."

As editor of the book, Kierkegaard has the same relationship to his other *I* as, for example, Constantin Constantius in *Repetition* has to "the young man." Just like Constantius, Kierkegaard in *From the Papers of One Still Living* takes the stance of clear, ironic, good sense, while Kierkegaard's "friend," the other *I*, in his "dissatisfaction with the world"[20] reminds us of the young man with his melancholy. The two characters have still another common trait: the other *I* has "his αδυτον"[21] (his impenetrable sanctuary), which is analogous to the closed-up-ness or reserve

[17] Ibid., p. 62.

[18] Ibid., p. 64; if this expression is permitted; reduced to absurdity for use by everyman.

[19] See pp. 30-33 above; see also Arild Christensen, "Der junge Kierkegaard," *Orbis litterarum*, XVIII, 1963, pp. 31ff.

[20] S. V., XIII, p. 46.   [21] Ibid., p. 47.

of the young man, who toward the end is able to communicate with Constantius only by letter, without Constantius's being able to answer. These two figures, the other *I* and the young man, represent the deeper level in the personality which is still brooding over possibilities; whereas Kierkegaard and Constantius in the respective works take clear, already-concluded positions. Mention could also be made of an unimportant similarity between Kierkegaard and Constantius—that both are named as being responsible for publication.

With respect to the art of communication, one can carry the similarity between the two books one step further and point out that essentially there are three persons involved. In *Repetition* this situation is clear: there we have Constantius, the young man, and, as the third, Kierkegaard himself, who is the real occasion for the book's coming to be. It can also be said that there are three persons in *From the Papers of One Still Living*: first Kierkegaard as ironist, then the other *I* representing the unclarified possibilities, and finally Kierkegaard as the actual person, who is more than the ironist.

The Concept of Irony, Kierkegaard's doctoral dissertation, may also be considered a polemical book because of its unilateral emphasis on Socrates as an ironist, which must incite a countering reply, and also because of its critical appraisal of individual authors in the German romantic movement.

As a piece of writing the book's dominant quality is its rigorous scholarliness. In none of his later books does Kierkegaard use such detailed scholarly documentation and argument as in *The Concept of Irony*. In reading this book one gets the definite impression that Kierkegaard wants to show that he has completely mastered the working procedures of the objective disciplines before tackling the more difficult tasks confronting him in his increasing concentration upon subjective actuality. This strictly scholarly procedure is noticeable particularly in the first part with its thorough textual analysis of the source material for our knowledge of Socrates, the works of Xenophon, Plato, and Aristophanes. Here Kierkegaard quite independently considers the possibilities in interpreting this material. In the context of his thorough, textually critical treatment of the writings on Socrates Kierkegaard makes an ironic comment on Hegel, who did not have the aptitude for such "hyper-criticism," the justification of which Kierkegaard recognizes. Neglect of this "hyper-criticism" had negative results for Hegel. "Although he is freed in this way from much prolixity, he nevertheless misses one thing or another that would be a necessary moment in a complete account. Hence that which suffered the injustice of being overlooked in this way occasionally asserts its right and interposes itself at another place."[22]

Since *The Concept of Irony* was a doctoral dissertation and above all had to have a purely scholarly character, it is quite understandable that Kierkegaard had to set his own name to it. Yet in this book, too, we may speak of a hidden pseudonymity.

In the first place it must be underscored that *the* Kierkegaard who makes an effort to demonstrate the principle of irony in Socrates himself plays the many strings of irony in this work, not only in numerous statements and observations, but also in the very structure of the book. Kierkegaard develops the first three chapters of the book apparently along the lines of Hegel's pattern, which propounds a gradation of the three most important categories: possibility, actuality, and necessity. The ironic turn becomes clear in the second part of *The Concept of Irony*. Here Kierkegaard inserts, with emphasis, his own pattern of the relation between the three categories. It is the same pattern he jotted down in his journals in 1840[23] and which he maintains throughout his whole authorship. In *The Concept of Irony* the relation between possibility—actuality and concept (necessity) is formulated as follows: "These two

[22] *The Concept of Irony*, p. 244.
[23] III A 1 (*J. and P.*, II, 1587).

moments are inseparable; for if the concept were not in the phenomenon, or rather, if it were not the case that the phenomenon is only intelligible and actual in and with the concept, and if the phenomenon were not in the concept, or rather, if it were not the case that the concept is only intelligible and actual in and with the phenomenon, then all knowledge would be impossible; since in the one case I would lack truth, and in the other, actuality."[24]

This states unequivocally that possibility as well as actuality contain the concept as the second element, that is, the category of necessity, in Kierkegaard's understanding of the word. With the establishment of this formula the whole Hegelian plan is completely discarded, since recognition of the unity of two opposing elements, actuality and concept, in existence [*Tilværelsen*] posits its paradoxical character, a characteristic completely opposite to Hegel's and which remains basic to Kierkegaard's whole view of existence [*Tilværelsen*].

Aside from emerging as a master of irony, Kierkegaard in *The Concept of Irony* shows two more aspects of his personality. The first of these may be called the observant psychologist. Kierkegaard calls Socrates "the *ironic observer*"[25] in relation to his environment, but in his dissertation Kierkegaard is himself just such an observer with regard to Socrates. Kierkegaard mentions the necessity of two kinds of "integral calculation" in order to fathom the person of Socrates, since this investigation must take into consideration the "special circumstance" that because of Socrates's ironical behavior a disparity is created between the external fact of his life and his essential nature. A trustworthy conception of Socrates must therefore use an integral double calculation. "Forming a conception of Socrates, therefore, is quite another matter than forming a conception of most other men. Here lies the necessity of the fact that Socrates can only be apprehended through an integral calculation. But as there are now thousands of

[24] *The Concept of Irony*, pp. 259-60.
[25] *Ibid.*, p. 215.

years between him and us, and since not even his contemporaries could grasp him in his immediacy, so it is easy to see how doubly difficult it is for us to reconstruct his existence, for we must endeavor to apprehend through a new integral calculation this already complicated conception."[26]

Kierkegaard's main task in the first part of the dissertation is, as a psychological observer, to demonstrate from the external data about Socrates that his position is irony.

The other aspect of Kierkegaard that we find in *The Concept of Irony*, later represented by a particular pseudonym, is the dialectician who seeks to correlate the numerous points of view. Kierkegaard emerges as a dialectician particularly in the second half of the dissertation, where the concept of irony is treated together with its many manifestations and modifications.

Thus Kierkegaard functions in *The Concept of Irony* in the triple role of ironist, observing psychologist, and dialectician.[27]

Kierkegaard's efforts to work through from external phenomenal actuality into the hidden actuality of the subject, which begins with irony, signifies that, as he sees it, the way must go from the quantitative determinants to the qualitative. Thus we find—especially in the first part of the dissertation, which tries to arrive at and explain Socrates's ironic position—several parallel thought-developments, all of which move from quantity to quality.[28] This movement is completely understandable when we consider that with respect to all previous forms and expressions of life irony represents a new quality. We now inspect a few of these thought-developments.

[26] Ibid., p. 50.

[27] See Niels Thulstrup, *Kierkegaards Forhold til Hegel* (Copenhagen, 1967), pp. 224-25.

[28] Already it seems as if Kierkegaard is working with a long-range plan; in *The Concept of Irony* he tries to get through with the sphere of quantitative qualifications in order to concentrate in the authorship on the qualitative.

Mention must first be made of Kierkegaard's discussion of certain dialectical forms prior to Socrates. All these attempts fall within a quantitative dialectic with the general characteristic that the individual still has not won independence from external objective forces. It is these external authorities which are most profoundly determinative for the individual. It can be said of all the dialectical forms which arise as a result of the individual's absolute dependence on external forces that they are based upon "the external dialectic of the good."[29] Kierkegaard points out that Xenophon, too, would list Socrates under this dialectical form and thereby drive Socrates's dialectical position "back to the bad infinity surrounding the empirical."[30]

Kierkegaard, however, believes that Socrates as a representative of irony goes beyond "bad infinity." The true infinity opens up before him, and thus he stands at the beginning of a new form of dialectic. In its full development this dialectic becomes qualitative dialectic. But since Kierkegaard in his dissertation limits Socrates's position to the standpoint of irony, he cannot concede Socrates this qualitative dialectic but claims for him the dialectical forms appropriate to irony: "an abstract dialectic"[31] or "a purely negative dialectic,"[32] consequently forms of dialectic which aspire beyond quantitative determinants but which as yet possess the new only in its abstract form or as the simple denial of quantitative relations. Kierkegaard defines the Socratic position with respect to dialectic more closely by stating that Socrates "has arrived at the Idea of dialectic, but does not possess the dialectic of the Idea."[33] Here Kierkegaard invokes Aristotle, who discusses this in his *Metaphysics*.[34] "Thus it is quite in order when Aristotle denies dialectic in the proper sense of the word to Socrates."[35]

29 *The Concept of Irony*, p. 59.
30 Ibid., p. 60. 31 Ibid., p. 154.
32 Ibid., p. 173. 33 Ibid., p. 196.
34 See Aristotle, *Metaphysics*, 1078.
35 *The Concept of Irony*, p. 152n.

This movement from quantity toward the new quality is apparent also in the treatment of morality, which will be considered in some detail here. Morality expresses the primacy of the race and the state over the individual; the individual respects the moral laws not merely because of the punishment which follows their violation but also because of modesty. Thus modesty acquires an important function as long as the normative center of gravity for human actions lies outside of the individual. Modesty thus becomes equivalent to conscience, which, appearing on a higher plane, begins first with irony's concentration on subjective actuality. Socrates moves the center of gravity to the individual himself and thereby dissolves the substantial relations of state and race. Leaning on Hegel's remarks about this Socratic transition, Kierkegaard says: "Socrates's position is that of subjectivity of inwardness, reflecting upon itself, and in its relation to itself it loosens and dissolves the established [*Bestaande*] in a surge of thought that swells up over it and washes it away while it itself sinks back into thought once more. In place of the modesty (αἰδώς) which forcefully yet mysteriously binds the individual to the reins of the state, there now appeared the decisiveness and certainty of subjectivity in itself."[36]

Not until there is this subjectivity which opens the perspective of the infinite can there be any mention of conscience or, more correctly, the first sprouting of conscience. Agreeing with Hegel, Kierkegaard sharpens this up: ". . . in conscience the finite subject renders itself infinite."[37] In his dissertation Kierkegaard uses Hegel's terminology to define the transition from the moral sphere to the new one; the transition is called a progression from objective morality or custom to subjective morality, and the moral individual in the second sense is defined thus: "The moral individual is here the negatively free individual. He is free because he is not bound by an 'other,' yet he is negatively free because he is not limited in an 'other.' "[38]

[36] Ibid., p. 190 (ed. tr.).   [37] Ibid., p. 245.
[38] Ibid., p. 248. For Hegel's important distinction between

But this *"moral freedom"* can end in "arbitrariness"; it contains "the possibility of good or evil." Hegel wants to lead the moral individual to the good by recommending that he enter again into a positive relation to the objective forces. Hegel distrusts negative freedom, which is the first form of conscience but which by reason of its arbitrariness can turn toward evil. Kierkegaard quotes Hegel's elaboration of this point: "Das Gewissen ist als formelle Subjectivität schlechthin diesz auf dem Sprunge zu seyn, ins Böse umzuschlagen."[39]

Kierkegaard now follows Hegel's path a good way before later repenting of it.[40] We quote a few of the statements in which Kierkegaard makes the greatest concessions in seeking a positive relationship after having won negative freedom. He says of Socrates, who stopped with the negativity of irony: "The individual must no longer act out of respect [modesty] for the law, but must consciously know why he acts. But this, as anyone can see, is a *negative determination*: it is negative towards the established [*Bestaaende*] as well as negative towards that deeper positivity, that which conditions both negatively and speculatively."[41] "He [Socrates] negated the state without ever arriving again at the higher form of the state wherein infinity is affirmed, as he

objective morality or *Sittlichkeit* (spontaneous virtue based on custom) and subjective morality or *Moralität* (the individual conscience), see G.W.F. Hegel, *Lectures on the History of Philosophy*, I-III (New York, Humanities Press, 1963), I, pp. 387f. and footnote.

[39] Ibid., p. 248. "To have conscience, if conscience is only formal subjectivity, is simply to be on the verge of slipping into evil."

[40] See VI B 35:24 (*J. and P.*, V); X³ A 477 (*J. and P.*, IV): "Influenced as I was by Hegel and all the moderns, without the maturity really to comprehend greatness, I could not resist pointing out somewhere in my dissertation that it was a defect on the part of Socrates to disregard the whole and only consider numerically the particulars." See also XI² A 108 (*J. and P.*, IV).

[41] *The Concept of Irony*, p. 249.

negatively required."[42] "The moral individual can never realize the good; only the positively free subject can have the good as infinitely positive, as his task, and realize it."[43]

Influenced by Hegel, then, Kierkegaard wanted to place Socrates back in the civil context. Here we have an analogy to the attitude we meet later in Judge William on a higher level, namely, that the individual, after a negative movement, returns to the positive values of life.

Ironically enough, however, the dissertation contains not only an endorsement of Hegel on this point but also remarks which foreshadow criticism of the positive solution the system can offer and which defend Socrates's remaining within the position of irony. This appears in the following: "In general, one is accustomed to finding irony, conceived ideally, assigned its place as a vanishing moment in the system and for this reason described very briefly. Accordingly, it is not easy to conceive [begribe] how an entire life may be spent in this, especially when the content of this life must be regarded as nothingness. But one forgets that a standpoint is never so ideal in life as it is in the system. We forget that irony, like every other standpoint in life, also has its tribulations, conflicts, defeats, and triumphs."[44]

Ways of knowing in the process of man's mental-spiritual development also involve transitions from a lower level (quantity) to a higher position (quality). Oddly enough, these transitions are presented only in *The Concept of Irony*. The explanation must be that after writing his dissertation he works primarily with the highest form of cognition, namely, reflection on the paradoxical character of actuality. The preceding forms of cognitive activity, treated in the dissertation, are the presupposition for being able to proceed to reflection on the category of the absurd.

Kierkegaard assumes the following steps in the cognitive activity of thought: (1) mythological reflection, (2) meta-

---

[42] Ibid., p. 253.   [43] Ibid.   [44] Ibid., p. 192.

phorical reflection, (3) representative or abstract reflection, (4) scientific reflection,[45] and (5) reflection on the category of the absurd. He lists Plato under representative reflection: "Because Plato never arrived at the speculative movement of thought, the mythical, or more precisely, the image, may still be a moment in the representation of the Idea. Plato's element is not thought but representation [*Forestillingen*]."[46] This remark is completely in agreement with Aristotle's interpretation of Plato as stopping with the abstract reproduction (ideas) of things without applying these ideas to empirical actuality as Aristotle did. This is why Plato also did not achieve scientific thought. Aristotle was the first to establish principles for scientific thought, even if Aristotle in his *Metaphysics* points to Socrates[47] as already having supplied the primary foundation by his search for the conceptual aspect of things.

Reflection on the actuality of the absurd presupposes familiarity with the preceding forms of thought, but it builds primarily on the presuppositions of scientific thinking. Only rigorous scientific thinking permits the category of the absurd to appear in all its distinctiveness. In his dissertation Kierkegaard merely suggests this highest form of thought by mentioning in the last page the central presupposition of this kind of thinking: "*Credo quia absurdum.*"[48]

In explaining Socrates's thoughts on the immortality of the soul, particularly as set down in *Phaedo*, Kierkegaard points to this same movement from quantity to quality. Socrates starts with the Greek view of man as a relation between body and soul. But Kierkegaard expands that which has validity for the Greek understanding of man to apply to all Hellenistic psychic life by presupposing "the necessity of a dichotomy for Hellenism."[49] By means of reflection the

---

[45] Ibid., p. 249.   [46] Ibid., p. 134.
[47] See Aristotle, *Metaphysics*, 1078 b.
[48] *The Concept of Irony*, p. 341.
[49] Ibid., p. 69.

Greeks create an ideal world alongside the actual world and thus effect a doubleness, a "dichotomy," with respect to all existence [*Tilværelsen*]. Ideality and actuality then stand as two aspects of existence [*Tilværelsen*]. But Socrates seeks at all points to reach a "trichotomy," a third and higher aspect which, however, because of remaining within the position of irony, has an abstract character. Applied to the relation between body and soul this means that Socrates attempts to show that there are elements to be found in the soul which take one beyond the conception of the soul as a purely quantitative (finite) entity. By concentrating on the content of the soul, the individual discovers the presence of certain "universal-representations," certain ideas which he could not have acquired simply by observing the physical world. These ideas, gained through recollection, must have been in the soul beforehand and must be recognized as having permanent validity. From this line of thinking Socrates is led to the assumption that the soul itself also possesses an eternal quality. Thus it may be said that Socrates is on the way to finding a third element in the relation between body and soul and is approaching the idea of man as "a synthesis of the temporal and the eternal."[50]

But since in his dissertation Kierkegaard confines Socrates to the position of irony, the synthesis cannot be posited in its proper significance; the eternal self as the third element of the synthesis is conceived only as an abstraction, with the result that the immortality of the soul is also understood abstractly. In the following comment Kierkegaard throws more light on the limitations of this synthesis by comparing it to the synthesis properly understood: "What we meet with here is not the eternal self-positing of self-consciousness that allows the universal to close tightly and firmly around the particular, viz. the individual; on the contrary, the universal flutters loosely about the particular."[51] Kierkegaard then clearly states that

[50] Ibid., p. 107.   [51] Ibid.

Christianity is the first to create the possibility for a "positivity"[52] by placing the whole question of human existence on an entirely different plane.

Kierkegaard sets forth these thoughts while examining Socrates's "proofs" for the immortality of the soul, and throughout this discussion Kierkegaard emphasizes that Socrates advances no further with his proofs than to indicate the third element of the synthesis as an abstract category. In examining Socrates's "proofs,"[53] Kierkegaard may have confirmed the idea, which from now on belongs to the fixed elements in his thinking, that on the whole one cannot achieve actuality itself by any proof—since proofs belong to the sphere of thought. The transition from thought-actuality to genuine actuality takes place by means of a "venture" and is no longer within the sphere of reflection but of faith. Kierkegaard quotes Socrates's observations in *Phaedo* on this "venture" of believing in the continued existence of the soul, but Kierkegaard does not make further use of this Socratic declaration in his dissertation.

Many similar transitions to an abstract quality could be cited in the dissertation. Kierkegaard treats in detail, for example, Socrates's presentation of an abstract conception of love in the *Symposium*.[54] Mention may also be made of Kierkegaard's assertion that with his irony Socrates neutralizes the difference between the tragic and the comic in finite (quantitative) terms. Here he again arrives at a unity which is "the abstract and negative unity in nothingness."[55]

Thus at every point, according to Kierkegaard, Socrates goes beyond quantity. Yet he does not reach quality in its positive form but stops at its abstract form.

After showing how the Socratic movement toward irony has an influence on the various parallel aspects of individ-

[52] Ibid., pp. 112-13.
[53] Ibid., pp. 104-11 and 140; see *Phaedo*, 114 d.
[54] *The Concept of Irony*, pp. 78ff.
[55] Ibid., p. 89.

ual life, Kierkegaard shows how the concept of irony itself undergoes a change in being elevated from its quantitative definition to a qualitatively new position in Socrates. Irony existed prior to Socrates, but in him it became a quality.

Generally speaking, the concept of irony can be defined as a disparity or a misrelation between "essence and phenomenon";[56] this definition is valid for all forms of irony. This disparity also characterizes the quantitative and relative forms of irony, which Kierkegaard classifies under the terms "*executive*" and "*contemplative*" irony.[57] The first of these forms has a more existential character, whereas the second is more theoretical, but both of these forms must be considered as still belonging under quantity, since they deal only with particular aspects of existence [*Tilværelsen*]. Not until irony "directs itself against *the whole of existence* [*Tilværelsen*]"[58] do we have "irony *sensu eminentiori*," that is, irony as a new quality. Elaborating on this higher form of irony, Kierkegaard says: "Irony *sensu eminentiori* directs itself not against this or that particular existence [*Tilværende*] but against the whole given actuality of a certain time and situation. It has, therefore, an a priority in itself and it is not by successively destroying one segment of actuality after the other that it arrives at its total view, but by virtue of the fact that it destroys in the particular. It is not this or that phenomenon but the totality of existence [*Tilværelse*] which it considers *sub specie ironiæ*."[59] With this, irony too is given a new qualitative definition.

The examples cited of the transition from quantity to quality in the process of Kierkegaard's working out the manifestations of irony show that Kierkegaard is already using a few of the viewpoints which form the basis of his dialectical method. Emerging most clearly of all is the viewpoint which gives subjective actuality precedence over the objective. The psychological and esthetic points of view are also mentioned, and Kierkegaard touches on "the

[56] Ibid., p. 272.
[58] Ibid., p. 274.
[57] Ibid., p. 271.
[59] Ibid., p. 271.

paradigmatic."[60] The significance of the paradigmatic appears first when the individual approaches the ethical or is within the sphere of the ethical. However, analogies to this are also found on the esthetic level, as in Themistocles's attempt to imitate Miltiades.

The standpoint of the synthesis also appears in the dissertation, but it is the standpoint of the stages which emerges most clearly. By neutralizing external objective actuality, Socrates arrives at irony as the confinium prior to the next positive position. Thus the line of the stages is extended positively beyond Socrates in the suggestion of a new level leading all the way to humor and the final position where man reaches the point of "skepticism"[61] about his own capacity.

But in *The Concept of Irony* Kierkegaard extends the line of the stages negatively as well when he gives a detailed description of irony's "second power,"[62] represented by the German romantic trend. In the comments on this irony we get an example of Kierkegaard's use of the law of repetition, according to which every new mental-spiritual level of development modifies all of life's existential factors. The concept of irony also undergoes such changes at important turning points in history. With a view to the manifestations of irony in the historical process Kierkegaard says: "To a certain extent every world-historical turning-point must also exhibit this formation, and it would certainly not be without historical interest to trace such a formation through world history." As an example he mentions the period about the time of the Reformation: "Without attempting this, however, I shall merely cite Cardanus, Campanella and Bruno as examples from the age nearest the Reformation. Erasmus of Rotterdam to a certain extent was also irony. The significance of this formation, I believe, has hitherto not been sufficiently recognized, and this is so much the more curious since

[60] Ibid., p. 116.   [61] Ibid., p. 341.   [62] Ibid., p. 260.

Hegel has treated the negative with such decided partiality."[63]

According to the cited passages and others, Kierkegaard considers irony to be an important element in world history; it precedes every new turn in the history of thought. Irony annihilates the obsolete life forms and prepares a place for the new. In advance of the new, which is the intellectual life's repetition on a higher level, irony carries out its negative task. To this extent it can be said that these repetitions will always have a negative and a positive side. This is also true of Socrates as presented in the dissertation. Although Kierkegaard concentrates one-sidedly in *The Concept of Irony* upon Socrates's negative ironical side, he nevertheless refers in many places to the positivity which forms the background for Socrates's efforts as an ironist. "But *irony* is *the beginning*, yet no more than a beginning; it is and it is not. Moreover, its polemic is a beginning that is equally a conclusion, for the destruction of the previous development is as much its conclusion as is the beginning of the new development, since this destruction is only possible because the new principle is already present as possibility."[64] Or the following remark about irony in general: "As the ironist does not have the new within his power, it might be asked how he destroys the old, and to this it must be answered: he *destroys* the given actuality *by* the given actuality *itself*. Still it must not be forgotten that the new principle is present in him κατα δυναμιν, as possibility."[65]

But the repetitions resulting from irony within the romantic movement, which Kierkegaard treats in detail in the second part of the dissertation, are characterized by a suppressing of the positive element in repetition. For this reason Kierkegaard calls these manifestations of irony unjustified. To be justified, irony must be relevant to the new. For the romantic movement this means that the ethi-

[63] Ibid., p. 278.   [64] Ibid., p. 237.   [65] Ibid., p. 279.

cal element should be included. For Socrates this element could be made clear only by way of infinite reflection; whereas the romantic authors had this in their tradition. If the ethical is added to irony as the positive element, it would move in the direction of humor. This is apparent in the difference between irony and humor. Irony signifies the misrelation between "essence and phenomenon," the misrelation between internal and external actuality; in humor, on the other hand, a person discovers the disparity between the eternal qualifications of his essence and his phenomenological actuality, and this misrelation is deepened further when he sees the difficulty of fulfilling the ethical requirement.[66] Irony may therefore always be used in criticizing world-historical conditions; but humor, on the other hand, which turns toward the individual's own actuality, cannot. This insight later plays a definite role in Kierkegaard's thought.[67]

Since the German authors mentioned in the dissertation circumvent the ethical, their irony develops only in negative forms and does not make for the repetition of mental-spiritual life on a higher plane. The fact that Kierkegaard depicts romantic irony in such detail and with such sympathetic insight reveals that it was his own problem—and that while working on his dissertation he was already struggling to understand how authentic repetition could arise upon the wholly negative foundation of this irony. Working with these problems helped to crystallize important aspects of his understanding of existence.

Kierkegaard's thorough study of the representatives of German romanticism teaches him first and foremost that they erred in their very point of departure and in their special application of this point of departure.

Kierkegaard agrees with Hegel that it was Kant and

[66] See III B 19 (*J. and P.*, II, 1731) for an account of the difference between irony and humor.

[67] Examples: Kierkegaard's attempt to reach the individual by humor and his use of irony in attacking an external actuality, as during the Church battle.

above all Fichte who provided the basis for German romanticism (see pp. 53-54 above). With his Copernican turn Kant moved the center of gravity from external actuality to man himself. Fichte went a step further and maintained that man himself, without reference to the given actuality, is the constitutive power which shapes his actuality. Fichte thereby opened the possibility for the infinity of the subject, but it was a *"negative infinity,* an infinity without finitude, an infinity void of all content."[68] Fichte's thought became unreal; if it was to achieve actuality, "it had to become concrete."[69]

In the following statement Kierkegaard articulates very precisely the transition from Fichte's standpoint to romanticism and his general criticism of romanticism: "The Fichtian principle that subjectivity, the *ego,* has *constitutive validity,* that it alone is the almighty, was seized upon by *Schlegel* and *Tieck* and with this they proceeded to operate in the world. But this involved a double predicament: first, it was to confound the empirical and finite ego with the eternal ego; and secondly, it was to confuse metaphysical actuality with historical actuality. Thus it was to apply an abortive *metaphysical* standpoint directly to *actuality.* Fichte would construct the world, but what he meant was a systematic construction; Schlegel and Tieck, on the other hand, would dispose of a world."[70]

Kierkegaard does not mention in this connection Solger, who, as the third representative for romanticism, is also treated very extensively in the dissertation. This omission may be due to the fact that Kierkegaard, like Hegel, has a "decided partiality"[71] for Solger. As far as Kierkegaard is concerned this partiality is probably due to his conviction that, in spite of his completely negative standpoint, Solger struggles tirelessly to get clear on the relationship of irony to esthetics and philosophy; thus he is constantly on the way to a positive element. Kierkegaard is also able to accept Solger's views on artistic creation: *"Irony* and *enthusiasm*

[68] *The Concept of Irony,* p. 290.
[69] Ibid., p. 292. [70] Ibid. [71] Ibid., p. 323.

are there set forth as the two factors necessary for artistic production, the two necessary conditions *for the artist.*"[72] Kierkegaard incorporates this standpoint into his reflections on artistic creation at the end of his dissertation.

Of the three representatives of romanticism Kierkegaard discusses, he is most severe with Friedrich Schlegel because of *Lucinde.* The novel strikes at the very aspects of life which for Kierkegaard are most central: the content of the moral and the ethical. Kierkegaard does not object to criticism of these relations, but then the positive and ethically binding side should also appear. On the other hand, he is easier on Tieck's fantastic and arbitrary experiments with poetry since they do not constitute a direct attack on the ethical. Kierkegaard takes these three representatives of romanticism in sequence, discussing Friedrich Schlegel, who has the most negative views, first, and concluding with Solger, who shows certain signs in the direction of a possible positivity.

By studying these three romantic poets Kierkegaard is also able to recognize his own romantic tendencies, and therefore his criticism of this movement in its various formations must be regarded as a showdown with himself.

The first attempts to vanquish romantic irony are described in the dissertation. Kierkegaard's next work, *Either/Or,* is still wholly under the rubric of this showdown.

But *The Concept of Irony* does not restrict itself solely to criticism of the romantic movement; it also refers many times to the positive way out. For example, it states (in complete accord with Judge William in *Either/Or*) that the path away from irony's negative standpoint to a new positive position goes through ethical action, which tries to return to concrete actuality. "Thus actuality acquires its validity *through action.* Yet action must not degenerate into a kind of stupid perseverance, but must have an a priority in itself so as not to become lost in a vacuous infinity."[73] There

---

[72] Ibid., p. 332.   [73] Ibid., p. 341.

is already a glint of an "Either/Or" in the dissertation when Kierkegaard on the one hand characterizes the ironist's negative yield in the following words: "*Boredom* is the *only continuity* the ironist has. Yes, boredom: this eternity void of content, this bliss without enjoyment, this superficial profundity, this hungry satiety,"[74] and on the other hand advances action in its a priority, that is, its ethical significance as a means of deliverance from the empty "boredom" of negative irony.

On the last pages of the dissertation Kierkegaard touches on irony's ministering function, which can take two directions. In both cases irony is dominated by a higher positive view of life.

In the first place irony, like resignation, can help the individual continually to free himself from the power and entanglements of finitude. Irony helps put things in their proper place. Kierkegaard defines this function of irony as follows: "*Irony now limits, renders finite, defines, and thereby yields truth, actuality*, and *content*; it *chastens* and *punishes* and thereby imparts *stability, character*, and *consistency*. Irony is a disciplinarian feared only by those who do not know it, but cherished by those who do."[75]

In addition to this existential meaning, irony also has significance, Kierkegaard believes, for poetic creativity. His remarks on this subject should be regarded as an important addition to the view of the poet we encountered in *From The Papers of One Still Living*, which takes the position that the poet who has gone beyond the lyrical, which is poetry's first level, must win for himself a view of life which can help him coordinate the different elements of the production into a unity. *The Concept of Irony* now names irony as the instrument whereby the poet coordinates and masters his productions. In his dissertation Kierkegaard points to both these prerequisites for poetic creation: a view of life and irony. Of the poet who leaves poetry's first stage behind him he says: "Indeed, the more

[74] Ibid., p. 302.   [75] Ibid., pp. 338f.

the poet has departed from this standpoint, the more necessary it becomes for him to have a total-view of the world, and in his own individual existence to be master over irony, that is, the more *necessary* it becomes for him to be in some measure a *philosopher*. If this is the case, the particular poetic production will not have a mere external relation to the poet, but he will see in the particular poem a moment in his own development. It was in this respect that Goethe's existence as a poet [*Digter-Existents*] was so great: he succeeded in making his existence as a poet [*Digter-Tilværelse*] congrue with his actuality. This again *requires irony*, but, be it noted, *mastered irony*."[76] As examples of a poetic use of irony Kierkegaard names, in addition to Goethe, Shakespeare and J. L. Heiberg.

For Kierkegaard, then, mastered irony becomes a condition for genuine poetic creation. In this way he brings the poet into close relation to the ironist. By the power of deliverance afforded by irony both of them are masters of the determinants of finitude.[77] From the above it follows that in his poetic activity the poet, with the helping hand of irony, is able to master all the manifestations and conflicts of human life lying on the plane of finitude. But the condition for this is that he must also have a positive view of life.

After the publication of the dissertation, Kierkegaard himself is led into the kind of poetic activity in which the

[76] Ibid., p. 337.

[77] Later Judge William discusses this close relationship between the standpoint of irony, which does not reach the positivity of the infinite, and the poet: "So when the spirit is not allowed to soar up into the eternal world of spirit it remains midway and rejoices in the pictures reflected in the clouds and weeps that they are so transitory. A poet-existence is therefore, as such, an unhappy existence, it is higher than finiteness and yet not infiniteness" (*Either/Or*, II, p. 214). From his universally human, ethical standpoint, which insists on action, Assessor Wilhelm must therefore declare that poetry can provide only "an imperfect reconciliation with life" (*Either/Or*, II, p. 277), an idea strongly emphasized in *The Concept of Irony* (p. 312).

services of irony prove to be inadequate. The conflicts and decisions to be dealt with in his authorship do not fall within the quantitative determinants of finitude but within the qualitative contradictions of a man's interior life. Only humor with its knowledge of the strife between these qualitative factors can give help or guidance here. This function of humor emerges very clearly in Kierkegaard's authorship, beginning with *Either/Or*.

At the beginning of his authorship proper, Kierkegaard is faced with three commingling[78] motivations, each demanding to be heard.

In the first place, enriched by his studies, he is tempted to enter into discussion of the issues of the day again, but this time as a profound dialectician who, under the pseudonym Climacus, would demonstrate how a specifically philosophical problem should be treated.

In the second place, he feels the need to resolve his own deeply personal experiences and conflicts in literary activity.

In the third place there is the question of how far should he go in seeking a pastorate or should he be merely an edifying author.

Let us look first at the dialectician and the poet in Kierkegaard's activity as a writer.

In 1842-43 Kierkegaard the dialectician considered publishing the treatise *"De omnibus dubitandum est"*[79] under the pseudonym Johannes Climacus. Without a doubt the following journal entry dated 1842 alludes to this: "For the most part Descartes has embodied his system in the first six meditations. So it is not always necessary to write systems. I want to publish 'Philosophical Deliberations' in pamphlets, and into them I can put all my interim thoughts. It perhaps would not be so bad to write in Latin."[80]

---

[78] See pp. 173ff. above.
[79] See IV B 1 (*Johannes Climacus, or De omnibus dubitandum est*).
[80] IV A 2 (*J. and P.*, V).

There are two things worth noting in this journal entry heralding the publication of "Philosophical Deliberations." In the first place Kierkegaard is disinclined "to write systems," consequently to offer his philosophical views in a package; this is understandable, since the very word "system" itself had acquired an odious ring for him. Secondly, he declares that he will limit his deliberations to "interim reflections." This could indicate that there were very specific phenomena in the sphere of philosophy in his day to which he would temporarily turn his attention.

By choosing the phrase *De omnibus dubitandum est* as the theme for his reflections, Kierkegaard seems this time to be taking polemical aim specifically at Martensen, who, during this period and out of his Hegelian presuppositions. excelled in the interpretation of Descartes's *De omnibus dubitandum est*.[81]

In all probability Kierkegaard wants to show in his "reflections" how irresponsibly certain philosophical concepts are used, in this case Descartes's pronouncement on doubt.

Kierkegaard-Climacus submits to rigorous analysis the following three statements he has heard in connection with Descartes's thesis: "1. *Philosophy begins with doubt. 2. One must have doubted in order to be brought to philosophize. 3. Modern philosophy begins with doubt.*"[82] In an extremely penetrating study of these assertions he points out the weakness in their formulation and their internal contradictions. Climacus's critical analysis of the three assertions and of other allegations Climacus had heard in connection with the statement *De omnibus dubitandum est* is exceedingly instructive. In great detail and with

[81] See II C 18 (*J. and P.*, V) and Martensen's *De autonomia conscientiae sui humanae* (Copenhagen, 1837), p. 19. Even as late as 1850 Kierkegaard wrote: "Martensen was just as dogmatically rigid when he lectured on *de omnibus dubitandum* as when he lectured on a dogma." X³ A 544 (*J. and P.*, III, 3107).

[82] *Johannes Climacus, or De omnibus dubitandum est*, p. 116.

consistent precision and unremitting perseverance he makes a practice of working with problems in order to achieve complete clarity. Climacus articulates his own views on this tenacity in arriving at an understanding of Descartes: "The phrase *De omnibus dubitandum est* is firmly fixed in my mind. I will strive to think it through with all my own powers and try to do what it tells me with all my passion. Come what will, let it bring me everything or nothing, let it make me wise or foolish, I will risk everything but I will not given up thinking."[83]

In his analysis of this thesis Climacus also exemplifies how logical thinking always discovers logical and existential fallacies and thereby in an indirect way rejects the inadequate basis for certain claims.

It is characteristic of Climacus that he tries in his criticism to relate Descartes's thesis to existence, for example when he thoroughly scrutinizes the question: "How does the individual relate to that thesis?"[84]

These critical deliberations comprise the larger portion of the treatise and are placed in the middle of it. In the first portion of the treatise Climacus gives some biographical information about how from early childhood he was led to a preoccupation with the strict laws of dialectic, which builds upon the principle of consistency.[85]

At the end of the treatise Climacus places his own methodical explanation of the problem of doubt, and it is characteristic of Climacus as a dialectician that he tries to resolve this question in organic connection with man's spiritual development. With an extremely foreshortened perspective he goes through the principal steps in this development and relates them to the question of doubt.

Climacus begins with immediacy; since immediacy expresses unity, doubt is not present in it. It is language, or

[83] IV B 1, p. 141 (*Johannes Climacus*, p. 142).

[84] IV B 1, p. 129 (*Johannes Climacus*, p. 130).

[85] Some of this information has already been used in describing Kierkegaard's attempt to build his dialectical method. See pp. 168ff. above.

more correctly, reflection which first splits immediacy into two opposite components: actuality and ideality. Thus the first prerequisite for the emergence of doubt is created. But the task then becomes one of creating a synthesis of the two opposites. Reflection takes on the task of bringing about a synthesis between the two opposite components of reality but is unable to create this synthesis by objective methods. There has to be a third element, which Climacus calls consciousness and which to him is identical with the self or spirit.

Essentially, this third element comes first with Christianity. Climacus points out that Christianity with its ethical demand first of all increases the tension between actuality and ideality; not until the next round does it also show the way to the genuine overcoming of doubt (or, designated more accurately, despair) by faith.

In the following important annotation to the thesis, Climacus pregnantly states this concluding position, at the same time showing the inadequacy of reasoning if the aim is to overcome doubt through a search for objective truth:

> Doubt is produced EITHER by bringing reality [actuality] into relation with ideality
>   this is the act of cognition
>   insofar as interest is involved, there is at most a
>   third in which I am interested—for example, the truth.
> OR by bringing ideality into relation with reality [actuality]
>   this is the ethical.
>   that in which I am interested is myself.
>   it is really Christianity which has brought this
>   doubt into the world, for in Christianity this self
>   received its meaning. —Doubt is conquered
>   not by the system but by faith, just as it is faith
>   which has brought doubt into the world.[86]

In his resolution of the problem of doubt, Climacus sketches the way from the lowest stage to man's encounter with Christianity. He bases this dialectical operation primarily on the idea of man as a potential possibility con-

[86] IV B 13:18 (*J. and P.*, I, 891).

sisting of two opposites which are separated by reflection but which can ultimately achieve immediacy on a qualitatively new plane.

Climacus breaks off his line of thinking in the treatise precisely at the point where such central concepts as repetition, memory, and faith in the wider sense of the word arise. In reading the two concluding sentences in the treatise, one cannot avoid the thought that Climacus suddenly has perceived that at the time it was too soon to come out with the whole arsenal of important existential qualifications which he could use later in a more detailed and larger context.

Kierkegaard abandons the idea of publishing the treatise *"De omnibus dubitandum est"* with the dialectician Climacus as the main character, but Climacus is assigned the role of being the leading and top-ranking pseudonym in the coming authorship. Climacus's dialectical position is also defined as being within the sphere of humor.

For a more explicit explanation of this change in definition and its results, the following may be said:

(1) Kierkegaard is justified in placing Climacus on the plane of humor, because Climacus, representing Kierkegaard's dialectic and possessing his dialectical knowledge, has penetrated Christianity's central qualifications, particularly the most important of them all—that the entry of Christianity into the world, its beginning, was "at once historical and eternal."[87] With this knowledge as background Climacus can draw a clear boundary between the domain of the human and Christianity. But this means that Climacus in any case theoretically controls the domain which according to Kierkegaard comes under humor, which lies in the confinium between the human and the Christian.

(2) Kierkegaard's own existential position directly prior to the beginning of the authorship and sometime after that

[87] IV B 1, p. 117 (*Johannes Climacus*, p. 119).

must be characterized as being within the sphere of humor. The collisions between the ethical as the universally human and Christian ethics into which he was hurled following the break with Regine matured him for the position of humor, and this position was the condition for the next: the leap into Christianity.

Humor gradually assumes several shapes in Kierkegaard —it appears in its theoretical form in Climacus, existentially in Kierkegaard himself, and acquires an auxiliary function when the working out of the authorship begins.

As already mentioned, Kierkegaard as author cannot himself follow the instructions he gives poets in *The Concept of Irony*—namely, that they should coordinate the authorship with the help of irony. His own productions are characterized by qualitative contradictions, and there irony's help must essentially fall short. Humor affords the first insight into the clash of these qualitative contradictions and into the resulting developments, and only with the help of humor does the poet who wants to depict the way to Christianity manage to portray the individual's inner struggles along this way.[88]

Such a depiction can never be made with the help of a system, since the position of humor always contains something incommensurable, inner contradictions which prevent direct communication. In his study of Socrates and especially of Hamann in 1837, Kierkegaard came to understand this condition and wrote: "Therefore the humanist

[88] It is difficult to determine to what extent Kierkegaard was aware at the very beginning of his authorship of Lessing's scruples about using Christianity as a theme in poetic productions (*"das christliche Trauerspiel"*), since Johannes de Silentio is the first to mention Lessing's name in this connection. On the other hand, it is perfectly justifiable to maintain that Kierkegaard's authorship, with humor in an auxiliary role, demonstrates how the individual's pathway to Christianity, where "the purely human side (*theologia viatorum*)" is stressed, can be sketched. See note on Lessing and reference to his remarks in *Fear and Trembling*, pp. 97-98.

can never actually become a systematizer either, for he regards every system as a renewed attempt to blow up the whole world with a single syllogism in the familiar Blicherian manner; whereas the humorist himself has come alive to the incommensurable which the philosopher can never figure out and therefore must despise. He lives in the abundance and is therefore sensitive to how much is always left over, even if he has expressed himself with all felicity (therefore the disinclination to write). The systematizer believes that he can say everything and that whatever cannot be said is erroneous and secondary."[89] The ideas in this journal entry become the foundation of Climacus the humorist's mode of presentation. It can further be said that Kierkegaard chooses Climacus to be the one who, with the aid of humor, is to exercise control over his poetic productions, because Climacus has a comprehensive view of the existential spheres and knows how to place the separate works in the right relation to each other. In this way he succeeds in creating a tension between the separate parts of the authorship. In order that Climacus may be able to carry out his commission satisfactorily, Kierkegaard bestows psychological insight on him as well. As far as depicting the separate and specific existential positions is concerned, Climacus avails himself of the pseudonyms subordinate to him.

This provisional account of the significance of humor in structuring Kierkegaard's authorship shows that it is not a kind of disingenuousness or a retrospective construction on the part of Climacus when he casts a backward look over the authorship up to *Concluding Unscientific Postscript* and makes the claim that the pseudonymous writers and their books, led by *Either/Or*, only carry out what he himself intended to carry out. More specifically, he says: ". . . for step by step, just as I was about to realize

[89] II A 140 (*J. and P.*, II, 1702). See also II A 111 (*J. and P.*, III, 2308); II A 138ff. (*J. and P.*, II, 1700); and II A 694 (*J. and P.*, II, 1719).

my resolve in action, out came a pseudonymous book which accomplished what I had intended."[90]

This also means that the whole portion of the authorship Climacus discusses in *Concluding Unscientific Postscript* is encompassed by one idea, one plan, with the purpose of sketching an existential movement from the lower levels to the boundaries of humor.

But this does not necessarily mean that Kierkegaard-Climacus knew in advance specifically what each book would be called and what particular form it would have, but he was clear about the methodical procedure and the line he would follow, as well as about the dialectical standpoint that would be used in building the authorship. The latter was given in the dialectical method worked out by Kierkegaard. The claim set forth here will be substantiated as we go through the books up to *Concluding Unscientific Postscript*.

For the time being Climacus recedes into the background, but because of his dialectical knowledge of the spheres of existence he determines their place in relation to each other as well as their sequence among the works which portray the specific existential positions. Because of his insight into the universal laws of existence, Climacus officiates, so to speak, in the role of a dialectical theoretician, while the assistant-pseudonyms chiefly reproduce the various existential views of life. Thereby Kierkegaard's authorship acquires a tension between the abstract and the concrete in addition to the progressive movement conditioned by the spiritual development.

The abstract line, represented primarily by Climacus, reaches the peak of abstraction in *Philosophical Fragments; Concluding Unscientific Postscript* aims at a fusion of the abstract and the concrete orientations. Vigilius Haufniensis's *The Concept of Anxiety* must also be included in the abstract line.

[90] *Postscript*, p. 225. See also Kierkegaard's discussion of this while working out "The Accounting" in 1849: X^5 B 168, p. 362 (*J. and P.*, V) and B 211, p. 394 (*J. and P.*, V).

The concrete line begins with *Either/Or*, continues through *Repetition* and *Fear and Trembling*, and culminates in *Stages on Life's Way*.

It is of utmost importance to be alert to this contrast between the abstract and the concrete for the following reasons: the abstract movement reproduces in foreshortened perspective the universally valid norms for human existence, because it describes a movement from the first immediate stage through the interim stage in the direction of Christianity; the concrete line, on the other hand, represented by many of the pseudonyms, chiefly describes Kierkegaard's own movement toward Christianity. The universal laws of existence in their abstract generality apply to all, but the individual must interpret his own existence in the light of these universal truths just as Kierkegaard did.

Although the concrete line primarily concerns Kierkegaard's own life, this does not mean that it does not have universal interest. Individual history has a constant relation to the universal laws of existence, and individual examples teach us how these universal qualifications shape and mold individual existence. Insight into this correspondence between abstract and concrete can prevent flagrant misinterpretation of Kierkegaard's authorship.

After giving up the idea of publishing "*De omnibus dubitandum est*," Kierkegaard, under the dialectical guidance of the humorist, Climacus, chooses to begin his authorship with his own concrete life-history. Climacus uses several pseudonyms who are able to depict with poetic authority the different stages in Kierkegaard's development. For this undertaking the dialectician requires the help of the poet, who is able to identify himself with the individual philosophies of life. With regard to his close relationship to the poet in the unfolding of the authorship, Climacus says later that he was obliged to "go forward completely *methodice*, as if a poet and a dialectician were watching"[91] every step.

[91] See *Postscript*, p. 216.

Kierkegaard, concurring with Daub, writes in 1838: "Life can be interpreted only after it has been experienced, just as Christ did not begin to expound the Scriptures and show how they taught of him until after his Resurrection."[92]

Just such an interpretation of his personal development, in which the crisis of his engagement takes a prominent place, is initiated by Kierkegaard in *Either/Or*, which introduces the concrete line of the authorship. This interpretation, to be penetrating and reliable, can be undertaken only on the basis of a life-view or, as Kierkegaard says, with the help of "a key" which can unlock the connection between the separate levels of development. Kierkegaard has just such a key in the dialectician Climacus's clear insight into the domain of humor, which forms the boundary for the human understanding of life, as well as in his knowledge of the positive newness which Christianity represents. Applied to Kierkegaard's life, the first part of *Either/Or* can be said to reproduce Kierkegaard's romantic period; the second part depicts a return to the form of Lutheran piety prevalent in his time, idealized in the person of Judge William. This return took place after his father's death and lasted until the day Kierkegaard perceived that he was prevented from realizing the universal.

Exemplified in the presentation of two opposite views of life, the polemical aims of *Either/Or* are in two directions. In the first part there is a showdown with the romantic movement, both in the external and the internal sense; the second part contains a polemical undertone against the ethical humanism which in the person of Judge William offers itself as the solution to all the difficulties, both in his life-view and in his life, and with which his friend in part one of *Either/Or* must struggle.

A quick reading of *Either/Or*—especially the first part— can give the impression that it is a conglomeration of fragmentary pieces without an organizing power behind the

---

[92] II A 725 (*J. and P.*, I, 1025). See also *From the Papers of One Still Living, S. V.*, XIII, p. 69: ". . . since, as Daub observes, life is understood backwards through the idea."

whole.[93] Kierkegaard later felt prompted to call attention to the fact that the opposite is the case: "Probably no one suspects that *Either/Or* has a plan from the first word to the last, since the preface makes a joke of it and does not say a word about the speculative." "Some think that *Either/Or* is a collection of loose papers I had lying in my desk. Bravo! —As a matter of fact, it was the reverse."[94]

Examining the two parts of the book separately, we note first that pseudonymous writer A., who is responsible for part one of the book, is an ironist but not like the types we find in *The Concept of Irony*. A.'s irony bears the marks of having come into existence by means of the particular presuppositions that drew Kierkegaard toward the romantic movement. This irony is characterized by the individual's being compelled into it by fate or misfortune; whereas it usually is theoretical reflection upon the contradictions and vanity of life which leads to irony. Kierkegaard himself states the difference between A.'s irony and other forms of irony by saying that it does not "have its base in futility but in mental depression and its predominance over actuality."[95] Thus two principal forms of irony are found in part one of *Either/Or*. The one is only negative and consists of the individual's using the liberating power of irony simply to experiment with life; the other, however, like Socratic irony, strives for a new positivity. But both these forms express that spontaneity or immediacy is lost.

Seen from an ethical point of view, the negative forms of irony must be designated as belonging under guilt; whereas the irony which is conditioned by fate and misfortune but is directed toward a positivity must, in its re-

[93] Even in 1936 Sven Clausen could write in a "*Forsinket Anmeldelse af 'Enten/Eller'*": "Regarded as a composition, *Either/Or* is extremely loose and shapeless." "Everything possible is thrown helter-skelter together." See Sven Clausen, *Udvalgte Tvangstanker* (Copenhagen, 1945), pp. 157, 158.

[94] IV A 214 and A 215 (*J. and P.*, V).

[95] IV A 216 (*J. and P.*, V). See also IV A 213 (*J. and P.*, I, 907).

lation to guilt, first go through a dialectical and existential clarification.

With the presentation of the negative forms of irony, ironist A. continues and concludes the study of the romantic authors begun in *The Concept of Irony*. In the renewed treatment of the forms of irony in *Either/Or*, Kierkegaard lets A. take them to their final logical conclusion. He corrects them, exposes their weaknesses, and makes apparent their untenability as a life-view. Finally he puts the results of his consistent thinking about these forms together in his own theory of irony.

The three ironic standpoints with which A. settles accounts in *Either/Or* are represented by Friedrich von Schlegel, Tieck, and Solger.

In his *Lucinde*,[96] Friedrich von Schlegel submits to debate the question of morality in the domain of the erotic. A. then shows how such a negation of morality in the domain of the erotic can assume many forms; beginning with the most primitive form, he ends by showing negation carried to its extreme consequences in Don Juan's genius. Passions and emotions in their negative forms dominate on this level.

The next step in this negation is formed by reflection's attempt to bring all human relationships, consequently the relationship between man and woman also, down to the level of finiteness, where all higher considerations lose their obligatory power. This point of view is presented in "The First Love" and "The Rotation Method."

The climax of the negative form of the erotic is reached in the "Diary of a Seducer," which A. ascribes to another pseudonym. Here the seduction takes place not through the primitive power of sensuality as in Don Juan but according to a systematic plan thought out to the least detail. It is this which precludes any extenuating aspects. Here, then, irony in connection with the erotic reaches its climax—that is, irony is overcome by itself.

[96] On the relationship between *Lucinde* and *Either/Or*, see Georg Brandes, *Søren Kierkegaard* (Copenhagen, 1877), p. 57.

According to this view, the "Diary of a Seducer" m
be considered a refutation of *Lucinde*, since it shows t
extreme consequences of carrying out the ironic standpoint
in this book.

In the case of Schlegel's *Lucinde* there may still be some
doubt as to how reprehensible this form of eroticism is,
but in its consistently logical development in the "Diary of
a Seducer" its moral character is evident. Ethics must here
express its clear condemnation. Climacus articulates this
when, referring to Johannes the Seducer in *Stages on Life's
Way*, he makes a statement which must also apply to
Johannes the Seducer in *Either/Or*: "Take such a figure
as Johannes the Seducer. Whoever needs that he should
become mad or shoot himself in order to be enabled to see
that his standpoint is perdition, does not see it, notwith-
standing, but merely imagines it. Whoever understands it,
understands it the instant the Seducer opens his mouth
to speak; he hears in every word the perdition and the
condemnation upon him."[97]

In addition to its aim of refuting Friedrich von Schlegel's
Lucinde, the "Diary of a Seducer" has two other aims:

(1) This diary intends to give a subtle psychological
presentation of the very background and possibility of such
a seduction. For this it is necessary to have a penetrating
insight into the characteristics of the masculine and the
feminine psyche in the domain of the erotic, an insight
which again must build on the deep and comprehensive
knowledge of human nature which Kierkegaard had acquired gradually. The "Diary of a Seducer" contains, therefore, valuable experiences and psychological observations.
Kierkegaard himself calls attention to this in a note written while working on *The Concept of Anxiety*. "If anyone
has any psychological interest in observations related to
this, I refer him to 'The Diary of a Seducer' in *Either/Or*.
If one looks at it closely, one sees that this is something
quite different from a novel, that it has completely differ-

[97] *Postscript*, pp. 263-64. The last two words [*over ham*] are
omitted in the present English translation.

ent categories up its sleeve, and, if one knows how to use it, it can serve as a preliminary study for a very serious and not merely superficial investigation. The seducer's secret is simply that he knows that woman is anxiety."[98]

(2) The "Diary of a Seducer" has the further intention of easing Regine's separation from Kierkegaard by giving her the idea that in her own situation Kierkegaard was a seducer. Kierkegaard sometime later declares: "*Either/Or*, especially the 'Diary of a Seducer,' was written for her sake, in order to clear her out of the relationship."[99]

Either/Or also touches on and corrects Tieck's ironic position. Tieck's main trait is a wallowing in poetic imagination unrestricted by any consideration of actuality. The end result of this overbalance of fantasy must inevitably be emptiness and boredom. Apparently A., with his leaping from one subject to another, is imitating this form of poetic irony; he, too, has an overbalance of imagination which makes him "melancholy,"[100] but A. nevertheless manages by means of irony's organizing power—which again draws upon a higher view of life—to connect the essays apparently tossed together at random in part one of *Either/Or*. In this way Tieck's form of irony is also overcome with the help of irony.

The presence of irony as an organizing principle is traceable still more clearly in the discussion of Solger's irony. We have already shown[101] that in *The Concept of Irony* Kierkegaard is attracted to Solger's speculative attempt to throw light on basic philosophical and dogmatic concepts, especially with respect to the nature of art and poetry and their task in the mental-spiritual life. But Solger was not equal to the task.

In *Either/Or* ironist A. proposes his own solution, specifically in the domain of the esthetic, where he feels at home. The questions with which Solger grappled without

[98] V B 53: 26 (*J. and P.*, V).
[99] X¹ A 266, p. 177 (*J. and P.*, V).
[100] IV A 213 (*J. and P.*, I, 907).
[101] See pp. 203-204 above.

arriving at a clarification A. now tries to solve in his own way along the following lines. Above all he asserts that art and poetry "lie in relativity";[102] higher than these is metaphysics, which regards things under the aspect of eternity. Metaphysics in the domain of knowledge is what irony is on the existential level. Both go beyond the qualifications of finiteness and point to ethics as the next level.

Following Lessing's example, which has gained a place in esthetics, A. separates the world of poetry and the world of the visual arts by referring to the fact "that art lies in the qualification of space, poetry in that of time, that art expresses repose, poetry movement."[103] Thus poetry is superior to art.

A whole scale of various art forms may be arranged. With Hegel's theoretical reflections on the problems of esthetics and a principle of classification in esthetics[104] as a point of departure, A. chooses art's relation to language as the principle of classification. Like language, all art forms can be considered as media for reproducing an ideal content, but language is the most concrete medium. In full accord with Hegel A. declares: "As a medium, language is the one absolutely spiritually qualified medium." And further: "In language the sensuous is as medium depressed to the level of a mere instrumentality and constantly negated. Such is not the case with the other media."[105]

As media, the various art forms must be regarded as abstract and their degrees of abstraction determined in relation to language. Thus we find an ascending scale of art forms, such as sculpture, architecture, and painting. Music is closest to language since like language it takes place in time and also can depict moods and passion. But

---

[102] *Either/Or*, I, p. 148.   [103] Ibid., p. 167.

[104] See Hegel's *Vorlesungen über die Aesthetik* (Berlin, 1835), pp. 3ff.; *The Philosophy of Fine Art*, tr. F.P.B. Osmaston, I-IV (London, Bell, 1920), I, Introduction, pp. 1ff.

[105] *Either/Or*, I, p. 65.

music, too, must be considered abstract in comparison with language.

A. makes a special application of this classification in trying to establish that with *Don Juan* Mozart succeeded in creating a musical work unique in its category, inasmuch as music, an abstract medium, here gets its proper object in the idea of Don Juan, who is "the most abstract idea conceivable" and whom A. calls "the sensuous genius."[106]

In an extension of the theory of language as the concrete medium lies the solution to the question which occupied Solger as well, namely, how the eternal can be communicated in the medium of the finite. The whole plan of *Either/Or* answers this by addressing the individual indirectly and confronting him with the choice between two contrasting views of life. However, this elaboration of the idea of language as a means of communication is no longer within the competence of the ironist but becomes a task for Climacus, who understands how to set the contrasts over against each other.

The most important of A.'s essays is "The Ancient Tragical Motif as Reflected in the Modern."[107] In this essay A.'s own ironic position is articulated. The task is to find the elements which can lead out and beyond the borders of the esthetic. To this end the tragic is chosen as the point of departure, since the tragic may possibly contain elements which cannot find their resolution in the domain of the esthetic.[108] A. introduces his investigations by relying upon Aristotle's and Hegel's ideas on tragedy, but with his wider perspective he explodes the esthetic conception of the tragic. Esthetics operates with relative standards for the tragic, but A. wants to go beyond the relative to the boundaries of the ethical. In its wider consequences this transition may be seen as a transubstantiation of the rela-

---

[106] Ibid., p. 55. [107] Ibid., p. 135.

[108] See Harold Høffding, *Den store Humor* (Copenhagen, 1916), pp. 100-104, and Julius Schousboe, *Om Begrebet Humor hos Søren Kierkegaard* (Copenhagen, 1925), pp. 26-27.

tive guilt within tragedy into its absolute form. This also means that the presupposition for repentance is created, since repentance can be related only to absolute guilt. The tragic guilt of the esthetic moves between innocence and guilt [*Uskyld og Skyld*]. "Between these two extremes lies the tragic. If the individual is entirely without guilt, the tragic interest is nullified, for the tragic collision is thereby *enervated*; if, on the other hand, he is absolutely guilty, he can no longer interest us tragically."[109] Tragic suffering and guilt therefore become completely analogous to "hereditary guilt"[110] (called original sin in theology). Guilt ranges from inheritance in the wider sense to individual guilt.[111] It is this transformation of hereditary guilt into individual guilt, whereby guilt gets an absolute character, which interests A. This question has special interest for the second group of ironic figures, to which A. himself belongs, the group called "Συμπαρανεκρωμενοι."[112]

This group consists of tragic figures who are struck by misfortune without the possibility of completely excluding individual guilt. This is in complete accord with the classical conception of the tragic. What is new in A.'s analysis is that one cannot come to the new positivity without the reality of repentance—that is, without the individual's assumption of responsibility for the entire guilt. But the esthetician can go no further than to point to the new correlations.

It is true of all the ironists in the second group that an external fate or power has destroyed the happiness of their first immediacy; they are all unhappy figures who are reduced to living in memory. Each of them finds he has a special problem: to what extent is a return to the first immediacy possible, or is there a way to repetition on a higher level.

[109] *Either/Or*, I, p. 142.   [110] Ibid., p. 148.
[111] This becomes the theme of *The Concept of Anxiety* [*Dread*].
[112] *Either/Or*, I, p. 135; the fellowship of buried lives.

The first examples cited are the sorrowing women[113] who have been betrayed by their lovers; their first immediate happiness is destroyed. Now they are bound by memory to endless reflecting on their past happiness without perceiving the way out which repentance, seen from a higher viewpoint, would be.

In the essay "The Unhappiest Man,"[114] A. presents his own situation, and as the esthete who is able to talk about the more or less of suffering he places himself on the highest level of suffering. First of all he names several other figures who have lost the first immediacy and confidence in life. A. begins with a character from the preceding series, the sorrowing maiden, and continues the series according to a principle which will show the intensification of suffering with each new figure. They file past in review: Niobe, King Oedipus, Job, the father[115] of the prodigal son, one who "denied his father and himself,"[116] a girl who reminds us of Regine, and last, "the chosen favorite of the realm of suffering,"[117] who must be the ironist A. himself.

The intensification of unhappiness in A. is due not merely to being obliged to live in memory, having just like the others lost everything, but to the hope of a repetition of the first immediacy, which still tempts him. Because of this he is unable to find the relief in pain, which only memory could supply; he is cast from memory to hope and from hope back to memory. He expresses it poetically in these words: ". . . in his memory confounded by the light of hope, in his hope deceived by the shadows of memory."[118] He stands, a tragic figure, at the line of demarcation of the esthetic, but he wants to return to the first immediacy. The answer to the question to what ex-

---

[113] Ibid., pp. 175ff.   [114] Ibid., pp. 215ff.

[115] Probably refers to Kierkegaard's father, particularly the words: ". . . he overtakes him, if only in death," since Kierkegaard and his father were reconciled just a few months before his father's death.

[116] See II A 234 (*J. and P.,* V).

[117] *Either/Or,* I, p. 227.   [118] Ibid.

tent this last possibility can be realized is touched upon in part two of *Either/Or* but is not given definitively until *Repetition*.

In addition to this theme—the possibility of repetition of the first immediacy—which requires resolution, there is another theme in *Either/Or* which also awaits unraveling. In part one of *Either/Or*[119] as well as in part two there is reference to a secret[120] which must not be revealed but which caused the unhappiness and prevented the person involved from realizing the universal. It is Johannes de Silentio who, using the indirect method in *Fear and Trembling*, attempts later to inform those who are capable of finding its hidden meaning. These two themes—the attempt to search backward for the first immediacy and the explication of the cause of the unhappiness—cannot be treated until A. is confronted with the solution of his difficulties offered by Judge William on the basis of his ethical humanism.

In the second part of *Either/Or* Judge William stands as a positive counterpart to all the standpoints of irony treated in part one. He addresses himself only to A., however, and disregards the figures conjured up by A., characters who are perhaps unfamiliar to him.

Judge William seems to have solved satisfactorily the question of the relation to the first immediacy and has reached the higher stage of the ethical. The way to the new standpoint goes through repentance, and speaking of himself Judge William says of this movement of repentance: ". . . I repent myself out of the whole of existence."[121] Through this movement he finds his eternal self and chooses himself in his "eternal validity."[122] From this new position he steps once more into relation to the immediate and now his efforts are toward the creation of an "equi-

[119] See the Antigone motif in *Either/Or*, I, pp. 158ff.; compare also III A 207 (*J. and P.*, V) and IV A 114 (*J. and P.*, V).

[120] *Either/Or*, II, p. 119.   [121] Ibid., p. 229.

[122] Ibid., p. 210.

librium between the esthetical and the ethical in the composition of personality."[123]

Judge William recommends to his young friend, ironist A., the same way to the new positivity. But on the whole it is easy to discern the deficiency in Judge William's proposal to A. and to all ironists. Judge William is completely ignorant of the collapse of immediacy presupposed by all irony. He had a happy relation to the first immediacy before he undertook the movement of repentance. But this means that his penitence is abstract in nature. Judge William has nothing concrete to repent. But repentance without a concretion is an illusory movement. For the ironist who has experienced the collapse of immediacy through his own guilt or through the ups and downs of life as well as his own guilt, the way ahead goes only through concrete, actual repentance.

It appears, therefore, that Judge William's position is inadequate for A., because A. himself, as well as the negative examples of irony, have gone beyond Judge William and his position of ethical humanism. The ironists are no longer able, like Judge William, to attempt a mediation between the esthetic and the ethical.

A. must therefore remain in the position of irony and end in demonic despair, or he must proceed along the concrete way of repentance and find a solution which is on a higher level than Judge William's attempt to mediate.

Applied to Kierkegaard's personal situation, this says that after turning away from the standpoint of irony he is unable to find reassurance in the prevailing religious-ethical attitude in Denmark; his relationship to his father in particular, which at first impelled him to look in this direction, later forces him to look for a deeper understand-

[123] Ibid., p. 159. Kierkegaard himself points out that this is an attempt at mediation, saying that in the first part of *Either/ Or* he wanted to present "the isolated elements in isolated subjectivity" and in the second part he wanted to "mediate." III B 130 (*J. and P.,* V).

ing of his position than he can find under Judge William's guidance.

Of Judge William's position it may be also said that he advances in all its fullness and ideality the ethical position based upon a common, truncated interpretation of Luther's doctrine of earthly vocations. This is why for him marriage and attitudes toward work have such a central position. As a result there are three groups of virtues: "the personal, the civic, and religious virtues,"[124] which in Judge William's view should always be related to each other, with civic virtues in first rank. He has little sensitivity for the personal virtues, and the religious virtues, especially those connected with repentance and the choice of self, take on an abstract quality. The result is that the esthetic gets the upper hand in the end when he tries to create an equilibrium between the esthetic and the ethical.

Theoretically, however, there is an order in Judge William's categories, including those involving his religious position. He sums this up in a very significant line which reads: ". . . the absolute as absolute can only be for the absolute."[125] This means that if the individual is to avoid the danger of ending up in the purely finite he must continually make the movement toward the infinite, the absolute, over and over again. Judge William gives a historical example of a relapse into finiteness after choosing the infinite—namely, the Jewish people: "Even the Jew who chose God did not choose absolutely, for he chose, indeed, the absolute, but did not choose it absolutely, and therefore it ceased to be the absolute and became a finite thing."[126] Ironically, a similar relapse is initiated by Judge William through his attempt to create an equilibrium between the esthetic and the ethical.[127]

The statement that "the absolute as absolute can only

[124] *Either/Or*, II, p. 266.   [125] Ibid., p. 217.
[126] Ibid., p. 218.
[127] This corresponds to the relapse into Judaism with which Kierkegaard later charges Danish Christendom.

be for the absolute" does not get its full dialectical and existential explication until the other works appear following *Either/Or*, but the presupposition for this is that repentance becomes concrete. Abstract repentance can never create the condition for the religious relationship.

However, it is clear to Judge William himself that in some instances the carrying out of his ethical views can run up against insurmountable difficulties. He mentions as a real obstacle the instance already touched upon in our discussion of A.'s wider perspectives—that there is a secret which cannot be directly stated. But marriage, according to Judge William, requires complete openness and is made impossible if such openness cannot be achieved. He speaks of this obstacle to his young friend, the ironist: "For my part I will mention only one case, that is, when the individual life is so complicated that it cannot reveal itself. If the history of your inward development possesses an unutterable content, or if your life has made you privy to secrets, in short, if in one way or another you have gulped down a secret which you cannot draw up except at the cost of your life, then never marry."[128] With this remark the Judge personally admits to A. that his standpoint is not adequate to A.'s problem.

Judge William further reveals his understanding of A.'s existential difficulties by sending him "a sermon" from one of his acquaintances, a "clergyman in Jutland." The Judge believes that this pastor has grasped in his sermon what he himself essentially wanted to say to A. The theme of the sermon is: *"The edification implied in the thought that as against God we are always in the wrong."*[129]

With the upbuilding or edifying thoughts in this sermon, the unhappy character who steps forth in the first word of the "Diapsalmata"[130] comes to a complete halt in his many reflections on the problem of suffering and unhappiness. Kierkegaard articulates the connection between the first diapsalm and the sermon very clearly in these words:

[128] *Either/Or*, II, p. 119. [129] Ibid., p 343.
[130] Ibid., p. 19.

"The first διαψαλμ is really the task of the entire work, which is not resolved until the last words of the sermon. An enormous dissonance is assumed, and then it says: Explain it."[131]

From the viewpoint of the dialectic of communication, it is important to be aware that the humorist Climacus, who stands consultatively behind the advancing authorship, has made use of two other pseudonymous writers in establishing the conflict in *Either/Or*, each of whom depicts the area he particularly represents. Ironist A. leads the esthetic to its collapse in its extreme positions, and Judge William, in addition to a description of the positive forms of immediacy,[132] gives a blending of these forms with the ethical position.

But the "Either/Or" occasioned by these two opposites still does not achieve the humanist's ideal, since the ethical is not essentially involved in an inner struggle within the person himself. For the present they stand face to face as incompatible: the ironist with his insight into the negative aspects of existence, around which his reflection continually hovers, and the Judge with his self-assured claim for an ethical position within the same existence.

As previously indicated, there are suggestions in *Either/Or* which foreshadow a new light on A.'s existential position. The question of the possibility of a return to the first spontaneity or immediacy is still open, but consideration of the deeper reasons for the collapse of immediacy in A. may expected. Only an understanding of these issues can provide a basis for A.'s concrete understanding of his position and help him to clarify his relation to guilt and repentance.

If *Repetition* is regarded as a development of A.'s position in *Either/Or*, it may be said that A. now understands that Judge William cannot fulfill his ethical view and that the Judge cannot help him essentially, because he does

[131] IV A 216 (*J. and P.*, V).   [132] *Either/Or*, II, pp. 184ff.

not know the difficulties which arise when one loses spontaneity or immediacy.

As an ironist, A. must use his own insight in making experimental observations to penetrate the personality more deeply. Only an ironist, standing at the boundary between the esthetic and the ethical and aware of the negative aspects of life, can be of help in showing the way to new possibilities. As the later works will show, the ironist and the humorist are particularly fitted for the task of helping the single individual. Each of the positions stands at the threshold between a stage already experienced and a new stage and looks both ahead and behind. The observing, experimental representatives of irony and humor possess a predominance of reflection and have gained sufficient knowledge to point to a further development, but they themselves cannot execute an existential movement, since for this more is needed than knowledge and reflection. Only feeling and passion can prompt and carry through a new existential movement.

Since the possibility of a new point of departure is raised in *Repetition*, a second element of the personality, in addition to irony as the observing and reflecting element, is necessary—namely, feeling and passion. This second element is represented in *Repetition* by "the young man."[133]

This marks a clash of interests in A.'s interior being, indicating that A. is moving in the direction of humor, and each of the two poles gets its own personal representative. Constantin Constantius is the ironist who through his psychological experiment maintains a comprehensive view of the movements made by his counterpart, "the young man."

A.'s position, now elucidated by the relation between Constantin Constantius and the young man, is clearer, as far as it goes, than in *Either/Or*. Constantin Constantius, through the young man's confidence in him, gets to know

---

[133] See VII[1] B 83 (*J. and P.*, V): ". . . in *Repetition* feeling and irony are kept separate, each in its representative: the young man and Constantin."

about very concrete things which more explicitly illuminate the position in which "the unhappiest man" found himself. Melancholy prevents "the young man" from living in immediacy, just as it prevents A. in *Either/Or*. Melancholy changes the present to a memory, with the result that the young man cannot realize the universal—that is, cannot marry, since all his love for the girl is changed to memory. In this way he is beyond the relation before he has entered into it. But like "the unhappiest man" he is driven from memory to hope.

From his ironic standpoint, Constantin Constantius recommends to the young man various ways of totally liberating himself from the girl. If the young man were to follow this advice, he would still remain in the position of irony and end in a demonic despair. But Constantin Constantius, as "a serviceable spirit" (*Repetition*, p. 154) merely wishes to measure, by means of his proposal, the depths of his love for the girl.

The young man feels an ethical obligation to the girl, and one may very well say that it is this ethical point of view which prevents him from following the advice of the ironist. Constantin Constantius, however, does know the possibility of another way, but it lies outside his domain. This second possibility is to seek a way back to the first immediacy by faith in the absurd, but feeling and passion must attempt to find this way out on their own initiative.

This brings along with it a temporary separation of the two sides of the personality. At this point the young man understands that he cannot be helped either by the cold calculations of irony or by philosophy, which still lies within the sphere of immanence. He now turns toward transcendence and begins to read about Job, who in his need also sought the transcendent. From Job the young man learns something very important for his future development—the, confident courage to complain to God about the wrong which, seen from universally human perspectives, has befallen him. Like Job, therefore, he fights to the end the battles between the human and the divine views of justice and learns to yield to God's righteousness. This important contribution from man's side in relation to God is expressed in these words: ". . . Job's significance is that the border conflicts incident to faith are fought out in him, and that the prodigious insurrection of the world and bellicose powers of passion are here set forth."[134] Job also expected repetition and got it. But how did it go with the young man?

Repetition touches on Kierkegaard's reflections during the time of his engagement and directly afterward as to whether the obstacles which changed his love for Regine to a memory could be taken away in faith that with God everything is possible. Kierkegaard quickly discovers, however, that his case, despite all its similarities to Job's, lies on a completely different plane. Job knew that before God he was "innocent and pure in his inmost heart";[135] his past caused no difficulties in grasping the extent of his guilt or innocence. The young man, however, is confronted by a lengthier reexamination of this question. With this background of insecurity, the possibility of repetition on Job's basis is precluded, but this negative conclusion is also an indispensable step which cannot be leapt over in concrete existence. In his existential need one is led to a real confrontation with the transcendent.

The book *Repetition* was supposed to demonstrate clearly the impossibility of a Job-like return to the happiness of the first immediacy. But this final result had to be changed, since news of Regine's new engagement reached Kierkegaard before the publication of *Repetition*. He no longer needed to inform Regine of the impossibility of a repetition according to the given presuppositions, since she herself demonstrated its impossibility by becoming engaged to another.[136]

[134] *Repetition*, p. 130.   [135] Ibid., p. 125.

[136] This explanation implies rejection of the assumption that Kierkegaard's accidental meeting with Regine in Frue Kirke April 16, 1843 (see Hirsch, *Kierkegaard-Studien*, I, pp. 255ff.) was the occasion for writing the two simultaneously published

The impossibility of repetition is not left as the final result, however; the other side, which had already developed in the break with Regine, must be advanced, namely, the impetus to poetic activity. Now this activity could develop without reference to Regine, and the young man calls liberation from the relationship to her a "repetition of the spirit." Since, however, it is not possible for the young man to carry through a repetition in the world of actuality, he is returned to memory. However, as Constantin Constantius remarks, through his movement toward the transcendent in testing the possibility of repetition, the young man wins "a religious tone" which will help him as a poet "to explain actuality"[137] and thereby serve the universal. Constantin Constantius explains that a poet is an exception "who represents the transition to the genuinely aristocratic exceptions, namely, the religious exceptions."[138] The young man does not, like Job on a lower level, become such a religious exception, but through relation to the transcendent he finds the Archimedean point from which

---

books *Repetition* and *Fear and Trembling*. Just about the time that Kierkegaard wrote about the meeting, he went more thoroughly into the obstacles which continually stood in the way of a marriage with Regine. "In the marriage ceremony I must take an oath—therefore I do not dare conceal anything. On the other hand there are things I cannot tell her. The fact that the divine enters into marriage is my ruin. If I do not let myself marry her, I offend her. If an unethical relationship can be justifiable—then I begin tomorrow. She has asked me, and for me that is enough. She can depend on me absolutely, but it is an unhappy existence. I am dancing upon a volcano and must let her dance along with me as long as it can last. This is why it is more humble of me to remain silent." IV A 133 (*J. and P.*, V); see also IV A 107 (*J. and P.*, V).

This note shows that the whole weight of the difficulties in realizing the marriage still rested upon Kierkegaard, and that out of regard for Regine he could not allow himself to begin a new venture which could end even more tragically than the first. Kierkegaard still had a long struggle ahead of him to gain clarity on his difficult position.

[137] *Repetition*, p. 155.   [138] Ibid., p. 154.

he can judge actuality. This becomes his temporary form of repetition, which Constantin Constantius calls "consciousness raised to the second power."[139]

Before Constantin Constantius takes leave of the reader, he points to the way which could lead the young man to a deeper experience of the religious, that is, lead him from being a poetic exception to the religious. Since Constantin Constantius remains essentially in the position of irony and it is only on the basis of this "presupposition of consciousness"[140] [*Bevidstheds-Forudsætning*] that he can help the young man win a new point of departure after the collapse of immediacy, he is not qualified to be an adviser and counselor in the impending religious struggles and crises, and he must hand the young man over to the observers who have even greater insight and experience with regard to the young man's inner conflicts than Constantin himself. In weighty sentences Constantin Constantius lets it be known that he is aware of the positions which go beyond the result he arrives at in *Repetition*. He directly anticipates the problems in *Fear and Trembling*, and especially in " 'Guilty?' / 'Not Guilty?' "[141] which depict the religious exception's process of coming into existence on a higher level.

Referring to the perspectives which could not be attained within the scope of the book *Repetition*, he says of the young man: "If he had had a deeper religious background, he would not have become a poet. Then everything would have acquired for him religious significance. The event in which he was ensnared would still have had significance for him, but then the shock would have come from higher spheres, and then also he would have been in possession of a very different sort of authority, even though it were bought by sufferings still more painful; he then would have acted with an iron consistency and firmness such as he did not show, he then would have gained a fact of consciousness to which he could constantly hold and which

[139] Ibid., p. 156.   [140] Ibid., p. 158.
[141] *Stages*, p. 179.

would never become ambiguous to him but would be profound earnestness because he himself had posited it by virtue of a God-relationship. The same instant the whole question about the temporal would have become indifferent to him; what is called reality would in a deeper sense be of no importance to him. He would have drained off religiously all the dreadful consequences contained in that occurrence. Though reality were to turn out differently, it would not change him essentially even if the worst were to come to pass; it would not dismay him more than he already was dismayed. He would then have understood with religious fear and trembling, but also with trust and confidence, what he had done from the very first, and what as a consequence of this he was morally bound to do later, even though this obligation were to prompt the strangest behavior."[142]

These observations mention both "the shock" which could come from "higher spheres" (the suspension of the ethical, the theme of *Fear and Trembling*) and a religious thinking through and taking over of all the dreadful consequences of his engagement to Regine and the breaking of this engagement. The completion of this last task is accomplished later by Quidam: "An absolute resolution bestows calmness, the resolution which has gone through the dialectic of fear makes one unafraid."[143] Here Quidam informs us that he has thought all the dreadful consequences through to their logical conclusion and is ready to assume the responsibility for them. This leads him to concrete repentance, which is the condition for the possibility of the second spontaneity, in which the reality of sin is assimilated. As the above quotation shows, Constantin Constantius can only suggest this relationship.

Johannes de Silentio, the author of *Fear and Trembling*, has advanced further existentially than Constantin Constantius. Despite his role as "a serviceable spirit,"[144] the

[142] *Repetition*, pp. 157-58.   [143] *Stages*, p. 360.
[144] *Repetition*, p. 154.

ironist Constantin Constantius was not sympathetic enough to identify wholly with the difficulties of an individual existing person. Johannes de Silentio has this sympathy, and by means of his capacity for "sympathetic insight"[145] he is able to discover hidden conflicts in the individual's life. With his sympathy for suffering and with his understanding of inner conflicts, Johannes de Silentio is closer to humor than to irony, and thus he forms a connecting link between Constantin Constantius's ironic standpoint and the position of Frater Taciturnus, the humorist.

Although Constantin was unsuccessful in penetrating the secret in the young man's life, Johannes de Silentio gets to know it but feels bound to silence. He is, however, willing to communicate the secret indirectly to anyone who manages to master the meaning of the message, just as Tarquinius's son understood his father's indirect discourse, but the messenger who brought the message understood nothing.[146]

The hidden meaning in *Fear and Trembling*, which was supposed to be deciphered primarily by Regine, could not consist in her learning *that* she was sacrificed as Isaac was sacrificed by Abraham, for she knew that, as did others, but in enlightening her as to *why* she had to be sacrificed. As will be seen later, Kierkegaard simply wanted to tell Regine that he himself was being sacrificed, and therefore he had to sacrifice her.

This theory is supported by Kierkegaard's declaration that the primary difficulty in a marriage between him and Regine was that he would have to initiate her into his relationship to his father. This is quite clearly stated in the following journal entry: "But if I were to have explained myself, I would have had to initiate her into terrible things, my relationship to my father, his melancholy, the eternal

[145] See pp. 29-33 above.
[146] See the motto for *Fear and Trembling* (p. 21) and E. Hirsch's study of Johannes de Silentio in *Teologisk Tidsskrift for den danske Folkekirke*, 1931, pp. 214ff.

night brooding within me, my going astray, my lusts and debauchery, which, however, in the eyes of God are perhaps not so glaring; for it was, after all, anxiety which brought me to go astray, and where was I to seek a safe stronghold when I knew or suspected that the only man I had admired for his strength was tottering."[147]

The last words in this entry indicate that Kierkegaard's flight into the esthetic life and away from Christianity was in a sense occasioned by the father. As a "modern" Antigone,[148] Kierkegaard felt bound to his father's memory not to speak directly about it to anyone, but since his conception of marriage required such a direct revelation, the way to marriage was blocked for him.

Further confirmation of the correctness of this theory is provided by the fact that sometime later, when Kierkegaard has a more detached view of his relations to his father and Regine and can confide more freely on paper, he attaches primary importance in his journal entries about Abraham and Isaac to what must have taken place between his father and him, and only secondary importance to what occurred between him and Regine.[149]

After the break with Regine in 1841 Kierkegaard wrote: "My sin is that I did not have faith, faith that for God all things are possible, but where is the borderline between that and tempting God; but my sin has never been that I did not love her."[150] And in 1843 he repeats: "If I had had faith, I would have stayed with Regine. Thanks to God, I now see that. I have been on the point of losing my mind these days."[151] These entries must be interpreted to mean that the essential obstacle to resuming the relationship to

[147] IV A 107, p. 43 (*J. and P.*, V).

[148] *Either/Or*, I, pp. 151-59. That Kierkegaard felt some similarity between himself and Antigone is also seen in ibid., p. 162, where he compares her with Epaminondas. He discusses this also in III B 179, 40 (*J. and P.*, V), where he certainly speaks of himself.

[149] See X⁴ A 338, 357, 458 (*J. and P.*, III, 3020, 3714; V); X⁵ A 132 (*J. and P.*, II, 2223).

[150] III A 166 (*J. and P.*, V).   [151] IV A 107 (*J. and P.*, V).

Regine was that he could not initiate her into the secrets of his life, since they concerned not only him but primarily the memory of his father. They are the same difficulties referred to at the end of the entry from 1843, just quoted.

All this shows that the chief problem for Johannes de Silentio, and thereby Kierkegaard, is not primarily that of Abraham but of Isaac. We must think of Kierkegaard as an Isaac who, unlike the Biblical Isaac, is aware that he is being sacrificed. This raises in him the difficult question of the future implications of this sacrifice, which in the first phase means the end of immediate happiness. All this must then be held together with the inheritance—the guilt and the responsibility he felt saddled with from his father.[152] His movement toward faith in order to achieve immediacy once again must therefore appear different from Abraham's.

Kierkegaard cannot, therefore, present Abraham as a paradigm of his relationship to Regine. Abraham was, after all, "the righteous man" and one could still approach him in "immediate categories,"[153] and Abraham, after having found faith, returns to a positive relation to the first immediacy. But for Kierkegaard-Isaac, the question of a return to the first immediacy on the given grounds remains highly problematical.

This difference between Abraham's situation regarding faith and the situation of one whose burden is the loss of immediacy and the problem of guilt[154] can best be illuminated by Johannes de Silentio's reflections on the relation

[152] See IV A 107, p. 43 (*J. and P.*, V) and VII¹ A 126 (*J. and P.*, V): "An old man who himself was extremely melancholy (why, I will not write down) gets a son in his old age, who inherits all this melancholy." The sacrifice also changed the son into "an old man." X¹ A 234 (*J. and P.*, V).

[153] *Fear and Trembling*, p. 108n.

[154] These two aspects, guilt and the ideal striving of one sacrificed, are reflected later in the relationship between Climacus and Anti-Climacus. See pp. 334-38 below.

between desire and duty:[155] a person can concentrate the whole content of his life in one desire, this desire expresses the direction of the life of immediacy; but the universal is supposed to sanction the wish and convert it into duty if the desire is to be more than an individual whim. It is fortunate if desire and duty merge, as they do with Abraham. His desire centers in love of Isaac, but he also has the duty to love Isaac. If a higher duty, duty to God, requires that he sacrifice Isaac, he undertakes through this sacrifice a double movement: he gives up his desire and at the same suspends the duty which the universal places upon him. This obedience to the higher demand becomes the condition for the next: to believe that Isaac can be had again "by virtue of the absurd."[156]

For an Isaac in the role of an Abraham who, as in Kierkegaard's case, is hindered by the responsibility and guilt of the past, a movement toward faith would appear otherwise; he, too, has but one wish, in which the first immediacy asserts itself, namely, the desire for Regine, but he does not have duty's sanction of this desire, especially since his reflections on duty regarding his previous life make it clear to him that he cannot bring this desire into harmony with the universal. He therefore gets involved in the contradiction with the universal that in his movement toward faith he cannot suspend the universal since it is suspended for him in advance by his previous life. It cannot be said that he is able to give up his wish, either, since his wish for the same reason is unjustified. In order to go further he must first root out all these connections in his life and get clear on the question of guilt; thus it is repentance and not resignation which can help him along the way to faith.

All this leads to the understanding that Kierkegaard's own position is represented in *Fear and Trembling* prima-

[155] Compactly treated in the footnote on p. 88, *Fear and Trembling*.
[156] Ibid., p. 48.

rily by means of the merman.[157] A new category, signifying a forward step compared to all the previous positions, surfaces with the merman. Johannes de Silentio points out that the merman, too, must "have recourse to the paradox," even though he can do this only with a point of departure different from that of Abraham. "For when the single individual by his guilt has gone outside the universal he can return to it only by virtue of having come as the individual into an absolute relationship with the absolute. Here I will make an observation by which I say more than was said at any point in the foregoing discussion. Sin is not the first immediacy, sin is a later immediacy. By sin the individual is already higher (in the direction of the demoniacal paradox) than the universal, because it is a contradiction on the part of the universal to impose itself upon a man who lacks the *conditio sine qua non*."[158]

With this observation Johannes de Silentio sets a period to all the previous efforts to return to the first spontaneity or immediacy in which the reality of sin is still not present. It can therefore be said that not only Abraham in *Fear and Trembling* but also Job and the young man, yes, even Judge William, had not seriously encountered the problem of sin, since their centers of gravity still lay in the first immediacy. Now Johannes de Silentio, who, significantly enough, himself forms an intermediate link between irony and humor, introduces a totally new view of things, in which the reality of sin is concretized in the merman. Now mention is made of "a later immediacy" which has the reality of sin as its presupposition. From now on the merman is used to make graphic the position which implies the possibility of moving to faith or remaining within the demonic.[159]

The merman's position is precisely the same as Kierkegaard's after he perceives that a return to the first immediacy is blocked off for him. The problem for the mer-

---

[157] Ibid., pp. 103ff.   [158] Ibid., pp. 108.
[159] See Edward Geismar, *Søren Kierkegaard*, I-VI (Copenhagen, 1927-28), II, pp. 6off.

man and Kierkegaard is their "preexistence,"[160] which can be understood only as the problem of guilt carried over from their past life. Before this can be cleared up they are both confronted by the possibility of the demonic. Only through repentance can they advance, but before the movement of repentance can be undertaken, certain questions must be answered: is their guilt dependent upon external factors such as heredity and environment or is it individual, the result of their own acts. Even if the individual is finally led to assume the entire guilt as his own, to get clear on the question of "not-guilty—guilty" is of existential importance to him. Only in this way can the individual become conscious of his dependent relation to the race (the universal), whereby the category of the single individual comes into view. This whole complex of problems points ahead to a more penetrating treatment of these questions; they get their radical disentanglement not only in *The Concept of Anxiety* but particularly in the third part of *Stages on Life's Way*.

In conclusion, two more observations regarding the existential progress that *Fear and Trembling* manifests in relation to *Repetition: Repetition* culminates in a poetic exception who wants to serve the universal; in *Fear and Trembling* the exception is in a religious category. As one who serves, the poetic exception is in continuous touch with the universal; the religious exception on the other hand is set outside the universal, and through his absolute isolation the individual breaks away from primary dependence on the race and becomes the single individual [*den Enkelte*]. There are, however, two opposite ways of being an exception, depending on whether one is led into isolation by faith or by guilt. An example of the first kind of isolation is Abraham, who in faith relates himself as the single individual absolutely to the absolute. The opposite example is the merman who through guilt has gone outside the universal and is on the way toward the demonic

[160] *Fear and Trembling*, p. 105.

paradox. The two positions confront each other like a new, sharpened "Either/Or," and the merman is farther along the way negatively than Abraham is positively.

The progress in *Fear and Trembling* compared with *Repetition* is detected also at another point. In *Repetition* remembering or recollection is referred to as the final position in "the ethical [pagan] life-view,"[161] but recollection is a very abstract expression within the human sphere. In *Fear and Trembling*, on the other hand, the account of the hero's struggle and resignation contains many examples of the highest ideality within the sphere of the human, and examples of tragic guilt are also given. In this way the human sphere is drawn into existential reflection more concretely than in *Repetition*. Both kinds of tragic conflicts mentioned here are placed in contrast to the religious exception. These conflicts can be understood by the universal, whereas the religious exception is deprived of such understanding. The presentation of these diversified examples of tragic conflicts in human life and the discussion of their contrast to the religious exception may not be the least important aspect of *Fear and Trembling*.

One of the essential reasons for presenting these tragic conflicts within the sphere of the human seems to be to point out that tragic guilt can be of such a nature that it cannot be fully and finally explained outside the religious sphere.[162]

With the figure of the merman in *Fear and Trembling*, the concrete-individual line approaches its temporary climax: through guilt the single individual is set outside the universal and negatively is higher than the universal. He

[161] *Repetition*, p. 34.

[162] Vigilius Haufniensis says something like this regarding these conflicts in *Fear and Trembling*: "There the author several times allows the wishful ideality of the esthetical to founder upon the exacting ideality of the ethical, in order by these collisions to let the religious ideality come to evidence, which is precisely the ideality of reality." *Concept of Anxiety* [*Dread*], p. 16n. See also note 108 above.

can first come into a positive relation to the universal when, "after having made the infinite movement of repentance, he makes still one more movement by virtue of the absurd."[163] In order that a positive relation to the universal can be created, he must have recourse to the religious, as the double movement described here. The first part of this double movement expresses that the merman has acknowledged sin as a reality in his life and now repents of it absolutely; the second part points to a power which through forgiveness can create the point of departure for a new immediacy and a new relation to the universal.

But the merman can also remain in the demonic sphere; he can "enter into an absolute relation to it."[164] With this last turn he moves away from faith.

The first is Kierkegaard's own way, with the continual possibility of switching over to its opposite, and this way is concretely presented in the third part of *Stages on Life's Way*.

But prior to *Stages on Life's Way*, two books are published which in a more theoretical and abstract manner touch on the questions the previous pseudonymous books have raised. Here the problem is guilt and forgiveness for the single individual and his relation to the absolute after he has gone beyond the boundaries of the universal. The human position will now be confronted in earnest by the position which lies outside its boundaries. The two books, *Philosophical Fragments* and *The Concept of Anxiety*, have the task of explaining the contrast between the human and the Christian. The "Either/Or" of Judge William still lies completely within the sphere of the human.

To understand the relation between *Philosophical Fragments* and *The Concept of Anxiety*, it will be helpful to recall a distinctive feature in Climacus's dialectical method. We know from *"De omnibus dubitandum est"* how Climacus began his dialectical exercises either from below

[163] *Fear and Trembling*, p. 109.
[164] Ibid., p. 106.

in order to come to "the higher thought," or from above, that is, from this "higher thought," in order to get back to the lower positions. This procedure illuminates the relation between *Philosophical Fragments* and *The Concept of Anxiety.*

In *Philosophical Fragments* Christianity is "the higher thought" which has consequences for all of human life. The whole of life is structured in relation to the reality which, from the human point of view, comes (to use Barth's expression) " 'senkrecht von oben.' "[165] The higher thought breaks into the patterns of human life and interrupts and illuminates them in a completely new way.

The Concept of Anxiety moves in the opposite direction. It begins at the lowest level with man in order to move to "the higher thought." In contrast to the movement *senkrecht von oben*, the movement in *The Concept of Anxiety* may be called an ascent, because it begins with the problem of the first man's guilt and then moves progressively upward to lead man to confrontation with Christianity.

The two books supplement each other in a very splendid and dialectically deliberate way.[166] *Philosophical Fragments* looks at man from a spiritual point of view; whereas *The Concept of Anxiety* reminds us that man is not only a spiritual being or has the possibility of becoming that but that he is also a being of flesh and blood and therefore through heredity and environment is deeply rooted in man-

---

[165] Karl Barth, *Der Römerbrief* (Zurich, 1947), p. 77; " 'vertical from above,' " *The Epistle to the Romans* (Oxford, Oxford University Press, 6th ed., 1933), p. 102.

[166] Torsten Bohlin was the first to note that *The Concept of Anxiety* and *Philosophical Fragments* "gå tillbaka till olika utgångspunkter" ("go back to different points of departure"), but since he did not discover the dialectical reasons for this, he thought that the incongruity of the two books was due to an error in Kierkegaard's thinking. See Torsten Bohlin, *Kierkegaards dogmatiska åskådning* (Stockholm, 1925), pp. 222ff. On the same problem see Eduard Geismar, *Søren Kierkegaard*, III, pp. 86ff., and E. Hirsch, *Kierkegaard-Studien*, II, pp. 112ff.

ifold anthropological presuppositions. If we disregard all these presuppositions and look upon man only from a spiritual point of view, we end in the empty space of abstraction.

In *Philosophical Fragments* the dialectician and principal pseudonym, Johannes Climacus, who up until now has directed the course of the authorship from the wings, appears on the scene, and now that the subordinate pseudonyms have laid the groundwork for an understanding of the difference between the human views of life and the life-view which points toward the transcendent, he himself completes the sharpest possible demarcation between the human and the Christian. This demarcation is sorely needed after Hegel had undertaken the previously discussed mediation between philosophy and theology.

Philosophical Fragments is the most abstract of all Kierkegaard's works. This abstract presentation was required in order to pose the problem as sharply as possible. A more historical-concrete account of this difference between the human and the Christian involves the danger that the boundaries would not be explicitly drawn. To achieve this, the question of difference has "to be simplified as much as possible" and treated in this simplified manner on an abstract plane. In a journal entry about *Philosophical Fragments* Kierkegaard speaks of the advantages of using an abstract procedure: "It is a dangerous pet-idea to want to be concrete immediately in answering an abstract question, whether the concretion consists of a resumé of some earlier philosopher's thought or the particularity of the historical. The concretion often has the effect of seductively depriving thought of the serenity and simplicity which are satisfied with thought itself. The mathematician is content with his numerical calculations and does not wish to use dollars, marks, or shillings in order to engage the participation of the materialist. But even though the concrete is more necessary than it is for the mathematician, one does not begin immediately by making the thought concrete but *in abstracto* clarifies the thought he wishes later to point out in the concrete."[167]

The whole plan of *Philosophical Fragments* has an ironic undertone, since there is something ironical about having to supply information on Christianity in relation to the human in a day when by means of "speculation" this seemingly had been understood in a profound and unsurpassed way. This time Johannes Climacus uses rational means to show the dubiousness of all attempts to bring the spheres of the human and the Christian closer together. Climacus therefore does not present himself as a believer; he is simply a dialectician who, thinking consistently, experimentally deals with a question. In his capacity as dialectician he must, unlike a believer, set forth the viewpoints of Christianity in the form of a hypothesis. On the basis of this hypothetical assumption he then draws the implicit logical conclusions regarding human knowledge and existence. The logical conclusions of the hypothesis are drawn with mathematical exactness; thus *Philosophical Fragments* is the book which best illustrates what Kierkegaard means by consistent thinking. In the books with a concrete content this consistency is more hidden.

Philosophical Fragments may be properly regarded as an elaboration and full explanation of the antitheses which Kierkegaard posed in the first of the theses in *The Concept of Irony*. The thesis in question reads: "*Similitudo Christum inter et Socratem in dissimilitudine præcipue est posita.*"[168]

Climacus later in "*De omnibus dubitandum est*" states clearly that the reason for the dissimilarity is that Christianity "had come into the world by a new beginning, and this beginning was at once historical and eternal. . . ."[169]

[167] V B 41, pp. 96ff. (*J. and P.*, II, 1606).
[168] *The Concept of Irony*, p. 348. ("The similarity between Christ and Socrates consists essentially in their dissimilarity." Ibid., p. 349.)
[169] P. 119.

With this it parts company qualitatively with all other religious and human approaches.

This unique character of Christianity, which contains the blending of the temporal and the eternal elements, is described in *Philosophical Fragments* with the words: "The historical made eternal, and the Eternal made historical"[170] and expresses God's Incarnation in time.

When Climacus from now on uses the designations "the God" and "the moment" for Christ, this also stresses the fusion of the two elements referred to in Christ's life. The designation "the God" points to a specific figure in history who is believed to be God, and "the moment" asserts the coming of the eternal into the temporal, for the moment is verily a synthesis of time and eternity.

Climacus now uses this dogma of the Incarnation of God as a hypothesis to elucidate the relationship between the human and the Christian. The hypothesis essentially claims that "the God" is truth. With this hypothetical pronouncement as his point of departure, Climacus uses a thought experiment first to find the implicit consequences of the hypothesis for the Socratic position and thereby for all human striving for the truth, and next to find what attitude man with his standpoint should take to the claim that "the God" is truth, together with how the single individual can become involved in "the God's" offer.

As far as the Socratic standpoint is concerned, Climacus maintains that if "the God" is truth, then Socrates's search and all human searching for truth must be declared to be untruth. Here an either/or applies. This negative judgment of man's situation prior to Christianity is, according to the hypothesis, based particularly on this, that with "the God" the historical and the eternal are fused into a unity; here the truth and the person are identical. With Socrates, however, the identity of a person and the eternal truth is out of the question. The truth which Socrates and all men

[170] *Philosophical Fragments*, p. 76.

can reach by "recollection" and introspection must first and foremost be understood as an objective quantity which must first be realized by man in order to be changed into a subjective truth.

In order not to confuse[171] the issue, Climacus in *Philosophical Fragments* does not get involved at all in the question of what results Socrates would achieve if he attempted to live according to his interior truth. Climacus simply wants to demonstrate that Socrates's position, seen on the basis of this hypothesis, must be declared to be untruth.

Not until *Concluding Unscientific Postscript* is the question of Socrates's attempt to realize the ethical demand broached. There Climacus demonstrates that man, by his very efforts to honor the eternal obligations, is led by the middle axiom that "subjectivity is truth" to the collapse of this subjectivity in the stage of humor, which ends with accentuating "the eternal recollection of guilt."[172] This, however, does not mean that the cleft between the human and the Christian is narrower in *Concluding Unscientific Postscript* than in *Philosophical Fragments*; it rather becomes more concrete. The difference here between the two books is that in *Philosophical Fragments* the distance is defined purely dogmatically and completely abstractly, while in *Concluding Unscientific Postscript* man's existential development is considered, showing that man in exerting himself to the uttermost ends in guilt, which, however, gets a totally new and decisive qualification only in Christianity.

In *Philosophical Fragments*, then, Climacus demonstrates that, viewed from the standpoint of Christianity, all Socratic and human interpretations of existence must be stamped as untrue, but he does not go further into the more concrete issues. Most of the book deals with the first and crucial difficulties a man comes up against in his encounter with Christianity. After showing Christianity's judgment of man, it deals with man's view of Christianity

[171] See *Postscript*, pp. 184-85n.
[172] Ibid., p. 492.

and the difficulties that arise when mankind meets a power that wants to transform it.

The first difficulty Climacus mentions in man's relation to Christianity lies in the sphere of thought, since Climacus as a thinker is especially alert to the difficulties on this side. He shows that with Christianity thought is placed before the "absolute paradox"[173] with which it cannot cope. Admittedly man, in the "passion of thought," tries to go beyond himself to discover "something that thought cannot think" but is unable by himself to find the possibility of the paradoxical actuality which "the God" represents.

In connection with the absolute paradox Climacus takes up the question of the extent to which it is possible to give proofs for the existence of God. This is denied in the simple argument we encountered earlier—that reason always operates with possibilities and therefore cannot reach the reality which God is presupposed to be except by a leap, but this means that there cannot be any proof of God.

A concentrated footnote to the next text points out how Spinoza, lacking the distinction between essence and being, consequently between thought and actuality, not only evades "the difficulty" in proofs of God's existence in that he "probes the depths of the God-idea in order to bring being out of it by way of thought," but does not come to grips at all with the difficult question related to "introducing God's ideal essence dialectically into the sphere of actual being,"[174] that is, the problem of "the God." Climacus's reproof of Spinoza does not apply only to this thinker, of course, but has a message to all who erase the line of demarcation between thought and being.

In confronting the absolute paradox, thought not only reaches its frontier with respect to proofs of God, but it

[173] *Philosophical Fragments*, p. 46; IV C 84 (*J. and P.*, III, 3074).

[174] *Philosophical Fragments*, pp. 51ff. See also the statement on the Incarnation: "by which the God's eternal essence is inflected in the dialectical determinations of coming into existence." Ibid., p. 109.

stands before an actuality which has two conflicting qualities, a compounding which shuns all attempts on the part
of reason to explain or understand. To come into a positive
relation to this new actuality an "organ" other than
thought is required, and therefore the supremacy of
thought must yield ground if the new is to come forward.
The new can be grasped only by faith, but in that case
the single individual has gone beyond the domain of
thought. The first presupposition for faith is that the understanding is taken prisoner, which appears in the following observation by Climacus on the coming into existence of faith: "It comes to pass when the Reason and the
Paradox encounter one another happily in the moment,
when the Reason sets itself aside and the Paradox bestows
itself, the third entity in which this union is realized (for it
is not realized in the Reason, since it is set aside; nor in the
Paradox, which bestows itself—hence it is realized *in* something) is that happy passion to which we will now assign
a name, though it is not the name that so much matters.
We shall call this passion: *Faith*."[175]

The requirement that the understanding be dethroned
by faith will meet opposition in man, and the expression
for this opposition is offense. Offense as the opposite of
faith thereby becomes an extremely important characterization of man's possible reaction to "the God's" offer.
Since Climacus in *Philosophical Fragments* deals with the
relation between the human and the Christian in the foreshortened perspective of abstraction, offense is presented
in its simple and primary form and solely in connection
with the paradox understood as a logical contradiction.
The full development of this concept, both with regard to
man as a synthesis and to the components of this synthesis
in "the God," comes in later works.[176]

[175] Ibid., p. 73.
[176] Offense with regard to man as a synthesis is depicted
later in *The Sickness Unto Death*; in *Practice in Christianity*
offense is seen from the point of view of the composite elements
in Christ.

The condition for faith and faith itself, which means that "the Paradox and Reason meet in the mutual understanding of their difference," are given to man by "the God" alone; but this presupposes that man is contemporary with "the God." Climacus then tries to show by consistent thinking that believers at all times are situated equally in regard to contemporaneity with Christ. His account has three main parts: first he designates the different forms of contemporaneity; next he explains freedom and the historical in relation to contemporaneity; and finally he shows how all "disciples" are placed on an equal footing in regard to being contemporary with "the God" when it is a matter of accepting faith from him.

(1) With regard to the first point, the three forms of contemporaneity are differentiated: (a) direct, immediate contemporaneity, which quite simply means that one was contemporary with a historical person or event. For Kierkegaard this kind of contemporaneity with regard to Christ does not play a substantial role until later. In *Philosophical Fragments* he is satisfied with merely touching on it briefly. (b) Contemporaneity with the eternal, a contemporaneity which has various aspects. A good example of this kind of contemporaneity is the Socratic position pointed out in *Philosophical Fragments*: by means of "recollection" man (Socrates) becomes contemporary with the eternal, which previously was present in him only potentially, and he can now enter into conscious relation with it. But the relation to God also belongs to this form of contemporaneity, which expresses that man becomes aware of being before the God who is always present. (c) The third form of contemporaneity is faith's contemporaneity with "the God" in "the autopsy of faith."[177] This last contemporaneity is paradoxical in nature since it contains two qualitative opposites: the eternal revealed at a specific point of time within history, where one cannot become contemporaneous with the eternal without the historical as the intermediary.

[177] *Philosophical Fragments*, p. 87.

The third form of contemporaneity, then, is related to the historical, and since the historical signifies a movement or a process of development, Climacus in the interpolated "Interlude" goes into the problem of history and freedom. At the same time these studies serve as the basis for the principal aim of this "Interlude"—namely, to make a distinct separation between "the direct and ordinary form of the historical" and "that historical fact"[178] which tells of "the God."

(2) With regard to the historical as a continuous movement, Climacus shows that it proceeds along parallel lines, one above the other; each lower level serves as possibility for the next higher level. Here Climacus is obviously in harmony with the Aristotelian view that a sphere of actuality becomes possibility for the next actuality, and so on, until an actuality is reached which can no longer become possibility since it is the underlying actuality. To explain more sharply this relation which concerns the historical as well as freedom, Climacus uses the pattern set forth in entry IV C 100 on the relation between "thought and being."[179]

As a logical development of this pattern, actuality is conceived as a unity of necessity and possibility (freedom), that is, necessity always accompanies possibility as one of the components of actuality. But during the historical development, which is always within the category of coming into existence [*Tilblivelsen*], the element of freedom (possibility) must be especially accentuated, since "all coming into existence takes place with freedom, not by necessity. Nothing comes into existence by virtue of a logical ground, but only by a cause. Every cause terminates in a freely effecting cause. The illusion occasioned by the intervening causes is that the coming into existence seems to be necessary; the truth about intervening causes is that

178 Ibid., p. 108.
179 IV C 100 (*J. and P.*, I, 197); on the concept "contemporaneity," see Per Lønning, *Samtidighedens Situation* (Oslo, 1954), pp. 151ff.

just as they themselves have come into existence they point back ultimately to a freely effecting cause. Even the possibility of deducing consequences from a law of nature gives no evidence for the necessity of any coming into existence, which is clear as soon as one reflects definitely on coming into existence."[180]

Climacus then shows how freedom comes more and more into the foreground in the higher forms of actuality. In the world of external nature there can be no question of freedom in the proper sense, although it also belongs within coming into existence, which includes everything that has come into existence. It is only in "historical coming into existence in the stricter sense,"[181] that is, in human history, that freedom comes to the fore and that time becomes significant for coming into existence, which cannot be said about external nature. For Climacus, who looks analytically at everything from the angle of eternity, all coming into existence in nature has no other meaning than to be the foundation for the next level, where man's decisions in time are made and time is thereby accentuated.

Turning then to the historical in the stricter sense, Climacus makes a point of rejecting with a thoroughgoing logical argument all attempts to regard historical events and, in general, the historical, as subject to necessity. He polemicizes not only against Hegel's view of "the course of world events as an inevitable development"[182] but against all attempts to eliminate freedom as co-determinative in historical developments.

In elaborating on the category of the historical (and it is quite apparent that he is familiar with the literature on this theme), he repudiates (with Hegel in mind) the viewpoint that necessity is entailed by the very concept "historical" because the historical, in being apprehended, is supposed to be changed into necessity. He summarizes his

[180] *Philosophical Fragments*, p. 93.
[181] Ibid., p. 94.
[182] This idea had already been criticized in I A 205 (*J. and P.*, II, 1232).

conclusion in the following sharp sentence: "If the object of apprehension is changed in the process of apprehension, the apprehension is changed into a misapprehension."[183]

Climacus's zeal for stressing the freedom aspect of the historical may also be interpreted as a defense of the reality of repentance.[184] Under the presupposition of a necessary historical development, repentance would become an illusion, since we cannot repent what has happened by necessity. Climacus makes an important distinction between the unchangeability of what has happened and the claim of its necessity; the first does not preclude the reality of repentance, but the other does.

Climacus goes on to show how reflection over that which has come into existence brings out the possibilities which were present before one of them was actualized through the individual's decision and thereby made historical. A prerequisite for understanding the historical in this way is a "sense for coming into existence," which Climacus amplifies in saying: "The historian thus again confronts the past, moved by the emotion which is the passionate sense for coming into existence: wonder. If the philosopher never finds occasion to wonder (and how could it occur to anyone to wonder at a necessary construction, except by a new kind of contradiction?) he has *eo ipso* nothing to do with the historical; for wherever the process of coming into existence is involved, as is the case in relation to the past, there the uncertainty attaching to the most certain of events (the uncertainty of coming into existence) can find expression only in this passion which is as necessary to the philosopher as it is worthy of him. (Plato, Aristotle.)"[185]

With these reflections Climacus undergirds the view that reflection on the historical as that which has come into existence does not eliminate the element of freedom in it.

Through this relation to freedom, the past continually preserves an element of uncertainty within itself; therefore

---

[183] *Philosophical Fragments,* pp. 98-99.
[184] Ibid., p. 96.   [185] Ibid., p. 99.

there can be no absolute proofs that what happened had to happen just so and not otherwise. This uncertainty about that which has occurred has the effect that there is a risk in making fixed claims about the coming into existence of the historical, that is, about the transition from "the manifold possible how" to a "thus." Only faith, which knows uncertainty and the possibilities of doubt, can at its own risk grasp the historical.

After discussing various aspects of the historical with special emphasis on freedom's part in it, Climacus proceeds to his central concern in the "Interlude," which is to show the difference between "the direct and ordinary form of the historical"[186] and the report that God has revealed himself in a historical person.

The difference is that the historical in the ordinary sense contains only the "contradiction" that one of the hypothetical possibilities was chosen at a risk and a transition from this possibility to its actualization was accomplished.

On the other hand, the report about "the God" contains a logical and ontological self-contradiction, since it asserts the unity of two incompatible qualities. The risk in believing the report will therefore be on a qualitatively higher plane than in believing the ordinary historical. Here the historical details become of minor importance compared with the report itself of the Incarnation.

Climacus expresses this particularly in his *"nota bene* on the page of universal history," which simply reports the following about "the God": " 'We have believed that in such and such a year the God appeared among us in the humble figure of a servant, that he lived and taught in our community, and finally died,' " and Climacus thinks that this "is more than enough"[187] to be the occasion for faith in a later disciple. With this formulation the content of Christianity is given "in its least possible minimum,"[188] and it is outdone only by Climacus's use of the word "moment" to designate the absolute paradox, a designation

---

[186] Ibid., p. 108.   [187] Ibid., p. 130.
[188] X⁶ B 121, p. 154 (*J. and P.*, V).

which expresses the paradox in the "most abbreviated form."[189]

With the *"nota bene* on the page of universal history" Climacus wishes to stress as the most important point that "the God" had lived as a historical figure at a specific time and yet was believed to be God. Therefore Climacus includes in this concise communication of "the content of Christianity" only the purely historical elements and omits the other dogmatic affirmations which concern faith in the Resurrection and the Ascension. Climacus is of the opinion that the first and greatest difficulty in Christianity is to believe that God once became this particular individual man.[190] The one who in faith first receives assurance of this will be led further to faith's assurance of the Resurrection and the Ascension. It must, however, be added that Climacus's brief "world-historical NB," in addition to what has been stated here, at the same time illuminates many other central points concerning Christianity;[191] but the most important is his emphasis on the historicity of Christianity.

Climacus is thinking of this primary and greatest difficulty when at the end of *Philosophical Fragments* he shows in some detail and through consistent thinking that where faith in the truth of Christianity is concerned the believers in all ages face the same crucial difficulty—namely, to believe the absurd. Climacus rejects all attempts to "prove" the truth of Christianity in order thereby to slip into Christianity more easily, since precisely by such "proofs" one erases the qualitative difference between the ordinary historical, which always can be made probable, and Christianity's historical side, which, seen from the point of view of reason as well as of history, represents the improbable.

---

[189] *Philosophical Fragments*, p. 64.

[190] The same view is later expressed by Anti-Climacus in *Practice [Training] in Christianity* (p. 84).

[191] One of the other points is discussed in Gregor Malantschuk, "Søren Kierkegaards Modifikationer af det kristelige" (*Dansk teologiske Tidsskrift*, XX, 1957, pp. 227ff.).

The *Concept of Anxiety* [*Dread*] supplements in a decisive way Climacus's analysis in *Philosophical Fragments* of Christianity's view of man and man's possible relationship to Christianity. Whereas the complex of problems in *Philosophical Fragments* moves on an abstract plane and views man only as a mental-spiritual being, Vigilius Haufniensis submits man to a psychological investigation. The single individual must constantly begin his development from below and, from the existential point of view, must go through a prolonged process before he has the courage and earnestness necessary to make the decision regarding Christianity. The individual is born with a certain intentional structure and tendencies which make up his psychosomatic given and is also exposed to environmental influences; these factors together have their significance in the individual's movement toward the understanding of existence which Christianity provides.

As a psychologist Vigilius Haufniensis in *The Concept of Anxiety* takes upon himself the task of depicting the mental-emotional aspects of man, and the whole content of this book may therefore be briefly characterized as a description of the "psychological, approximating states"[192] which precede Christianity's qualification of human existence. But Vigilius Haufniensis points unflaggingly to the fact that the actual transition from these mental-emotional positions to the new position which Christianity offers can occur only by a qualitative leap.

None of Kierkegaard's other works uses the category of the leap to the degree that *The Concept of Anxiety* does. This is in line with the whole complex of problems in this book, which concerns the relation of the race and the individual to guilt and the individual's movement toward personal guilt. Only the individual can really come under guilt, since only the individual can provide the basis for qualitative determinants, whereas the race will always belong under the objective (the quantitative). Vigilius

[192] *The Concept of Anxiety* [*Dread*], p. 105 (ed. tr.).

Haufniensis expresses this by saying that "the sinfulness of the race proceeds by quantitative determinants, while the individual by the qualitative leap participates in it."[193] Concerning the essential affinity of the individual, of individuality, with quality, Kierkegaard states: "There is really only one single quality—individuality. Everything revolves round this, and this is why everyone understands qualitatively with regard to himself what he understands quantitatively with regard to others. Individuality does this, but not everyone wants to have it."[194] Vigilius Haufniensis pursues further the thought presented by the earlier pseudonymous writers, namely, that guilt establishes the new quality which finally leads the individual out of the domain of the race and the universal, as, for example, in the case of the merman. The extensive use of the category of the leap in *The Concept of Anxiety* points specifically to the individual's participation in guilt. In a decisive sense the qualitative leap appears only in relation to Christianity.

In explaining the "psychological, approximating states" which lie prior to the qualitative leap into Christianity, Vigilius Haufniensis uses a well-considered dialectical procedure with special emphasis on the laws of existence, according to which no level of existence can be leaped over, since this would only bring confusion into human existence. Therefore he begins with the lower forms of existence and proceeds to the higher ones, which are then confronted by Christianity. It must be interposed here that this depiction of the levels of human existence [*Tilværelse*] also has an abstract quality, since it would go too far afield to give in a single book concrete characterizations of the separate levels, but the very fact that we are dealing with a psychological theme gives the book a less abstract character than *Philosophical Fragments*.

The main concern of Vigilius Haufniensis is to show how Christianity's dogma of original sin may be treated from a psychological point of view.

[193] Ibid., p. 31.
[194] V A 53 (*J. and P.*, II, 1986).

Before giving his positive contribution to the resolution of this question, Vigilius Haufniensis takes a few shots at the view of the relation of faith to the philosophy in Hegel-influenced dogmatics; here Vigilius Haufniensis is in complete harmony with Climacus in *Philosophical Fragments*, who draws the sharpest possible line between faith and knowledge. After briefly going through the formulation of the doctrine of original sin in the dogmatics of various churches, Vigilius Haufniensis takes a somewhat critical attitude to these formulations, since none of them considers the mental-emotional aspects of original sin.

Prior to stating his view on the connection between mental-emotional states and original sin, he defines more precisely certain definitions important for his interpretation—such as "the first sin," "the concept of innocence," and "the concept of the fall." Vigilius Haufniensis begins pondering original sin so far down the scale that he also touches on the difference between the animal and the human individual. He points to the underlying difference between animal and man as being that in the animal world the particular specimen of the species only repeats the characteristics of the species without contributing anything new to the development; whereas with man there begins a development which constantly creates new elements which alter the race and by changing the race preforms the new individuals. Vigilius Haufniensis believes firmly that the whole creative process which takes place in the single individual, which again influences the race, is due to man's connection with the eternal, which continually asserts itself more and more in the course of history. The essential difference between animal and man, then, is that the animal is but a transient, temporal being; whereas man is destined for eternity.

Man's attachment to the eternal also means that he is related to freedom—that is, has the possibility of determining his own movements himself; whereas the animal is bound to drives and instincts.

In his original state man, too, is bound to nature, living

only in the present, in the moment. The new state begins through the human individual's capacity to rise, through reflection, above nature, and to view the future as a possibility which both attracts him and frightens him. In this way the category of possibility comes to have crucial significance for all of human existence. Freedom makes its appearance with possibility, for not until the individual is confronted by possibility, or more correctly, by possibilities, can there be any question of a movement which is no longer determined by purely instinctive reactions and drives. Since possibility always concerns the future with its drawing power and its uncertainty, the state of the individual corresponding to possibility will be anxiety, which both desires and fears possibility.

Through his experience of anxiety and possibility, which are the distinguishing marks of freedom, the individual moves away from the original "immediate unity with his natural condition,"[195] where he lived in innocence and ignorance, and moves in the direction of knowledge and guilt.

The knowledge toward which the individual is moving is knowledge of the eternal, which the individual is supposed to possess as his own, but as long as this knowledge has not been attained, the individual continues to remain in the mental-emotional sphere. And even if a man meets the eternal as an external reality, without the dawn of the eternal in the individual himself through this meeting, he continues to remain in the mental-emotional sphere.

This establishing of frontiers with the aid of the eternal also has significance for Vigilius Haufniensis's more specific characterization of the two important concepts: anxiety and possibility.

Haufniensis places anxiety on the mental-emotional level; on a higher level, where spirit appears, despair, and later offense, correspond to anxiety and melancholy. Of anxiety's transition into melancholy, Vigilius Haufniensis

---

[195] *The Concept of Anxiety* [*Dread*], p. 37.

says: "Anxiety has here the same significance melancholy
has at a far later point where freedom, after having passed
through imperfect forms of its history, has to come to itself in a deeper sense."[196] And in the footnote to this he
refers to Judge William's description of the esthete's melancholy and despair in part one of *Either/Or*.

Vigilius Haufniensis is unable to find a new name for
possibility in the higher spiritual sphere and therefore calls
possibility on the mental-emotional level "possibility of
possibility."[197] Only the expression "possibility" is adequate
for the spiritual sphere of human existence and is legitimately used by Anti-Climacus in depicting this sphere in
The Sickness Unto Death.

In the progressive movement of the individual's historical development, anxiety and also "possibility of possibility" undergo a quantitative change within their boundaries.
On the lower level anxiety is mild "in its sweet feeling of
apprehension,"[198] later "more reflective"[199] and greater. A
similar change takes place with possibility; on the lower
levels the content of possibility, seen from a higher point
of view, is like a dream world; later the possibility becomes
more concrete.

However, possibility and anxiety do not follow an
ascending line but on every level take many shapes. With
reference to this Vigilius Haufniensis declares: ". . . in
possibility everything is possible, and he who truly was
brought up by possibility has comprehended the dreadful
as well as the smiling."[200] At the same time this statement
points up that the shapes of possibility and the expressions
of anxiety can be divided into two kinds: the negative with
its somber background and terror, and the positive with
its genial appearance, or they may be designated as the
possibilities of happiness and of unhappiness. Vigilius
Haufniensis's interest lies in the domain of negative possibilities, since they most clearly touch on the problem of
original sin, inasmuch as the problem of the first unhap-

[196] Ibid., p. 39. [197] Ibid., p. 38. [198] Ibid.
[199] Ibid., p. 47. [200] Ibid., p. 140.

piness and guilt, as previously indicated,[201] unambiguously points in this direction. But the positive possibilities also contain elements of anxiety and uncertainty, since there is no guarantee of a happy future, for "terror, perdition, annihilation dwell next door to every man. . . ."[202]

Vigilius Haufniensis shows further how the negative possibilities, which the race in the historical process must take over from the transgressions and guilt of the single individuals, wield an ever stronger influence upon succeeding individuals. This is extensively treated by Vigilius Haufniensis after he has attempted to interpret the Old Testament's account of the fall from his psychological point of view and demonstrated that sin still continues to enter the race in the same way, and therefore the story of the fall has current significance for every man. Before discussing under the heading "subjective anxiety" the influence of possibility and anxiety on the single individual through the race, he embarks on the subject he calls "objective anxiety." Objective anxiety expresses that not only the individual man but all existence [*Tilværelsen*] suffers the results of the fall.[203]

The special interest Vigilius Haufniensis displays in depicting subjective anxiety is consistent with Kierkegaard's prevailing tendency to concentrate on subjective actuality.

In discussing subjective anxiety, Vigilius Haufniensis shows how the influence of anxiety and possibility during the historical development of the race takes two directions as *"the consequence of the fact of generation"*[204] and as *"the consequence of the historical situation,"*[205] or in other words, as the consequence of heredity and environment.

[201] See pp. 222-25 above.

[202] *The Concept of Anxiety* [*Dread*], p. 140.

[203] A short but very clear account of what Kierkegaard understood by the fall and its consequences for the single individual and the race is given in *Edifying Discourses*, II, pp. 27ff. Vigilius Haufniensis refers to Romans 8:22 with regard to objective anxiety.

[204] *The Concept of Anxiety* [*Dread*], p. 56.

[205] Ibid., p. 66.

Under heredity Vigilius Haufniensis first discusses the factors which propagate the inheritance from generation to generation. Man and woman are the factors which carry the generation's inheritance further, and Vigilius Haufniensis describes more specifically their mental-emotional differences and their relation to anxiety. This leads to the question of sexuality, which Vigilius Haufniensis handles step-by-step according to the characteristic Kierkegaardian dialectic.

Vigilius Haufniensis begins by pointing out the sexual differences between animal and man. The animal is "enthralled in the blindness of instinct and acts blindly";[206] man begins in ignorance and innocence also in regard to the sexual but gradually becomes more conscious. The first reaction of spirit to the sexual is modesty: "The real significance of modesty is that spirit, so to speak, cannot recognize itself as the extreme point of the synthesis."[207] Spirit is here understood in its expanded meaning, therefore also as its harbinger on the lower level.

The sexual impulse reaches a certain climax when it is united with the erotic, such as love between man and woman. But the erotic still does not represent the spiritual, being merely "the union of the psychical and the physical," with beauty as its visible expression. The new spiritual element is first heralded in Socrates's conception, which from his ironic point of view has "neutralized" the significance of the erotic and beauty. But Christianity was the first to want "to lead the spirit further"[208] and therefore suspends the erotic, as Haufniensis says, in order to subjugate the sexual and the erotic to responsibility and to the demands of the spirit.

In discussing anxiety Vigilius Haufniensis considers it most important to point out that heredity can make the individual suffer the negative consequences of heredity. "What the Scripture teaches, that God visits the sins of the fathers upon the children unto the third and fourth

[206] Ibid., p. 61. [207] Ibid.
[208] Ibid., p. 63.

generation, life itself proclaims in a loud enough voice."[209] Through the guilt of the father the individual seems predestined to perpetrate the transgressions himself, and possibility therefore seems to become actualized without the individual's consent. Vigilius Haufniensis says of these negative possibilities in their highest potency: "The frightful maximum here is that anxiety about sin produces sin."[210]

But Vigilius Haufniensis, since he presupposes the freedom of the individual, cannot go so far that in some cases he grants that heredity completely predisposes the individual to fall, since on the one hand this would destroy the individual as an independent being and on the other hand would destroy the leap from possibility to actuality, which he continually stresses.

The other area in which the race can influence the single individual negatively is the environment with its knowledge of negativity and the resulting "power of example."[211] But no matter how powerful this influence, it, too, for the same reasons can never become absolute.

In discussing the problem of anxiety Vigilius Haufniensis makes a penetrating analysis of the relation between time and eternity. From a dialectical point of view it is quite appropriate to take up the question in this book. Anxiety and possibility imply that the individual rises above his original ties to momentary actuality and by means of reflection forms ideas not only of his past but primarily of his future. In this way the whole question of time arises for the individual, and time does not embrace merely the present but the past and the future. According to Haufniensis this new movement signifies at the same time that the eternal in man, even if as yet inadequate, begins to assert itself in the historical development of the individual. The individual, who is constituted as a synthesis of time and eternity, thereby moves in the direction of a greater understanding of the eternal as a qualification of

[209] Ibid., p. 65.   [210] Ibid. (ed. tr.).
[211] Ibid., p. 67.

his being. But at the same time the eternal as the transcendent can reveal itself as a reality beyond the compass of the human, something Vigilius Haufniensis also points out. He treats both these modes of the eternal in discussing the problem of time and also in later sections.

Regarding the problem of time and eternity, Vigilius Haufniensis scrutinizes three widely separated viewpoints, showing the three different positions in man's gradual movement toward greater accentuation of the eternal. These three world-historical positions are represented by paganism, Judaism, and Christianity. Every new and intensified appearance of the eternal has a retroactive significance for the understanding of time and temporal existence.

In paganism, where the eternal shows itself only in its first, imperfect form, the temporal itself has little meaning. It is regarded as "non-being,"[212] and the highest paganism can come with respect to the problem of time and eternity is to conceive of the eternal as an abstraction, an analogue to philosophy's achievement in the field of ontology.[213]

A new level is introduced in Judaism; temporality is demarcated by the recognition of a transcendence which lies above and beyond the temporal. But this partially abstract perception of eternity still does not have a decisive influence upon an accentuation of the meaning of time.

Not until the coming of Christianity does something totally new appear in its fullness, and then time and decisions in time also acquire infinite weight for the single individual. Vigilius Haufniensis points out that only this

[212] Ibid., p. 74.

[213] See p. 100 above. Of Christianity's gradually more concrete estimate of this "non-being" Vigilius Haufniensis declares: "The Christian now takes the position that non-being is everywhere present as the Nothing out of which all is created, as appearance and vanity, as sin, as sensuousness divorced from the spirit, as the temporal forgotten by eternity; wherefore the whole point is to do away with it and get being in its stead." *The Concept of Anxiety* [*Dread*], p. 74. We recognize the line from the creation account through Judaism to Christianity.

understanding of the relation between time and eternity, with an infinite accentuation of the past as well as of the future, permits Christianity's important dogmatic qualifications, such as conversion, reconciliation, resurrection, and judgment, to come into their own.

The next passages in Vigilius Haufniensis's account of the problem of anxiety are interesting in that they show how the single individual must first of all, now or later, dialectically and existentially move through the levels of paganism and Judaism in order to reach a real meeting with Christianity. Here Vigilius Haufniensis-Kierkegaard is unmistakably building upon his own experiences from earliest childhood, when he fought his way out of anxiety and the dark suspicion of a connection between racial guilt and his own guilt in order to reach the Christian view of life—in short, from the period of his life when the burning question for him was "to what extent it is fate and to what extent guilt"[214] that leads him into his existential difficulties.

Significantly, the description of the way toward Christianity is introduced by a criticism of his own age, which is charged with "absence of spirit" or is called "paganism . . . within Christianity,"[215] in which there certainly is familiarity with Christianity but only as knowledge, as "rote learning,"[216] without any relevance of this knowledge to existence. Vigilius Haufniensis believes that original paganism is preferable to paganism in Christendom because "the former is oriented *towards* spirit, the latter is oriented *away* from spirit."[217] This last state engenders "the anxiety of absence of spirit."

The rest of the book describes the various movements through the levels of paganism and Judaism to a confrontation with Christianity and the consequences of such a confrontation.

Dialectically and existentially, it is very important to note that during this whole progressive movement Vigilius

---

[214] *The Concept of Anxiety* [*Dread*], p. 107.
[215] Ibid., p. 83.   [216] Ibid., p. 85.   [217] Ibid.

Haufniensis gives a detailed account only of man's mental-emotional possibilities on the esthetic plane and merely approaches the frontier of the spiritual in man.[218] On the other hand, a gradually increasing attention is given to the "object of anxiety"[219] in portraying the positions of paganism, Judaism, and Christianity.

In discussing paganism Vigilius Haufniensis shows that the spiritual does not really make its appearance here. The synthesis contains only a unity of body and soul; thus man is still entirely on the psychosomatic level. At this level fate is the highest power and is the object of anxiety which sets limits to externally oriented activity. The essential scope of anxiety lies within paganism, since the individual as yet has not come into relation to the eternal, and fate does not express anything eternal, either. Therefore, according to Vigilius Haufniensis, man still lives in ignorance, which characterizes the stage in which anxiety essentially dominates. Regarded from a higher viewpoint, fate is a nothing, and thus it can be said that man's anxiety in paganism is an anxiety about nothing.[220] In the next stages it is different.

Vigilius Haufniensis believes that the majority of men do not discover this connection between anxiety and fate, since in their anxiety for the future they are related to anxiety through middle terms and external interests. This is why Napoleon as a genius of action is used as an example of anxiety about fate and nothing. Napoleon did not need to consider intermediaries and therefore stood face to face with fate and all its ambiguities and contingencies seen from a historical point of view. Various elements in Napoleon's relation to fate are portrayed.

The element of contingency or chance which fate contains is one of the two essential aspects in the definition of fate. According to Kierkegaard, represented by Vigilius Haufniensis, all things and all circumstances have an

[218] See p. 283 below.
[219] *The Concept of Anxiety* [*Dread*], pp. 92, 99.
[220] Ibid., p. 87.

essence-aspect and a being-aspect; contingency is fate's being-aspect, whereas its essence comes under necessity, which is characteristic of all essence-determinants. For this reason Vigilius Haufniensis defines fate as "a unity of necessity and contingency."[221]

The genius and any other man can go beyond the domain of fate only by "a religious collecting of oneself,"[222] which here means by turning away from external actuality and concentrating on one's interiority. Vigilius Haufniensis stresses "what torments"[223] the individual (genius) will go through by this turning back into himself. One is tempted at this point to think that for the aspect of Kierkegaard's personality represented by Vigilius Haufniensis the possibility is open for an expansion of genius into the external world, but that he chooses a religious concentrating, which, in Haufniensis's opinion, changes the spontaneous genius into a "religious genius," which agrees with Kierkegaard's conception of himself as a religious genius.[224] The religious genius is considered in the discussion of the next level, anxiety in Judaism.

In a decisive way Judaism is farther advanced than paganism in that the object of anxiety is a "something."[225] In Judaism man has knowledge of a transcendent power and can come under the qualification of guilt, which was not possible in paganism. It is impossible to be guilty in relation to fate.

The fact that man comes within the category of anxiety also in Judaism is bound up with Judaism's not having gone beyond the psychological level. Progress can take place only if a person, after coming into relation with an eternal transcendent power, finds his way to an eternal decision in his own interior being. This means that, face to face with God, he must go through the absolute move-

---

[221] Ibid., p. 87 (ed. tr.).   [222] Ibid., p. 91 (ed. tr.).

[223] Ibid., p. 92.

[224] To avoid a misunderstanding of this expression, see ibid., p. 102, and X² A 578 (*J. and P.*, II, 2092).

[225] *The Concept of Anxiety* [Dread], p. 92.

ment of repentance and come totally under guilt. Vigilius Haufniensis's conclusion is really only an elaboration of the law of existence Judge William formulates in these words: ". . . for the absolute as absolute can only be for the absolute."[226] This means that if through relation to the eternal a person does not become conscious of his own eternal qualification, he falls back into the qualifications of finiteness.[227]

To explain more explicitly man's relation to the transcendental power, Vigilius Haufniensis uses the religious genius. In the following words he further explains his motivations for using the genius as an example of how "individualities" within Christianity must, during their historical evolution, repeat the previous stages before reaching the level of Christianity: "Here again [the] genius evinces clearly what in less original men exists in such a way that it cannot easily be reduced to categories. By and large the genius differs from other men merely in the fact that within his historical presuppositions he consciously begins just as originally as Adam did. Every time a genius is born, existence as it were is put to the test, for he surveys and lives through all the past until he catches up with himself."[228]

Here in all clarity it is stated that in order to attain the higher levels every individual must live through the preceding level in his existence, but that the genius experiences the repetition of "universal history"[229] in a more complete way.

The religious genius Vigilius Haufniensis now uses as an example is different from the genius on the level of immediacy in that he turns away from the external to his

[226] *Either/Or*, II, p. 217; see pp. 294, 310 below.
[227] On this point these words from *Either/Or* may be cited again: "Even the Jew who chose God did not choose absolutely, for he chose, indeed, the absolute, but did not choose it absolutely, and thereby it ceased to be the absolute and became a finite thing" (*Either/Or*, II, p. 218).
[228] *The Concept of Anxiety* [*Dread*], pp. 93-99.
[229] Ibid., p. 93

inward self, where he meets God through conscience. "For by the fact that he turns toward himself he turns *eo ipso* toward God, and it is a well-established ceremonial convention that if the finite spirit would see God it must begin by being guilty. In turning toward himself he discovers guilt."[230]

In this way the question of freedom and responsibility becomes acute for the religious genius, and he discovers his own guilt on a constantly greater scale. This discovery of his guilt reaches its climax when the individual (the genius) takes upon himself in possibility all temporal guilt as his own. "At last it is as if the guilt of the whole world united to make him guilty, or in other words, as if by becoming guilty he became guilty of the guilt of the whole world."[231] Here the individual reaches the boundary line of the psychological and can go no farther by himself.

Christianity is the first to confirm that what the single individual has discovered as his possibilities in guilt is also an actuality. Christianity places the single individual in the category of sin and seeks to enlighten him on the difference *"in concreto"*[232] between good and evil; this distinction could not even be found in paganism, and in Judaism it was given only in its abstract form.

In Christianity the single individual is confronted by "the qualitative leap" in its decisive meaning, and here two fundamental approaches are possible: (1) Either the person flatly refuses to submit to Christianity's characterization of himself as sinner; he then suffers from "anxiety over the evil," essentially marked by his unwillingness to admit his absolute weakness, even if he is not unsympathetic toward Christianity. Vigilius Haufniensis says of this positivity in "anxiety over the evil": "This formation,

---

[230] Ibid., p. 96.

[231] Ibid., p. 98. Here one could draw a parallel to Father Zossima's words in Dostoevski's *Brothers Karamozov* "that we are all guilty in everything."

[232] *The Concept of Anxiety* [Dread], p. 99.

viewed from a higher standpoint, is in the good,"[233] and therefore the individual has anxiety over the evil.

(2) Or one is in flight from Christianity, wants to avoid meeting it and tries to build up a defense against it. This attitude Vigilius Haufniensis characterizes as "anxiety over the good," and he believes that in this expression he has found "a key which opens the door wherever there is a trace of the phenomenon"[234] of the demonic.

In describing the position "anxiety over the evil," in which the individual is still unwilling to acknowledge his total guilt, Vigilius Haufniensis gives examples which in a gradually ascending scale show man's impotence before sin. This impotence culminates in a condition where even repentance prior to the fall cannot prevent it. Vigilius Haufniensis alleges that anxiety is at its peak in this condition.

It is then shown that only "faith" can create a new point of departure. Faith alone can conquer anxiety and place man in the right relation to repentance. With this the transition from the mental-emotional level to the spiritual sphere is accomplished. Vigilius Haufniensis also calls attention to the fact that "everything that has here been expounded belongs to the sphere of psychology,"[235] which has the task of describing man's condition before sin entered as a new qualification by way of Christianity.

The demonic as "anxiety over the good" pertains primarily to man's mental-emotional side, but in his repeated denial of the eternal and defense of himself against it the demonic also takes on spiritual forms. Therefore Vigilius Haufniensis declares that the demonic "belongs to all spheres, the somatic, the psychic, the pneumatic."[236]

In clarifying the nature of the demonic under these three points of view, Vigilius Haufniensis gives a most penetrating and comprehensive description of man's attempt to avoid coming into existential contact with Christianity.

[233] Ibid., p. 106.
[235] Ibid., p. 104.
[234] Ibid., p. 113n.
[236] Ibid., p. 109.

The section "Freedom lost pneumatically" may be regarded as an announcement of further treatment of the problem of anxiety, which is done dialectically in *The Sickness Unto Death*. The higher expression of anxiety, when it comes in contact with the eternal, becomes despair (which later may be intensified to offense), the different forms of which are presented in *The Sickness Unto Death*. Vigilius Haufniensis's "Schema for the exclusion or the lack of inwardness" forms a connecting link to the first section of *The Sickness Unto Death*. Both positions call attention to the misrelation which arises in man when the elements of the synthesis, the eternal and the temporal, do not come into proper relation to each other. But in *The Concept of Anxiety* this is viewed predominantly from the mental-emotional side, and one is compelled again and again to admire the sensitive dialectical differentiation with which Vigilius Haufniensis is able to describe the manifold aspects of this misrelation or "the exclusion of inwardness" in man.

Vigilius Haufniensis concludes *The Concept of Anxiety* by pointing out that not only the person who by inheritance and situations is thrown into anxiety can move toward a higher spiritual position but also one who in a quiet life has been spared these external stimuli. The latter, as "possibility's pupil,"[237] "assaults the infinite"[238] by identifying with another's unhappiness and guilt. He will discover this by anxiety, which becomes for him "a ministering spirit,"[239] and he will also experience that all the possibilities of anxiety can be overcome by "the anticipation of faith."[240]

Compared to the books discussed up to now, *Stages on Life's Way* is a much more ample representation of the dialectical points of view. This is due in the first place to the intention in the preceding books to depict only single levels of development, and secondly, to the fact that the

[237] Ibid., p. 143 (ed. tr.).   [238] Ibid., p. 144.
[239] Ibid., p. 142 (ed. tr.).   [240] Ibid., p. 141.

individual (A.), moving through these levels, has not as yet reached his high point. Not until *Stages on Life's Way* is a comprehensive survey made of the prior points of view, and here the person portrayed reaches an understanding of his difficulties in existence. In the most important part of *Stages on Life's Way*, " 'Guilty?'/'Not Guilty?' ", the struggling individual reaches a decision and from his newly won position can survey the levels he has left behind in his existential movement. In fact, *Stages* provides an example of what is meant by Climacus's expression, *"the simultaneity of the individual factors of subjectivity in the existing subject."*[241] The human subject possesses in this simultaneity all the elements of his experience. Through the reproduction of these elements the law of repetition comes to play an important role, since it reveals how the past stages look in a new light.

By beginning with the third and most important section of *Stages*, it is possible to show how the newly won position bears on the past positions in a transforming way. In " 'Guilty?'/'Not Guilty?' " we have the temporary culmination of the existential movement which is introduced in *Either/Or* with "the unhappiest man's" complex of problems, which Judge William tries vainly to resolve in the second part of *Either/Or*. Within the sphere of ethical humanism, the next attempt to resolve these same difficulties is made in *Repetition*, where the unhappy man looks for a solution by immersing himself in the book of Job in order to find a way back to the repetition of his lost first spontaneity. But the way back to the first happiness of immediacy and to a positive relation to the universal is blocked off for the unhappy man. In *Fear and Trembling* the unhappy individual compares his situation to Abraham's, who lost everything but in faith won it back. But here the realization breaks through that his similarity to Abraham is inadequate since the unhappy man is placed outside the universal because of a guilt, and his first move-

[241] *Postscript,* p. 307.

ment cannot be the movement of resignation, as with Abraham, but must be the movement of repentance. This position coincides with the merman's, who carries a guilt from his "preexistence." As long as he does not make the movement of repentance, he must be regarded as the prototype of Quidam in the third part of *Stages*. Quidam begins as a demonic figure, but later is "a demoniac in a religious direction,"[242] which also means that the healing process has started. All the characters prior to Quidam represent the concrete line in Kierkegaard's authorship up to *Concluding Unscientific Postscript*, and in Quidam's account of his existential position this concretion reaches its culminating point. Through Quidam's portrayal of his life history we get the most ample concrete characterization of the nature of the difficulties which prevented all those other characters from coming into a positive relation to the universal.

The humorist Quidam concentrates entirely upon his interior actuality, which is, in fact, a task for the humorist since the obstacles arise within. The dialectically important point about Quidam is that without a pseudonym as intermediary he himself sketches his progress from his demonic position toward the religious. With this sketch Quidam himself as an individual reproduces the double movement. This is characteristic of the position of humor, where the person is dealing chiefly with his own inner struggles and where the external factors can only be an occasion. In Quidam, therefore, we have a concrete example of "double-reflection" in its highest form, namely, in its function during an existential process. This is confirmed by the following journal entry: "This experiment (Guilty?/Not Guilty?) is the first attempt in all the pseudonymous books at an existential dialectic in double-reflection. It is not the communication which is in the form of double-reflection (for all pseudonyms are that), *but* the existing person himself exists in this. Thus he does not give up immediacy but

[242] *Stages*, p. 363.

keeps it and yet gives it up, keeps love's desire and yet gives it up."[243]

Farther along in the same entry and in the one following, it appears that Kierkegaard, as early as the writing of *Either/Or*, considered it his task to work out "the experiment" but, as he says, in order that it "might be done in proper categories enormous detours would have to be made."[244] He traveled these "detours" in the preceding authorship in order to depict first the levels up to the stage of humor. "The experiment is the only thing which has had considerable preliminary work prior to its being written. Already while writing *Either/Or* I had it in mind and a lyrical hint was frequently and casually dropped there."

Kierkegaard's pseudonyms describe the "detours" particularly in *Repetition* and *Fear and Trembling*. Concerning the course of this description, which begins with A.'s position as the exception in *Either/Or* and ends with a definitive clarification of the same position through Quidam, Kierkegaard writes: "In every one of the pseudonymous works the theme of 'the single individual' appears—yes, certainly, and the following is one of several ways: the pseudonymous writers concentrate upon working out the universal, the single individual [*den Enkelte*], the special individual [*den særlige Enkelte*], the exception, in order to find the meaning of the special individual in his suffering and his extraordinariness.

"The Judge in *Either/Or* had already posed this with respect to the exception from being married.

"Then came *Fear and Trembling—Repetition*, the psychological experiment—all commentaries on the category: the single individual.

"But in relation to the reading public, the pseudonymous writers themselves as well as the books affirm the category of the single individual."[245]

We will now take a closer look at Quidam's complex of

[243] VII¹ B 83, p. 276 (*J. and P.*, V).
[244] VII¹ B 84 (*J. and P.*, V).
[245] X¹ A 139 (*J. and P.*, V); see *The Point of View*, p. 124.

problems. He relates the story of his engagement by first of all recollecting it; this he does in the morning. Next he concentrates on what has been recollected, utilizing the rigorous viewpoints of ethics; this he does at night. Thus a conflict between the elements of the given actuality and the guiding and judging demands of ethics is introduced, and this becomes the content of "a story of suffering." By this interior confrontation between the given actuality and ethics he is led to the conclusion that not only did the engagement under the given presupposition have to be broken but that he at the same time became guilty in relation to his beloved. The guilt here has a definite concrete shape, and the possible repentance must also be entirely concrete.

In his depiction of the way to an understanding of the concrete guilt, he points out that this last solution—breaking the engagement—was the only one possible for him. The example of Job could take him no further. Unlike Job, he could not turn back to the first immediacy. To use Job as a paradigm was also dubious because the struggling individual in this case was as yet involved with the transcendental as something external; the individual as yet had no consciousness of the kind of ethics in which God communicates with man through the ethical in the form of conscience. Quidam says: "Hence it is a weak point in the structure of the Book of Job that God appears in the clouds and also appears as the most accomplished dialectician; for what makes God the terrible dialectician He is, is precisely the fact that one has Him at very much closer quarters, and therewith the softest whisper is more blissful, and the softest whisper is more terrible, than seeing Him enthroned upon the clouds and hearing Him in the thunder. Hence one cannot argue dialectically with Him, for all the dialectical power in the soul of the man concerned God uses against this man."[246]

Alluding to Abraham and other examples, Quidam

[246] *Stages*, p. 292.

speaks also of "a teleological suspension of the ethical,"[247] but now there is a clearer recognition of the difficulties bound up with "a collision of suspension with relation to a present actuality,"[248] for example, how difficult it can be to decide if and when the suspension can be discontinued.

Quidam generally alleges "melancholy"[249] to be the source of the obstacles against which his ethical insight must contend and where a clarification must be worked for. This melancholy was also encountered in the individual forerunners to Quidam. The pseudonymous publisher of "A Story of Suffering," the observer Frater Taciturnus, explains that "therefore melancholy must have accompanied him through the previous stages."[250]

Quidam, however, does not leave us high and dry with respect to the origin of this melancholy. In "the passages entered the fifth of each month"[251] we find the secret sources of the melancholy. But Quidam does not entirely lift the veil from the secret. The more deeply hidden causes of his difficulties he mentions only indirectly and in symbolic form, as indicated by Frater Taciturnus: "In order to throw light upon his reserve I have introduced in the diary passages in which he gropes as it were after an expression for his own reserve. He never expresses himself directly but indirectly."[252]

Of these inserted passages[253] it can briefly be said that they represent the negative sides in man, attributable to heredity, environment, and individual guilt, the very forms of guilt discussed by Vigilius Haufniensis in *The Concept of Anxiety*. These negative elements permit the individual to remain doubtful about the degree to which he is guilty or not-guilty, until he, as in "A Story of Suffering," penetrates them with ethical passion and takes them upon himself

[247] Ibid., pp. 218f.   [248] Ibid., p. 245.
[249] Ibid., pp. 345, 357ff.   [250] Ibid., p. 390.
[251] V B 148:25 (*J. and P.*, V).
[252] *Stages*, p. 389.
[253] See Lina Zeuthen, *Søren Kierkegaards hemmelige Note* (Copenhagen, 1951).

as his own guilt. Because of their indirect form[254] these inserted passages must be interpreted circumspectly, but particular ones clearly point to heredity or paternal influences.

With his indirect account in the inserted passages of the various reasons for his melancholy, Quidam empties the "preexistence" in which his prototype, the merman, was imprisoned, and Quidam can now move toward the second higher immediacy after having lost the first.

At the end of the book the humorous observer, Frater Taciturnus, who has an auxiliary function with respect to Quidam, characterizes from many angles this progress toward the new immediacy and relates it primarily to the tragic, which in its highest form as tragic guilt contributes the last position within the domain of the purely human. This tragic position, however, still contains the unresolved question of guilty or not-guilty, but the religious position cannot be satisfied with anything less than bringing the person totally within the sphere of guilt. As long as guilt does not have this absolute character, repentance also is "dialectically prevented from coming to a head,"[255] according to Frater Taciturnus in a chapter heading. But, as we have seen, the tragic in unhappy love has its deepest cause in psychological givens of heredity and environment; therefore Frater Taciturnus can go on in his chapter heading and say: ". . . *the last confine between the esthetic and the religious lies in the psychological.*" Frater Taciturnus's reflections at the end of the book call attention to the psychological side, which is confronted with the ethical during the personality's movement toward the religious, understood as the second immediacy,[256] which can be found only through Christianity.

From this extreme point in Quidam's movement toward the religious we return to the first part of *Stages*. Here we find a repetition of the various positions described in the preceding works, but now seen in the light of Quidam's

254 V B 148:29 (*J. and P.*, V).

255 *Stages*, p. 404.   256 Ibid., p. 435.

standpoint, representing the final position of humor. The viewpoint of the five esthetes in "*In vino veritas*" is a negative counterpart to Quidam's positive movement toward the religious, and it is actually the relation between these two opposite positions which forms a new "Either/Or" in *Stages on Life's Way*, of which Kierkegaard says: "*Three stages and still an Either/Or.*"[257] Judge William's standpoint, as the second stage placed between the esthetic and the religious stages, has lost its alternative character and finds itself, as will be seen, in a defensive position in relation to the others, even if it stands closer to Quidam's movement toward the religious.

What we note particularly in the standpoints repeated in "*In vino veritas*" is that they are not only the obviously demonic attitudes, such as Johannes the Seducer's, characterized as such, but that the originally positive attitudes, now looked at from a higher stage, are now also considered to be demonic. This applies to Constantin Constantius as well, who has an assisting role in *Repetition* and despite his ironic attitude reveals an understanding of the movement toward the transcendent, which the young man finally attempts. But in "*In vino veritas*" Constantin Constantius falls within the category of the demonic. The same applies to Victor Eremita, who represents resignation. Resignation has a positive significance on certain levels in the existential movement, but as a fixed standpoint without relation to the next higher position it also falls within the demonic. The one person in this group of esthetes judged most leniently is the young man; Climacus later says of him that he is still "a hopeful case,"[258] whereas it would be "ridiculous" to try "to warn Victor Eremita, Constantin Constantius, the fashion tailor, or a Johannes the Seducer. . . ."[259]

Through these characters the humorist now evaluates his own earlier thoughts and positions in the esthetic period. The distortion of these attitudes is demonstrated

[257] VI B 41:10 (*J. and P.*, V).
[258] *Postscript*, p. 264.   [259] Ibid., p. 263.

by the one-sided characterization of woman;[260] she is denied the possibility of the existentially deeper meaning in life which she does have, according to Judge William's view. After Quidam has himself undertaken a movement away from his esthetic past, the viewpoints of the esthetes remain as "a recollection."[261] William's universally human-ethical standpoint in *Stages*, compared to his position in *Either/Or*, reveals some changes. In *Either/Or*, says Kierkegaard, ". . . there were only two positions and the Judge was completely victorious";[262] in *Stages* there are three positions and the Judge, who finds himself in the middle between the esthetic and the religious positions, must defend himself against both sides. From what he says, he is completely unsympathetic with the five esthetes, but this is not simply a sign of strength on his part, for he himself is in danger of slipping over into the esthetic category; in fact, he is more and more taken up with purely temporal interests. On the other hand, he does show great understanding of the difficulties which the religious exception, alias Quidam, will encounter on his way, but warns strongly against setting foot in the "narrow pass" the exception must go through. The most important point

[260] Kierkegaard uses the title of Henrich Steffens's book *Caricaturen des Heiligsten* (Leipzig, 1819) to characterize the speeches in which the five esthetes express their views on woman: "The purpose of the 5 speakers in '*In vino veritas*,' all of whom are *Karrikaturen des Heiligsten*, is to illuminate women essentially but nevertheless falsely. The Young Man understands women solely from the point of view of sex; Constantin Constantius considers the psychic aspect: faithlessness —that is, of frivolousness; Victor Eremita conceives of the female sex psychically as sex, her significance for the male, i.e., that there is none; the milliner considers the sensual aspect outside the essentially erotic in the vanity which is more pronounced in a woman's relationship to women, for as an author has said, women do not adorn themselves for men but for each other; Johannes the Seducer considers the purely sensual factor with respect to the erotic." V A 110 (*J. and P.*, V).

[261] *Stages*, p. 25; *Postscript*, p. 265.

[262] VI A 41 (*J. and P.*, V).

in the Judge's changed attitude in *Stages*, however, is his perception that marriage, which he has heatedly defended against all attacks, is not "the highest life."[263] With this, the basis for the attitude he has had up to now and for his emphasis on the idea of secular vocation as most important in life goes to pieces. The Judge now stands divided and "struggling in life"[264] between the radical points of view, yet realizing that the next positive movement from his position can only occur in the direction of the religious.

If the Judge's stage is conceived as one of the simultaneous factors in "the existing subjectivity," then this means that as far as the existing humorist Quidam is concerned he must on the one hand look upon the Judge's stance of ethical humanism as a stage already transcended but at the same time must recognize that it was from this stage, rising up before him as a tempting possibility, that he moved toward religious actuality. Therefore this stage also is included among the "simultaneous factors."[265] Looking at it from a higher level, one could say that through the presentation of the Judge's position of ethical humanism the point is advanced that this view is on the way to resolution and must end either in a demonic position or be renewed by a decisive relation to Christianity.

While *Stages* depicts "the simultaneity of factors in the existing individual" who moves through the domain of humor, which is "very extensive, precisely as constituting the boundary of the religious,"[266] Climacus in *Concluding Unscientific Postscript* gives a detailed account of all the dialectical and existential factors treated in the authorship up to this point. Dialectically, *Concluding Unscientific Postscript* is chiefly characterized by Climacus's arrangement of two developmental sequences alongside one another: the individual-concrete and the universal-abstract. Regarding the first sequence, Climacus himself indicates

---

[263] *Stages*, p. 166.
[265] *Postscript*, p. 307.
[264] VI A 41 (*J. and P.*, V).
[266] Ibid., p. 403.

the necessity of giving a concrete example of such a developmental sequence as a countermove to the speculative thinking of the day, and he has followed with interest the different pseudonyms's presentation of this line,[267] reaching its high point in Quidam's position. In *Concluding Unscientific Postscript* Climacus introduces this individual-concrete sequence with his discussion of "a contemporary effort in Danish literature," which is placed after Climacus's criticism of Hegelian speculation. The universal-abstract sequence of development in *Concluding Unscientific Postscript* is a widening and deepening of the purely abstract Socratic standpoint in *Philosophical Fragments* together with several common views from the preceding works, a widening and a deepening that eventually embraces the sum total of human existential experience prior to its meeting with the specifically Christian[268] religiousness.

In Climacus's conception of the relation between these two existence-sequences, the description of an individual-concrete line of development holds only for a single individual and thus cannot serve as a paradigm for other individuals. The individual points of departure may in fact be quite different for different individuals, since every one has his distinctive mark and his distinctive given of heredity and environment. Moreover, in his existence the individual is continually faced with the choice between two opposite possibilities, for there is no absolute certainty in existence. For these reasons a description of the individual-concrete line can only be given by the individual concerned. Nor can the individual-concrete line ever be looked upon as concluded as long as the individual is in existence. It is with this last condition in mind that Climacus states that "no system of existence [*Tilværelsens*] can be given."[269] This cannot be completed as long as there are any single individuals, because every existence always means an incompleteness, hence the impossibility of a

---

[267] Ibid., pp. 224ff.; X⁵ B 168, p. 362 (*J. and P.*, V), and B 211, p. 394 (*J. and P.*, V).

[268] *Postscript*, p. 494.   [269] Ibid., pp. 99, 107 (ed. tr.).

system. The pseudonyms have shown how such an individual-concrete sequence of development looks in existence. But every individual existential movement must be regarded from universal dialectical points of view and in such a way that they may be used to orient the particular existing individual. Climacus propounds these dialectical points of view particularly in the theory of the stages, and he now uses them to give an expanded account of the Socratic position in *Philosophical Fragments*. In *Concluding Unscientific Postscript* he deals chiefly with the universal sequence. Because the other pseudonyms had worked extensively and satisfactorily with the individual sequence, Climacus neither could nor needed to do anything but briefly touch on it in the inserted "appendix." Since this line has already been discussed, we will go immediately to a more detailed account of the universal-abstract sequence.

A quick comparison of *Philosophical Fragments* and *Concluding Unscientific Postscript* clearly indicates that in the later work Climacus attaches primary importance to a widening and a deepening of the sphere of the human. In the earlier work, treatment of the Socratic point of view, designated by the letter A in contrast to Christianity designated by the letter B (similar to the later distinction between Religiousness A and B), takes up only a small part of the book. The remainder of the book treats Christianity's qualitatively new point of view and man's confrontation by it. In *Concluding Unscientific Postscript*, however, the introduction to Section A and Section A itself occupy a central position, and only at the end is Religiousness B briefly skimmed over. Thus it is clear that Climacus's chief aim is to give extensive treatment of the human, amplifying the very abstract and one-sided demarcation of the domain of the human in *Philosophical Fragments*; he does not need to pay special attention to the psychological givens of human existence, since they are described in detail in *The Concept of Anxiety*. Climacus can be satisfied with merely mentioning this book in his "appendix" and touching on its main points in a few observations.[270] In *Concluding Unscientific Postscript*, therefore, man is depicted as being in contact with the eternal, which means that we find ourselves beyond the borders of the psychological in the narrower sense of the word.[271]

In contrast to *Philosophical Fragments, Concluding Unscientific Postscript* develops in such a way that first of all the consciousness of the eternal, Socratically understood as a man-inhabiting possibility, and then Christianity's offer of "an eternal happiness" evoke the greatest existential effort on man's part to realize these eternal qualifications in his existence. But at the farthest frontier and at its highest potentiation, this effort discloses man's total impotence and total guilt in relation to the absolute good which man wanted to attain by himself. With its qualitatively new category Christianity is prepared to explain to man that he is a sinner. For Climacus the central concept in this "approximation" of the human to Christianity, which can be attained only by a leap, is appropriation. Out of this concept the separate stages of this "approximation" can be more specifically defined.

Since the concept of appropriation is the key concept for Climacus, and despite his respect for the purely objective disciplines where appropriation plays no role, he concentrates on those truths which can be appropriated by the subject and in which appropriation plays an essential part. This can be said only of the ethical norms which Christian as well as humanistic ethics propounds, and of the religious, understood as an offer of "repetition" (salvation), consequently of a qualitative change in man through

[270] Mention is made of Socrates's lack of the presuppositions for recognizing original sin and of its important supplemental significance on the way toward Christianity. Ibid., pp. 186-87, 470, 517.

[271] Kierkegaard divides the psychological in three main ways: man's mental-emotional states in an ordinary sense, man's condition in his contact with the man-inhabiting eternal, and collisions arising from Christianity. See pp. 36, 260-61 above.

his qualification as sinner and through the offer of salvation.

Climacus's interest in appropriation as the essential in the realms of ethics and Christianity places him in opposition to all those in Christendom to think that the most important task in Christianity is to provide an objective version of Christian doctrine. Their efforts go into creating a reliable point of departure for the faith. Climacus runs through the principal forms of these efforts. The Catholic Church secures itself in the last resort by the authority of a completed objective view of Christianity. Protestantism attempts to create an objective and dependable foundation for the Christian faith by means of comprehensive historical and exigetical studies. In Denmark Grundtvig tries to give a brief objective recapitulation of Christian teaching in his theory of the Christian congregation's unaltered confession of faith through the ages and "the word in connection with the sacraments."[272] Climacus also mentions how men want to "prove" the truth of Christianity by the fact that it has lasted all these centuries. Finally he discusses speculative attempts to secure the foundations of Christianity by means of Hegelian philosophy.

Climacus points out the barrenness of these efforts and the mistaken zeal that is manifested; it may be said in general that the weakness in all these attempts resides in man's wanting to find absolute objective security where such a thing simply cannot be had. Christianity's fundamental claim is that it is founded on a historical fact, but for all things historical it holds that one can never be completely sure of their truth, at most one can only attain an approximation. But even if a person thought it possible to find an objective certainty about the truth of Christianity, he would still be faced by the essential difficulty in Christianity—namely, how does the individual person become a Christian.

But Climacus still has an argument up his sleeve which

[272] *Postscript,* p. 37.

reveals the dubiousness of all attempts to render the truth of Christianity probable first of all before relating existentially to it. In *Philosophical Fragments* he shows that the coming of "the God does not fall under the ordinary historical point of view, since the fact of Christianity—from the standpoint of the historical—must be regarded as an absurdity. All attempts to render Christianity probable in the ordinary historical way must therefore fail. They are attempts to make Christianity into an objective, contradiction-free truth on the same plane with all other objective truths. But in doing this one forgets that Christianity is separated from the contradiction-free, objective truths by a cleft with which only "the leap" can cope, and that as a consequence there is no "direct and immediate transition"[273] to Christianity. Climacus shows that where two qualitative opposites are placed together in existence, objective thinking discovers a contradiction to which it is not equal and before which it must halt. This situation is primarily true of Christianity, but there is a lesser similarity to it in the Socratic position. In the *Postscript* Climacus finds this similarity through an elaboration of the Socratic standpoint in *Philosophical Fragments* by having Socrates actualize in existence the truth arrived at by "recollection." As long as one is satisfied to assume that Socrates has "the eternal essential truth" only as "recollection," there is, from the objective point of view, no contradiction. In that case Socrates simply possesses an abstract truth, and there is no genuine contradiction between him as person and this truth.[274] Not until he wants to apply this truth in his personal existence and bring it in relation to his concrete situation does the contradiction, the paradox,[275] appear— namely, that the eternal wants to transform his temporal life and that there must therefore be a synthesis of the two opposite qualities. Now Socrates, as this single individual stands not related to an abstract concept of truth but related to truth as an ethical demand. Looking objec-

[273] Ibid., p. 47. [274] Ibid., p. 184. [275] Ibid., p. 183.

tively at this situation, one can say that in his existential attempt Socrates abandons objective certainty and stands face to face with an "objective uncertainty." Climacus therefore defines Socratic existence in these words: ". . . *objective uncertainty held fast in an appropriation process of the most passionate inwardness is the truth, the highest truth attainable for an existing individual.*"[276]

Christianity can also be viewed objectively, but such an objective approach results in the "certainty" that Christianity is the absurd. Thus a strictly scientific-scholarly approach leads to completely different results than those usually aimed at in attempts to "prove" the truth of Christianity objectively. This also means that those attempts are based on misunderstanding and superficial thinking. By way of such an objective scrutiny, however, one may differentiate precisely between the Socratic and the Christian spheres of existence. Climacus says of the distinction: "When Socrates believed that there was a God, he held fast to the objective uncertainty with the whole passion of his inwardness, and it is precisely in this contradiction and in this risk that faith is rooted. Now it is otherwise. Instead of the objective uncertainty, there is here a certainty, namely, that objectively it is absurd, and this absurdity held fast in the passion of inwardness is faith."[277]

In working out this question Climacus refers to Lessing, who to a degree was aware of the obstacles the existing individual runs up against in the encounter with Christianity. Moreover, Lessing knew the difficulty of communicating religious experience directly; he spoke of "the leap" as a condition for becoming a Christian, and in his way suggested that appropriation is a prolonged process.

After discussing Lessing, Climacus gives his own ideas

[276] Ibid., p. 182.

[277] Ibid., p. 188. Seen from the viewpoint of the stages, these situations look like this: in the esthetic stage a person relates to the probable, in the ethical stage to the uncertain, since the ethical as the eternal cannot be given ocular proof, and in the religious stage to the improbable (the absurd).

on the difficulties which confront the subject when he wants to appropriate the truth. Climacus stipulates the first level of this appropriation with the words: "Subjectivity, inwardness is truth."[278] Climacus begins with a substantiation of this position, ascribing it to Socrates, after which by means of painstaking dialectical reflection he leads the existing individual through many levels of existence to a final confrontation with Christianity, where it is acknowledged that "subjectivity is untruth."[279] With these two contrasting statements the abstract claim in *Philosophical Fragments* that Socrates achieved the truth of "recollection" and that Christianity changes this position into untruth is existentially expressed. In the statement "subjectivity is truth," Socrates is conceded much more than before, far more than the Socratic position in *Philosophical Fragments*. In a long footnote Climacus speaks plainly of "an analogue to faith *sensu eminentiori*"[280] in Socrates. Climacus could not make this claim in *Philosophical Fragments*, where the main point was to place the human position in sharp contrast to Christianity, since this claim would merely confuse the issue. But now, where throughout the whole book it is demonstrated that the Socratic point of departure, not only when regarded from the angle of abstraction but, which is more important, in an existential sense, leads to the collapse of the human, Climacus can very well give Socrates the con-

[278] Ibid., p. 183.   [279] Ibid., p. 185.

[280] Ibid., p. 185n. With this Kierkegaard gives the last of the four aspects of Socrates analogous to Kierkegaard's division of himself into pseudonyms. In the first (*The Concept of Irony*) Socrates is consistently set forth as an ironist, without regard to his achieving "the good" (*The Concept of Irony*, p. 254), as the foundation for the ethical; in *Either/Or* Socrates is referred to as an ethicist who strives in the domain of personal ethics "to develop himself into a paragon of virtue" (*Either/Or*, II, p. 244). We find the third aspect in *Philosophical Fragments*, where Socrates represents the abstract truth of recollection, while in the fourth and last aspect we see Socrates's ethics carried to its final conclusion. See Himmelstrup, *Søren Kierkegaards Opfattelse af Sokrates*.

cession which also represents a break with the objectivity of Christendom. This concession, however, is weakened in the following pages by showing that Socrates still did not know the frailty of human nature, which man first learns from the doctrine of "original sin."

With this progression the Socratic standpoint in *Philosophical Fragments* is expanded to embrace all the levels of the human until its confrontation with Christianity.

By the transition from the purely objective point of view · to the subjective appropriation of the truth, Climacus strongly emphasizes the significance of the ethical as a personal matter and sharply differentiates it from the thinking which places "the world-historical"[281] in the foreground. A person's ethical development may take three directions: the civic, the personal, and the religious,[282] and Climacus attaches the greatest importance to personal ethics. This is in complete agreement with Socratic ethics, where civic ethics and "civic life"[283] have lost primary importance. Climacus moves along the same lines, and therefore actions which have their goal only in external actuality become secondary. For this reason he must also direct his penetrating and detailed criticism against overestimating the world-historical. The most important events do not occur in the external world but in subjectivity, which finds the laws for its ethical action within itself. For Climacus the ethical signifies at the same time a private coknowledge or "complicity with God."[284] Climacus joins these two sides, the ethical grounding in the person himself and the relation to God: ". . . the ethical is a correlative to individuality, and that to such a degree that each individual apprehends the ethical essentially only in himself because the ethical is his complicity with God."

After Climacus has put the world-historical in second place by concluding, "First then the ethical, the task of becoming subjective, and afterwards the world-histori-

---

[281] *Postscript*, p. 121.
[283] Ibid., p. 245.

[282] *Either/Or*, II, p. 266.
[284] *Postscript*, p. 138.

cal,"[285] he points to the central questions the ethical subject comes up against when he deliberates on his own situation. Among these questions, which concern all men,
Climacus reckons these: ". . . *what it means to die.*"[286]
". . . *what does it mean to be immortal?*"[287] ". . . *what does
it mean that I am to thank God for the good He bestows
upon me?*"[288] ". . . *what does it mean to get married?*"[289]

Through a concentration upon these existential questions the transition from purely world-historical views to
the central concerns of the subject is accomplished, and
he may now begin with ethical earnestness to draw the
consequences for his own life out of this concentration
within himself. The subjective appropriation of the insight
he has won, which in the first round may be defined entirely objectively, leads to the subject's being completely
influenced and marked by this insight; it becomes his essential existential truth, which, from the subject's side, is
the meaning of "subjectivity is truth." But the expression
"truth is subjectivity"[290] says exactly the same thing, understood as the transition from insight into the truth to
its appropriation by the subject. This process of appropriation is then placed in relation to Christianity with its re-
valuation of human standards. In the insert "Appendix,
A Glance at a Contemporary Effort in Danish Literature,"[291] Climacus discusses the pseudonymously given examples of how the process of appropriation takes place in
a single existing individual who must wrestle particularly
with the problem: *"What does it mean to get married?"*
All the central existential questions can be resolved only
by each person for himself.

Climacus next sets himself the task of broadly sketching
the course of individual development which in the other
pseudonyms' portrayals, as far as they go, culminates in the

[285] Ibid., p. 142.   [286] Ibid., p. 147.
[287] Ibid., p. 152.   [288] Ibid., p. 158.
[289] Ibid., p. 160.   [290] Ibid., pp. 169-224.
[291] Ibid., pp. 225-66.

position reached by Quidam, who moves through the stage of humor toward "the boundary of the religious."[292]

Before sketching the universal points of view for the existential movement of the individual, Climacus gives a very full account of questions concerning the relation between thought and being, but with special emphasis on being. This whole discussion must be understood as an attempt to understand the ontological, both in its relation to the sphere of the human and to Christianity. The question of being had been treated by Climacus in *Philosophical Fragments* in a primarily abstract way, whereby being can in fact embrace everything and nothing,[293] that is, being has no gradations. But it must be added that there are certain intimations of the possibility of gradations of being. For example: "Or is the difficulty increased by the fact that the non-being which precedes the new birth contains more being than the non-being which preceded the first birth?"[294] Here the very expression "more being" is used. This question is set forth more clearly by Frater Taciturnus, who, in an important passage about the ontological, states the principal difference between abstract being and being which assumes concrete forms and thereby acquires gradations. Frater Taciturnus writes: "The metaphysical is abstraction, there is no man who exists metaphysically. The metaphysical, ontology *is* but does not *exist*; for when it exists it is in the esthetic, in the ethical, in the religious, and when it *is* it is the abstraction of or the *prius* for the esthetic, the ethical, the religious."[295] Here we note that the abstract-ontological is given with the copula "is"; but being which is defined only by the copula "is" "does not *exist*," that is, it can signify all and nothing, since it is so comprehensive that it does not contain any concretion.[296] The more concrete-ontological is

[292] Ibid., p. 403.
[293] *Philosophical Fragments*, pp. 50ff. (especially footnote, pp. 51-52).
[294] Ibid., p. 25.   [295] *Stages*, p. 430.
[296] Kierkegaard's pseudonyms, in their statements on abstract

expressed with "exists," and "when it exists it is in the esthetic, in the ethical, in the religious." Then being enters into the corresponding concretions, which Frater Taciturnus merely names according to the three main viewpoints of the stages. Not until *Concluding Unscientific Postscript*[297] does Climacus give a comprehensive account of the ontological by treating the special forms of being as they are found in each of the three stages. With this he provides a solid foundation for possible further work with the ontological within the different spheres of existence, work made necessary particularly because of the confusion Hegel's "pure thought"[298] had occasioned by setting aside concrete actuality.

After treating the ontological, Climacus discusses the importance for the existing individual of maintaining "the simultaneity of the individual factors,"[299] after which he himself appears as the "subjective thinker."[300] Next he once again makes a sharp distinction between speculative thought, which wants to comprehend everything, and Christianity, which as the absurd *factum* sets a limit to all speculative comprehension. From these brief explanations he goes on to the presentation of the level of the human during the process of approximating the Christian.

---

being, could find support in the clear characterization of it given by Paul M. Møller in his lectures on ontology in 1837. "Being can be regarded simply as the copula with a completely indeterminable subject. It declares neither that something is nor what it is. X is X is the formula whereby this complete absence of determinativeness is expressed." "Completely indeterminate being is still nothing. In ordinary language one is justified in speaking this way." "The movement of ontological thinking really begins with the observation that being is nothing, or more accurately, that for us it is still nothing." See *Efterladte Skrifter af Poul M. Møller*, I-II (Copenhagen, 1839-43), III, p. 349.

[297] *Postscript*, pp. 267-322; see also the epistemological observations, pp. 169-224.

[298] Ibid., pp. 275-82.   [299] Ibid., p. 307.

[300] Ibid., p. 312.

The goal which Climacus advances for the individual moving toward Christianity is "an eternal happiness,"[301] which is completely analogous to "an eternal consciousness"[302] which Climacus in *Philosophical Fragments* has given as one of the principal points in the single individual's relation to Christianity. The individual has the task of pathos-filled involvement in the ethical-religious striving related to eternal happiness as the highest good. Climacus says of this pathos: "In relation to an eternal happiness as the absolute good, pathos is not a matter of words, but of permitting this conception to transform the entire existence of the individual."[303]

"Resignation"[304] is named as the first condition for this transformation of the individual by pathos. Through resignation the single individual liberates himself from finite goals; these must take second place, and the eternal comes to the foreground. This outlook during the progressive movement is expressed with the words: ". . . relating himself at one and the same time absolutely to the absolute τελος and relatively to relative ends."[305] But in a wider sense this means *The Dying Away From the Life of Immediacy While Still Remaining in the Finite.*[306] What Climacus here postulates as a universal rule the concrete individuals in the works of the other pseudonymous writers have already tested in their lives. The problem of "the unhappiest man"[307] was his having lost the first immediacy or spontaneity and not being able to return to it; he is obliged thereafter to move through different existential levels toward the second immediacy,[308] which only Christianity is capable of creating. This movement, which the concrete individual makes because of his unhappy situation, Climacus seeks to make a universal law which applies to everyone who wants to draw near to Christianity.

[301] Ibid., p. 323.
[302] See title page of *Philosophical Fragments*.
[303] *Postscript*, p. 347.   [304] Ibid., pp. 353, 396.
[305] Ibid., p. 386.   [306] Ibid.
[307] *Either/Or*, I, pp. 215-28.   [308] *Stages*, pp. 435-36.

It may be inserted here that just as "the unhappiest man" was further advanced in existence than Judge William, so also Climacus's universal sequence is more advanced compared with the Judge's position, for although the Judge as an ethicist begins his existence with repentance, which stands higher in the context of the stages than resignation, he nevertheless attempts to create a "balance" between the esthetic and the ethical. For Climacus there can be no question of any balance between the two, since the esthetic and the finite goals are clearly placed elsewhere.

It ought to be added here that only by ". . . the ideal task: the simultaneous maintenance of an absolute relationship to the absolute, and a relative relationship to the relative"[309] does the sentence from part two of *Either/Or*— "the absolute as absolute can only be for the absolute"— get real meaning. For Judge William this sentence merely expresses a choice: ". . . I posit the absolute and I myself am the absolute";[310] in *Concluding Unscientific Postscript* it is no longer simply a matter of choosing the absolute but also of inwardly appropriating the absolute as one's own. During this appropriation process the individual discovers, however, that his orientation takes the opposite direction, that is, he is bound to the relative goals. Climacus explains: "The actual individual is [stuck] fast in the immediate and is insofar really absolutely committed to relative ends."[311] When the individual attempts to liberate himself from his bondage to immediacy, suffering is the consequence, and the individual experiences existentially that the grounds of suffering lie in his attachment to the temporal. But there are, however, several other kinds of suffering in existence, and Climacus scrutinizes them in order to define more explicitly the suffering which comes in "dying away to the life of immediacy." This suffering is characterized by its sustained continuance, because the

309 *Postscript*, p. 386.
310 *Either/Or*, II, p. 217; see p. 269 above and p. 310 below.
311 *Postscript*, p. 386.

task here is infinite; thus it is dissociated from the forms of suffering on the esthetic plane. Climacus considers this sustained suffering to be religious suffering, and he also distinguishes between this suffering and the suffering to which man can become exposed by his ethical-religious action in the external world.

Strictly speaking, then, when the apostles,[312] by obeying God more than men, exposed themselves to persecution, this suffering was not religious, and Climacus believes that "by and large, very little is said in the New Testament"[313] about the religious suffering which centers in the subject's internal battle with himself. This suffering is more akin to the suffering Paul knew and called "the thorn in the flesh."[314] The religious suffering is always related to the eternal bliss which Paul experienced in ecstasy. And even if one must guard against offhandedly juxtaposing the pathos-filled relation to the eternal truth with Paul's ecstasy, and his thorn in the flesh with the suffering involved in pathos-filled striving, there is nevertheless an analogy between them, which Climacus puts this way: "We others must be content with lesser experiences, but the relationship remains entirely the same. The religious individual is not necessarily caught up into the third heaven, but neither does he know the suffering which constitutes the thorn in the flesh. The religious individual sustains a relationship to an eternal happiness, and the sign of this relationship is suffering, and suffering is its essential expression—for the existing individual."[315]

Climacus next discusses how a person who in earnest practices resignation and "dying away to the life of immediacy" learns that he achieves nothing by himself and is as "nothing before God."[316] Climacus gives examples of how difficult it is to apply this in his life.

There is a still higher expression than religious suffering as the mark of the relationship to the eternal salva-

---

[312] Ibid., p. 405; Acts 5:41.   [313] *Postscript*, p. 405.
[314] Ibid., p. 406.   [315] Ibid., p. 407.
[316] Ibid., p. 412.

beyond recollection

tion—namely, guilt. Here again Climacus draws a parallel to the concrete-individual sequence in which the single individual with his suffering as the point of departure struggles forward through the maze of "guilty, not-guilty" to the personal assumption of guilt. This assumption means "the deepest possible immersion in existence,"[317] and it leads the individual on to a new and higher plane.

In *Concluding Unscientific Postscript* Climacus simplifies this process by leaving out the many specific factors entering into the concrete-individual movement and simply lets guilt appear as a new and essential determinant in a universally valid form. He points up the fact that the slightest delay in the process of "dying away to the life of immediacy" places the individual under guilt, and this guilt becomes a "totality-qualification."[318] He substantiates this more specifically: "The very least guilt—even if from that time on the individual were an angel—when it is put together with a relationship to the eternal happiness, is enough, for the composition determines the quality."[319] The individual is thereby "forever" caught[320] in total guilt and is thereby bound to "the eternal memory of sin-consciousness." It is easy to see that the single individual in this position has gone far beyond Socratic "recollection," which as yet has not become encumbered with the negative factors of guilt. But this movement, as Climacus sketches it now, lies also in the domain of humor, although far from the Socratic sphere of experience which he designates as "ethics with irony as incognito."[321] However, through this reflection over "the eternal memory of sin-consciousness" the single individual can remain in the domain of humor without drawing from it the final conclusion for his existence. Essentially this conclusion can first be drawn when the sin-consciousness is concerned with completely concrete factors, as in the case of Quidam.

[317] Ibid., p. 473 (ed. tr.).　　[318] Ibid., p. 471 (ed. tr.).
[319] Ibid., pp. 471f.　　[320] Ibid., p. 475.
[321] Ibid., p. 473n.

Climacus calls this last position within the domain of the human "hidden inwardness."[322] All the possibilities of the human are exhausted in it; in "self-annihilation before God"[323] the individual acknowledges his total impotence. This last position is designated Religiousness A. The person now stands before "the specifically Christian" religiousness, Religiousness B, with its absurd claim about God in time. Climacus characteristically compares Religiousness A to Religiousness B by saying that "even if it [Religiousness A] had not been exemplified in paganism, it could have been, because it has only human nature in general as its assumption, whereas the religiousness which has the dialectical in the second instance cannot have been before itself, nor even after it has come can it be said to have been able to have been before it was."[324] This assumption that Religiousness A could have been possible in paganism may be understood at face value and ironically. Taken at face value, it means that Climacus, with dialectical consistency, has brought human existence to its farthest boundary; at the same time it would be very ironic that an existing individual in this finally developed form, which had already been possible in paganism, is not to be found even in Christendom; this latter point is clearly evident in his critical observations on the various religious conditions in his own day as well as in the past.

But at the same time we must note that Religiousness A not only belongs to paganism but also forms a necessary transition to Christianity in a decisive sense. "Religiousness A must first be present in the individual before there can be any question of becoming aware of the dialectic of B." And further: "Religiousness A can exist in paganism, and in Christianity it can be the religiousness of everyone who is not decisively Christian, whether be he baptized or no."[325] The fact that Religiousness A can appear in paganism and also be considered a preparatory step to Christianity, strictly speaking, can be explained by

---

[322] Ibid., p. 492.   [323] Ibid., p. 507.
[324] Ibid., p. 496.   [325] Ibid., pp. 494-95.

the fact that Climacus in Religiousness B, intensifies the ethical-religious conceptions which certainly are to be found partially in paganism but which Christianity potentiates anew. In order to lead the human sequence to its collapse, Climacus has specifically used the ethical-religious categories of Christianity; only by using these in existence does a person's consciousness of total guilt and his impotence in expressing the relation to "eternal happiness" become apparent.

The essential distinction between Religiousness A and B can therefore best be adduced if Religiousness A, with its border on the confinium of humor, is regarded as dominated by the ethical-religious demands of Christianity; whereas Religiousness B is thoroughly dependent upon the saving work of Christ, offered to the person who has exhausted his own possibilities. In going from Religiousness A to Religiousness B, the single individual comes into a completely new "existence-medium"[326] by breaking "with the understanding, and with thinking, and with immanence, in order to lose the last foothold of immanence, eternity, behind one, and to exist constantly on the extremest verge of existence by virtue of the absurd."[327]

Continuing his discussion of the transition from the human to the Christian, Climacus again goes into the dialectical difficulties in man's relationship to Christianity already touched upon in *Philosophical Fragments*. In considering sin as "the new existence-medium" in Christianity, he refers to the lesser analogy to it advanced in *The Concept of Anxiety* by Vigilius Haufniensis—namely, that to

[326] Ibid., p. 516.

[327] Ibid., p. 505 (ed. tr.). Man is a synthesis of the temporal and the eternal. Therefore the eternal as immanence is "behind one" and is in contrast to Christ the eternal, the paradoxically transcendent in time (therefore by virtue of the absurd). "Behind one" refers to the eternal as the high stage of humor and "the eternal recollection of guilt" (*Postscript*, pp. 492-93), which as "Religion A" can be fulfilled and healed only by a breach with immanence and by a faith-relation to the paradox of the transcendent in time.

the individual weighed down by the burden of racial guilt it ultimately seems as if "the guilt of the whole world were united in order to make him guilty, or in other words, as if by becoming guilty he became guilty of the guilt of the whole world."[328]

And of the religious genius who experiences this guilt in a more primitive manner, it is said that: ". . . by himself he sinks before himself into the abyss of the consciousness of sin."

The distinction between the sin-consciousness discussed in *Concluding Unscientific Postscript*, which depicts the person as existing "by virtue of the absurd,"[329] and the guilt-consciousness in which the individual feels guilty of the guilt of the whole race, can be defined more explicitly as follows: the guilt of the race which the individual takes upon himself as his own is only the possibility of guilt, with which the individual identifies himself, yet without having arrived at the consciousness of the ethical as the eternal within him; this ethical point is the boundary toward which the individual is moving. In *Concluding Unscientific Postscript*, however, the ethical consciousness and knowledge of the eternal in the person is presupposed, and it is from this point of departure that the single individual begins his attempt to penetrate the temporal with eternity's demands, ultimately leading to an existential experience of his total guilt, which Christianity sharpens and heightens into sin-consciousness, giving a new and radical characterization of man. Putting it briefly, the distinction between the two kinds of guilt-consciousness, the one in *The Concept of Anxiety* and the one in *Concluding Unscientific Postscript*, is that in the first the individual sees his own possibilities only in the guilt of the race; whereas in the second the single individual comes to acknowledge his own incapacity in the face of the eternal ethical requirement, resulting in the knowledge of his own absolute guilt. In the first case, then, the movement starts from the

[328] *The Concept of Anxiety* [*Dread*], p. 98 (ed. tr.).
[329] *Postscript*, p. 505.

individual's finite premises, such as heredity and environment; in the second, from the single individual's knowledge of what is ethically required of him. These two forms illustrate on the existential plane the axiom that man is a synthesis of body-soul and spirit; *The Concept of Anxiety* represents primarily the body-mind elements in the synthesis, while in *Concluding Unscientific Postscript* the dominant emphasis is upon the ethical as corresponding to the spiritual.

Of the two forms of guilt-consciousness the one produced by man's ethical striving is the more profound and the more decisive since it has as its origin the single individual's experience of his boundaries and limitations; a person is thereby kept from self-inflation and is prepared to see the newness which Christianity offers as his only deliverance. But the other side of guilt-consciousness must not be forgotten, either, and Climacus reminds us of it in two places,[330] calling it "a second isolation" in relation to the isolation which sin occasions on the ethical and religious planes. The second isolation is caused by the burden of the race's heritage.

That both of these aspects of guilt must be taken into account is clearly shown in the third part of *Stages On Life's Way*, where in Quidam we have an example of a concrete, existing person and we do not move within abstract qualifications as in *Concluding Unscientific Postscript* and partially also in *The Concept of Anxiety*. Quidam, too, is engaged in a strenuous struggle to understand the heavy heritage that the race has laid upon him, and at the same time he seeks to arrive at a personal ethical understanding. Therefore, when Quidam concludes his account of his suffering by saying that he has made "a resolution which has gone through the dialectic of fear,"[331] he means that he has attempted (although with negative results) in a concrete way to relate the guilt of the race,

[330] Ibid., pp. 186, 516-18, and also in the discussion of the pseudonymous books, p. 239.
[331] *Stages*, p. 360.

which has prevented him from realizing the universal, and the ethical requirement. Without going into the many aspects of Quidam's inner struggle, ending with his resolution to break the engagement, it may be said that Quidam's attempt to join the consequences of original sin to the ethical requirement are futile, for he must at the same time take upon himself the concrete guilt for the broken engagement. Thus original sin as well as ethics takes him to the boundaries of the human; in his existence he reaches the dividing line between Religiousness A and B, and his problem now is to reach the second immediacy.

This movement toward Christianity in *Stages on Life's Way* as well as in *Concluding Unscientific Postscript* can be filled out by looking at Kierkegaard's own statements about his relation to Christianity at that time and comparing his position with the various positions of Climacus, Frater Taciturnus, and Quidam, which, since they lie within the sphere of humor, are an approximation to Christianity. In fact these three pseudonyms represent aspects of Kierkegaard's personality since they denote Kierkegaard's various dialectical and existential positions, and it may be of some value to look at them in relation to Kierkegaard's own life.

As a dialectician and psychologist Climacus has the most comprehensive view of the spheres of existence, but as a dialectician he lacks the passion for a decisive movement toward Christianity. He therefore serves as an example of the truth that even the most comprehensive and farsighted dialectical thinking cannot bring a man farther along existentially; for this, passion and a bond to concrete forms of guilt are necessary. Frater Taciturnus voices the truth that when the single individual concentrates upon his inner conflicts and tries to understand them, there has to be an observer who can explain the manifold factors in these conflicts, all of which still are dominated by the contrast between the eternal and the temporal. As we have seen, the ironic observer discovers the conflicts arising in the transition from external actuality to a concentration upon the inner life; the humorist's task as observer concerns the conflicts which are centered entirely upon man's inner life, where the contrast of the eternal and the temporal is an interior actuality within the person himself. Moreover, an observer's strength lies in reflection, even though his reflection is closer to life than that of the dialectician. But the main point is that the observer, too, as observer, remains within the realm of knowledge and does not get involved in existence.

Quidam,[332] the third of the humorous figures, is differentiated essentially from Climacus and Frater Taciturnus by being an existing personality with a concrete guilt which compels him to move out of the position of humor in the direction of Christianity. This alone reveals that he is the one most like Kierkegaard, whose concern was to draw close to Christianity in a decisive way, step by step in the struggle with concrete difficulties. But just as Quidam is only next door to Religiousness B and does not take the decisive last step of becoming a Christian in the Kierkegaardian sense, so Kierkegaard for a time did not do so either. A few remarks by Kierkegaard together with some notes to *Concluding Unscientific Postscript* will clearly illustrate this.

In journal entry X² A 163 (*J. and P.*, V) Kierkegaard writes: "*Johannes Climacus* was actually a contemplative piece, for when I wrote it I was contemplating the possibility of not letting myself be taken over by Christianity, even if it was my honest intention to devote my whole life and daily diligence to the cause of Christianity, to do everything, to do nothing else but expound and interpret it, even though I were to become like the legendary Wandering Jew, myself not a Christian in the final and most decisive sense of the word and yet leading others to Christianity." The assertion is repeated in a later journal entry.[333]

[332] See N. H. Søe, "Der Quidam des Experiments als religiøser Typus," *Orbis litterarum*, X, 1955, pp. 259-67.
[333] X³ A 258 (*J. and P.*, V).

While writing *Concluding Unscientific Postscript*, Kierkegaard is in the same position as Quidam, who also has not taken the decisive step but finds himself in the existential movement toward Christianity. In a draft of *Concluding Unscientific Postscript* we find a slightly humorous glimpse into what it was that prevented the decisive step. It states there (this is omitted in the text [p. 210] of *Concluding Unscientific Postscript*): ". . . that, like that Wandering Jew in a beautiful legend, I should lead the pilgrims to the promised land and not enter myself, that I should guide men to the truth of Christianity and that as my punishment for going astray in my younger days I myself would not enter in but would venture only to be an omen of an incomparable future."[334] In this entry we have both the idea of the Wandering Jew (as in X^2 A 163), who by his continuing in sin symbolizes for Kierkegaard despair, and a more concrete statement of the obstacle itself: "punishment for going astray in my younger days." Both of these clearly express that Kierkegaard has not yet come to believe the forgiveness of sins. But to believe the forgiveness of sin means first of all that the single individual relates to the specifically Christian after he has received the gift of a new immediacy, even though he and his dialectical talents have, like Climacus, completely entered the service of Christianity.

This, perhaps, is the place for a comment which will explain how this duality is possible—that Kierkegaard is totally committed to Christianity and still prefers not to be called a Christian. Kierkegaard makes a sharp distinction between believing in Christ as the revelation of God and in believing the forgiveness of one's sins. For an intellectual person it is a leap to believe in Christ as the absurd truth, and this is the first and the most decisive step. But it is possible to believe in Christ without being willing to believe the forgiveness of sins.[335] It must be re-

[334] VI B 40:33 (*J. and P.*, V).
[335] Whether Luther found himself in a similar situation, I am not competent to say, but this much is clear—long before

membered that for Kierkegaard the way of faith is a long and troubled passage, which can be put down "on paper" easily enough, but this paper version does not include the existential problems. Kierkegaard expresses himself quite clearly on these two main steps on the Christian journey: faith in Christ and believing the forgiveness of sins through Christ.[336] This, too, is found in a draft of *Concluding Unscientific Postscript*. "The forgiveness of sin is indeed a paradox insofar as the eternal truth is related to an existing person; it is a paradox insofar as the eternal truth is related to the person botched up in time and by time and who nevertheless is an existing person (because the qualification of sin existence is registered and accentuated a second time), but forgiveness of sin is really a paradox only when it is linked to the appearance of the God [*Guden*], to the fact that God has existed [*existeret*]. For the paradox always arises by the joining of existing and the eternal truth, but the more often this occurs the more paradox."[337] This view of faith in Christ and believing the forgiveness of sins as two different steps can be deduced from many other statements.

Kierkegaard approaches the second step of faith, believing the forgiveness of sins, a few years later. The first indication of it is found in several journal entries in 1848[338] at a time of preoccupation with the question of the forgiveness of sins. "And only now, now in my thirty-fifth year, with the help of heavy sufferings and the bitterness of repentance, have I perhaps learned enough about dying

he could believe the forgiveness of his sins Luther believed in Christ as God's Son.

[336] *Stages*, p. 434; *Postscript*, p. 469. Concerning his contribution to the characterization of faith Kierkegaard says: "I venture to claim that in my writings accurate dialectical qualifications of specific points are set forth such as have not been known before." X² A 596 (*J. and P.*, V).

[337] VI B 45 (*J. and P.*, III, 3085); *Postscript*, p. 201.

[338] VIII¹ A 640-53 (see collations of entries in *J. and P.*, II, III, and V); see also entries in *Armed Neutrality and An Open Letter*, pp. 57-66.

away from the world so that I can rightly speak of finding my whole life and my salvation through faith in the forgiveness of sins."[339]

In conclusion it may be said that at the time around the publication of *Concluding Unscientific Postscript* Kierkegaard is aligned with Quidam, and both are moving toward the second immediacy, which is not forthcoming until believing the forgiveness of sins has created the condition for it. It may also be said that part of what Kierkegaard is seeking in his subsequent intense absorption in the Christian-ethical side of existence is certitude about forgiveness.

During the movement toward Christianity which Climacus discusses in *Concluding Unscientific Postscript*, the significance of subjectivity and the subjective side of appropriation are more and more strongly accentuated. The same is true in the comprehensive, concluding presentation of the difference between the objective view of Christianity and, as Climacus points out, the constant Christian presupposition of a process of appropriation by the individual. But it is clear to Climacus, however, that the very fact that he has been able to give a comprehensive and accurate description of the process of appropriation means that his emphasis on subjectivity also acquires an objective side. Climacus's admission of objectivity simultaneous with his decisive emphasis on subjectivity can be explained by the fact that basic to his view of the relation subjective-objective is a distinction between the quantitative dialectic and the qualitative dialectic with which he operates in *Concluding Unscientific Postscript*.

The quantitative dialectic embraces all the qualifications of the finite, and its goal is to produce a so-called objective knowledge containing a greater or lesser degree of probability. In the quantitative dialectic the principle of identity is the highest principle, since all the kinds of content with which the quantitative dialectic is concerned lie within a

[339] VIII[1] A 663 (*J. and P.*, II, 1215).

homogeneous category: finiteness. Here, therefore, all the determinants of content are seen from a comprehensive viewpoint, are "one and the same."[340] In a wider sense all the objective intellectual disciplines are embraced by this category and belong with it under the quantitative dialectic; in Climacus's *Schema* the historical disciplines are placed at the top.

On a totally different plane, however, lies "the qualitative dialectic,"[341] concerned with ethical and Christian-ethical concepts. Absolute incompatibilities make their appearance in this sphere, and the principle of identity cannot be used here as the highest norm, since it can only cope with relative incompatibilities and must explain a composition of two absolute incompatibilities as absurd. These absolute opposites will always be present during the process of the single individual's appropriation of the absolute truth, but above all during the process of appropriating Christianity as a historical fact. In the appropriation the subjective factor comes to the fore, quite in contrast to what happens in the objective disciplines, and here the objective "What" is not decisive, but rather the subjective "How" of the appropriation. But the fact that the constant struggle of appropriation between two absolutely incompatible qualities can be described indicates that the "How" of the appropriation also has an objective "What." Climacus gives examples of this earlier in his characterization of the fact of Christianity, looked at from the angle of objectivity.[342] This objective view of the two contradicting components of the absurd can, however, be carried through for the whole range of appropriation, which Climacus discusses in detail in his closing remarks in *Concluding Unscientific Postscript* on the relation between the objective and the subjective.[343]

In a journal entry in 1849 Kierkegaard wonders that no one has become aware of this connection. He writes: "In

[340] VII¹ A 84 (*J. and P.*, I, 759).
[341] *Postscript*, p. 348.   [342] Ibid., p. 188.
[343] Ibid., pp. 54off.

all the usual talk that Johannes Climacus is mere subjectivity, etc., it has been completely overlooked that he, in addition to all his other concretions, points out in one of the last sections that the remarkable thing is that there is a How with the characteristic that when the How is scrupulously rendered the What is also given, that this is the How of 'faith.' Right here, at its very maximum, inwardness is shown to be objectivity. And this, then, is a turning of the subjectivity-principle which, as far as I know, has never before been carried through or accomplished in this way."[344]

It would be a mistake to draw the conclusion from this that Climacus-Kierkegaard places objectivity in the sphere of the absurd on equal footing with subjectivity. Just as one must strive for objectivity in the objective disciplines, so one must give subjectivity precedence in the sphere of the absurd. Kierkegaard voices this clearly in the following sentence: "Objectivity is believed to be superior to subjectivity, but it is just the opposite; that is to say, an objectivity which is within a corresponding subjectivity is the finale."[345]

The pseudonymous books up to and including *Concluding Unscientific Postscript*, using the dialectical method, give a survey of the different levels of existence and their respective ranks. Since the upbuilding [opbyggende] or edifying part of the authorship begins at the same time as the pseudonymous and continues on a parallel line with it, it is reasonable to discuss the relation of dialectic to this side of Kierkegaard's production also. The principal pseudonym, Climacus, makes some important observations about this which undoubtedly are in harmony with Kierkegaard's own opinions. One of the most important of Climacus's observations reads thus: "For dialectic is in its

[344] X² A 299 (*J. and P.*, IV).
[345] X¹ A 146 (*J. and P.*, V); compare entry from 1835: "The genuine philosopher is subjective to the highest degree." I A 77 (*J. and P.*, V).

truth a benevolent helper which discovers and assists in finding where the absolute object of faith and worship is— there, namely, where the difference between knowledge and ignorance collapses in absolute worship with a consciousness of ignorance, there where the resistance of an objective uncertainty tortures forth the passionate certainty of faith, there when the conflict of right and wrong collapses in absolute worship with absolute subjection. Dialectic itself does not see the absolute, but it leads, as it were, the individual up to it, and says: 'Here it must be, that I guarantee; when you worship here, you worship God.' "[346]

As the above quotation clearly shows, dialectic plays a not insignificant role in the upbuilding works, helping the single individual to perceive clearly what it means to worship in the right way. In giving these opinions on the relation of dialectic to the upbuilding or edifying, Climacus gives final form to an idea which Kierkegaard once posed as a question needing an answer. Kierkegaard writes in 1831: "It takes some time before we really settle down and feel at home (know where everything has its place) in the divine economy. We grope around amid a multiplicity of moods, do not even know how we should pray; Christ does not take on any definite configuration in us—we do not know what the cooperation of the Spirit means, etc."[347] We will now see how the dialectical viewpoints apply in Kierkegaard's upbuilding works, without, however, going into the many other exceedingly important questions which lie beyond the scope of this study.

The fact that Kierkegaard progresses dialectically in the development of the upbuilding or edifying authorship is shown at the outset by its parallelism with the pseudonymous authorship. This "doubleness,"[348] as Kierkegaard calls it later, has its origin in Kierkegaard's understanding of existence as proceeding in multiple collateral series. Among the multiplicity of viewpoints standing in collateral

[346] *Postscript*, pp. 438-39.   [347] II A 756 (*J. and P.*, IV).
[348] *The Point of View*, pp. 10ff. (ed. tr.).

connection with each other and under which human existence can be scrutinized, a man's intimate religious life
and outlook must be regarded as the most important. The
religious upbuilding as the most central line runs parallel
to other collateral viewpoints, for example, that man is a
synthesis of freedom and necessity, of finitude and infinitude, etc., but these collateral linkages receive the most
detailed treatment in the pseudonymous authorship. Although reasoning from other than dialectical points of
view, Hirsch has already demonstrated this parallelism in
a convincing manner by pointing to a congruity between
the progress of the pseudonymous works and the upbuilding portion of the authorship.[349]

In the upbuilding literature other dialectical points of
view appear just as distinctly as this continuous parallelism, but in contrast to the parallelism these points of view
determine the structure of the edifying from within. To
name a few:

(1) The application of the idea of the synthesis and in
a wider sense of the doctrine of the stages

(2) A gradually stronger intensification of subjectivity,
which reaches its climax in the confrontation with Christianity

(3) Use of the law of repetition, which modifies all the
existential approaches on the basis of the new insight and
experience which every new position during the progress-
ing movement brings with it

(4) An alternate use of the abstract and the concrete,
with the paradigmatic as the most distinct form of the
concrete.

In addition to these dialectical viewpoints, the upbuilding literature also makes use of the dialectic of communication. Kierkegaard's scrupulous declaration in the upbuilding works of his own position relative to these works
and his designation of the specific upbuilding categories
which apply to each work correspond to the pseudony-

[349] For more on this see E. Hirsch, *Kierkegaard-Studien*, I, pp.
266ff., 649ff., 831ff.

mous works as an expression of Kierkegaard's imagined or fulfilled existential possibilities.

Our first task is to show how these dialectical viewpoints appear in and leave their mark upon the upbuilding or edifying works.

The eighteen edifying discourses deal with a person's first confrontation with the eternal and are addressed to the person who as yet is on the esthetic level and point to the eternal as the fixed point in all the changes and vicissitudes of temporal life. The very first discourse points out that only the eternal can cope with the temporal: "By what means does he then conquer the changing conditions? Through the eternal."[350] The eternal is now defined in two directions. Multiple definition is prominent also in the pseudonymous authorship, but it now is used in a more concrete and existential way. In his spiritual development man encounters the eternal as the transcendent outside of himself and also as the eternal within man. A person must learn to understand both aspects of the eternal, "for the absolute as absolute can only be for the absolute."[351] In other words, at the same time that a person involves himself with God he must seek to grow steadily in an understanding of himself and of the possibility of the eternal in himself. These two directions—the movement toward the transcendent and toward the eternal in man himself—together form the movement of faith. According to Kierkegaard, faith is always related to the eternal and must never be understood as a fixed state or something static, but, like other qualifications of existence, must be regarded as a dialectical-existential movement through several demarcated positions and levels. Thus Job is an example of a man who is fighting "border conflicts"[352] on the way to faith. Abraham's faith occupies a higher position, and is already next door to the position of

[350] *Edifying Discourses*, I, p. 21.
[351] *Either/Or*, II, p. 217 (ed. tr.); see pp. 269, 294 above.
[352] *Repetition*, p. 130.

faith implied in the eighteen edifying discourses. But there are continually new positions within the movement of faith, until it ultimately comes to Christ as the object of faith. Therefore it can be said that the upbuilding works, with the exception of *The Sickness Unto Death*, published later, delineate the stages on the way of faith. At the same time this movement of faith gives ever stronger expression to the realization of the synthesis which is supposed to unite the eternal with the temporal; the nonappearance of the synthesis means therefore that faith, too, is not present, a condition marked by anxiety, despair, or offense.

The eighteen discourses, then, are addressed to the person on the esthetic plane in Christendom and attempt to bring about an interior realignment in him through confrontation with the eternal. Through affirmation of the eternal the discourses try to guide the reader in the following directions: he must learn to regard everything as a gift from above, whatever his lot;[353] he must have a forgiving disposition toward his fellow man;[354] he must expect to be "strengthened in the inner man";[355] he must learn to bear heavy misfortunes in patience.[356] Above all, the discourses aim to help the single individual to an inner steadfastness ("win God in constancy") in order that, persevering, he can preserve his soul despite the manifold temptations of this world.[357] This steadfastness forms in man the first shoot toward becoming a self through relation to the eternal. But one still remains in the domain of the esthetic, even when he is in contact with the religious through the eternal, since the ethical as the eternal still is not present. The perspective is widened, however, by introducing a reality other than the reality of this world; this is called "the expectation of an eternal happiness,"[358] an idea which

[353] *Edifying Discourses*, II, pp. 27ff.
[354] Ibid., I, pp. 61ff.   [355] Ibid., pp. 94ff.
[356] Ibid., II, pp. 7ff.
[357] Ibid., p. 67; III, pp. 7ff., 71ff.
[358] Ibid., pp. 95ff.

again has significance for the understanding of temporal existence as a time of preparation.

The most penetrating reflections are found in the last four of the eighteen edifying discourses. They prepare the transition to the reality of the ethical as Kierkegaard understands it and to an existential understanding of man as a spiritual being. In the first of these four discourses the claim is made that in the search to *"know himself"*[359] a person discovers "the deeper self" within, which clashes with "the first self," representing one's temporal desires and his urge to assert himself in the external world. In the discovery of the deeper self, hitherto hidden spiritual elements in the physical-psychical synthesis appear, and through this new component a person learns that he "is capable of nothing" by himself. Kierkegaard here is in the same thought-world touched on by his pseudonyms, but in this edifying discourse he gives a plain and direct reason for this condition. Kierkegaard points out that as long as a man still lives without knowledge of the deeper self, he believes that he himself is able to accomplish something in the world if external conditions or fate do not prevent it. But through the deeper self he learns that he is capable of nothing, for when the deeper self, which intends to be the guiding force in man, tries to liberate the first self from absolute dependence on the surrounding world, it becomes clear that the deeper self with its most extreme efforts is able to do no more than prevent the first self from snatching at temporal things.[360] While the first self is being overcome in this duel, the deeper self also uses up all its powers. In this way it becomes apparent that all by himself, that is, by his deeper self, one cannot conquer himself, and also that a new point of departure for further

[359] Ibid., IV, p. 29.

[360] Climacus articulates this truth with special clarity in this sentence: "It is quite simply a psychological fact that the same energy which when directed outwardly accomplishes this or that, requires a still greater energy in order to check its outward striving." *Postscript*, p. 453.

spiritual development can be created.[361] Kierkegaard points out further that the deeper self not only ends with a negative result in the external world but that it cannot by itself become master of all the temptations the self generates and is exposed to. In relation to his own inner actuality, too, a person ends in the knowledge that he is capable of nothing. This last experience, in a way analogous to the declaration in *The Concept of Anxiety* that one must recognize his weakness in the face of the temptation of the possibilities,[362] is stated in the following words: "If he conquers the temptation which his environment presents to him, this does not prove that he would conquer if the temptation came in the most terrible form that his mind can conceive. But only when it presents itself to him in this magnitude does he really learn to know himself. In this manner it is present to his inner self, and hence he knows in himself what he has perhaps failed to learn from the world, that he can do absolutely nothing."[363]

Through this knowledge of himself a person learns that he is not his own master; he is capable neither of overcoming himself in every situation nor of doing the good in the eternal sense. He can do both only through faith in God. With this train of thought Kierkegaard wants to show that it is the experience of the deeper self in the existential sphere that leads a person to faith in God. "Whoever can do nothing of himself cannot undertake the least enterprise without God's help or without coming to notice that there is a God."[364] Only through faith in God is a man capable of doing "ever more and more."[365] It is plain to see in Kierkegaard's study of the deeper self how closely he links the eternal in man to faith in a transcendent power.

In the second of the four discourses, "The Thorn in the Flesh," attention is again called to man's frailty, which,

[361] See analogy in *Fear and Trembling* (p. 66) between resignation and faith.

[362] *The Concept of Anxiety* [*Dread*], p. 98.

[363] *Edifying Discourses*, IV, p. 39.

[364] Ibid., p. 42.   [365] Ibid., pp. 45-46 (ed. tr.).

however, is considered from a new angle. It shows that the suffering from the thorn is connected with the experience of "bliss," as was the case with Paul.[366] The experience of bliss does not in fact protect against anxiety about temporal temptations and relapse into sin. On the contrary, it makes them more present. But this very anxiety about a possible relapse prevents a man from becoming arrogant because of having experienced bliss even in this temporal existence.

The third discourse, entitled "Against Cowardice," stresses the importance for the spiritual life of a continual renewal of resolution. The resolution should prompt a man anticipating God's help to make every effort to actualize the good. "Do for God what you can, then God will do for you what you cannot."[367]

The last of the eighteen edifying discourses stresses that one ought not try by means of prayer to change God's will in order to attain his temporal desires. It is not God who is supposed to change his mind according to man's wish, but man must himself be changed by being able to renounce his wish even if it is his one and only and to him his most important wish. The goal this discourse sets for man is to be "nothing" before God, that is, to be liberated from the pressure of his desires in order through prayer to become obedient to God's will. It affirms that man conquers through his prayer because "God conquers."[368]

Seen from the point of view of dialectic, the eighteen discourses are still within the scope of the esthetic, but in two directions they touch on the eternal as the expression for the religious: the eternal in man and the transcendent. Again, the idea of man as a synthesis of two opposite qualities has its first formulation in these discourses. Here, too, is the first attempt to lead the individual, still totally attached to externality, to become the single individual, which can occur only through the relationship to God. There is still no trace in the eighteen edifying discourses

---

[366] Ibid., p. 58.   [367] Ibid., p. 102.   [368] Ibid., p. 143.

of the law of repetition, since man here continues to remain within the same closed area, and repetition presupposes transition to a new existential point of departure.

In the *Three Discourses on Imagined Occasions* Kierkegaard selects three of life's most central problems as subjects for penetrating study. These problems are: man's search for God, marriage, and death. In order to throw the fullest light on his subject, Kierkegaard characteristically uses the same procedure in these discourses as in the dialectic—that is, thinking a thought in all its implications.[369] Perhaps it was this preponderance of the dialectical in the discourses which led to the omission of the predicate "upbuilding," although on the whole the discourses are in an edifying or upbuilding mode. The fact that Kierkegaard originally thought of publishing these discourses under the pseudonym Johannes de Silentio[370] could indicate that Kierkegaard thereby wished to demonstrate the predominance of the dialectical.

Concentration on the central existential questions which relate to all men has the goal (which is also the case with Climacus)[371] of helping man to pass over from the purely objective view of existence to a subjectively interested approach, the only way in which a person can become a subject or the single individual. It is also significant that the next portion of the upbuilding literature is addressed to the single individual [*den Enkelte*].

In the first discourse, entitled "On the Occasion of a Confessional Service," the theme is: "What it means to seek God." Here Kierkegaard gives a detailed, coherent account of how the thought of God must go through many levels from its infant beginning before it becomes clarified, and of how in the relationship to the divine man's highest

[369] See VII¹ A 13 (*J. and P.*, I, 155); IX A 42 (*J. and P.*, V).
[370] See VI B 128, 132-34 (*J. and P.*, V).
[371] This transition is indicated very clearly by the fact that Climacus, after discussing these same existential questions (*Postscript*, pp. 147-61) in the next chapter goes into a discussion of "subjectivity."

expression is faith in a personal God who makes his demand upon man and teaches him his own inadequacy and sin. Kierkegaard characterizes it thus: "The object sought is therefore given. God is near enough, but *no one can see God without purity, and sin is impurity, and therefore no one can take cognizance of God without becoming a sinner.*"[372]

Kierkegaard goes on to show that sin must not be generalized but that one must begin concretely with the particular sin in order "to trace a connection from this or that particular sin,"[373] something Kierkegaard thereafter calls an "unfathomable connection." Having learned from his own experience, Kierkegaard finally warns against getting hung up [*blive hængende*] on the particular sin. "To repent of a trivial generality is a contradiction like offering the most profound passion a feast of superficialities; but to stick fast in remorse for some particular transgression is to repent on one's own responsibility, not before God, and to weaken one's resolve is self-love in melancholy of spirit."[374]

In the discourse "On the Occasion of a Wedding" we find Kierkegaard's numerous thoughts on marriage, on carrying through an ideal of marriage and the responsibility attached to marriage. Kierkegaard's pseudonyms, such as Judge William and others, also discuss many aspects of marriage in considerable detail, but all of them look at this question from their own quite specific existential positions. In the discourse "On the Occasion of a Wedding" Kierkegaard looks at marriage in terms of principles; he points consistently to the manifold difficulties of implementing an ideal marriage and stresses the significance of the resolution in overcoming these difficulties. The upbuilding aspect of this discourse consists in pointing out that only with the help of God can one stick to his resolution; "with God's help the resolution will certainly conquer all."[375]

[372] *Thoughts on Crucial Situations*, p. 25.
[373] Ibid., p. 31.   [374] Ibid., p. 34.   [375] Ibid., p. 70.

In the discourse "At the Side of a Grave" Kierkegaard reflects on death from various perspectives in order to show what man ought to learn from death, which sets an irrevocable period to every man's life. By earnestly thinking about death and the uncertainty of death one learns to use his life properly. "For when conceived in earnestness death gives energy to live as nothing else does. . . ."[376] But "death itself explains nothing";[377] it teaches merely that every man's life comes to an end. A person must himself find or choose a meaning for death and thereby an explanation of life. There are, after all, many interpretations of death as the conclusion of the temporal life. Of the most earnest of them Kierkegaard says: "The explanation has also used other interpretative names; it has called death a transition, a transformation, a suffering, a struggle, the last struggle, a punishment, the wages of sin. Each of these explanations contains an entire view of life."[378] The explanation acquires value only when it also "finds retroactive power in life"[379] and at the same time prepares man for "life's final examination," which "is equally difficult for all."[380]

In *Three Discourses on Imagined Occasions* the dialectical is clearly placed in the service of the upbuilding in illuminating the three central issues of existence. Thinking through these questions must be regarded as the first reaching out of a helping hand to the single individuals who, by means of "occasions" or situations, are faced with these questions which are common and inescapable for all men. The subjective responsibility involved in furthering a man's development in becoming the single individual is awakened through confrontation with these questions.

In the upbuilding or edifying works just discussed the center of gravity is in the esthetic, which, however, continually comes in touch with the religious, understood as knowledge of the eternal in man himself and of God;

[376] Ibid., p. 90.   [377] Ibid., p. 107.   [378] Ibid., p. 110.
[379] Ibid.   [380] Ibid., p. 114.

this knowledge is influential in the realignment of man. The religiousness with which man is confronted is still not Christianity. According to Kierkegaard's dialectic of existence, Christian-religiousness presupposes that a person has come in contact with the ethical and also that he has made the attempt to carry it out. As already mentioned, the ethical has two points of origin: man's consciousness of the eternal in himself and the transcendent power. In the wider sense the first point of departure must be called Socratic, but with Kierkegaard it is deepened by the Old and New Testament conception of God. At the first point of origin a person concentrates primarily on the knowledge of the eternal as the good in and for itself and on actualizing this *in concreto* by willing the good. This starting point, however, lacks the authority which can come only from the transcendent power through the command's unconditioned "You shall." The latter form of the ethical is the highest and it is therefore entirely understandable, dialectically speaking, that Kierkegaard first of all explains the first form of the ethical, which he does in *Edifying Discourses in Various Spirits* and then gives a full account of the second form in the next upbuilding work, *Works of Love*.

One becomes the single individual in the Kierkegaardian meaning of the word only through his attempts at the ethical in both its forms, which means that he no longer holds the laws of social morality and propriety to be the highest norms but rather the eternal's unchangeable claim. It is therefore quite in order that Kierkegaard introduces his account of the ethical in the first discourse in *Edifying Discourses in Various Spirits* with an address to "that single individual."[381] With the subtitle of the discourses, "in various spirits," Kierkegaard wishes to draw attention to the various specific viewpoints from which these discourses address the single individual.

The first portion deals exclusively with the form of the ethical which arises out of man's concentration on his

[381] See Preface to *Purity of Heart* (ed. tr.).

eternal consciousness, although Kierkegaard does link this form of the ethical with religious elements taken from Christianity. He writes of this part of the book: "The design is essentially ethical-ironic and thereby upbuilding, Socratic."[382] The terms "ethical-ironic" and "Socratic" denote not only Kierkegaard's systematic method of procedure but also indicate existential positions. The term "Socratic" also means that concentration on the eternal is a continuation of the way to subjectivity which began with Socrates and the final goal of which is "the single individual," a goal which is reached for the first time, however, in the intensification of the claims by Christianity. The phrase "ethical-ironic" alludes to the scrupulously executed demarcation of the domain of the ethical from the domain where finite teleology prevails and where "providence" has its abode. Essentially Kierkegaard is here depicting in the sphere of the upbuilding the same basic change with respect to goals for human action as Climacus gives in the formula "to relate himself at one and the same time absolutely to the absolute and relatively to the relative,"[383] but with the difference that the eternal in the first section of *Edifying Discourses in Various Spirits* is placed more decisively in the foreground. This is clearly seen in the urging and prompting "to will one thing"[384] which runs through the entire first section of the book. But "to will one thing," namely the good, implies a "no" to all finite goals and a concentration on the eternal, which is always one and the same. But man, who is bound to the multiplicities of this world and forgets the one thing needful, is judged by this strong emphasis on eternity's ethical standards. The final result of man's self-searching in the light of the eternal and in relation to God is repentance, which corresponds exactly to the experience of the single individual's attempts to implement the formula (*Postscript*) quoted above.

[382] VIII¹ A 15 (*J. and P.*, V).
[383] *Postscript*, p. 386 (ed. tr.).
[384] *Purity of Heart*, p. 53 and throughout.

In the second section, "What We Learn from the Lilies of the Field and the Birds of the Air" (in the current English translation together with section three, "The Gospel of Suffering"), Kierkegaard wants to lead the single individual out of the negative position of repentance, whereby one has repented himself out of life's positive relations, back to these relations. This is strongly reminiscent of Judge William in part two of *Either/Or*, who, after completing the movement toward repentance, returns to life's concrete elements.[385] This return to the previous positions is an expression of Kierkegaard's dialectical law of repetition, according to which all the preceding levels are seen in the light of that which the person has most recently attained. Here for the first time Kierkegaard uses this law in his upbuilding or edifying works. He repeats the edifying within the esthetic sphere from the new perspective, and then the ethical is also repeated, but not as a judging authority (as before), but as a positive prompting. The discourse ends with the third stage, the religious, in which one is counseled to hold fast to God alone and seek "first the kingdom of God and His righteousness."[386] Of the repetition carried out in the three parts of this second section Kierkegaard remarks briefly: "The structure of the three discourses about the lilies and the birds is that the first is esthetic, the second ethical, the third religious."[387]

The third section of the discourses, "The Gospel of Suffering," also leads a person back to concrete tasks. Here the ethical appears in its most concrete form, which occurs when the ethical is taught by a paradigm, because the paradigm in an altogether concrete way illustrates particular levels in life.[388] The paradigm is Christ, and the example of

---

[385] *Either/Or*, II, pp. 219-21.
[386] *The Gospel of Suffering*, p. 231.
[387] VIII[1] A 1 (*J. and P.*, V).
[388] A kind of paradigm, the lilies and the birds, is also used in the second portion, but the dissimilarity of "the school-

Christ is used to show how man is to bear his suffering, which "directs a man's attention *inward*" and "then the instruction in it begins."[389] Of his delineation of suffering in "The Gospel of Suffering" Kierkegaard writes that he "leaves the suffering indefinite."[390] This means that here Kierkegaard does *not* make a distinction between different kinds of suffering but takes them all as one. But nevertheless the sufferings Kierkegaard writes about in "The Gospel of Suffering" can be divided into three groups,[391] two of which Kierkegaard later discusses in detail in two sections of *Christian Discourses*. The three kinds of sufferings distinctly named in "The Gospel of Suffering" are: (1) universally human, "unavoidable suffering,"[392] such as sickness and death, (2) involuntary, "innocent suffering," and (3) the suffering[393] a person is exposed to by confessing his Christian faith; Kierkegaard calls this last suffering the "specifically Christian."[394] Of the three kinds of suffering[395] "innocent suffering" refers directly to Kierkegaard's own life. In the pseudonymous authors this kind of suffering is

---

masters," the lilies and the birds, to man makes the whole thing definitely humorous. Kierkegaard writes on this: "As soon as the teacher takes a lower position within the very same genus and stands below the learner, the situation becomes humorous." And further: "But the situation becomes even more humorous when the teacher and the learner do not have even the same genus in common but in qualitative heterogeneity are related inversely to one another. This is the definitely humorous relation. The lilies and the birds." VIII[1] A 15 (*J. and P.*, V).

[389] *The Gospel of Suffering*, p. 55.

[390] VIII[1] A 504 (*J. and P.*, IV).

[391] Kierkegaard does not mention here the religious suffering discussed in *Postscript* (pp. 410-12) and in the discourse "The Thorn in the Flesh" (*Edifying Discourses*, IV, pp. 49-73), which expresses that man is related to an eternal happiness."

[392] VIII[1] A 259 (*J. and P.*, IV).

[393] *The Gospel of Suffering*, p. 139.

[394] VIII[1] A 259 (*J. and P.*, IV).

[395] Compare Arild Christensen, "Romantismens og Søren Kierkegaards Opfattelse af Lidelsen," *Kierkegaardiana*, I, 1955, pp. 28-41.

represented by, for example, "the unhappiest man" and by the various aspects of Quidam's suffering in " 'Guilty?'/ 'Not Guilty?' " It is also worth noting that in "The Gospel of Suffering" "innocent suffering" is made the focus in the most penetrating of the seven discourses, namely, the fourth discourse. It is this suffering which can lead to rebellion against God and to a demonic power if it is not borne meekly. In the fourth discourse Kierkegaard points to the only help there is to conquer this kind of suffering, namely, one's perception that *"in relation to God a man always suffers as being guilty."*[396] Only Christ suffered in every way as innocent. With Christ as prototype, a person must learn to bear all suffering; but in stressing that Christ alone "was without guilt *before God"*[397] Kierkegaard makes a qualitative distinction between Christ and every other man, and thereby he points to Christ not merely as prototype but also as Savior. In his extensive explanation of how Christianity changes suffering to joy, Kierkegaard still does not come any closer to the question of the Atonement in Christ. Before this can be done, the ethical must be intensified even more strongly through the transcendent command of active love to one's fellowmen, which comes in the next book, *Works of Love*.

Of those who might not be able to understand this steady and consistent carrying through of the ethical development whereby the Atonement comes to occupy its proper place, Kierkegaard writes: "In all likelihood the wiseacres who know how to rattle off everything will charge my *Christian Discourses* with not containing the Atonement. Consequently, after 5 years of having the chance to learn from me how maieutically I proceed, they have remained every bit as wise—will probably go on being that. First the first, and then the next."[398] This statement with reference to the edifying works is an expression of the dialectical principle

[396] *The Gospel of Suffering*, p. 67. See also very end of *Either/Or*, II.
[397] *The Gospel of Suffering*, p. 73.
[398] VIII¹ A 49 (*J. and P.*, V).

employed especially in the pseudonymous works: "pursue a conclusion single-mindedly to the uttermost."[399]

The higher level of the ethical in *Works of Love* in relation to the *Edifying Discourses in Various Spirits* comes out clearly in the principal differences between the two books. *Edifying Discourses in Various Spirits*, with its starting point in the words from Ecclesiastes—"He has made everything beautiful in its time; also he has put eternity into man's mind"[400]—affirms that man can make "the decision" for this eternal "by willing one thing," which means to will the eternal. *Works of Love*, on the other hand, presents God as coming as an outside power with his authoritative "You *shall* love." And this command did not "arise in any man's heart";[401] this can be pronounced only by God.

In explaining what it means "to will one thing" all the time Kierkegaard mentions "double-mindedness" as the opposite of "to will one thing." Kierkegaard uses the phrase "double-mindedness," which he found in the Epistle of James,[402] to cover the concept of despair. In *Works of Love*, however, he points out that the negative response to the command "You *shall* love" expresses itself in offense.[403] Of the negative terms "despair" and "offense," offense appears in a more advanced stage in a person's spiritual development, since it belongs to the specifically Christian sphere.

Writing in *Edifying Discourses in Various Spirits* Kierkegaard says of the single individual: "this consciousness of being an individual is the primary consciousness in a man, which is his eternal consciousness."[404] Here the category of the single individual is linked to a man's "eternal consciousness." In *Works of Love*, on the other hand, the single individual is elevated to a qualitatively new level in that the single individual here is addressed by God with

[399] X⁶ B 127, p. 169 (*J. and P.*, V).
[400] *Purity of Heart*, p. 36; Ecclesiastes 3:11.
[401] *Works of Love*, p. 40.   [402] James 4:8.
[403] *Works of Love*, p. 41.   [404] *Purity of Heart*, p. 193.

"you" [*Du*], which sets a man in a personal and decisive relationship to God.

One more essential difference may be mentioned. In *Edifying Discourses in Various Spirits* man is primarily concerned with himself, either as willing or as suffering; in *Works of Love* his attention is turned toward God and the neighbor, even though the interior battle of self-denial must be present as the presupposition for neighbor-love.

In *Works of Love* the ethical Christian ideal is carried to its highest point, and to reach this high point Kierkegaard employs his usual dialectical procedure of beginning his deliberations on the lower levels in order finally to describe the highest position. This is done on three levels. (1) First of all he distinguishes the Christian love implied in the command to love one's neighbor from the purely human forms of love, especially from its highest forms as erotic love and friendship, and shows what forces in the sphere of the human determine relationships among men. Of these he mentions: "impulse . . . feeling and inclination with one or another discriminating alloy of duty, natural relationship, right,"[405] and the calculation of the understanding.

(2) In contrast to this, it is shown that Christian love always has God as the "middle term"; a person relates to the neighbor only through God. At the same time Kierkegaard specifies the nature of Christian love by pointing out that it is "the fulfilling of the law"[406] and "a matter of conscience,"[407] and that it reaches out to all men and is a constant obligation toward the neighbor.

(3) Not until "the second series" or part two of *Works of Love* is Christian love described as it begins to function. Continuing Paul's words about love in I Corinthians, Chapter 13, Kierkegaard shows the different aspects of Christian love. Kierkegaard's own words, which he used in one of the eighteen edifying discourses, namely, "Love Shall

[405] *Works of Love*, p. 144.   [406] Ibid., pp. 99ff.
[407] Ibid., pp. 136ff.

Cover a Multitude of Sins,"[408] may be used to present love's demands. There he declares: "We shall speak as to the perfect."[409] And further: "If there was someone who did not feel himself perfect, the speech made no difference."[410] Kierkegaard knows that the ideal is placed so high that only the "perfect" would be able to carry it out. But love's demands are addressed to all. Through their absoluteness, then, love's demands have two aspects. The first—that their presentation carries a convicting power; a person must be brought to see how far away he is from the ideal and be humbled under the ideal. This is the goal of the description of love at work. Seen in this light, Kierkegaard is right in saying that *Works of Love* contains "a powerful polemic."[411]

But there is another aspect as well. Strongly convinced that the first Christians, especially the apostles, made more effort to actualize these ideal demands than was the case in later generations, Kierkegaard also ascribes an existential meaning to these demands. It is significant that he singles out the apostle John as an example of one "who was perfected in love."[412] The apostle has become "one with the commandment"[413] about loving.

If these two aspects (ideal and existential) of love were applied to Climacus' differentiation between religiousness A and B, it could be said that the ethical, especially in the first section (*Purity of Heart*) of *Edifying Discourses in Various Spirits*, falls entirely under religiousness A. The Christian ethic in *Works of Love* falls under religiousness B as well as under A. In the first case ethics is essentially an imperative with convicting power and prepares man for the consciousness of sin; in the second case, after man has come under the consciousness of sin and forgiveness, it becomes an indicative ethic, a prompting, motivating power.

[408] *Edifying Discourses*, I, pp. 61-90.
[409] Ibid., p. 66.   [410] Ibid., p. 76.
[411] VIII[1] A 559 (*J. and P.*, V).
[412] *Works of Love*, p. 344.   [413] Ibid.

After having the viewpoints of Christian ethics reach their climax in *Works of Love*, Kierkegaard uses his law of repetition in exactly the same way as in the first part of *Edifying Discourses in Various Spirits*, where he carried the ethical to its ultimate conclusion. In part one of *Christian Discourses* he goes back to the previous levels as he repeats the parable of the lilies and the birds, but now from a higher point of view, that is, with the Christian ethic in *Works of Love* as background. This higher viewpoint comes out in the conflict between paganism and Christianity running through all seven discourses in part one. True to his dialectical method, he begins with elementary human problems such as the cares of poverty and gradually ascends to cares with more and more of a spiritual cast, such as the "cares of presumption,"[414] "the cares of self-torment,"[415] and the "cares of irresolution, fickleness, disconsolateness."[416] Through all this the contrast between paganism and Christianity comes out more sharply, with the result that the discourses have a polemic thrust. Part two, "Joyful Notes in the Strife of Suffering," also contains a repetition. Kierkegaard isolates "innocent suffering,"[417] which was also touched on in *Edifying Discourses in Various Spirits*, and now shows how the single individual by holding fast to God and eternity not only overcomes it but that these sufferings become significant for his spiritual growth. It could be added here that at the time Kierkegaard wrote *Christian Discourses* he was seeking to understand "innocent suffering," to which he felt bound, and to win a cheerful courage and boldness with respect to it. He comes to the resolution that the danger is not in "innocent suffering" but in the sin. Therefore he formulates the sentence which is repeated for every single discourse, that "sin alone is man's corruption,"[418] the underlying theme for these discourses.

---

[414] *Christian Discourses*, p. 17.
[415] Ibid., p. 73.   [416] Ibid., p. 83.
[417] VIII¹ A 504 (*J. and P.*, IV).
[418] *Christian Discourses*, p. 107.

In part three, "Thoughts Which Wound from Behind—
for Upbuilding," Kierkegaard aims to depict the specifically
Christian suffering, voluntary suffering. He says of it
". . . voluntarily to give up all is Christian."[419] In a journal
entry he says more specifically: "To suffer patiently is not
specifically Christian at all—but freely to choose the suffering which one could also avoid, freely to choose it in the
interest of the good cause—this is Christian. I wonder if
many pagans did not also suffer patiently. Moreover, what
similarity is there between suffering patiently (unavoidable
suffering) and this, that Christ was God and yet chose to
suffer?"[420]

But it is clear to Kierkegaard that pointing out this kind
of suffering implies a strong polemic against his age and
the view of Christianity prevalent in his age.[421] He has
strong doubts about how right he is in including this part,
for after "the powerful polemic in *Works of Love*" he actually wanted to strike "a milder tone."[422] But his last judgment with respect to this third part and thereby with respect to its relation to the three other parts of *Christian
Discourses* is that "Without the third section *Christian Discourses* is much too mild, for me not truly in character;
they are mild enough as it is. And how in the world would
I get a more felicitous juxtaposition than with the enormous thrust in section three—and the hidden inwardness
in the fourth, simply because it is the communion on Fri-
day."[423] And he adds in the same note: "Then, too, without
the third section *Christian Discourses* is much too repeti-
tious." Kierkegaard refers here to the repetitions of the
previous discourses. Of the seven discourses in part three,
five deal directly or indirectly with voluntary suffering.
But also in the discourse, "The Resurrection of the Dead

[419] Ibid., p. 186.
[420] VIII¹ A 259 (*J. and P.*, IV).
[421] See, for example, VIII¹ A 486 (*J. and P.*, V) and A 559
(*J. and P.*, V).
[422] VIII¹ A 558 (*J. and P.*, V).
[423] VIII¹ A 560 (*J. and P.*, V).

Is at Hand, of the Just—and of the Unjust"[424] Kierkegaard tries to remind the single individual of the judgment the gospel speaks of and to lead him to greater responsibility and earnestness. The seventh discourse, "He Was Believed on in the World,"[425] with its added "confession of faith,"[426] has a strongly personal character, since Kierkegaard no doubt wants to express through this that he now puts all his trust in Christ through faith in the forgiveness of sins. It is, in fact, in the spring of 1848 that the question of the forgiveness of sins looms up existentially for him. Several days prior to the publication of *Christian Discourses* he writes: "My whole nature is changed. My concealment and reserve are broken—I am free to speak.

Great God, grant me grace!"[427]

Although doubt moderates his hope a few days later, the following journal entry in all probability is an accurate statement of his position at that time with respect to Christianity: "I do believe in the forgiveness of sins, but I interpret this, as before, to mean that I must bear my punishment of remaining in this painful prison of reserve all my life, in a more profound sense separated from the company of other men; yet this is mitigated by the thought that God has forgiven me."[428] This indicates that his melancholy, which until now had stood in the way of accepting faith in the forgiveness of sins, is not totally overcome, but that he has reached, nevertheless, the second immediacy, where Christ is in the center of the single individual's life, as expressed in the "confession of faith" above.

From the fourth part of *Christian Discourses* it might seem that Kierkegaard is approaching a final phase in his authorship. This could perhaps be confirmed by the fact that some four months after the publication of *Christian Discourses* he published his last purely esthetic pseudony-

[424] *Christian Discourses*, pp. 210ff.
[425] Ibid., pp. 239ff.   [426] Ibid., p. 248.
[427] VIII¹ A 640 (*J. and P.*, V).
[428] VIII¹ A 645 (*J. and P.*, V).

mous work as a serial in *The Fatherland*, calling it *The Crisis and a Crisis in the Life of an Actress*.[429] Up to this point the upbuilding or edifying series and the pseudonymous authorship have gone along together. Until the publishing of *Concluding Unscientific Postscript*, the pseudonymous authorship is more strongly represented; from the subsequent period of his immersion in Christian religious themes there are two books which must be classified with the esthetic writings—namely, *Two Ages: the Age of Revolution and the Present Age. A Literary Review*,[430] following *Concluding Unscientific Postscript*, and *The Crisis and a Crisis in the Life of an Actress*. The first of these books contains in addition to excellent literary criticism a penetrating analysis of the reasons for the leveling process which Kierkegaard believes to be under way in his day. In publishing the second purely esthetic work, *The Crisis and a Crisis in the Life of an Actress*, an esthetic analysis of Madame Heiberg and her art, Kierkegaard wishes to emphasize that he has finally come to the end of the line running parallel to the upbuilding literature. "After two years during which religious works only were published, there follows a little esthetic article. Hence assurance was provided both first and last against an interpretation of the phenomenon which supposes an esthetic author who with the lapse of time has changed and become a religious author."[431]

Despite the apparent finality of these works, Kierkegaard has not reached the end of his authorship. He still has not discussed the very important Christian theme: offense. In depicting the movement toward Christianity Climacus had, in fact, mentioned this concept and related it to faith, but as a humorist he was not qualified to give a detailed explanation of the concept "offense." The concept "contempo-

---

[429] *S. V.*, X, pp. 319-44, now in English under the title *Crisis in the Life of an Actress*. See Bibliography.

[430] *S. V.*, VIII, pp. 3-104, part of which is in English under the title *The Present Age*. See Bibliography.

[431] *The Point of View*, p. 12.

raneity" also requires a study, especially after Kierkegaard, through constant emphasis upon the ethical requirements, perceives that accentuating direct contemporaneity could reinforce these requirements by putting them under the paradigmatic in such a way that Christ's earthly existence forms the paradigm. It is Kierkegaard's existential experiences as a Christian, especially in the conflict with *The Corsair*, which bring this out more strongly. His theoretical knowledge about Christianity is gradually enlarged to an existential insight into certain central Christian truths, so that he can write: "Everything involved in 'imitation,' dying to the world, being born again, and so on, I myself was not aware of in 1848."[432]

This new vision of what Christianity requires of the man who has reached the new immediacy is now illustrated in Kierkegaard's usual dialectical way on the various existential levels in man's development—this time in the little work, *The Lilies of the Field and the Birds of the Air*. In these discourses, corresponding to the three stages, we meet the same theme as in the second part ("What We Learn from the Lilies of the Field and the Birds of the Air") of *Edifying Discourses in Various Spirits*, but the later discourses imply the consciousness of the new immediacy which is expressed in the fourth part of *Christian Discourses*. In a journal entry from about the time of the publication of *Christian Discourses*, Kierkegaard clearly declares that the next collection of discourses will make a distinction between poetry as an example of the highest esthetic immediacy and Christianity as "the poetry of eternity" (that is, religious immediacy). Kierkegaard had personally experienced this in his own life, and a few words from the entry are addressed primarily to himself: "Immediacy or spontaneity is poetically the very thing we desire to return to (we want our childhood again etc.), but from a Christian point of view immediacy is lost, and it

[432] X⁴ A 553, p. 372 (*J. and P.*, II, 1942).

ought not be *yearned* for again but should be attained again."[433]

Therefore Kierkegaard begins the first discourse by stressing *silence*,[434] by which the first immediacy is promptly put in second place. Silence is analogous to resignation, and unconditioned silence means that the spontaneous, immediate man's hankering to have his desires fulfilled must become silent in order that he may become sensitive and responsive to what God wants to say to him. The ethical in the second discourse accentuates *obedience*[435] after he has made the leap from the multiplicity of the esthetic to the choice of God. The demotion of the esthetic as inessential compared with God is clearly heard in these sentences: "There is an either/or: either *God*/or . . . the rest is indifferent. Whatsoever a man chooses, when he does not choose God, he has missed the either/or, he is in perdition with his either/or. So then: either *God*/. . . . no stress falls upon the second term, except by reason of opposition to God, whereby the stress is laid infinitely upon God, so that properly it is God who, as Himself the object of the choice, makes the decision tense, so that the choice becomes truly an either/or."[436]

The third discourse sets joy[437] in the center, a joy which is distinct from the spontaneous, immediate man's fleeting joys in having his desires fulfilled. "The absolute joy"[438] is reached only through the relationship to God, and a person can hold fast to it through all situations if he obeys the apostle's words: "Cast *all* your cares *upon* God."[439] Throughout the repetition of the three stages on a higher plane, Kierkegaard refrains from touching on the heaviest sorrow, "sorrow for sin,"[440] which he strongly stresses in part two

[433] VIII¹ A 643 (*J. and P.*, II, 1942).

[434] *The Lilies of the Field and the Birds of the Air*, together with *Christian Discourses*, p. 322.

[435] Ibid., p. 336.   [436] Ibid., p. 333.

[437] Ibid., p. 347.   [438] Ibid., p. 353.

[439] Ibid., p. 352. See I Peter 5:7.

[440] *The Lilies of the Field*, p. 354.

of *Christian Discourses* and which is given detailed consideration later when he amplifies the concept of offense in *Practice [Training] in Christianity.*

Prior to this work and prior to an intensification of the ethical toward the paradigmatic, two works appear (under the pseudonym H. H.) with the joint covering-title *Two Minor Ethical-Religious Treatises*: "Has a Man the Right To Let Himself Be Put to Death for the Truth?"[441] and "Of the Difference between a Genius and an Apostle."[442] In these two treatises Kierkegaard ponders his position, with the imminent sharpening of the Christian requirements in mind. He is aided in clarifying his own position by the situation of Pastor Adler, who had claimed a direct revelation from Christ. In *The Book on Adler*[443] Kierkegaard submits Adler's claim to a thorough investigation and simultaneously sets down his own views concerning the concept of revelation, strongly emphasizing the enormous responsibility which accompanies a direct order from God. Kierkegaard himself never claims to have had such a direct revelation; he regards himself as merely a genius concerned with religion and obliged to get his instructions indirectly, by eavesdropping.

In the little treatise "Of the Difference between a Genius and an Apostle" Kierkegaard shows that there is a qualitative difference between the two. By being chosen directly by Christ, as the apostles were, or called by a revelation, as Paul was, an apostle gets *"his divine authority"* and is in an *"absolute, paradoxical teleology."*[444] The genius, however, is on a lower level and represents merely the highest in the development of the human race. But as Vigilius Haufniensis points out, a secular genius or a genius in

[441] In English translation together with *The Present Age* (1940 edition). See Bibliography.

[442] Ibid. (also in 1962 edition).

[443] *The Book on Adler* takes up most of Volume VII² of the *Papirer*, and the major part is in English translation under the title *On Authority and Revelation*. See Bibliography.

[444] *The Present Age*, p. 91.

the esthetic sphere can make the transition to the religious sphere and become a religious genius[445] who has the possibility of being placed in the service of the religious, as was the case with Kierkegaard. As a religious genius using his own experiences he knows how to give a new and original presentation of the way to Christianity. But at the same time that he tightens up the Christian ideals, the question of how far he himself should venture out in his life becomes more acute. For the apostle or for the one who receives a direct call this question does not exist; even if such a person exposes himself to personal danger, he is simply obeying God's orders. But one who has only his conscience to guide the extent of his venturing out and to decide whether other men are permitted to become guilty of his death cannot avoid painful dialectical deliberations. These questions are dealt with in the second treatise: "Has a Man the Right To Let Himself Be Put to Death for the Truth?" The pseudonymous writer H. H. strongly emphasizes that the question here is not whether this man has the courage to let himself be put to death—this deliberation lies on a lower level—but how the single individual before God can defend letting other men become guilty of his death. In concentrating on this question Kierkegaard learns to know his limitations and the solution to his next task. On the one hand it is clear to him that Christianity has far greater requirements than he had advanced hitherto, and on the other hand he perceives that he cannot personally fulfill these highest demands of Christianity. Kierkegaard attempts to solve this problem by introducing a new pseudonym who will represent Christianity in its more rigorous form and be a contrast to Kierkegaard's own position as a Christian.

[445] Compare to Vigilius Haufniensis's comment on Talleyrand as a genius: "If such a genius had disdained the temporal as the immediate, had turned toward himself and toward the divine, what a religious genius might have come out of it!" *The Concept of Anxiety* [*Dread*], pp. 91f. On genius and the religious, see note 224 above.

The name of the new pseudonymous writer appears for the first time in a journal entry of 1848: "If I should need a new pseudonym in the future he shall be called Anticlimacus. And then he must be recklessly ironical and humorous.[446] The choice of the name "Anticlimacus" shows that Kierkegaard intends to set up a contrast to the principal pseudonym Climacus himself and not to one of the pseudonyms subordinate to Climacus. He is supposed to take a position in contrast to that of Climacus, since Climacus merely presents the levels in the direction of Christianity but without wanting to call himself a Christian and without being able to come any closer to the decisive Christian qualifications. This means that Anti-Climacus (as spelled later) is supposed to introduce a movement going far beyond the domain of humor which Climacus represents and that now the discussion is supposed to be unambiguous and without the humorist's retraction of what has been said. Just the contemplated emphasis on imitation would have to lead to the repudiation of humor, for the viewpoint of humor would pay no attention to external recognizable signs in the process of ethical-religious development, which is precisely what one would do if imitation were to come to the foreground. Thus humor and likewise hidden inwardness (the next position after humor) step back to make room for the visible decisions related to imitation.

When Kierkegaard in his first note about Anti-Climacus says that he must be "ironical and humorous," he is thinking of the form in which Anti-Climacus should set forth his views. The fact that Kierkegaard places "ironical" first must be understood to mean that irony in particular should be brought to bear as the form of attack, which is also understandable, given the condition that irony has its proper role in showing up disparity in the external actuality; whereas humor turns toward man's interior actuality. As will be seen, this transition from the stage of humor to Anti-Climacus's ironical-humorous standpoint finally ends

[446] IX A 9 (*J. and P.*, V).

in the purely ironic form during Kierkegaard's attack upon the external form of Christendom.

Thus the main difference between Climacus and Anti-Climacus is that the former "drowns everything in humor; therefore he himself retracts his book." Anti-Climacus, on the other hand, is "thetic,"[447] that is, he does not retract his stand but stands by it. The relationship could also be expressed by saying that Anti-Climacus has made the decisive leap into Christianity, and Climacus continually recoils from it.

There is a further difference in that Climacus represents the solid difficulties in becoming a Christian, which is why all the pseudonyms subordinate to him are most concerned with man's psychological side, namely with the individual's thralldom to heredity and environment. Quidam in Frater Taciturnus's presentation is the first to reach a position where the *"psychological"*[448] seeks its religious expression through repentance. In contrast to Climacus, who is interested in finding the difficulties in existence,[449] Anti-Climacus wants to advance the ideal demands as sharply and clearly as possible. But the genuine union of these two directions is constituted only by a spiritually striving individual. The tension between these two opposite poles is found to an exceptional degree in Kierkegaard. Many examples could be cited, but we mention only one in *The Concept of Anxiety* which clearly revolves around Kierkegaard himself. It refers to a struggle with "closed-up-ness" or "reserve" [*Indesluttethed*], which places the individual in the sphere of guilt, and to the exceptional difficulty of this struggle. Of the individual who comes up against these exceptional difficulties Vigilius Haufniensis says: "In order that this phenomenon may occur the individual must be such a blending of purity and impurity as seldom is encountered."[450] The impurity provides the concrete difficulties which Climacus deals with through the subordinate

---

[447] X[1] A 530 (*J. and P.*, V).   [448] *Stages*, p. 404.
[449] *Postscript*, p. 166.
[450] *The Concept of Anxiety* [*Dread*], p. 114.

pseudonyms and which first involve original sin and second the individual's own delinquencies. On the other hand, purity alludes to the always-present ideal demands. Seen from this perspective, Climacus's relation to Anti-Climacus is like that between actuality and ideality in a man's life.[451]

Despite these differences between Climacus and Anti-Climacus, they do have a similarity: both are dialecticians, the one with his center of gravity in the human and the other in the distinctively Christian. A clear indication of this similarity and dissimilarity between the two pseudonyms is found in Anti-Climacus's short but extremely important essay from 1849: "Climacus and Anti-Climacus, a Dialectical Discovery."[452] It goes on to say of the relation between the two pseudonyms: "For we are related to each other, but we are not twins, we are opposites." The contrast is indicated more explicitly when Climacus says "that he is not a Christian," but Anti-Climacus says of himself that he "in hidden inwardness is . . . an extraordinary Christian such as there has never been." It is worth noting that Anti-Climacus describes his position as "hidden inwardness" in the same breath with the blunt words about being such an "extraordinary Christian." Regarding the special kind of relationship between them, he says: "If it should happen sometime that we switched identities at the instant of contact so that I would say of myself what Johannes says of himself, and conversely, it would make no difference. Just one thing is impossible—that we both say the same thing about ourselves; on the other hand it is possible that we both could vanish." This declares that by the very fact of their representing contrasting viewpoints they are inextricably bound to each other in that they complement each other. In the next sentence the nature of this "relationship" is illuminated when Anti-

[451] The high ideality was especially due to the circumstance that Kierkegaard was, "religiously understood, even as a child, prepledged [*forlovet*]" to service in the cause of Christ. X[5] B 153 (*J. and P.*, V). See also X[1] A 272 (*J. and P.*, V).

[452] X[6] B 48 (*J. and P.*, V).

Climacus says of himself and of Climacus: "Actually, we do not exist, but he who does come to be simply and plainly a genuine Christian will be able to speak of us two brothers —opposites—just as the sailor speaks of the twins by which he steers." In other words, the two pseudonyms do not duplicate a concrete individual actuality since they, like "the twins"[453] in the constellation, exist only as points of orientation. This establishes the abstract character of the two pseudonyms; both of them are dialecticians who only advance universal laws for the orienting of the single individual. Anti-Climacus concludes his essay by saying that while sailors' stories are not always true, the story of the two contrasting pseudonyms has reality to the extent that everyone who wants to be "the true Christian" will discover these contrasts.

These two orienting viewpoints propounded by the dialecticians Climacus and Anti-Climacus presuppose an individual life for which they can be guiding principles. Together with Climacus the subordinate pseudonyms dealt with such an existence, but we will also encounter this individual line in Anti-Climacus. But since here it is a matter of a Christian existence, this approach does not need to fight its way, with the aid of pseudonyms, out of the multiplicity of esthetic and ethical attitudes, which are especially characteristic of the first two stages, but faces the one task of practicing [indøve] Christianity. If we turn to Kierkegaard's own situation while preparing to use Anti-Climacus for this high-tension interpretation of Christianity, his position may be described something like this: he has gone beyond the stage of humor, but he does not want to be paired with Anti-Climacus. Kierkegaard very briefly defines his existential position with these words: "I would

[453] Twin brothers. See Acts 28:11. H. Mosbech's *Kommentar til Apostlenes Gerninger* (Copenhagen, 1929) states that "the twins (*Dioskurerne*) designates Zeus's twin sons by Leda: Castor and Pollux; they were regarded as half-gods and were the patron deities of seafarers; a constellation bore their name and was connected with them, and sailors used it to steer by."

place myself higher than Johannes Climacus, lower than Anti-Climacus."[454] In the same entry Kierkegaard says that the fact that Anti-Climacus confuses himself with his "ideality" can be interpreted as the demonic in him. Kierkegaard goes on to say of Anti-Climacus: ". . . but his portrayal of ideality may be entirely true, and I humble myself before it."

According to what has been said, Anti-Climacus, in explaining what it means to be a Christian, must, like Climacus before him, be attentive to the universal and to the individual approach. Without the latter he would himself be guilty of the purely abstract presentation which Climacus combatted through his subordinate pseudonyms.

The deeper insight into Christian existence that Kierkegaard believes he has found after 1848 must continue to have a tensing influence on the two approaches.

Despite Kierkegaard's satisfaction with the choice of the pseudonym "Anti-Climacus," whose important function in the authorship is readily clear to him, he is not spared—as his journals reveal—many painful thoughts about how closely related his own person should be to this pseudonym as he uses it in his two works *The Sickness Unto Death* and *Practice [Training] in Christianity*.[455]

These two books, Kierkegaard's last two substantial works, can be looked at together as a sharpened *Either/Or* carried through to its final logical conclusion, which goes much farther than the first *Either/Or* in Judge William's attempt to create an *"equilibrium"* between the contrasting alternatives. In *The Sickness Unto Death*, despair and offense, faith's negative opposites, are taken on an ascending scale to their extreme forms; in contrast to this, *Practice in Christianity* presents the struggle of faith and Christian pathos at the highest level. In the first book time and the single individual are supposed to be manifest; in the second, the ideal demands are set forth.

[454] X¹ A 517 (*J. and P.,* V).
[455] See X¹ A 422 (*J. and P.,* V); X² A 89 (*J. and P.,* V); X² A 147 (*J. and P.,* V).

The structure of *The Sickness Unto Death* embodies a very clearly designed progressive dialectical movement; of all the authorship this work most obviously carries through the development of a theme. *Practice in Christianity* came about through the joining together of some separate pieces,[456] but Anti-Climacus manages to give this work, too, a dialectical, cohesive structure.

The Sickness Unto Death may be looked upon as a continuation of *The Concept of Anxiety*. Since *The Concept of Anxiety* begins on the lowest level[457] with the portrayal of the human situation and the resulting forms of misrelation in the synthesis expressed in anxiety, and since *The Sickness Unto Death* deals with the higher forms of this misrelation, these two books are best suited to demonstrate the continuous dialectical line which certainly also runs through the other books in Kierkegaard's authorship but comes out particularly in these two books with all the clarity and convincing power one could wish. In order to show the progressive dialectical connection between these two books, we go back to the central viewpoints in *The Concept of Anxiety* to show how they find their next and complete development in *The Sickness Unto Death*.

Throughout the exposition Vigilius Haufniensis consistently maintains his stated goal of describing the nature and forms of anxiety. According to him the domain of anxiety lies within the scope of man's mental-physical synthesis. Vigilius Haufniensis places the individual who finds himself in this state in relation to the three highest external powers man has encountered in his world-historical journey. In paganism fate was considered to be the final authority in existence. In Judaism it was God as the transcendent power who stood behind everything; in Christianity man meets God as the concrete revelation in time.

By bringing the individual located on the mental-emotional level into relation with the three powers, Vigilius Haufniensis gets three completely different forms of anxi-

---

[456] X¹ A 422 (*J. and P.*, V).
[457] See *The Concept of Anxiety* [*Dread*], pp. 37-41.

ety. The anxiety over fate is defined as anxiety over nothing, since fate, seen from a higher point of view, is a nothing. The relation to the personal transcendent power involves anxiety over guilt. In the single individual's meeting with the revealed truth, he is concretely enlightened about the good, whereby the ambiguity of anxiety disappears and anxiety goes in two directions: either as "anxiety over evil" or as "anxiety over good."

With this procedural method Vigilius Haufniensis is able to encompass all forms of anxiety in his portrayal, but in order to do it consistently he has to refrain altogether from considering the eternal in man; the individual must be kept within the scope of the mental-physical synthesis all along the way. Consequently the development in this portrayal of successively more negative forms of anxiety takes place through the individual's confrontation with the eternal *outside of man*. It must be interpolated here that the belief in fate as the utmost power in immanence is analogous to man's belief in the eternal. If in *The Concept of Anxiety* Vigilius Haufniensis had taken into consideration the factor of the eternal *in man*, he would have come upon the category of despair as well as the category of anxiety, since despair expresses the misrelation within man himself between his eternal and temporal components. Without a doubt Vigilius Haufniensis avoids mixing the two conceptual spheres on purely dialectical grounds, but he does, however, finally arrive at the point in *The Concept of Anxiety* where he presents a *"Schema for the exclusion or the lack of inwardness"*[458] as the dividing line between anxiety on the one side and despair and also offense on the other side. Inwardness means that a person turns toward his inner center; he discovers the eternal within himself, but by excluding this inwardness he ends in despair. Vigilius Haufniensis on this occasion mentions offense rather than despair, but this is also in

[458] Ibid., p. 126.

order, since the important thing for Vigilius Haufniensis is not to bring the eternal element in man to the fore but to confront man with Christ, but the negative form of this relation is always offense. Thus Vigilius Haufniensis has dialectical reasons for not naming despair as the form of misrelation in the synthesis arising after a man through self-examination has found the eternal within himself, without, however, trying to actualize it.

But Kierkegaard already had a clear conception of the forms of despair, and even though Judge William does not pursue them further, they are used in *Either/Or*. The negative level of offense following upon despair, which Vigilius Haufniensis just reaches and which points beyond the domain of anxiety, had already been defined basically by Climacus. *The Sickness Unto Death*, therefore, begins where Vigilius Haufniensis ends, namely, with an emphasis upon the two subsequent regions and the concepts despair and offense.

Since the problem of anxiety is examined so thoroughly in *The Concept of Anxiety*, Anti-Climacus-Kierkegaard does not need to go into this subject any further but merely repeats the position in *The Concept of Anxiety* very briefly and uses it as background for the reflections to follow. However, in his preliminary draft of *The Sickness Unto Death* Kierkegaard gives some detailed and excellent similarities and dissimilarities between the two books. Kierkegaard makes a special effort here to distinguish between despair and anxiety as the antecedent position which still belongs under "the composition of the mental and the physical." Here Kierkegaard does not use the terms "anxiety" to characterize this domain—but "dizziness" [*Svimmelhed*]. Vigilius Haufniensis had already pointed out the close correspondence between anxiety and dizziness in saying: "One may liken anxiety to dizziness." And further: "Thus anxiety is the dizziness of freedom which occurs when the spirit would posit the synthesis, and freedom then gazes down into its own possibility and grasps at finiteness for support."[459] The expression "dizziness" is another name for the same state, but the term "anxiety" puts more stress on the element of "choice" and "dizziness" stresses the element of cognition—yet both lie on the same plane. Despair is a more advanced stage than anxiety and dizziness: "in all despair there is an interplay of finitude and infinitude, of the divine and the human, of freedom and necessity."[460]

Anxiety and dizziness still lie within the scope of relative contrasts, the contrast between body and mind [*Sjæl*], where the mind or soul as yet contains the eternal element only potentially, but in despair the qualitative contrast comes to the fore, since the eternal element in man is now accentuated as a contrast to the synthesis between mind and body alone.

Anti-Climacus touches very briefly in *The Sickness Unto Death* on the stage of anxiety, since here everything is looked at from the point of view that man can acquire or has knowledge of the eternal within him. Therefore it is also understandable that Kierkegaard intends to exclude the complex of problems related to anxiety and original sin from his study of despair in *The Sickness Unto Death*. In entries for *The Sickness Unto Death* he writes: "It is best to remove the allusions to the dogma of original sin which are found especially in chapter II (and anywhere else they are found). It would take me too far out, or farther than is needed here or is useful."[461] But in the second chapter referred to he does allow two allusions to anxiety and original sin to remain and underscores their significance for an account of sin, "the dialectic of sin,"[462] since the possibility of sin begins with anxiety; "sin pre-

---

[459] *The Concept of Anxiety* [Dread], p. 55 (ed. tr., S. V., IV, p. 331).
[460] VIII² B 168, p. 261 (*J. and P.*, I, 749).
[461] VIII² B 166 (*J. and P.*, V).
[462] *The Sickness Unto Death*, pp. 232, 251.

supposes itself" through anxiety and thereafter is "explained by the doctrine of original sin."[463]

In introducing the core definition of the concept of despair in *The Sickness Unto Death*, Anti-Climacus presents a whole new aspect of the relation between anxiety and despair: "In the relation between two, the relation is the third as a negative unity, and the two relate themselves to the relation, and in the relation to the relation. Within the definition of mind, the relation between mind and body is such a relation. If, however, the relation relates itself to itself, then this relation is the positive third, and this is the self."[464]

In this formulation of the two levels of the synthesis, attention is directed to all the elements which are part of these syntheses. In addition to what is called "the relation between two" on the first level of the synthesis, a third is also set forth, "a negative unity," whereby the first synthesis acquires three parts, the third part of which corresponds to the expression "the first self,"[465] which Kierkegaard uses in his edifying works. The adjective "negative" signifies that the third element, like the first synthesis as a unit, still lies on the plane of the finite. In Kierkegaard's dialectical language, finiteness always falls within negativity and only with the eternal is there a positivity.

On the next level of the synthesis, which is constituted by spirit (the self) as "the positive third," corresponding to "the deeper self"[466] in the edifying works, Anti-Climacus does not clearly state the content of the three parts making up the synthesis but develops this in the succeeding expositions. The first part is finiteness, including all three elements from the previous synthesis, that is the mind-body, and the "negative unity," or the "first self." The second part is represented by infinity or possibility; with

[463] Ibid., p. 220.
[464] Ibid., p. 146 (ed. tr., S. V., XI, p. 127).
[465] *Edifying Discourses*, IV, pp. 95-96.
[466] Ibid., p. 35.

this part the eternal in man comes to the fore and as such must be interpreted as the ethical in the proper sense, which from its side poses a task for man. Spirit is the positive third part which is to form a unity between the two first parts and set the synthesis in motion. The term "the positive third" expresses the element of the eternal, by which the spirit (the self) is set in close relationship to the second part, which represents the eternal as requirement. The spirit's (self's) actuating function is marked by ever greater consciousness and transparency as the synthesis comes into existence, but this consciousness and transparency may also be present even if the person fails to realize the goal of the synthesis. In both eventualities, it still holds for the self that "the more consciousness, the more self; the more consciousness, the more will, and the more will the more self."[467]

With this emphasis on all the elements of the synthesis, two features of Kierkegaard's dialectic become clear: (1) the higher form of the synthesis, which assimilates all the previous parts of the development, provides a good example of *"the simultaneity of the individual factors"*[468] on each higher level. (2) The ethical as the central concern in all Kierkegaard's dialectical and existential deliberations also emerges clearly now by forming the second part of the synthesis. The ethical is more clearly established through Anti-Climacus's characterization of the way the transition to the higher synthesis takes place. "Accordingly the development consists of infinitely moving away from oneself in the process of infinitizing oneself and of infinitely returning to oneself in the process of finitizing."[469] This statement delineates the double movement of infinity, which is the prerequisite for actualizing the higher synthesis, and it must be regarded as a principal formula for all Kierkegaard's earlier dialectical explanations of the application

[467] *The Sickness Unto Death,* p. 162; see also p. 175.
[468] *Postscript,* p. 307.
[469] *The Sickness Unto Death,* pp. 162-63 (ed. tr., S. V., XI, p. 143).

of the ethical in existence. The goal during the actualizing of the synthesis is defined from now on as follows: "in relating itself to itself and in willing to be itself, the self is grounded transparently in the power that established it."[470]

This declaration of the goal for the actualized synthesis now serves as the point of departure for a sketching of the misrelation in the synthesis which arises when it is not constituted by spirit. This lack of the right relation between the parts of the synthesis leads to different forms of despair, which Anti-Climacus designates under one phrase as "the sickness unto death." Anti-Climacus then describes the ever more intensified forms of despair, step by step. He begins with the two parallel parts in the synthesis: "finitude-infinitude"[471] and "possibility-necessity"[472] in order then to introduce spirit as the third part. Before spirit is introduced as an element, one may speak only of "figurative despair,"[473] which means that one has still not gained knowledge of the eternal; it must be regarded as a border area of the domain of anxiety. With the incorporation of spirit as the third element come the two principal forms of despair, which arise through a person's either submitting to the power of finitude or the "abuse of the eternal."[474] The two forms of despair are called: "in despair not to will to be oneself" or "in despair to will to be oneself."[475]

Through the two principal forms of despair[476] Anti-Climacus comes to the group of qualifications which presuppose the single individual's knowledge of the eternal within himself,[477] and which therefore had to be left out of *The Concept of Anxiety*. As this side of man's relation to

[470] Ibid., p. 147 (ed. tr., S. V., XI, p. 143).
[471] Ibid., pp. 162ff.
[472] Ibid., p. 168.
[473] Ibid., p. 146 (ed. tr., S. V., XI, p. 127).
[474] Ibid., p. 201.
[475] Ibid., pp. 146, 180ff. (ed. tr., S. V., XI, pp. 127, 159-60).
[476] All these forms of despair are still within the scope of the Socratic-human.
[477] One finds the eternal only within himself; observation of the external yields only relativity.

the eternal now gets its proper place, Anti-Climacus returns to the theme followed in *The Concept of Anxiety*, namely the person's confrontation with the eternal as an external and transcendent reality. This comes in the second part of the book, and we note that Anti-Climacus at first does not refer to God as a transcendent reality but to "the conception of God," an expression which places God between immanence and transcendence; as mere idea God is immanent; as the object of faith he is transcendent. Despair in relation to God is defined as sin: "Sin is this: *before God, or with the conception of God, in despair not to will to be oneself, or in despair to will to be oneself*."[478] The emphasis is on "before God." This level also has its gradations, as Anti-Climacus says: "The more conception of God, the more self; the more self, the more conception of God. Only when the self as this definite individual is conscious of existing before God, only then is it the infinite self, and then this self sins before God."[479] The next higher level is the relation to a transcendent power which enlightens man about his condition, that despair is sin. Of this it is said: "After having been informed by a revelation from God what sin is, then before God in despair not to will to be oneself or before God in despair to will to be oneself" is to sin.[480] The final and decisive qualification comes when a person is brought into relation with Christ as Savior, and here the heart of the matter is believing the forgiveness of sins. Here again there is a potentiation. "As was said in the foregoing, 'The more conception of God, the more self,' so here it is true that the more conception of Christ, the more self."[481] In the relation to Christ, despair as sin becomes offense, and Anti-Climacus shows how offense at Christ can assume ever more intense forms, up to the deliberate attack on the truth of Christianity. This position of offense is defined by Anti-Climacus as "sin against the Holy Ghost."[482]

[478] *The Sickness Unto Death*, p. 208 (ed. tr., S. V., XI, p. 189).
[479] Ibid., p. 211.   [480] Ibid., p. 232.
[481] Ibid., p. 245.   [482] Ibid., p. 262.

In brief, all the forms of despair and offense can be classified on the following three principal levels: on the first
level comes "the break with the good," on the second "the
break with repentance,"[483] the third is the break with faith
in Christ and the forgiveness of sins.[484]

Offense and despair are presented in *The Sickness Unto
Death* in their purely negative forms, consequently not as
"the means of healing."[485] All these forms describe man's
flight from the eternal both as an inner and as a transcendent reality. But Kierkegaard has provided (particularly in
the first part of *Edifying Discourses in Various Spirits*) a
portrayal of the way despair can act as a means of healing.
The single individual who is ready to "will one thing" also
must struggle with "double-mindedness,"[486] that is despair,
but it is shown how despair is something which the single
individual can overcome and be cured of only by "willing
one thing." Offense, too, can be thought of as "a means of
healing" when it is regarded as a transition for the one who
is on his way to Christianity. We thereby get two kinds of
offense: in the one a person gradually moves farther away
from faith; he encounters the other on the way of faith;
this other form is presented in *Practice in Christianity*.
Thus Kierkegaard sharply distinguishes the negative forms
of despair from the positive.

Practice in Christianity consists of three parts which
Kierkegaard had worked on separately and in the beginning regarded as three different works, as is clearly indicated in the following journal entry: "The three works:
'Come to Me'; 'Blessed is He Who is Not Offended'; 'From
on High He Will Draw All Men Unto Himself' will be pseudonymous. Either all three in one volume under the common title, *Practice in Christianity*,—Essay by ——, or each

---

483 Ibid., p. 241 (ed. tr., S. V., XI, p. 219).
484 Ibid., pp. 244-62.
485 Ibid., p. 143 (ed. tr., S. V., XI, p. 118).
486 *Purity of Heart*, pp. 53-67.

one separately."[487] A unification was easy to achieve since all three parts are dominated by the thought of contemporaneity [*Samtidighed*] with Christ. Anti-Climacus here goes more deeply into the thoughts on contemporaneity which Climacus sets forth in *Philosophical Fragments*. This takes two directions: first, the form of contemporaneity central to *Philosophical Fragments*, namely, contemporaneity with Christ in "the *autopsy* of faith,"[488] is dealt with in such a way that the difficulties come out clearly; this is accomplished by an extensive consideration of the concept "offense," which is posited as an unavoidable possibility in one's meeting with Christ as Savior; second, Anti-Climacus decisively stresses immediate contemporaneity with Christ as man; this form of contemporaneity is just mentioned in *Philosophical Fragments* but without a development of the implications.[489]

This change in the conception of contemporaneity is completed in 1848. Now Kierkegaard understands it as his task to place man in "the situation of contemporaneity" with the Christ who at one time walked on this earth as this definite individual man. The transition to a new use of the concept of contemporaneity comes out especially in two journal entries, later followed by many others. In the first entry Kierkegaard speaks of the necessity and difficulty of giving a new account of the concept of contemporaneity: "It is a matter neither more nor less than a revision of Christianity; it is a matter of getting rid of 1800 years as if they had never been. I believe fully and firmly that I shall succeed; the whole thing is as clear as day to me. Yet I note all the more soberly that if there is the very slightest impatience and self-assertiveness, then I shall not be able to do it, then my thoughts will be confused."[490] And in the next entry on this he says: "Out with history. In with the situation of contemporaneity. This is the cri-

[487] X¹ A 422 (*J. and P.*, V).
[488] *Philosophical Fragments*, p. 87.
[489] Ibid., pp. 68-88.   [490] IX A 72 (*J. and P.*, V).

terion: as I judge anything contemporaneously, so am I. All this subsequent chatter is a delusion.

"This is really the direction in which my whole productivity has tended. This is why I use experiments instead of *actual* histories.

"Luther's mistake was that he did not go back far enough, did not make a person contemporary enough with Christ.

"The possibility of offense then becomes that which is to judge Christendom."[491] Of the means by which such a "situation of contemporaneity" can be brought about Kierkegaard says: "But now, aided by imagination, everyone should be able to bring this sacred history so close that he becomes contemporary with it."[492]

Using his poetic and dialectical imagination, Anti-Climacus in the first part of *Practice in Christianity* confronts the reader with Christ, but as yet he does not distinguish between the two aspects of this contemporaneity—Christ as the object of faith and Christ as a man who takes his place on the lowest level in existence. The first aspect is completed in "the *autopsy* of faith"; here Christ stands in the center as Savior. The other aspect accentuates Christ's purely human existence and points to Christ as prototype. These two aspects are then handled separately in the following sections.

Anti-Climacus can make this distinction because of his premise that in the Incarnation of Christ there are two clearly distinguishable forms of degradation. (1) The first degradation, which Anti-Climacus calls the essential one and which in connection with Kierkegaard's other remarks about it could be called the qualitative degradation, is God's degradation from being God to becoming man. This degradation may be called the essential one because the distance between God and man is infinite. "For it is always

IX A 95 (*J. and P.*, I, 691).
X⁴ A 609, p. 426 (*J. and P.*, IV).

a degradation for God to be man, even though He were Emperor of all emperors; and essentially He is not more degraded by being a poor, lowly man, mocked and (as the Scripture adds) spit upon."[493] (2) But God's degradation was not only to become man; he also chose a degradation within the relativities of this world when he chose not to be an emperor but took upon himself the form of a servant. In contrast to the first we could call this a quantitative degradation. With this degradation God chooses the most thankless position in existence in order to be "behind" all men so that no man will be able to complain that Christ in his earthly existence had a better position than he.

The first degradation cannot be seen; only the man is seen and not that this man is also God. But the other degradation can be seen by anyone who wants to see it. The first degradation involves the absolute paradox, and the way to the paradox is not direct; only faith is equal to it. But the other paradox is clear and open to everyone. Anti-Climacus says of it: "The loftiness"—that is, the fact that God was in this man, "must not be of the direct sort," but "lowliness must be of the direct sort." Man can relate himself to loftiness only in faith and worship; whereas lowliness directly invites imitation. The following quotation clearly illuminates the relationship between Christ as Savior and Christ as prototype: "The prototype lies infinitely close to man in lowliness and degradation, and yet infinitely far away in loftiness, even more distant than if it were merely far distant in loftiness, because in order to reach it, to determine one's character in likeness to it, one must go through lowliness and degradation, for there is

[493] *Practice [Training] in Christianity*, p. 43 (ed. tr., S. V., XII, p. 38). Climacus says (*Postscript*, p. 528): "The paradox consists principally in the fact that God, the Eternal, came into existence in time as a particular man. Whether this particular man is a servant or an emperor is neither here nor there, it is no more adequate for God to be king than to be beggar; it is not a greater humiliation for God to become a beggar than to become an emperor."

absolutely no other way—this constitutes a still greater distance, really an infinite distance. In this way 'the prototype' is in a sense *behind*, more deeply pressed down in lowliness and degradation than any man has ever been, and in another sense *before*, infinitely exalted. But 'the prototype' must be behind to be able to catch and to embrace all; if there were even one person who in fact could offer less or duck underneath by showing that in lowliness and degradation he is situated still lower, then the prototype is not 'the prototype'; then it is only a deficient prototype, that is, only a prototype for a great mass of men. The prototype must be *unconditionally* behind, behind all, and it must be *behind* in order to drive forward those who are to be fashioned according to it."[494]

Thus under "the prototype" Anti-Climacus considers Christ "merely as man,"[495] but he nevertheless continually points to the unity of Savior and prototype in Christ: "Christ came to the world for the purpose of saving the world, and at the same time (this is implicit in his first purpose) to be 'the prototype,' to leave behind him footprints for the one who would attach himself to him and who consequently must become an 'imitator,' a 'follower,' the correlative of 'footprints.' "[496] It is clear that Anti-Climacus isolates Christ's quantitative degradation in order to accentuate imitation; this goes together with Christ's ever stronger intensification of the ethical demands, which reach their highest in imitation. Of this ethical side of imitation Kierkegaard writes in a journal entry: "Christ as the prototype is still a form of the law, yes, the law raised to a higher level. . . ."[497] The demands of this law are most effective when a person becomes contemporary with Christ as the prototype; this contemporaneity becomes "the most rigorous examination ever possible. If this were to be per-

[494] *Practice [Training] in Christianity*, p. 232 (ed. tr., S. V., XII, p. 218).
[495] Ibid., p. 181.
[496] Ibid., p. 232 (ed. tr., S. V., XII, p. 218).
[497] X^2 A 451 (*J. and P.*, II, 1654).

petual, then the Jews were under milder judgment under the law."

In the second part of *Practice in Christianity*, Anti-Climacus deals with a person's relationship to Christ as Savior and goes through the possibilities for offense implicit in this relationship. The forms of offense depicted in *Practice in Christianity* are distinct from the forms of despair in *The Sickness Unto Death* in that they no longer express man's continual flight away from Christ but must be understood as stations which must be passed through as possibilities on the way to an ever stronger attachment to Christ in faith. Offense here may be regarded as a "means of healing."

There is yet another difference between the forms of offense in the two works. In *The Sickness Unto Death* the possibility of offense was present in man on the basis of the composition of the human synthesis; when a person refuses to bring the elements of the synthesis into right relation to each other, the meeting with Christ must then release ever stronger forms of offense. In the last two sections of *Practice in Christianity* the individual is presented as being on the way of faith, and the difficulties for him lie in the compounding of God and man in the person of Christ. The two major possibilities of offense, characterized as follows: *"The possibility of essential offense in relation to loftiness, that an individual man speaks or acts as though he were God, says of himself that he is God, therefore in relation to the qualification of God in the composite God-man,"*[498] and *"The possibility of essential offense in relation to lowliness, that one who gives Himself out to be God appears to be a low class, poor, suffering, and finally impotent man,"*[499] cannot be avoided by any person who wants to be a Christian. In going through these principal forms of offense, Anti-Climacus points out that even the disciples, who were called by Christ, could not

[498] *Practice [Training] in Christianity*, p. 96 (ed. tr., S. V., XII, p. 90).

[499] Ibid., p. 105 (ed. tr., S. V., XII, p. 98).

escape offense. The inevitability of offense with respect to Christ is due to man's not being equal to the composition of the person of Christ and that there cannot be any direct assurance that Christ is God. Only faith can overcome the possibilities of offense. The impossibility of Christ's being able to communicate directly to man as God and the need for the leap of faith as the middle term are fully discussed by Anti-Climacus when he deals with Christ's "absolute unrecognizableness" ("Incognito").[500] Anti-Climacus also points out that for Christ "the mystery of suffering"[501] lies in the impossibility of his communicating directly to man; Christ comes with salvation to man, but the possibility of offense and thereby also of damnation is present. Anti-Climacus says of this suffering: "No man can comprehend this suffering, and the wish to comprehend it is presumptuous."[502] This is the suffering Christ as Savior must bear, and this suffering cannot exist for man, because it lies beyond the scope of the human.

But on the other hand, man can and shall share in and learn from the suffering which Christ endured as the poor, scorned man. This becomes the principal theme in the third part of *Practice in Christianity*. From on high Christ will draw man to himself through the same degradation which he experienced on earth. Anti-Climacus varies and illuminates this theme from all sides. Here it is also possible to see the idea of the stages applied. A person begins on the plane of the visible and is drawn toward the invisible.

In all these accounts of a man's difficulties in relation to Christianity, Anti-Climacus is describing universal aspects of existence, just as Climacus does in *Concluding Unscientific Postscript*. But Anti-Climacus does not forget the individual approach, which for Climacus is presented by the pseudonyms subordinate to him. Without the individual approach Anti-Climacus could be accused of giving an abstract presentation. In the example of the child[503] influenced at an early age toward a rigorous form of Chris-

---

[500] Ibid., p. 127.
[502] Ibid., p. 138.
[501] Ibid., p. 136.
[503] Ibid., pp. 174-79.

tianity, Anti-Climacus provides a concrete individual supplement to his abstract account. Beginning with the impact of religion on the child, a story is told of an entire life stamped by the highest ideal demands and an attempt to actualize them. Anti-Climacus also has traces of an individual approach in the conclusion of the first part and in the beginning of the second part of *The Sickness Unto Death*. Typically, he concludes the first part with a discussion of a "slip of the pen"[504] similar to one at the end of Quidam's diary,[505] an allusion to Kierkegaard's fate of being set outside universal. This complex of problems is supplemented in the first pages of the second section of *The Sickness Unto Death* by an account of Kierkegaard's struggle to understand his poet-existence and the task which "the thorn in the flesh" poses for him.[506] Anti-Climacus does not need to go into this more deeply since it is treated adequately by Climacus's pseudonyms, who had described the single individual's struggle with the concrete difficulties involved in the approach to being a Christian. Anti-Climacus's most important task is just the opposite—namely, to stress the ideal demands.

Thus Climacus and Anti-Climacus complement each other in portraying individual existence, for this can be portrayed in its wholeness only by placing the actual difficulties side by side with the ideal requirements. It must be said, however, that individual existence, as sketched by Climacus's pseudonyms and by Anti-Climacus, has many extraordinary features. Granted that each individual existence is different and can never fully be a paradigm for other existences, it still must be said that individual existence as presented in Kierkegaard's works is too complicated (because of the great contrasts between the actual difficulties and the ideal requirements) to be a paradigm (see pp. 366-70 below).

With *Practice in Christianity* the Christian demands are

---

[504] *The Sickness Unto Death*, p. 207.
[505] *Stages*, pp. 361-62.
[506] *The Sickness Unto Death*, pp. 208-10.

pressed "to the highest ideality"[507] in order that the single individual might learn through this ideal the right use of grace. In all his dialectical and existential presentations Kierkegaard always considers the doctrine of grace to be the ultimate and most central doctrine. His own existential experiences had fully taught him how little a man can accomplish.[508] Therefore, after publishing *The Sickness Unto Death* and before publishing *Practice in Christianity*, he establishes a "fulcrum," in which grace is emphasized. Concerning the three discourses, "The High Priest," "The Publican," and "The Woman That Was a Sinner," which appeared in the intervening period, he writes: "I must have a fulcrum, but I cannot use a pseudonym as a fulcrum; they are parallel to Anti-Climacus; and the position of 'Discourses at the Communion on Fridays' is once and for all designated as the fulcrum of the authorship."[509] The fulcrum consists of the thoughts about the Atonement set forth in the short discourses. But Kierkegaard also ends his authorship proper with thoughts about the Atonement, as we see in *An Edifying Discourse* and *Two Discourses at the Communion on Fridays*. In *An Edifying Discourse* "the woman that was a sinner" becomes the example of one who has arrived at the perception that *"with respect to finding forgiveness* [a person] *is able to do nothing."*[510] In this discourse we find thoughts about Christ as prototype similar to those set forth in *Practice in Christianity*. Even an aspect of the possibility of offense is intimated: "In his lifetime Christ is primarily the prototype for his contemporaries, even though he is the Savior, and even though his life is suffering, so that he may be said to bear the sins of the world, even during his lifetime, but what stands out is that he is the prototype. And since Christianity is not a

[507] *Practice [Training] in Christianity*, p. 7, editor's (Kierkegaard's) preface.

[508] See X¹ A 132, 135 (*J. and P.*, I, 693, 236); X¹ A 134 (*J. and P.*, IV).

[509] X² A 148 (*J. and P.*, V).

[510] *Practice [Training] in Christianity*, p. 268.

doctrine such that it is the same no matter who the proclaimer is but is related to the proclaimer and to the extent that his life expresses the doctrine, it would be all too clear that when Christ proclaims Christianity and does it as the prototype, no one is able to keep up with him entirely—they fall away, even the apostles."[511] The Atonement is the principal subject of the *Two Discourses at the Communion on Fridays*. This is powerfully voiced in the statement: "If justice were to become furious, what more could it want? There is, after all, full satisfaction; if in your repentance and brokenness you expect to get justice outside yourself as an aid in finding out what the guilt is, there is, after all, full satisfaction, one who makes full satisfaction and completely covers all your guilt, making sight of it impossible, impossible for justice and thereby also for repentance in you or over yourself, for repentance also loses its eyesight when justice, to which it appeals, says: I can see nothing."[512] Here it is vigorously emphasized that guilt and repentance are overcome by "one who makes full satisfaction." The discourse does not imply that there will be no guilt and repentance again, but the Atonement always has the power to get rid of it.

With grace as the fulcrum, Kierkegaard's dialectical reflections must also find a resting point. All his dialectical and existential thinking works toward this final and decisive boundary for all dialectic. The ethical requirement and the whole "dialectic of sin" find their resolution here. To that extent the dialectic has reached a firm place on which to stand.

Kierkegaard's last two books before the Church conflict, *For Self-Examination* and *Judge for Yourselves!*, the first of which was published about a month after the *Two Discourses at the Communion on Fridays*, and the other not until 1876 by Kierkegaard's brother, do not really belong

---

[511] "An Edifying Discourse," together with ibid., p. 270 (ed. tr., S. V., XII, p. 258).

[512] *Two Discourses at the Communion on Fridays*, together with *Judge For Yourselves!*, p. 22 (ed. tr., S. V., XII, p. 287).

in the connected sequence of the upbuilding authorship. As their titles indicate, both books have the special function of alerting the contemporary age to the question asked earlier, especially in the upbuilding works: What does it mean to be a Christian? They are like a forewarning of the criticism of the Church and Christendom in general which is quietly being prepared. The thought of imitation [*Efterfølgelsen*] in particular is strongly stressed in these two books—a thought from which the most decisive implications are drawn regarding the Christian life. These two books also herald a period in which the qualitative dialectic is no longer in the foreground, but rather the quantitative dialectic.

After seeing how Kierkegaard applies the various dialectical viewpoints in his upbuilding works also, it is appropriate to discuss Kierkegaard's conception of his own relation to this literature. As mentioned, Kierkegaard designates this position by using very specific characteristic terms for the various works in the upbuilding literature. For Kierkegaard this designation is even more important than the ranking of the pseudonyms in the esthetic authorship, since that part of the authorship occupies a lower level, and for him the esthetic, viewed existentially, is a mastered sphere at the time he begins his authorship; whereas the parallel religious sequences become steadily more pertinent to him.

By repeatedly using the expression "without authority,"[513] Kierkegaard wants to emphasize that his upbuilding

[513] It is interesting to note the stipulation "without authority" applied in *Two Ages . . . A Literary Review* to "men of distinction" who have "understood the diabolical principle of the levelling process" (*The Present Age*, p. 62) and, unrecognizable, work against it. In *On My Work as an Author* (together with *The Point of View*, p. 142) there is a similar thought: "The genius is without authority." In both instances he is thinking also of himself, and emphasis on the connection between the genius and "men of distinction" and the expression "without authority" would certainly help throw light on Kierkegaard's own position from the beginning of his authorship.

or edifying works are not "sermons";[514] to preach sermons requires ordination.[515] In the beginning he uses the predicate *opbyggende* (upbuilding, constructive, edifying) to characterize his discourses. This predicate is generally used for the upbuilding works running parallel with the esthetic authorship. The name changes in the later religiously toned writing; for example, the second part of *Edifying Discourses in Various Spirits* is simply called "Discourses" and the third part is called "Christian Discourses." *Works of Love* is called "Some Christian Reflections in the Form of Discourses," and Kierkegaard explains very clearly in his journals how he distinguishes between an "upbuilding discourse and reflections."[516] Next come *Christian Discourses* and *The Lilies of the Field and the Birds of the Air, Three Godly Discourses. The Sickness Unto Death* is designated "For Upbuilding and Awakening" and *Practice in Christianity* "For Awakening and Increase of Inwardness." The next three discourses, *An Edifying Discourse* and *Two Discourses at the Communion on Fridays*, again come under the designation "upbuilding." Of his own attitude to these distinctions within the upbuilding literature, and also its place in the authorship, he says: "There is a stretch which is mine: the upbuilding; behind and ahead lie the lower and the higher pseudonymity; the upbuilding is mine, not the esthetic, neither [the pseudonymous works] for upbuilding nor, still less, those

[514] *Edifying Discourses*, I. Preface.

[515] The concepts "authority" and "ordination" are deepened and enlarged during the development of the authorship, in line with a presentation of the greater requirements for the Christian life. For a detailed account see Valter Lindstrom, *Efterføljelsens teologi hos Søren Kierkegaard* (Stockholm, 1956), pp. 242ff. This deepening finally shatters the current external conceptions of the meaning of ordination: "A Christian pastor I have never known." IX A 283 (*J. and P.*, V).

[516] VIII¹ A 293 (*J. and P.*, 641). See *Works of Love*, pp. 199-212, for further discussion of "upbuilding," also translators' introduction, pp. 11-13.

for awakening."[517] This comment tallies with several others, among them the very familiar "I would place myself higher than Johannes Climacus, lower than Anti-Climacus."[518] This new characterization of the various upbuilding works shows how important it is for Kierkegaard to be able to state clearly his own existential position in the ever more intensified religious sequence of works.

The clear dialectical coherence of Kierkegaard's authorship, in the upbuilding portion as well as in the esthetic, compels us to return once again to the question whether Kierkegaard, through the structuring of his authorship, does not finally present a rounded out view of existence and man such that it must be called a "system."[519] This interpretation must again be completely rejected, since it should be clear from this view of the authorship that Kierkegaard in describing existence sets forth ever stronger contrasts, which is in contrast to system-formation, which mediates the contrasts. This increasing sharpening of the contrasts is clearly discernible, as we have seen in a comparison between the "Either/Or" of his first work and the "Either/Or" expressed in *The Sickness Unto Death* and *Practice in Christianity*. In the early work (particularly in Volume II of *Either/Or*) it may be somewhat legitimate to speak of an attempt at mediation between the two contrasts presented in *Either/Or*; in the later two works the two qualitative contrasts, perdition and faith, are carried to their extremes.

Although the idea that Kierkegaard has created a "system" must be rejected, one should be continually aware that an account of a progressive movement which with the help of a qualitative dialectic poses ever more decisive contrasts, placing a person in the tension of choice and final decision, does give us a coherent survey of existence. It is this coherence that Kierkegaard had in mind and expected people to look for in his authorship: "Thus there

[517] X¹ A 593 (*J. and P.*, V).   [518] X¹ A 517 (*J. and P.*, V).
[519] See pp. 169-72 above.

will be no judgment of my work as an author at all; no one has faith enough in it to look for a total plan in the whole—nor the time or ability. The judgment will be that I have changed a little over the years.

"So it will be. For me it is very sad, I know deep within me that it holds together in a different way, that there is a totality in the whole (especially since it was by the aid of Governance) and that there is truly something more to be said about it than this poor comment that the author changed."[520] And again: "It is one idea, this continuity from *Either/Or* to Anti-Climacus, the idea of religiousness in reflection."[521] He himself describes the procedure by which this coherence and unity in the authorship may be demonstrated: "If anything should be said about my work as an author, it could be done in such a way that a third person is formed, the author, who would be a synthesis of myself and the pseudonym, and he would speak directly about it. Then only an introduction would be needed in which this author would be introduced, and then he would say everything in the first person. The introduction would point out that the whole authorship was a unity; but I would not be the pseudonym, nor the pseudonym I; therefore this 'author' would be a synthesis of the pseudonym and me."[522] The basic origin of the unity-idea is Kierkegaard's conception that Christianity alone is able to provide a true explanation of existence. It is not only in the beginning that this is a guiding thought for Kierkegaard, when, for example, he says that "Christianity explains the world,"[523] but later he also clearly voices the same thought when he relates it to the problem of suffering in the world: "No, Christianity is still the only explanation of existence which holds water."[524] Consequently, only Christianity brings unity and meaning to existence, but the same Christianity also places every single individual before the qualitative

---

[520] X^1 A 116 (*J. and P.*, V).   [521] X^6 B 4:3 (*J. and P.*, V).
[522] X^1 A 300 (*J. and P.*, V).
[523] II A 517 (*J. and P.*, III, 3275).
[524] IX A 358 (*J. and P.*, I, 1052).

choice and gives him a task for eternity; therefore existence cannot be understood as finalized. Kierkegaard also
speaks of his own task in this connection as "casting Christianity completely and wholly into reflection,"[525] that is,
into the form of possibility which creates the condition for
choosing. This interpretation of the unity-idea prevents all
systematic finalizing.

In order to understand Kierkegaard's literary production
in his journals during the last years and culminating in
his attack upon the Church, it must be clear that one of
the many essential features of his dialectical method is to
describe the concepts of existence and their connection
with each other on an ascending scale. Applied in the
sphere of the ethical and the religious, this method provides the following clearly designated levels, leading to an
understanding of the use he later makes of the idea of
imitation. On the lowest level Kierkegaard places civic and
social morality, to which he will not concede the name of
ethics. The ethical emerges for the first time in human
existence through the single individual's discovering the
eternal within himself and relating himself to it. Kierkegaard and his pseudonyms deal in great detail with this
level,[526] the final gradation of which is the individual's
awareness that he falls short in his attempt to realize the
ethical in his existence. On the next level the ethical comes
as an imperative from a transcendent power who speaks
to man with the "You shall" of his authoritative law and
love. This ethical "You *shall* love,"[527] which a person can
never reach by himself, is expressed with particular clarity

[525] IX A 226, p. 123 (*J. and P.*, V); see X² A 106 (*J. and P.*,
V): "To cast Christianity into reflection. . . ."

[526] Even in *Practice [Training] in Christianity* (p. 160) this
level is named as the condition for being able to be drawn by
Christ. It states there: "Hence Christ would first and foremost
help every man to become himself, would require of him first
and foremost that by entering into himself he should become
himself, so as then to draw him unto Himself."

[527] *Works of Love*, p. 40.

in *Works of Love*, where the ethical in the Christian meaning of the word is treated in detail. In the attempt to
realize this "You *shall* love," one discovers his weakness
and sin in a qualitatively new way. On the last level the
ethical appears in the figure of Christ as the prototype,
who with his concrete example makes his demands on
the single individual in an extraordinarily searching way.
The distance between a person's ability and the ideal is at
its greatest here, which makes man's need of grace especially obvious. The transition to each of these levels presupposes a movement of infinity on man's part, which on
an ascending scale is termed irony, resignation, and repentance.

With the publication of *Practice in Christianity* Kierkegaard's pseudonym Anti-Climacus advances the idea of
imitation as the final and most concrete form of the ethical,
thereby preparing the way for the proper use of grace. By
emphasizing Christ as the prototype, the claim on man is
"pressed up to the highest ideality."[528] Kierkegaard, however, does not stop with this position as formulated in
Practice in Christianity but in his journals intensifies the
idea of imitation still more in order to draw out new and
more comprehensive implications, which he then uses for
a critical examination of the religious conditions in Christendom. We shall now try to show (a) how Kierkegaard,
despite his already strong emphasis on imitation in *Practice in Christianity*, continues to draw out the further implications of this idea; (b) how he justifies doing what
finally leads to a wholly negative and polemical attitude
toward the condition of human existence; and (c) the
forms of communication in which he uses the idea of imitation in his decisive critique of the idolatry of Christendom.

(a) Numerous and repeated expressions in the journals
witness to the fact that once again it is Kierkegaard's struggle against the abuse of grace which makes him bring

[528] *Practice [Training] in Christianity*, editor's (Kierkegaard's)
preface, p. 7 (ed. tr., S. V., XIII, p. I).

out additional negative comparisons of life in Christendom with the imitation of Christ. For Kierkegaard there is an indissoluble connection between law and grace. Grace, therefore, comes into its own only against the background of the requirements. If this connection is broken, there is danger of a kind of mysticism in which Christ does indeed come in contact with man as a "tangent"[529] or an "idea,"[530] but not as "the idea" that comes into the world and influences concrete human existence. As long as Kierkegaard assumes that the so-called "hidden inwardness" embraces the ethical claims which through their normative and evaluative function constitute a condition for the proper use of grace, he does not need to emphasize the claims in an especially decisive way. But the conviction that "hidden inwardness" does not in itself have the tension between the components which an individual's struggle to actualize the ethical claims should imply leads Kierkegaard to accentuate the ethical and imitation. Kierkegaard is entirely on the right track in saying that to the degree that the higher ethical claims are given up, to the same degree a person will regard merely social and civic morality as the highest norm for his life, but in this way grace also loses its original meaning. Kierkegaard speaks very plainly about this relationship: "We have completely abolished imitation, and at most we hold to the paltriness called social morality. In this way men cannot become properly humbled so that they genuinely feel the need of 'grace,' because the requirement is no more than 'social morality,' which they fulfill tolerably well."[531] For Kierkegaard it remains firmly established that there is no use for grace if social and civic morality are the highest norm for human life; it all ends, to use his own word for it, in "nonsense." Transgressing civic and social morality produces guilt only in the context of the state or society, and in that case there

[529] X¹ A 49 (*J. and P.*, I, 327); X⁴ A 28 (*J. and P.*, I, 528); and XI² A 53 (*J. and P.*, II, 1444).
[530] X⁴ A 354, p. 206 (*J. and P.*, II, 1904).
[531] X⁴ A 349 (*J. and P.*, II, 1902).

is no sense in speaking of guilt or sin as understood in a religious perspective.

Kierkegaard believes that this abuse of grace, which he underlines in numerous and frequently very stinging terms, takes place in Protestantism especially, particularly because here—and rightly so—grace is placed in the center for the Christian. Furthermore, it is clear to Kierkegaard that the abuse of the "principle of faith" is more difficult to demonstrate than the abuse of "the principle of works," which is "simpler"[532] and therefore is more apparent. In this connection he points out the weak points in both of the two great religious communities, Catholicism and Protestantism: "When Catholicism degenerates, what form of corruption is likely to appear? Surface sanctity. When Protestantism degenerates, what form of corruption will appear? The answer is easy: spiritless secularism."[533] He gives this simple instruction, addressed to Protestantism: "But now in our time it is clear that what must come to the fore is the aspect of Christ as prototype. The main point is to have learned from the Middle Ages to avoid the errors of this approach. But it is this side which must come to the fore, because the Lutheran emphasis on faith has now simply become a fig leaf for the most unchristian shirking."[534]

In spite of his powerful polemical offensive against the abuse of grace, Kierkegaard continually maintains that grace is definitive, and he can speak in a very mild and sympathetic way of the relation between imitation and grace in the midst of man's existential difficulties and in the situation of death: "No, the Atonement and grace are and remain definitive. All striving toward imitation, when the moment of death brings it to an end and one stands before God, will be sheer paltriness—therefore Atonement and grace are needed. Furthermore, as long as there is striving, the Atonement will constantly be needed to pre-

---

[532] XI² A 301 (*J. and P.*, III, 2543).
[533] XI² A 305, p. 325 (*J. and P.*, III, 3617).
[534] X¹ A 154 (*J. and P.*, III, 2481).

vent this striving from being transformed into agonizing anxiety in which a man is burned up, so to speak, and less than ever begins to strive. Finally, while there is striving, every other second a mistake is made, something is neglected, there is sin—therefore the Atonement is unconditionally needed.

"Although it is the utmost strenuousness, imitation should be like a jest, a childlike act—if it is to mean something in earnest, that is, be of any value before God—the Atonement is the earnestness. It is detestable, however, for a man to want to use grace, 'since all is grace,' to avoid all striving."[535]

Kierkegaard wants to prevent Christianity from becoming an "idea in the abstract sense," whereby one "interprets rigorousness as pride, and then going scot-free is supposed to be commendable humility."[536] It is this "cunning humility"[537] which in a "refined"[538] way would misuse grace that he is gunning for. Kierkegaard himself frequently stresses that "it is God who gives everything,"[539] but this does not mean exemption from "the tension of life,"[540] because "in order to become spirit one must go through crises which make us, from a human point of view, as unhappy as possible."[541] But grace remains definitive for Kierkegaard, and it is important in this connection to be aware that even during the conflict with the Church, in which Kierkegaard carries the requirement of imitation to its most extreme form, he reminds us of the possibility he sets forth in *Practice in Christianity*, that a person "admits that this is the requirement, and then has recourse to grace."[542]

(b) Kierkegaard's most violent criticism of Christendom is bound up not only with his emphasis during his last

[535] X⁴ A 491 (*J. and P.*, II, 1909).
[536] X⁴ A 354, p. 206 (*J. and P.*, II, 1799).
[537] XI² A 326 (*J. and P.*, III, 2682).
[538] X⁴ A 521 (*J. and P.*, II, 1913).
[539] X¹ A 59 (*J. and P.*, II, 1383).
[540] XI¹ A 572 (*J. and P.*, III, 2554).
[541] X³ A 526 (*J. and P.*, V).
[542] *Attack upon "Christendom,"* p. 243.

years on martyrdom as the Christian's standard but also with his emphasis on Christ as "prototype" with all its negative implications for the way life has been organized. In his accentuation of imitation, the focus is no longer on what Christ said about imitation—words which may be interpreted in various ways—but on Christ's own life as an example to imitate. Already in 1843[543] Kierkegaard pondered the question of how far Christ's own life should provide a paradigm for the Christian life. It was already clear to him that "Christ's coming implied a polemic against existence" and that "Christ's life had a negative-polemical relationship to Church and state." But Kierkegaard was brought up to think that it was "greater" to conform to the universally human conditions than to relate polemically to existence. At that time he faced "the most difficult of problems," which he could not resolve in a satisfactory way. In his later years Kierkegaard no longer faces such problems. Christ is now unhesitatingly taken as the prototype, but in doing this Kierkegaard comes to regard the positive relation to life not as "greater" than Christ's negative relation, but as subordinate. The martyr as the proper example of true Christianity must also be measured by Christ as the prototype. The martyrs are only "derived prototypes," but Christ is "the prototype."

Since Christ's degradation within the relativities of this world is obvious, his earthly existence can be used as paradigm, whereas Christ's degradation from God to man is a matter only for faith and worship, and here to talk of a paradigm would be blasphemy. Christ's visible degradation, however, has an absolute character. No one can outdo Christ in this respect;[544] Christ must always be "behind" every man. For this very reason, through his attempt to be like "the prototype," a person will discover his limits and his distance from the ideal. This helps one to "train the need for grace."[545] Thus "the prototype" itself prepares

[543] IV A 62 (*J. and P.*, III, 3076).
[544] X² A 317 (*J. and P.*, II, 1859).
[545] X⁴ A 369 (*J. and P.*, II, 1906).

a person for " 'the Redeemer.' " " 'The prototype' slays all, as it were, for no one achieves it. 'The Redeemer' wants to save all.

"Yet Christ is both, and that swindle which takes redemption and grace in vain is not Christianity."[546]

By using "the prototype" as He walked on earth emancipated from finite concerns, Kierkegaard is able to criticize most concretely the Christendom which in his opinion had ended by being completely attached to finite goals. Christ's life with its polemical-negative relation to the structures of life must be seen as a higher analogy of the movement of infinity which is constantly repeated. Previously Kierkegaard had always directed men to a return to life's concrete tasks. He does not, however, continue this during his attack on the Church; there is only one mitigation, the discourse "The Unchangeableness of God," which points back to his first upbuilding discourses. The way in which the idea of imitation is carried through during the attack upon the Church strongly indicates that at the end Kierkegaard wants to show that the old order has to go and that men are again standing "at the beginning."[547]

(c) In making Christ's visible degradation the measure of the Christian life, Kierkegaard can no longer use the qualitative dialectic. This dialectic, after all, directs all its attention to man's inner actuality; by presenting contrasting existential positions it impels man to choose between them, and furthermore it delineates levels of absence of inwardness and of growth in inwardness. In this way the qualitative dialectic concentrates entirely on inwardness and cannot be used in judging Christendom's external condition as compared with Christ's visible degradation. To make this judgment Kierkegaard has to resort to the quantitative dialect, which makes a point of bringing out visible differences.

In using the quantitative dialectic, Kierkegaard himself stands in the position of hidden inwardness, inasmuch as

[546] XI[1] A 492 (*J. and P.*, II, 1934).
[547] XI[1] A 505 (*J. and P.*, V).

he admits his own existential distance from this new ideal for the Christian life, an ideal already heralded by Anti-Climacus. He expected the same admission from the Christians of his day.

Concerning the transition from the qualitative dialectic to the quantitative dialectic and the necessity for such a transition, he writes: "Assume that that illusion 'Christendom' is truth, that it must be left standing: then unrecognizability is the maximum. If, however, the illusion must go, then it gets down to this: you actually are not Christians—then there must be recognizability." And further: "If the illusion 'Christendom' is truth, if the kind of preaching prevalent in Christendom is the way it should be, then we are all Christians and we can only speak of becoming more inward: then the maieutic method and unrecognizability are the maximum.

"But suppose now (something I was not aware of at first) that the preaching prevalent in Christendom leaves out something essential to the proclamation of Christianity —'imitation, dying away to the world, being born again etc.' —then we in Christendom are not Christians, and here the emphasis must be on recognizability."[548]

With this observation Kierkegaard announces the application of the quantitative dialectic, in which external characteristics come to play a significant role. In comparing Christ's visible degradation and Christendom's external condition, Kierkegaard places in confrontation two life-positions which have diametrically opposite aims. The trend in Christendom, which Kierkegaard also calls a relapse into Judaism and paganism,[549] was toward greater external power, influence, and status in the world; Christ's life, however, moved in the direction of greater renunciation, powerlessness, and suffering. This is why these two views of life, the universally human and Christ's, cannot be compared directly. "The more the phenomenon, the

---

[548] X⁴ A 558 (*J. and P.*, V).

[549] See X³ A 276 (*J. and P.*, II, 1867) and A 506 (*J. and P.*, II, 1174) with references.

appearance, expresses that here God cannot possibly be present, the closer he is; inversely, the more the phenomenon, the appearance, expresses that God is very near, the farther away he is." And more concretely: "Everything that strengthens the appearance distances God. At the time when there were no churches and the few Christians gathered together in catacombs as refugees and persecutees, God was closer to actuality. Then came churches, so many churches, such great, splendid churches: to the same degree God was distanced. For God's nearness is related inversely to phenomenon, and this ascending scale (churches, many churches, splendid churches) is an increase in the sphere of appearance."[550] Conversely, he says very concretely of Christ: "The least possible of all places or phenomena—one solitary, destitute, abandoned human being—this is the place for God; to such an extent does God relate negatively to appearance; and if God is to be present in this man, he must make him more unhappy, humanly speaking—to such an extent does God relate negatively to appearances; he has to have as little appearance as possible, and in addition he must negate this little bit."[551]

According to this principle of comparison, external progress in the individual's life must necessarily mean an ever increasing distance from the ideal. The final implication of this judgment of the universally human enterprise would be a disavowing of every positive relation to the values of human life, whereby the single individual would be placed outside of the universal altogether. However, Kierkegaard does not draw this extreme conclusion: "*Christianity is a Kingdom not of this World* yet it wants to have a place in this world—right here is the paradox and the collision; it wants to have a place, but again not as a kingdom of this world." And he continues by deepening this thought, at the same time showing how Catholicism and Protestantism have tried to solve this

[550] XI² A 51, p. 59 (*J. and P.*, III, 3099).
[551] XI² A 52 (*J. and P.*, III, 3100).

question: "This is the way it is in the New Testament. Christendom naturally has not been able to go along with this; it was all too strenuous. Therefore they have *either* made it into a kingdom of this world (Catholicism) whereby the Christian collisions vanish, and direct recognizability, which is pleasing to men, becomes the rule, or they have transposed Christianity into hidden inwardness, an adequate form, if you will, of not being a kingdom of this world, but yet not the Christian form, not the paradox, and again they avoid the Christian collisions." This, that Christianity "wants to have a place in this world," "a visible discernible place,"[552] Kierkegaard designates as a "paradoxical recognizability," which means that "everything Christian is the direct opposite of the directly human."[553] In his last journal entries Kierkegaard strongly emphasizes this clash between the purely human and the Christian.

When Kierkegaard thinks about the special task to which he must apply the quantitative dialectic, he conceives of himself as a "Christian auditor" who is supposed "to 'know' the counterfeits."[554] The qualifications he ascribes to this auditor correspond to his own acquired qualifications.

During all this activity there is a receding of humor as the factor determining the form of communication and presentation in the development of the authorship; humor always permits a more lenient interpretation of human existence. But now irony enters the scene and takes command during Kierkegaard's preparation of critical material aimed at Christendom.[555] Kierkegaard also compares his task to Socrates's, but he knows that "the irony with respect to Christianity has one element more than Socratic irony has, inasmuch as men in Christendom not only imagine themselves to be human beings (here, of course, Socrates stops) but also imagine themselves to be some-

---

[552] XI² A 80 (*J. and P.*, I, 614).

[553] XI² A 213 (*J. and P.*, V).   [554] XI² A 36 (*J. and P.*, V).

[555] See Malantschuk-Søe's, Villads Christensen's, and P. G. Lindhardt's books on the attack on the Church.

thing historically concrete, which being a Christian is."[556] The comparison with Socrates is very characteristic of Kierkegaard's last period; like Socrates he is convinced that he has to fight against the outlived and emptied forms, which must be renewed from within. Thus Kierkegaard carries out the task which is analogous on a higher level to the task Socrates carried out and which Kierkegaard depicts in his doctoral dissertation, *The Concept of Irony*. This also means that with his last writings Kierkegaard wants to be instrumental in destroying "the phenomenon" Christendom in order to make room for the dawn of the new. This procedure cannot in itself be called upbuilding, but it was not supposed to be; Kierkegaard could point to the new form of upbuilding which would follow the demolition of the old forms by referring to his earlier books,[557] of which the esthetic books indirectly contain upbuilding elements while the upbuilding or edifying literature speaks about it directly.

In my account of the relation between dialectic and existence in Søren Kierkegaard, the first portion is a consideration of the period prior to Kierkegaard's preparations for attacking the Church; in this earlier period the qualitative dialectic is central, and it is this dialectic that has been my concern; it is also the nerve in Kierkegaard's whole authorship. The quantitative dialectic plays a role only during the brief period when Kierkegaard prepares himself for and carries out the task which to the very end he believes had been laid upon him.

[556] XI² A 189 (*J. and P.*, II, 1767).
[557] See, for example, *Attack upon "Christendom,"* p. 53, and XI³ B 195 (*J. and P.*, V), where Kierkegaard points to the fact that he has been working for fourteen years on an interrelated authorship and that he "always has a past accomplishment to refer to."

Bibliography

Editions referred to in the Notes of Kierkegaard's works in English translation, listed in order of first publication or time of writing

The Concept of Irony, tr. Lee Capel. New York: Harper and Row, 1966; Bloomington: Indiana University Press, 1968. (*Om Begrebet Ironi*, by S. A. Kierkegaard, 1841.)

Either/Or, I, tr. David F. Swenson and Lillian Marvin Swenson; II, tr. Walter Lowrie; 2nd ed. rev. Howard A. Johnson. Garden City: Doubleday, 1959. (*Enten-Eller*, I-II, ed. Victor Eremita, 1843.)

Johannes Climacus, or De omnibus dubitandum est, and *A Sermon*, tr. T. H. Croxall. London: Adam and Charles Black, 1958. ("Johannes Climacus eller De omnibus dubitandum est," written 1842-43, unpubl., *Papirer* IV B I; *Demis—Prœdiken*, 1844, unpubl., IV C I.)

Edifying Discourses, I-IV, tr. David F. Swenson and Lillian Marvin Swenson. Minneapolis: Augsburg Publishing House, 1943-46. (*Opbyggelige Taler*, by S. Kierkegaard, 1843, 1844.)

Fear and Trembling (with *The Sickness Unto Death*), tr. Walter Lowrie. Garden City: Doubleday, 1954. (*Frygt og Bæven*, by Johannes de Silentio, 1843.)

Repetition, tr. Walter Lowrie, Princeton: Princeton University Press, 1941. (*Gjentagelsen*, by Constantin Constantius, 1843.)

Philosophical Fragments, tr. David F. Swenson, 2nd ed. rev. Howard Hong. Princeton: Princeton University Press, 1962. (*Philosophiske Smuler*, by Johannes Climacus, ed. S. Kierkegaard, 1844.)

The Concept of Anxiety [Dread], tr. Walter Lowrie. 2nd ed. Princeton: Princeton University Press, 1957. (*Begrebet Angest*, by Vigilius Haufniensis, ed. S. Kierkegaard, 1844.)

Thoughts on Crucial Situations in Human Life, tr. David F. Swenson, ed. Lillian Marvin Swenson. Minneapolis:

374 *Bibliography*

Augsburg Publishing House, 1941. (*Tre Taler ved tænkte Leiligheder*, by S. Kierkegaard, 1845.)

Stages on Life's Way, tr. Walter Lowrie. Princeton: Princeton University Press, 1940. (*Stadier paa Livets Vej*, ed. Hilarius Bogbinder, 1845.)

Concluding Unscientific Postscript, tr. David F. Swenson and Walter Lowrie. Princeton: Princeton University Press for American-Scandinavian Foundation, 1941. (*Afsluttende uvidenskabelig Efterskrift*, by Johannes Climacus, ed. S. Kierkegaard, 1846.)

The Present Age [part of *Two Ages: the Age of Revolution and the Present Age. A Literary Review] and Two Minor Ethico-Religious Treatises*, tr. Alexander Dru, Walter Lowrie. London and New York: Oxford University Press, 1940. (*En literair Anmeldelse, To Tidsaldre*, by S. Kierkegaard, 1846; *Tvende ethisk-religieuse Smaa-Afhandlinger*, by H. H., 1849.)

On Authority and Revelation, The Book on Adler, tr. Walter Lowrie. Princeton: Princeton University Press, 1955. ("Bogen om Adler," written 1846-47, unpubl., *Papirer* VII² B 235.)

Purity of Heart, tr. Douglas Steere. 2nd ed. New York: Harper, 1948. (*Opbyggelige Taler i forskjellig Aand*, by S. Kierkegaard, pt. 1. "En Leiligheds-Tale," 1847.)

The Gospel of Suffering and *The Lilies of the Field*, tr. David F. Swenson and Lillian Marvin Swenson. Minneapolis: Augsburg Publishing House, 1948. (*Opbyggelige Taler i forskjellig Aand*, by S. Kierkegaard, pt. 3, "Lidelsernes Evangelium"; pt. 2, "Hvad vi lære af Lilierne paa Marken og af Himmelens Fugle," 1847.)

Works of Love, tr. Howard and Edna Hong. New York: Harper and Row, 1962. (*Kjerlighedens Gjerninger*, by S. Kierkegaard, 1847.)

Crisis in the Life of an Actress, tr. Stephen Crites. New York: Harper and Row, 1967. (*Krisen og en Krise i en Skuespillerindes Liv*, by Inter et Inter, *Fædrelandet*, Nos. 188-91, July 24-27, 1848.)

Christian Discourses, including also *The Lilies of the Field and the Birds of the Air* and *Three Discourses at the Communion on Fridays*, tr. Walter Lowrie. London and New York: Oxford University Press, 1939. (*Christelige*

Taler, by S. Kierkegaard, 1848; *Lilien paa Marken og Fuglen under Himlen*, by S. Kierkegaard, 1849; "YppersteprÆsten"—"Tolderen"—"Synderinden", tre Taler ved Altergangen om Fredagen, by S. Kierkegaard, 1849.)

The Sickness Unto Death (with *Fear and Trembling*), tr. Walter Lowrie. New York: Doubleday, 1954. (*Sygdommen til DØden*, by Anti-Climacus, ed. S. Kierkegaard, 1849.)

Practice [Training] in Christianity, including also *The Woman Who Was a Sinner*, tr. Walter Lowrie. London and New York: Oxford University Press, 1941; repr. Princeton: Princeton University Press, 1944. (*IndØvelse i Christendom*, by Anti-Climacus, ed. S. Kierkegaard, 1850; *En opbyggelig Tale*, by S. Kierkegaard, 1850.)

Armed Neutrality and *An Open Letter*, tr. Howard V. Hong and Edna H. Hong. Bloomington and London: Indiana University Press, 1968. (*Den bevæbnede Neutralitet*, written 1848-49, publ. 1965; *Foranledigt ved en Yttring af Dr. Rudelbach mig betræffende, Fædrelandet*, No. 26, January 31, 1851.)

The Point of View . . . , including "Two Notes about 'the Individual' " and *On My Work as an Author*, tr. Walter Lowrie. London and New York: Oxford University Press, 1939. (*Synspunktet for min Forfatter-Virksomhed*, by S. Kierkegaard, written 1848, publ. 1859; *Om min Forfatter-Virksomhed*, by S. Kierkegaard, 1851.)

For Self-Examination, tr. Edna and Howard Hong. Minneapolis: Augsburg Publishing House, 1940. (*Til SelvprØvelse*, by S. Kierkegaard, 1851.)

Judge for Yourselves! in *For Self-Examination* and *Judge for Yourselves! . . .* , including also *Two Discourses at the Communion on Fridays* and *The Unchangeableness of God* (tr. David F. Swenson), tr. Walter Lowrie. Princeton: Princeton University Press, 1944. (*Dommer Selv!* by S. Kierkegaard, 1852; *To Taler ved Altergangen om Fredagen*, by S. Kierkegaard, 1851; *Guds Uforanderlighed*, by S. Kierkegaard, 1855.)

Kierkegaard's Attack upon "Christendom," 1854-1855, tr. Walter Lowrie. Princeton: Princeton University Press, 1944. (*Bladartikler* I-XXI, by S. Kierkegaard, *Fædrelandet*, 1854-55; *Dette skal siges, saa være det da sagt*, by S.

Kierkegaard, 1855; *Øieblikket*, by S. Kierkegaard, 1-9, 1855; 10, unpubl., *S.V.*, XIV; *Hvad Christus dømmer om officiel Christendom*, by S. Kierkegaard, 1855.)

The Journals of Søren Kierkegaard . . . a Selection . . ., tr. Alexander Dru. London and New York: Oxford University Press, 1938. (From *Søren Kierkegaards Papirer*, I-XI¹ in 18 volumes, 1909-36.)

The Last Years, tr. Ronald C. Smith. New York: Harper and Row, 1965. (From *Papirer* XI¹-XI³, 1936-48.)

Søren Kierkegaard's Journals and Papers, tr. Howard V. Hong and Edna H. Hong. Bloomington and London: Indiana University Press, I, 1967; II, 1970; III-V in preparation. (From *Papirer* I-XI³, suppl. vols. XII, XIII, 1969-70, and *Breve og Aktstykker vedrørende Søren Kierkegaard*, ed. Niels Thulstrup, I-II, 1953-54.)

At various times in recent years over twenty-five paperback editions of twenty Kierkegaard titles in English translation have appeared. For paperback editions currently available, see the latest issue of *Paperback Books in Print*, published by R. R. Bowker Co., 1180 Avenue of the Americas, New York, N.Y.

General works on Kierkegaard are listed in the Bibliography of *Søren Kierkegaard's Journals and Papers*, I, pp. 482-88. Studies of a more limited and specific nature are listed in the appropriate section of topical notes in each volume of *Søren Kierkegaard's Journals and Papers*.

Index